Newspaperman

A memoir by Don Hatfield

Newspaperman
a memoir

DON HATFIELD

Bowen Books

Copyright © 2018 Don Hatfield

ISBN:1986794997
ISBN-13:9781986794992

TO SANDY

*The love of my life
who made everything possible*

"The problem with you, Mr. Hatfield, is that you like people too much. You probably ought to be in public relations."

ACKNOWLEDGMENTS

I am grateful to the team of Pamela and Charlie Bowen, for their friendship and for encouraging me in the writing of this book, Pamela for her always sound editing and advice, Charlie for actually bringing it into existence. I must give credit to the gifted glass artist Kelsey Murphy for badgering me into resuming and completing this work. And I owe a huge debt of gratitude to George H. Clark, my editor and mentor who believed in me in those early years, to John C. Quinn, editor extraordinaire and the "Conscience of Gannett," my boss and my friend, and of course to the late, great sports columnist, Ernie Salvatore, who started it all by hiring an 18-year-old kid with dreams. Finally, I must express my great appreciation to all those who worked with me and for me over the years. You taught me more than you will ever know, and you helped make it fun.

Don Hatfield
April 2018

CONTENTS

1
TIMING IS EVERYTHING

When I walked into the newsroom of the Huntington, West Virginia newspapers in June of 1953, a few days before my eighteenth birthday, I had no thoughts of someday running the place. I hoped to talk my way into a copy boy job for the summer--good experience for one who planned to major in journalism when entering college that fall. And someday, with a little luck, maybe, just maybe, I could find a job as a sportswriter. What greater life could there be?

The newsroom served both the morning Herald-Dispatch and the afternoon Huntington Advertiser as well as the combined Sunday Herald-Advertiser. I told the receptionist I was looking for the editor and was ushered through the newsroom and left standing outside a corner office as she went inside. The newsroom looked just the way I had imagined: desks with typewriters and paste pots, men and women with heads down, their fingers flying over typewriter keys or gripping thick copy pencils, some of their faces familiar to me from their columns. I felt both uneasy and yet somehow at home.

After a moment I was led into the office and

stood facing a desk behind which sat a white-haired man with a friendly smile. His name was Clyde Wellman and he was editor of the Advertiser. He did not seem at all surprised to see a strange kid standing in front of him. He asked what he could do for me.

I explained, somewhat nervously, that I wanted to be a newspaperman someday, that I had just graduated from high school, was planning to enter college in the fall, and hoped to find a job as a copy boy for the summer.

He asked me which high school and what kind of grades I had made and what I did there. I told him I had graduated with honors from Huntington Vinson, had played football, basketball and baseball, and that I liked to read and to write. "I read both Huntington newspapers every day. I know all the bylines."

He nodded, then stood and walked to the door and called to a man sitting at a nearby desk whom I recognized as John R. Brown, the Advertiser's long-time sports editor and columnist. "Aren't we looking for a copy boy?"

"Just hired one. But Ernie's looking for somebody."

"Ask him to come in for a minute."

Walking back to his desk the editor explained that John R. Brown had just been moved to city editor and that Ernie Salvatore, a reporter and Sunday television columnist, had been made sports editor and was looking for a part-time assistant.

Salvatore came to the office door. Italian, dark

hair, glasses, big smile, big hands, white shirt and tie like all the other men in the newsroom. Thirty-two years of age, I learned. We were introduced, my situation was explained, and Ernie told me to follow him--which, as it turns out, I did for the next seven years.

But on that morning, we talked for nearly an hour. He said he was from Greenwich, Connecticut--"Actually, Cos Cob; that's a part of Greenwich." His team was the Yankees. He had gone to Marshall College, as it was known then, had joined the newspaper as a reporter and then had become Sunday TV columnist. I told him I read his column every week, which of course pleased him. We talked about the local sports scene, about my playing in high school. He asked if I planned to play in college. Before I could answer, he said, "Once you trade in your spikes for a typewriter, kid, you can't go back." And he laughed. I would hear that again sometime later when injuring an ankle in an independent league baseball game.

He offered me the job that morning. Twenty hours per week, seventy-five cents an hour. Minimum wage. When we parted he said, "Oh, by the way, kid; you can type, can't you?"

Oh yes, of course, I said. Funny he would ask that, especially since, as I soon learned, he could type only with three fingers, two of them held together, sitting staring down at the keyboard as if the keys were threatening to move.

When I left the newsroom that day I had every confidence that already I had found my life's work.

My timing had been incredible.   For whatever reason, that would occur throughout my career.

And so it began, a life in newspapers that would last for nearly five decades, from the Fifties to the end of the Twentieth Century, a life in which that eighteen-year-old from Wayne County, West Virginia would become editor, publisher, a regional vice   president in the largest newspaper chain in America, an officer in The Associated Press's national editors organization, the president of newspaper associations in both West Virginia and Arizona, and a member of the Arizona Newspapers Hall of Fame. It would be a life that saw enormous change, from Linotype machines to computers, printed pages to on-line web sites, of successes and failures, controversy and tragedy, good times and bad, of meeting extraordinary people and ordinary people, Presidents and senators, of listening and learning and all the while observing the great and terribly swift passage of time.

2
LEARNING THE ROPES ... SORT OF

I expected the sports assistant's job to be mostly clerical, handling statistics and the daily sports calendar and running errands. But from Day One I was given small, then larger, writing assignments—a few briefs, a few rewrites, and then an actual story. "You're not bad, kid," Salvatore said. "Comes pretty natural to you, doesn't it?"

It did. I had devoured the sports pages since I had been a small boy. The morning Herald-dispatch, the afternoon Huntington Advertiser, the Sunday Herald-Advertiser, and the short-lived tabloid Daily News. All came into our modest house in the west end every day. And with them Life Magazine and occasionally the Sporting News and even the Baseball Register and in late summer several pre-season football magazines. I read them all and my father and I discussed them. And when my father took me to Cincinnati to see the Reds play, we often picked up a copy of the Cincinnati Enquirer. And early on I knew I wanted to be a sportswriter someday. I read every story and column thoroughly and I practiced writing stories and columns in the styles the writers used. So by the time I sat at the small desk beside the larger one belonging to Ernie Salvatore, I had a sense of how sports stories were written. I knew the difference between game stories and features and between reporting and column writing. I knew the nicknames of all the teams, local and national. I had something of a grasp of what was important in a sports story and what was not.

W. S. "Dez" Reynolds, the *Advertiser's* managing editor, and John R. Brown, the new city editor, must have noticed. At the end of my first week in sports they asked if I would be interested in moving over to city side for an additional twenty hours per week. Twenty hours in sports, twenty on city side--forty hours a week and that meant thirty dollars a week. I was on my way.

"Hey, don't get married to the kid," Salvatore told Brown. "I saw him first."

I was given a city desk beside veteran police reporter Jack Hardin, who a few years later would win a national reporting award for bringing in an escaped killer he had interviewed. Each day I worked from 5:30 a.m. to 9:30 a.m. in sports, then moved across the room to my desk beside Hardin. I was somewhat in awe sitting beside him until early on he asked me how to spell a couple of grade-school-level words.

However, sitting beside Hardin was an education in itself. Just listening to him working the phones would have been worth a journalism seminar. The city directory and the telephone book were his tools. When the police radio crackled the report of some accident or crime, Hardin would check the address and then phone next door. "What's going on over there?" he would ask.

After a few days Hardin said it was time to take me to the police station and "introduce you around." We met every cop in the building, including the chief, and we got the grand tour. It ended with a police lieutenant taking me into a locker room and opening a large metal locker in which were stacked countless bottles of whiskey, all confiscated.

"Have one," the lieutenant said. "Bourbon okay? Got more of that than anything."

Fine. Bourbon was fine, I said. How would I know? I was eighteen. I had only recently had my first beer.

"Congratulations on your new job," the lieutenant went on. "Stick with ol' Jack here; he knows it all."

"Yes, I will," I said. "Thank you very much."

But I spent no more time at the police station. My city assignments were much milder and much less important. The United Way, the Extension Service, rewrites, small features. Not nearly as much fun as sports. But good training. Brown was an excellent city editor, especially in shaping up copy. He would call me over after he'd edited one of my stories and go over it word for word, explaining what questions should have been asked that weren't, what words would be better than those I had chosen. He was deliberate and to the point without humiliating or embarrassing the kid that I was.

The written word, it soon became apparent, was holy in this newsroom. Proper grammar was not only expected, but assumed—far different from what one finds in most of today's newspapers and on television news. Every editor knew the language, even if a couple of the reporters did not. I was impressed.

Newspapers in those days, and for many years after, were structured according to departments, and some had more than others. In Huntington in the 1950's, The Advertiser's newsroom consisted of the city desk, sports department, women's department and the news desk. Other newspapers had additional departments. The Herald-Dispatch, for example, had a regional desk operation for news coverage that extended into Ohio, Kentucky and southern West Virginia. Some newspapers had business news departments, some features or arts-and-entertainment departments. But this was the Advertiser and we were a small afternoon daily.

City reporters were assigned beats and were expected to check them every day and produce stories if stories were merited. They wrote their stories on typewriters bolted into folding desk tops, using copy paper cut from newsprint. Each page measured somewhat less than letter size and was called a "take." A common order from the city editor to a reporter was to "give me three takes on that" or "hold that to two takes," and so on. Once completed the stories were turned into the city desk where they received their first editing. Sometimes they came back with orders to change something here or there or ask more questions or to start over. Again, language was holy.

The same held true in the sports and women's departments.

The city, sports and women's departments all produced their own pages, drawing them up on paper dummies, selecting all the content, editing all the stories and writing all the headlines. Each department had its own editor and reporters and the city desk also had an assistant editor.

The news desk produced all the remaining pages in the paper, including the front page. It was headed by the news editor, who made up the front page and sat in the "slot" or center, surrounded by copy editors who edited stories and wrote headlines, and the telegraph editor who was responsible for gathering all the national and world stories pouring over the various wire service teletype machines.

Each department functioned with a daily news budget—a list of stories available for that day's paper. Local news budgets were put together by the respective editor of that department, while national and world budgets, including sports, were put together by wire service editors in New York and elsewhere.

Each day on most newspapers the editors would meet well before deadline to discuss what should go into that day's paper and where it should go. Primary attention, of course, would be given to the front page, the window of the newspaper. What stories, local or otherwise, were important enough or significant enough to be there? And given the space inside that day's paper, what stories could be held, and what should be tossed? There was never enough space for everything.

The Advertiser in those days did not bother with a daily news meeting of all editors. The city editor sat just a few feet from the news desk and the news editor would simply turn and say "Got anything for me today?" But that would soon change.

In The Advertiser's sports department, a staff of only two people—Ernie Salvatore and myself—I soon learned to do things other than writing stories and compiling statistics. Gradually, Salvatore began showing me how to dummy up news pages, edit wire and local copy, and even write headlines.

Headlines involved family of type, column width and point size, and had to be written to fit. Most newspapers were formatted in eight-column pages in those days, and makeup tended to be vertical, which resulted in many one-column heads, limiting the number of letters one could use. That's why, Salvatore said, nicknames had become prevalent over the years. "'Ike' will fit in a one-column head. Eisenhower will not."

We used to joke about the need for rubber type so we could have an easier time writing heads. It never occurred to us that in the future computers would measure headlines and place them on a page with no concern whatsoever as to whether they would fit or not because they could be reduced or enlarged by computers and cameras.

It all became another of my lessons to be learned, while I was writing sports, shuttling over to city side to do a little city reporting, and shuttling back.

3
NOT ALL THE ANIMALS
ARE IN THEIR CAGES

Newsrooms are, in many ways, strange places. A coaching friend of mine who occasionally dropped by our offices once remarked: "This place is a zoo. If you built a fence around it and charged admission, you'd make a fortune."

He was speaking about the individuals who inhabit newsrooms. And certainly this was an interesting newsroom full of interesting characters.

City reporters wandered in and out, pounded out stories on deadline, cussed a bit, told stories after deadline, and sometimes bet each other on who would get a page one byline that day. One grizzled reporter, who took pride in telling stories about his days in Chicago confronting Dillinger and others, would come to the office early in the morning, then stretch out atop a large desk in the library and sleep. When he later phoned home he would say, "Hello Wife? This is Maxwell speaking." He wore two hearing aids and always had both belt and suspenders on his trousers. One day he was walking down the street when he saw the director of the Chamber of Commerce approaching. "How's business?" he asked. "Never better," came the reply. And with that the reporter dashed back to the newsroom where he began a story, "The director of the Chamber of Commerce said today business has never been better."

The morning paper, meanwhile, had a city reporter who wore a black hat, black suit, grey throwback spats over his black shoes, and carried a black cane "so they will always remember me."

But in many ways both were good reporters. And fortunately, such excesses were not found often in the newsroom. Mostly one heard reporters muse, "I wonder what that s.o.b. is up to?" Or "I wonder what is going on over there?" Or "I wonder what all that means?" They were curious—and curiosity was an important quality that unfortunately has faded in newsrooms over the years.

Humor was another important quality, although sometimes it could be cruel. A couple of fellow reporters occasionally played a trick on their partly deaf colleague by mouthing words silently in his presence, then as he quickly turned up his hearing aid to full volume, shouting "Isn't that right, Max?" which sent him reeling.

Beginning reporters were a particular target. There were no guards at the entrances of the newspaper building in those days, and local citizens frequently came into the newsroom, some delivering news releases, some to register complaints, and some to report a story that they felt should be published. Not all those who came into the newsroom were, shall we say, legitimate news sources.

There was this stereotypical "little old lady," white-haired, thin, always in a house dress, who came by fairly regularly. She would approach an editor or reporter and nearly always began her story with: "I talked to God last night." She would go on to explain that God had told her to come to the newspaper and have a reporter do a story on some impending disaster. Veteran reporters humored her, took notes, thanked her for coming, and she went away happy. If there happened to be a new, young reporter who had come aboard since the woman's last visit, the veterans would send her over to him. And they would sit back and watch the rookie listen to the woman's story, gradually grow uncomfortable, pause, clear his throat, then look around the newsroom wondering what to do, his eyes silently pleading for help. It was their entertainment for the day.

One day the woman came in, offered her usual explanation: "I talked to God last night." And a reporter said, "And what did God tell you last night?"

"He wanted me to announce our engagement. We're going to be married."

The reporter sent the poor soul to the women's department to pick up a wedding and engagement form, which she happily took home to fill out. Afterward, James R. Haworth, a brilliant wordsmith who had been city editor and was then a columnist, facetiously wrote, in the manner of 1920's society news:

"Miss Sally Jones today announced her engagement to Mr. George W. God of Huntington and Heaven." He finished this way: "After the wedding trip they will reside."

He did not, of course, publish the short piece, but it made its rounds in the newsroom for years after.

Haworth was among those most responsible for the high standards of language and grammar found in the newsroom at that time. He had guided many young reporters down the proper paths of literacy. His columns, which unfortunately were much too few, were witty and wonderfully readable. I remember one in particular, written about his trip to Africa. It began this way:

"You could tell by his gait he was a seafaring man."

It ended: "Thus did James R. Haworth arrive in Cape Town."

The sports departments were certainly not without their characters. Although The Advertiser sports staff consisted only of Salvatore and myself, nearby sat the sports columnist of the Herald-Dispatch, Duke Ridgley.

Duke Ridgley was an icon before the word became over-used. I had read his columns as long as I could remember, and I had even been in a few of them. Salvatore introduced us that first week, and Duke smiled and said of me, "I know all about him, Ernie. He's a good kid." Which made my day.

Ridgley had been something of a legend since

his own playing days when as a shortstop he had cut a silver dollar-sized piece out of the palm of his glove—"so I can feel the ball better." He had written articles on local baseball and sold them to the Herald-Dispatch and somehow had moved on to writing columns for the paper. He soon developed quite a following. His columns were filled with names of local players. One day as he and I walked down the street he was approached by a man who thanked him for writing about his son, then proceeded to correct some of the facts: it was not that date, but another date, not that game, but another game, and the score was wrong. "Did I spell his name correctly?" Duke asked. Why, yes, the man said. "That's all that matters," Duke said, and we walked on.

He dressed in a very flamboyant style: White shirt, loud wide tie often bearing red or yellow flowers, rust or yellow trousers, sport coats that might be light blue, yellow, rust or beige, and a large, floppy, rust-colored hat with a small feather.

He smoked almost constantly, and he would sit at his desk writing his column until his cigarette became ashes and fell on his shirt and tie. More than once he leapt to his feet to put out a fire in his waste basket, started from his cigarette and discarded chemically-treated wire photos. Then he would go back to his typewriter.

Duke's finished columns always totaled several pages of copy, but instead of clipping them together he would turn to the paste pot on his desk and paste them all together. Then he would drape the lengthy sheet over his desk lamp to dry. And yes, it too caught fire occasionally.

Duke was often sought to speak at local sports banquets and other meetings. And he usually ended each talk with this: "And you can bet your bottom dollar that I will be a fan of (name your team) as long as there's a one-way street in Charleston and the grass grows blue in Kentucky."

When there was a big game featuring a local team he would write, "And you can bet your bottom dollar I'll be there in person rooting for the (name your team)." On one such occasion I was assigned to cover the very game he had written about, so I asked if he'd like to share a ride. "Naw," he said. "I'm not going there. I'm going up to see Ohio State play."

On the other hand, he once gave me this bit of advice: "Don't ever forget the kids, Don. They'll make you, if you let them. They're the important things anyway."

Duke Ridgley was not the only character in that newsroom. On the other side of the room sat another popular columnist who had become something of an icon herself. Her name was Catherine Bliss Enslow and she headed the "Soc" (for Society) pages produced in The Advertiser She was a large woman who leaned to one side then the other as she walked. She carried a large paper shopping bag instead of a brief case, and she often could be heard whistling "Un Bel Di" from "Madame Butterfly" as she walked. In the office, she would lean back in a faded and stuffed reclining office chair, cigarette holder clenched in her teeth reminiscent of FDR.

From the first day I met her, she called me "Boy." That continued through the years even after I grew older and became her boss. In her final days she worked at home and she would call: "Boy, send somebody over to get my column."

Catherine Bliss Enslow had friends and contacts in New York, Washington, Lexington and Louisville. She frequented the Greenbrier, the magnificent resort in southern West Virginia. She loved to point out that she had met the Duke and Duchess of Windsor there, and spoke of them as if they were friends.

Her columns were "society" columns in the truest and oldest class-conscious sense of the word. There were no black faces, no black names in Catherine Bliss Enslow's columns. And when finally age required that she give up the column, it was not replaced.

For that matter, there were few black faces and black names anywhere in the pages of Huntington's two main daily newspapers, except occasionally in the sports pages. I promised myself that someday that would not be the case.

4
WHITE FACE IN THE CROWD

That first summer of my life as a newspaperman flew by, and with it my city reporting internship—but not, fortunately, my part-time sports writing job. In fact, with a full schedule of college and high school sports looming, Ernie Salvatore was able to convince the managing editor that he needed a fulltime sportswriter, and that I was ready.

"What about your college?" the managing editor asked.

"We'll work it out," Salvatore said quickly.

He put together a loose schedule. I would work from 5:30 a.m. until 7:45 a.m., then hurry off to classes (Marshall College was only six blocks from the newsroom). I would return to the newsroom in the late afternoon and I would cover high school games on Thursday and Friday nights and write up the games once they were over. Salvatore accounted for everything but sleep.

And now I was about to embark on my first game assignment—covering a Douglass High

School football game at Fairfield Stadium.

Douglass was an all-black school located just off Sixteenth Street in an area referred to by most of the white people in town as "the colored section." It was autumn of 1953 and integration had not yet arrived in Huntington.

Fairfield Stadium was the home of Marshall College as well as three city high schools---the all-white Huntington High and Huntington East as well as the all-black Douglass. Marshall got Saturdays, Huntington High and Huntington East shared Friday nights, and Douglass got Thursday nights. Fairfield was called "the old brickyard" for good reasons: its outer walls were made of brick, and it actually sat on the site of an old brickyard. The stadium seated about fifteen thousand but was rarely close to being full, even for college games.

I entered the stadium with press card and notebook in hand, wearing a brown tweed sports jacket, charcoal flannel pants and a white shirt and striped tie, all newly purchased ("on time," as we said then) for college and for my job. It was early September and far too warm for the clothes I wore but I never considered removing even my coat. I wanted to look professional—and older.

I walked up concrete steps to the press box and settled into a folding chair and looked out over the stadium and the sidelines. The Douglass players were going through their pre-game drills as were their opponents at the other end of the field. There was a small crowd, mostly on the home side of the stadium, and a few supporters of the opposing team on the opposite side. As I watched the fans joke and move around and talk with each other it suddenly occurred to me that the only white faces in the stadium, as far as I could tell, were mine and that of the public address announcer, a   local disc jockey whose side job was to work all Fairfield games. I knew him from our years of playing youth baseball. I wasn't sure whether he knew I was now working for the newspaper but he waved and called from his booth: "Nice threads."

"I'm covering the game," I said.   And he nodded.

I turned back to the field and thought of having played here myself only two years before as a member of the visiting Huntington Vinson team against Huntington High.. Now I was returning as a real, fulltime sportswriter. Amazing.

Ernie Salvatore was transforming the way sports was being written in Huntington, and he expected me to be part of that.   Television has changed everything, he said. It's no longer enough to report the score and describe the game. Now we need to go behind the scenes, interview coaches and players.   Besides that, we're an afternoon paper; we've got to get stuff the morning papers haven't had.

Salvatore had another idea, a departure from the past which was bound to shake things up. Douglass, he said, is just as much a part of Huntington as the other city schools and just as deserving of coverage.   Hence my presence at this opening game.

I recorded every down and every play and tried to observe the entire scene, taking notes for "color," as he had trained me to do. And when the game was over I walked down the stadium steps onto the cinder track surrounding the field, to interview the coaches and some of the players. I still remember the looks on the faces of the players as I--this young white boy--walked toward them.   I introduced myself to the veteran Douglass coach, a gentle man named Zelma Davis, and explained that I was the new sportswriter from the evening paper.

"You are most welcome," he said. And I was treated with respect and even kindness, which proved to be rare in the life of a sportswriter.

I returned to the office and wrote my story and left it for Salvatore.   The following morning he asked, "How did it go last night, kid?"

"Fine. Is the story okay?"

"Yeah. A couple of things I touched up. Good quotes, though. Lead was fine."

"Great. Thanks."

"Your first time covering a game."

"Right."

"There'll be a lot more."

And there were. Douglass's home football games on Thursday nights, other high school games throughout the region on Friday nights. There were ten high school football teams in the immediate area and I was the only one from our newspaper to cover them. Each week Salvatore designated which team I should cover in person, giving priority to the larger and more successful teams. I called as many coaches of the other local teams as possible for stories on their games, and rewrote game stories from the morning paper.

I had played against many of the coaches and players I found myself now covering. That had both an upside and a downside. The coaches by now knew I was representing the newspaper. On the other hand, they also knew I was young and thus did not have the same respect for me they would have had for Salvatore or an older writer.

During the pre-season I had walked onto the Barboursville High School field to do a feature and was met by the coach, Dick Ware. He took one look at me and laughed and for a moment I was unnerved. "Last time I saw you on this field you were lying under this bench here," he said. He was right. I had been returning the second half kickoff down the sideline only to be met by two of his biggest linemen, and they knocked me there.

"I'll bet I remember it better than you do," I said. And we both laughed and things went all right after that.

It was tougher the first few times I returned to my old school and entered the locker room to face some of my former teammates. I did not get a warm welcome, as one might expect. Rather, I was peppered with complaints that I was not giving the team enough coverage.

I worked six and sometimes seven days a week as well as covering games on Thursday and Friday nights. I wrote several stories every week, both pre-game and post-game, kept weekly statistics, and learned to edit copy. Salvatore covered Marshall, edited all local and wire stories, laid out the pages, wrote most of the headlines and ran our small department. Through necessity he tossed more and more things my way. And I came to think of myself as pretty important, as being already beyond such matters as beginning college journalism classes.

It was an attitude unfortunately made somewhat obvious to my journalism professor. He was a giant of a man, white-haired with a white pointed goatee, and he had only three percent vision, which caused him to walk, he said, like a drunken sailor. His name was Page Pitt. One morning after I arrived he told the class: "Mr. Hatfield here is already a professional newspaper man. Don, tell them everything you know about newspapers." And he stood and left the room.

Every student looked at me, waiting for the great truths I would pass along. I had no idea what to say and it suddenly occurred to me that I really had little to offer. "I don't really know all that much," I said. "I've just been working part-time at the paper this summer." It was a good lesson for me--as he knew it would be.

By the time football season ended basketball was getting under way. Once again I found myself at Douglass High School, this time standing in line outside the Douglass gym waiting to get inside to cover the game. It was a small gym, its bleachers packed with students and adults alike. I could see no empty seat and certainly there was no press row. Again, I was the only white face in the crowd, and in this space and in the midst of its bright lights I really stood out. Again, I had been here before as a player—just the previous year, in fact. Our Vinson High team had played Douglass each of the past two years, in this gym, in the small Vinson gym, and even in the city's 6,500-seat Memorial Field House as the featured game of the week.

I stood tentatively wondering what to do when a familiar face approached. It belonged to Bill Congleton, an outstanding Douglass athlete against whom I had played. "Hey there, Don," he said. "Come on in. Let me find you a place to sit." He walked to the front row of bleachers near the players bench and asked someone to move and gestured for me to sit there. "Good to have you," he said. "Good to see you again."

Bill Congleton would be a part of my life for years to come. He became a leader in civil rights. He helped me as a young managing editor of the "honky press" during a time of great strife. He assisted me in recruiting young black journalists. And when many years later my wife and I moved from the suburbs into the city, just three blocks from his house, he came by our home frequently, sometimes just dropping in with a bottle of Scotch to sit and talk, sometimes to bring by Marshall basketball recruits.. He invited us to his house as well, where we dined on wonderful fried wild game. He taught me many things without even knowing it.

But on this night in 1953 he was finding me a place to sit in a jammed high school basketball arena so I could cover the game.

I settled in and watched the athletes warm up. And there, still in a Douglass uniform, was the skinny kid with the knee brace who just the year before had torched me for twenty-six points. His name was Harold Greer and he was back for his senior year.

"That's the guy who humiliated me here last year," I told Congleton.

"Harold has grown since last year," Congleton said. "He's improved a lot too. He's going to Marshall next year."

That was a surprise. Marshall had no black athletes, had never had black athletes or even black students. And this skinny kid from Douglass was going to change all that? Break the barrier?

"Marshall? Great. Can I write that?"

"Better get it from Marshall and from Harold," Congleton said. Right, I thought.

Greer took over the game immediately. He was quick, confident, had a great jump shot and could drive to the basket. Marshall would be lucky to have him if, indeed, that came about.

Harold Greer—or Hal, as he came to be known-- did go to Marshall, the first black athlete to do so. He quickly became a star, one of the most flexible, dependable, intelligent players in school history. In his senior year when the Thundering Herd was short on big men, he even played center. And he was named captain.

"Think we should mention he's the first black captain of a Marshall sport?" Salvatore asked me. "Think we should mention that he's black?"

"They always mention it on the news pages when it's bad news," I said.

"That's a damned good point," Salvatore said. So we did.

When Hal Greer, the skinny kid from Sixteenth Street, graduated from Marshall he went to the NBA. He became an All-Star with the Philadelphia 76ers and played for many years, finishing his career as one of the highest scorers in league history.

After Greer's retirement from the NBA Bill Congleton and a few other friends and supporters in Huntington pointed out that every school Hal Greer had attended—elementary, high school and college —was located along Sixteenth Street. They put together a proposal that Sixteenth Street be changed to Hal Greer Boulevard. City Council approved. Today the street is indeed known as Hal Greer Boulevard. The elementary school is no longer there. The building that was Douglass is no longer used as a high school. Marshall College has become Marshall University. And its Old Main sits facing Hal Greer Boulevard.

The thought occurs to me now how much of a role Douglass High School, this small all-black school in the "colored part of town," played in my life. I grew up in a poor neighborhood in the west end where there were no blacks—none in my schools, none within miles. I played in all-white summer youth baseball leagues. All my high school opponents in football, basketball and baseball were all-white schools. And then beginning with my junior year there were the basketball games against Douglass. Those games were close and hard-fought and the Douglass players were not only good athletes but "good guys," as we said back then. Then it turned out that my first assignment as a young sports writer was to cover Douglass football and that my first basketball assignment took place in the Douglass gym.

And there were the people I met there--not just the players, but coaches like Zelma Davis, Joe Slash and George France, each of whom presented a new and different kind of person to me. Davis, the grey, grandfatherly-type who said little, who possessed great manners and in his few words, great wisdom. Slash, highly educated, articulate, kind, the personification of the word "gentleman," and who became principal and later superintendent of all county schools. And France. Well, George France was another matter. An outstanding basketball coach whose teams ran opponents out of the gym, France was an arrogant, aggressive, straight-up coach who was as honest to me as any coach I ever covered. After a tough basketball loss, he sometimes would point to the color of his skin and say, "That's what it was. The refs don't like our black boys." I would say, "George, you don't want to say that," and he would look at me and shake his head and say, "Ah Don," as if I were too naïve to understand. Many people disliked George France. I understood that. But I did not. I once was told that in a meeting of area coaches who were criticizing our newspaper's coverage in general and my stories in particular, France stood up and said, "Well, I think he does a pretty good job." It probably didn't earn him any new friends. But I appreciated it.

And of course there was Congleton, my old basketball opponent who opened doors, shared information only he had, provided tips, helped me recruit black reporters, who came to my house for drinks and conversation. And on whose front porch one night I was shown an old scrapbook in which were pasted many newspaper clippings and photographs. In one he and I were going up for a rebound in the old Vinson gym.

"Look at that," I said over our scotches. "I'm out-rebounding you."

"No way," he said. "It's the angle of the photograph."

My friend, who decades later was the first person I thought of and called when Barack Obama was elected president of the United States. I knew that for him this night was the realization of a once seemingly far-fetched dream for which he had fought and sacrificed and endured enormous hardships. He was ill but took my call.

"You did it," I said.

"We all did it," he said.

5
A GROWING LESSON – OR TWO

It wasn't called "March Madness" in those days, especially on the high school level. But March meant Tournament Time. And in the spring of that first year, it so happened that the West Virginia State High School Basketball Tournament was scheduled for Huntington's Memorial Field House. Being the lone high school basketball writer on our paper, I naturally got the assignment. I also got some advice from the boss.

"This Beckley team has won the state championship five years in a row," Salvatore said. "That's the big story here. If they win this year, that's six, and that will tie a national record for their coach, Jerome Van Meter. Now, what we want to focus on is him. If he ties the national record, how does it feel? What does he think? And if it happens that he loses, well then, how does he feel? How does it feel to lose when you're this close?"

Right, I thought. Got it.

"So get close so you can talk to him after the game, win or lose," Salvatore said.

Right.

Press row was right on the floor, not far from the teams' benches. To my right was the bench of Woodrow Wilson High School of Beckley. And there he sat, "the old Grey Eagle," as they called him in Beckley, the almost legendary Jerome Van Meter. White hair. Distinguished. A kind yet stern face.

His team was opening against a good Huntington High School team. I sat with my note pad and portable typewriter watching Van Meter as well as the action on the court. The game was close all the way, and Huntington High was leading late. Could it be that Beckley would be upset in its very first game? That the streak would end?

I left press row and crept down behind the Beckley bench, right behind Van Meter. Ernie Salvatore's words rang in my ear. "How does it feel to lose when you're this close?"

I looked at the clock and then at the court and then at the back of van Meter's head. Only seconds were left. And then it was over. Woodrow Wilson had lost and so had Jerome Van Meter's chance for a national record.

Van Meter jumped from the bench, hands to his head, and spun around--only to see me in his face. Before he could even breathe I shouted: "Coach— how does it feel to lose?"

He looked at me in disbelief. "WHAT?!"

I was stunned, not only with his reaction but in the sudden realization of what I had said and how I said it. "I mean…"

"Oh my God!"

"I'm sorry…"

I backed away and he turned to his players and comforted them and they walked off the floor together. And I crawled away slinking toward press row. I sat there for some time, embarrassed and reluctant to approach him again for quotes, toying with my typewriter thinking how stupid I had been. I watched as the teams scheduled for the next game came onto the floor. And then I saw Van Meter emerge from the dressing room and walk toward press row. He pulled himself up beside me and leaned close. He spoke softly.

"I'm sorry if I was rude to you. But, son, don't ever come up to a coach that soon after he's lost such an important game."

'I know. I'm sorry. I…"

"All right then. Now what was it you wanted to ask me?"

What a gentleman, I thought later. What class. And what a lesson to learn. It was one I never forgot. Have some concern for the person you're interviewing. Recognize the need for time and space. Be aware of how you pose the questions. Timing, as I have said, is everything.

Not every coach is as kind or as classy as Jerome Van Meter was in those days.

The Marshall College head coach at the time, Cam Henderson, was even more of a legend than Van Meter. He had won a national championship— the NAIB—a few years before. Part of his legend, if one could believe it, was that he had invented both the zone defense, necessitated by a wet floor from a leaky ceiling, and the fast break. Whatever the truth, he had been a consistent winner and a cold, aloof,

Sphinx-like coach.

I had not covered a college game at that point. But Salvatore was in New York covering the Huntington Golden Gloves team, which our newspaper sponsored, and I was filling in. This time I waited outside the locker room after the game until Henderson emerged. And then I walked up to him and said, with as much confidence as I could muster, "Coach, I'd like to talk to you about tonight's game. I'm filling in for Ernie Salvatore."

He looked at me, deepening the ever-present frown he always wore, sighed and, putting his massive hand on my shoulder, said, "Son, you see all those people over there running around with statistics in their hands? You go over there and they'll give you everything you need to write your story." And with that he turned abruptly and walked away.

Not quite what I had envisioned. Not quite as successful as I had planned, nor what, I was sure, Salvatore had expected. I had failed.

It wasn't the first time. And it wouldn't be the last.

Sent to cover the Tri-State Men's Softball Tournament, I was given the opportunity to make a few extra bucks by serving as the chief scorekeeper. (This was not considered unethical in those days, any more than taking a bottle of free booze from a cop.) Somewhere along the way I lost track of a run and added an out. To this day I have no idea how that happened. I only remember angry men with softball bats yelling at me from the fence that separated field from bleachers and press box.   I never changed the scorebook and in great anger they resumed playing. Fortunately the angry team won after all, so my huge error had not cost the game. I had been wrong, all right. Still don't know quite how or where.

But one learns over time, from small things to larger things. I learned in covering literally hundreds of Golden Gloves amateur fights not to wear my best tie and jacket because in sitting at ringside, which I did, blood sometimes comes splattering your way. I learned to cover copy paper so it would not be ruined, to put my hat behind me, and to carry a few paper towels.

The Golden Gloves was big in those days, with stables of young boxing hopefuls coming to Huntington for this regional tournament. Winners in each class of the open division went on to New York where they fought other young fighters, some of whom became world champions.

The Golden Gloves tournament was quite a scene, a mix of all kinds of young people—some poor, from broken homes and all but uneducated, others middle-class, educated, a few even in college. Some in the novice division were scared and learned something about themselves when they climbed into the ring. Others toughed it out and advanced.

I not only learned how to report on dozens of fights a night, but also how to deal with the participants, particularly the younger ones. Mostly I learned to listen, to those who were scared and to those who were pretending to be cool, the greatest fighters to come down the pike.

I learned there were different sets of unwritten rules and policies in covering different sports. In golf, one spoke softly, if one spoke at all, and presented an understanding and appreciation for this "gentleman's game." At the opposite end of that spectrum was so-called professional wrestling, or "rasslin'," where I learned it was no big deal to be given the results on paper before the matches began.

And I learned that high school sports were not college sports and certainly were not professional sports. There was an enormous leap in covering professional hockey, for example, especially minor league professional hockey.

The Huntington Hornets had seemingly dropped out of the sky, moving to our city from Grand Rapids, Michigan. They competed in the International Hockey League, a high minor—or "amateur" league, as they called it, even though all the players were paid. Cincinnati, Fort Wayne, Indianapolis and Toledo were some of the teams in the league, so this was not kid stuff.

Salvatore called me over and informed me I was now our newspaper's hockey writer. I told him I knew nothing about hockey, had never seen a hockey game or match or whatever it was called. He said I could learn. I did.

Covering gnarly, sweaty, profane hockey players when you're still quite young and wide-eyed is not the most fun thing to do. But it is educational.

I learned once again to be careful how I posed a question, and when. I learned to avoid the player who was smashing his hockey stick into his locker and to talk with another player until he cooled off. I learned not to accept as gospel everything every player told me, especially about the coach. And when one afternoon I had to check out a report and went looking for a couple of the players, I learned it is not wise to follow them to the house of a couple of women with somewhat relaxed morals.

I also learned never to be late. Driving to Cincinnati to cover a Hornets game, I got lost trying to find the arena. I arrived just after the game had started, but it was already Cincinnati Mohawks 1, Huntington Hornets 0. Unfortunately, that was the only goal scored that night. And I hadn't even seen it. I asked others how the goal had been scored, and went on from there.

The hockey team left after one year and that was the end of my hockey writing career.

By that time, The Advertiser sports department had grown. Salvatore and I knew that with so many local sports events, we needed help. Ernie said we could only afford a part-timer. I convinced him to give a friend of mine a chance. Walt Leonhart had been my closest friend in high school and had just spent six months in the Army. He had enrolled at Marshall as a journalism major. He knew sports and had always been good with words and I convinced Salvatore that he was the right person for the part-time job.

I took Walt to a Douglass game so he could observe how I took notes and interviewed coaches and then returned to write the story (I still have a photo of the two of us at a Douglass game). In a short while, Ernie gave Walt the opportunity to write.

His vocabulary, as I knew, was outstanding. What I did not know was that his spelling and grammar were not. But we worked through it and it was good having my friend there. He had been the class clown in high school and as long as I could remember, funny things had happened to him. I was never sure which were truly unexpected and which were staged for laughs. On The Advertiser, he twice had problems with paper spikes. One day, having seen both Salvatore and me stashing copy on a spike, he tried it, only to have the spike run through the palm of his hand. On another occasion, bending to sit down, he bumped his forehead on a spike and sat back, surprised, blood running down his face. Everyone laughed, as did he, and I told myself, Well, that's Walter.

I think he could   have been a valuable sportswriter because of his intelligence and an ability to talk with people and ask good questions. But he decided to change his major and go into education, hoping to become a coach. He did just that, becoming basketball coach at our old high school, and then softball coach at a high school in Florida where he won a state championship.

Ernie next turned to a sportswriter from The Parthenon, Marshall's student newspaper. His name was Lowell Cade and, being a local boy from Wayne County, he became a key part of the staff. He eventually would become sports editor of The Advertiser, and today a special sports award is presented in his name.

Soon we added another Marshall student named Tom Miller to bring our staff to four. And that staff produced, in my opinion, the best local sports section in the state, despite larger staffs elsewhere We worked long and hard, came up with good stories and quotes, and soon The Advertiser became *the* newspaper for local sports.

Miller later became a top-flight investigative reporter. He was featured in a national book on investigative reporters, won many awards and thousands of dollars in his reporting, and became the political correspondent for The Herald-Dispatch.

With these additions, I became assistant sports editor and sports columnist and edited many stories each day, including those written by Miller and Cade. One day I went to Cade, copy in hand, and said, "Lowell, you can't do this."

He looked at me with wide eyes and said simply, "I did."

6
A LITTLE BIT OF HISTORY

The Huntington Advertiser and The Herald-Dispatch had interesting histories. They would have an even more interesting future over the next sixty years. But like most young people, I gave little thought to either past or future. The present was everything.

The city of Huntington at that time was an attractive, busy, thriving city, stretched along the banks of the Ohio River but protected from the river by a floodwall which had been erected following the devastating floods of 1937. Downtown Huntington boasted three major hotels, three others of lesser size, three department stores, and several movie theaters including the historic Keith-Albee, a virtual palace built in 1927. Fourth Avenue offered several high quality men's and women's shops and on both Fourth and Third Avenues were shoe stores, jewelry stores and many other retail establishments.

At the eastern end of Fourth Avenue sat Marshall College, with an enrollment at that time of about two thousand. On Fifth Avenue, at 25th Street, sat the new Memorial Field House, where high school and college basketball games were played and concerts held.

South of downtown, beyond the railroad tracks and accessible by six underpasses or, as we called them then, "viaducts," was a residential area called the South Side. It boasted the city's largest high school, Huntington High, a sizeable and handsome building. In its center was Ritter Park, a lovely area of trees walking paths, ponds and an outdoor amphitheater and surrounded by fine homes. However, to the east of the park, from 16th Street further east to nearly 20th Street and from 8th Avenue stretching south for several blocks, was a quite different area, a mixture of lesser houses, apartments, and government low-cost projects, and largely occupied by many belonging to the city's black community. It stood in sharp contrast to that other part of the South Side, in cultural and economic matters, although its high school, Douglas, was an outstanding school with excellent faculty.

Huntington was one of four major cities on the Ohio River, the others being Pittsburgh, Cincinnati and Louisville. It was, and is, the largest inland port in America in terms of tonnage, primarily because of the coal shipped by rail from the state's southern coal fields to be loaded on barges which carried it both up river and down river.

It was, both historically and economically, a railroad town, having been selected by Collis P. Huntington, its namesake, to be the western terminus of his Chesapeake and Ohio Railroad.

The city actually got its start as a settlement called Holderby's Landing in 1775. In 1799 another settlement, called Guyandotte, was founded on the eastern bank of the Guyandotte River, where it met the Ohio River. In 1837 Marshall Academy was born, to become Marshall Normal School, then Marshall College, then Marshall University. And in 1871, it all came together with the incorporation of the city of Huntington.

And now, in the 1950's, it was a good place to live and work, with a population of more than 80,000 in the city and over 100,000 in the county. The Huntington newspapers' past, like that of most newspapers, included multiple startups, mergers and consolidations, sales and purchases, moves, changes in product, changes in policies, and even a joint operating agreement—a JOA. I had no idea what that was or what it meant. But it would prove to be a huge part of my career at more than one location.

The Advertiser was born as a weekly newspaper in 1875 from a merger of the Weekly Independent and the Cabell Press, and became a daily in 1889. The Herald was founded in 1890, but struggled, and in 1893 was purchased by Col. Joseph Harvey Long, a printer from Pennsylvania who had been working on newspapers in Wheeling, West Virginia. Col. Long would become a legendary figure in Huntington. First, he built up the failing Herald, establishing it as a strong Republican voice in the area which, it was believed, was instrumental in electing several Republicans to local offices. Then in 1895 he sold the Herald and purchased The Advertiser, and established it as a strong voice for Democrats. In 1904 another newspaper, the Huntington Dispatch, was launched. And in 1909 the Herald and the Dispatch merged with a stock company assuming ownership.

The Advertiser and the Herald-Dispatch competed strongly. Col. Long became a huge part of the community, even being commissioned post master in 1916, an office he held for five years before resigning to concentrate on his growing newspaper business. Meanwhile, the Herald-Dispatch was changing hands, with Dave Gideon assuming ownership in 1919.

The two newspapers competed in many ways. In 1924 Col. Long purchased property at the corner of Fifth Avenue and Tenth Street for a sparkling new building for the Advertiser. Then the Herald-Dispatch announced plans for its own new building just a few doors down, also on Fifth Avenue.

After a few years of rivalry, in 1927 owners of the two newspapers agreed to combine their business operations in order to increase their profits. They formed the Huntington Publishing Co. and consolidated all operations in The Advertiser's new building. Col. Long would serve as chairman of the new company and publisher of The Advertiser. Gideon would serve as company president and publisher of the Herald-Dispatch. The venture enjoyed considerable success for many years.

When in 1953 I walked into the building looking for a job, Col. Long was still alive and still serving as publisher, at least in name. Although past ninety and feeble, he maintained his familiar corner office on the first floor, coming there on most days for a few hours. White-haired and leaning forward on his cane, he occasionally emerged into the front lobby to look around. I saw him a few times but never met him. I did hear that one day he saw Ernie Salvatore come in the front entrance and turned to John R. Brown, who happened to be nearby. "Brownie?" he said. "Who is that man?"

"Colonel, that's your sports editor, Ernie Salvatore," Brown said.

The colonel nodded and went back to his office.

Col. Long died in 1958 at the age of ninety-five and was replaced as publisher by one of his sons, Walker Long. Dave Gideon had died in 1950 and had been replaced as publisher of the Herald-Dispatch by his nephew, William Birke.

I had arrived too late to know Gideon but I did know Bill Birke even though he was publisher of "the other" newspaper. Although I was there for the last days of Col. Long, I always considered Walker Long my publisher, even before he became that officially.

The joint agreement was not altered by the new publishers, as far as I know. After all, it was making money for both sides, with costly duplication and redundancy being eliminated—one circulation department instead of two, one advertising department, one business department, and above all, one printing press and one building. Only the news and editorial functions were separate, and even they shared one newsroom.

Despite this lack of financial competition between two companies, such operations have been permitted by the government because they allow two newspapers to survive and thus "preserve two separate and distinct voices in the community."

Over the years many have claimed that this is a violation of anti-trust laws. There have been several court tests. The most famous went to the United States Supreme Court, which agreed. However, before joint operations around the country could be dissolved, Congress stepped in and passed new legislation, referred to as the "Surviving Newspaper Act." It permitted a joint newspaper operation to exist if one side could prove that without it one of the newspapers would fail—and, if both papers were "separate and competing," thus providing two voices in the community.

There was no question the two Huntington newspapers were different. The Advertiser continued to be the Democratic newspaper, the Herald-Dispatch the Republican paper. That was true not only on the editorial pages, but even in the political news that was published. Democrat news went in the afternoon paper, Republican news in the morning paper. The distinction went so far as to the coverage of elections, in which The Advertiser ran photos of only Democrat winners, the Herald-Dispatch pictures of only Republican winners.

The Huntington newspaper joint agreement had been established years before the court tests and the change in legislation. But there had always been general agreement that the news staffs and news content must be kept separate. And yet, here was this one newsroom with no walls in which existed these two "separate and competing" news staffs.

I have been involved with other JOA's over the years, and not one of them put the two "separate and competing" news staffs in the same room. If there is another somewhere in this country which did, I am not aware of it.

As if that weren't strange enough, there was only one photo department, and it served not only both news rooms but the advertising department as well. No competition there.

Fortunately, not everyone worked in the newsroom at the same time. Morning newspapers were put together at night, afternoon papers in the morning. Certain reporters and writers on both staffs crossed over at various hours for various reasons, but the sports, city, and news desks did not function at the same time.

The two top editors, it should be noted, were there at the same time, and they did occupy separate offices. But theirs were the only walls to be found in the newsroom.

Still, even without physical walls, territories and boundaries were clearly marked and clearly understood. There were partial partitions, and Advertiser desks occupied one side of the room, Herald-Dispatch desks the other, and Sunday staff desks were in between. The photo department moved around a good bit, from one storage-like room to another.

Of course, rules that applied in 1927 when the Huntington joint operation was formed were far different from those of recent years. In fact, when I arrived on the scene, the Huntington Publishing Co. was an agency that owned not only both newspapers, but the main local television station (WSAZ-TV) and top-ranked radio station (also WSAZ) as well. In later years the government would not allow the same company to own all those "voices" in the same community and the radio and TV stations had to be sold.

But those were only a few of the major changes to come to the Huntington newspapers in the next several years.

7
NEW MAN IN TOWN

The down time on a daily newspaper in those days was between and after deadlines. There might be only a few minutes between first and second edition deadlines, but in that time newsroom staffers relaxed for the most part and caught up on each other's news. There was more time after final edition deadline, but that was also time to work on an advance for the next day, or to join each other in a nearby bar.

I was fortunate in making friends despite my youth and learned a lot from them--and not just about newspapers. John McClane was a copy editor who handled our entertainment pages and he and I immediately became friends. We were both interested in the arts, especially in theater, and we often talked after deadline. McClane much preferred handling wire stories out of New York than local stories. New York was his dream. He spent every vacation there. Someday, he would say, I'm going to live there. He treated me like an adult more than some of the others did. And even though he had little interest in sports, he also talked frequently with Ernie Salvatore. They both loved New York and talked often about restaurants and shows and the wonders of the great city.

Estelle "Bill" Belanger held the title of city editor of the Sunday Herald-Advertiser and wrote a Sunday column on a variety of matters, called "Dubbing In." But her first love, like McClane's, was the arts, and again it was this that led to our becoming friends as well. She was not at all interested in sports, was in fact somewhat resentful of the attention given sports, and was astonished to find that a member of the sports staff cared about anything beyond sports. When she discovered that I did, we quickly found things to talk about. If the arts were the first love in Belanger's life, boats were the second. She had built a charming small brick house across the Ohio River and from there she could watch the large commercial river craft go by with their heavy loads of barges, as well as the many pleasure boats. At that time she did not own a boat of her own, but several of her friends did and she would go boating with them.

From both McClane and Belanger, I learned what was current, especially on Broadway and in books. Part of me had always wanted to be a novelist, in addition to my dream of becoming a sportswriter, and Bill Belanger was someone I could talk with about that. She would become a special person in my life.

Another person with whom I could talk about nearly every subject from golf to movies to baseball to women was Bob Rine, a reporter who had worked in Wheeling before coming to The Advertiser. A sophisticated lover of classical music, good martinis, good books and golf, Rine had actually been a professional umpire who not only worked in the minor leagues but also served as an instructor in the then-famous George Barr school for umpiring. He was not a large man, which may have kept him out of the major leagues, and he gave up the business and became a newspaper man. He happened to be a very good one, too.

And then there was Salvatore, not only my boss, but gradually becoming my friend. If Bob Rine was a man who appreciated martinis, Salvatore was an absolute connoisseur. While I never came to appreciate that particular drink as much as he, in years to come we would become great drinking partners, and pretty good at it.

In summers Ernie would spend his vacation back in Greenwich and work as a summer replacement copy editor on the New York Times. He hoped that someday it would pay off in a permanent job offer. A few years later it would; but oddly enough, after thinking about it a while he turned the job down and stayed in Huntington.

McClane, on the other hand, took his modest savings, left The Advertiser and Huntington and moved to New York where he found a job in public relations.

So these were my colleagues and my close friends in those early days. I was very fortunate.

It was about this time that there appeared a new editor in the newsroom, Clyde Wellman having retired. His name was George Henry Clark, and he had been city editor of a newspaper in Washington, D. C., which had folded. Clark returned to West Virginia, his native state, to take the top newsroom job at the Advertiser. His title would be managing editor, with Dez Reynolds moving to editorial page editor. I never knew how that came about, whether Clark had applied for the position or was recruited. But he was a most welcome addition.

I was busy trying to combine college with work. And my priority was clearly my work. He asked me about that one day and when I confessed that I really would like to give up class and concentrate on my job, he nodded. Then he told me it was important for me to continue going to class and to study, and that if I needed help to come to him.

He was a gentle man, tall and lanky, with greying hair and glasses. He had an exceptionally kind face and a wonderful sense of humor. I liked being in his presence and undoubtedly went into his office more than I should have. I liked and admired everything about him--his obvious intelligence, the way he spoke to people, the kind way he talked to his wife on the phone if she happened to call when I was in his office.

One morning after deadline but before class, he discovered me with my head over a book, and apparently I was frowning. He asked what I was reading. I held up Chaucer's *The Canterbury Tales.* His face lit up. "Wonderful," he said. "I know you must be enjoying it."

"To tell the truth," I said, "I can't always make out what's going on."

He picked up the book and turned to "The Miller's Tale." "Ahh, look at this one," he said. And he read aloud with a lilt in his voice and an accent as if he had never left the shores of England. I sat back, surprised, and he talked about the story and read the words, "Aback he start," and laughed as if reading it for the first time.

That this experienced newspaperman from the big city could be so interested in something assigned in my college classes impressed me.

But everything George Clark said impressed me. We talked many times, about music and books and his personal favorites, about my studies. And sometimes he would muse about "the many mysteries of life."

"Life is so goddam beautiful," he said suddenly one day, with great passion, as though someone was arguing the matter. I did not know how to respond. I said "Yes, it is."

I valued our talks greatly and came to trust him like no other person.

He bought a small farm with an old farmhouse on the outskirts of Huntington. He drove in and back each day, which struck me as strange for someone who had lived so long in a big city. He was always upbeat, always understanding, always aware of what was going on in the newsroom—no easy achievement. I did not know at that time that he suffered from debilitating migraines. He never complained.

By this time Salvatore trusted me to put out the Monday sports section by myself so he could take the day off. At first he left me with a preliminary sports front showing where I should place the Associated Press's college football roundup, the pro football roundup, and local college and high school stories. I completed the pages, selected and handled the photos, edited the stories and wrote the headlines, and then took everything to the then managing editor, Dez Reynolds, for final approval. I assumed Reynolds knew what the sports section was all about, what it should contain, how it should look. I was surprised when he examined the daily sports calendar and said, "This is too long; can't you cut it?"

Well, I thought in my young arrogance, I guess I could cancel some events. But I said, "Not really. It's supposed to include all the local events in town as well as those games on television. It has to be consistent each day."

He said, "Oh."

When George Clark took over the managing editor's job, he never asked to see the Monday pages before I sent them to composing, and I never offered. He did ask each Monday whether I needed any help, an offer I always declined, but he never looked over my shoulder.

Clark was busy improving the newspaper, hiring educated and experienced reporters and changing the way things were done. That sometimes involved standing up to other departments in the building such as Production and Circulation, which had long had the final say about deadlines and press starts. "We've got to get the news in the paper," he would say, "even if we have to delay press start."

His first change involved the World Series. Most Series games at that time were day games, and Clark wanted to hold press start so we could get the final score, with story and summaries, in that day's paper. He won, and we did just that.

His next such victory came during the State High School Basketball Tournament being played at Memorial Field House just a mile or so from our newspaper offices. By delaying deadlines and press starts, we were able to get in final scores of the early afternoon games, with stories. And we delivered copies to the arena before the start of the next game.

Not such a big deal, perhaps, but something that had not been done before at the Huntington papers.

One afternoon he asked if I had ever thought about moving out of the sports department. He said he thought I had a future in newspapers that could extend beyond sports. I told him that being a sportswriter had been my dream since boyhood and I couldn't see myself doing anything else on a newspaper. He said he understood, but if I ever changed my mind to let him know.

I had never given such a move a thought until he mentioned it. Now I did. Still, I could not see myself as being a city reporter or some kind of editor. Nor could I even imagine working for some other part of the newspaper--definitely not on the

business side where making money was the priority.
I was a journalist, after all. I was pure.

8
HERE COMES THE SUN

I saw her first in the Student Union. Like all freshmen she was wearing this tiny green beanie. It went well with her green plaid jumper and skirt and white blouse.

She was beautiful. Dark hair and great brown eyes and a smile that would have sent Mona Lisa back to the minor leagues.

I was mesmerized.

She was sitting with friends in a booth. I moved to the adjacent booth to get a closer look at her name tag—again, something found on all freshmen at that time—without being too obvious..

It said "Sandra Soto."

Soto?   What kind of name was Soto? Japanese? She didn't look Japanese.

I wondered how best to approach her.   A fraternity dance was coming up—my first since joining Sigma Phi Epsilon--and I thought about asking her. On the other hand, she was just a freshman, and I wasn't sure I should take her to a dance with lots of older guys and their dates. Besides, I had not even met her.

I kept glancing at her trying to eavesdrop, again without being obvious. She was cheerful and laughed without being loud, and I really couldn't hear what she was saying, although mostly she seemed to be listening. Finally she left with a couple of other girls and I was left to kick myself for not having done something, anything, to make her aware of my existence in the world.

I called an older girl I knew from high school and took her to the dance. And there I was astonished to discover that the fraternity president— a senior, no less--had brought none other than the beautiful freshman I had seen in the Union as his date. That could have been me, I told myself. Well, maybe. Maybe not.

I watched as they took the floor to dance and after a while got up my nerve to cut in. Our fraternity president graciously bowed and gave me her hand and I moved in and introduced myself. As we danced I told her that I had noticed her in the Union and (why in God's name did I tell her this?) thought about inviting her to this dance, but had not.

She was not impressed. That was not the right thing to say.

When the dance was over she returned to her date and I returned to mine and had a lousy time the rest of the night.

A few days later I saw her again in the Union and this time among those sitting with her was a girl with whom I had graduated high school named

Gladys Varney. I waited patiently until they parted, and then hurried to catch up with my old schoolmate.

"I need a favor. That girl you were just with, Sandra Soto…"

"Yes, she's really nice."

"Yes. Well, I've got to meet her. I mean, I've met her, but I've got to get a date with her. I think I screwed up when I met her at the Sig Ep dance last week. Can you help me out? Tell her I'm not totally stupid, or something?"

"I'll see what I can do," Gladys said.

I went to the Union every day and on the third day found Gladys. "She's staying in Laidley Hall," she said. "Give her a call. She's expecting it."

"Great, great. Thanks a million."

When I called Sandra Soto at Laidley Hall, I told her I would like to get to know her. We could go to a movie or get a bite to eat or do whatever. She surprised me by saying she would be going to church that Sunday evening and perhaps I could give her a ride back to her dormitory.

It didn't sound like much of a date to me. But a start is a start.

I waited in front of the church in my faded blue '49 Ford convertible. She had said she would be coming out the side entrance. I got out of the car and stood leaning against the door, arms folded, trying to look cool, and watched for her. After a while she emerged from the church and turned my way. I waved and smiled and said "Hello there" and opened the car door for her. She was carrying a

Bible and some papers and was smiling, eyes bright, and she said "Thank you" and slid into the front seat.

"How was church?" I said, and she said, "Fine." And I was surprised to discover that I was somewhat nervous. I asked if she'd like to stop at a drive-in restaurant for a sandwich or milk shake on the way back to the dorm and she said that would be all right, but there was a curfew. She couldn't be late. I promised she would not be late.

Suddenly she exclaimed "Ohhh!" and I jumped and she said "Look at that moon!" And I soon learned that here was a person unlike any I had known. Sandra Gail Soto. Intelligent, Incredible enthusiasm for life. Full of laughter and energy. *Alive.*

She came from the southern part of the state, from a small coal mining community called Ameagle, named "for the American Eagle Coal Company," she explained. She was half-Spanish, on her father's side—hence the "Soto"—and half Polish/Austrian on her mother's, whose maiden name had been "Chingle." She was attending college on scholarship. And she was a few months away from her eighteenth birthday. A child. No, a woman—but child-like. A quality she never lost.

We talked about music and plays and books and sports. I spoke of seeing a road company performance of "South Pacific," of loving theater and classical music and good books. And she talked about her studies in voice and piano and dance, and of her family, especially her father. I was instantly jealous, as stupid as that can be, because she spoke of him with such admiration and reverence and love, and I worried that no one would ever take his place with her. But I quickly dismissed that from my mind; this was, after all, our first time being together.

When she left the car to enter Laidley Hall, I told her I would like very much to see her again. She said to give her a call.

What I was thinking even then was that I did not want this very special girl, this unique person, to get away from me.

I called every day. She took my calls on a pay phone in the hall and we talked until she had to return to her room to study. I saw her every week, for lunch, for movies, for drives through the park and in the country, for late afternoon meals at Wiggins' drive-in, where we splurged on spaghetti. And we talked about every subject imaginable.

Fortunately for me, she was no stranger to sports, her father having seen to that. She was one of three daughters and had no brothers, so having no sons her father took his oldest daughter to all kinds of sports events--boxing matches and football, basketball and baseball games. She was familiar with the words I used in talking about my sports writing job. She even had an appreciation for it.

On Friday nights she accompanied me to the high school game to which I had been assigned. If I had to sit in the press box, she would sit outside but nearby; usually we sat together. And she would wait after the game while I interviewed the coaches.

One Friday night she attended a game involving my old high school with my mother and father, and she waited with them while I walked across the field to see the opposing coach. The head majorette of the visiting team was a girl I had dated and some time before we had made an agreement to meet at this game and go out afterward. As I walked toward the coach, the girl ran across the field and announced that she was ready for our date. I had totally forgotten. I stammered that I was sorry, but that I was with someone else and that someone was waiting for me in the stands. The girl was stunned, looked daggers through me, turned in her white boots and marched off the field. I never saw her again, nor did I see any other girl. I never wanted to see anyone else, and never did.

When Christmas break came, Sandra Gail Soto returned to her home in Ameagle, deep in the mountains of Raleigh County, West Virginia. A few days before Christmas I drove there, accompanied by my cousin Jim Wilkes, to see her and meet her family. They were all friendly, but every one of them looked at me with some suspicion. Who was this person come to see (and God forbid, take away) their Sandra Galina?

She had turned eighteen only days before.

That spring I asked her to accept my fraternity pin, and in those days "being pinned" was interpreted by many as "engaged to be engaged." We were serenaded outside Laidley Hall by members of the fraternity. And in the days and weeks to come we were together almost constantly.

When summer came she did not return to Ameagle. Instead, with the help of those at the newspaper office, she found a job with the local Chamber of commerce. When autumn came and it was time to return to college, she stayed on as a part-time secretary. Working and carrying twenty-one hours in college and seeing me every day, she hardly had time to sleep. But she never complained, a style and quality that never faded.

Soon I wanted to replace the frat pin with a real engagement ring, but she balked. She did not want to talk about marriage. She was only eighteen. Her parents expected her to get a degree and do great things. I gave that little thought. I only wanted to make sure she did not get away.

"You don't want to marry me," she said. "I don't like anything about marriage. I don't like cooking, I don't like cleaning, I don't like the idea of staying at home."

"I don't want a cook or a cleaning lady," I said. "I just want you." "Besides," I added one day, hoping to make her laugh, "I need somebody to keep score for me when I cover games."

We were married the following summer, in June 1955. She was nineteen. She had to get her parents' written permission. We drove to Daytona Beach, Florida for our honeymoon–on borrowed money. On our return, we were talking about our future together. And I was talking about perhaps someday being promoted to sports editor.

"Sports editor?" she said. "I hope you want to be something more than just a sports editor."

I couldn't believe what I was hearing. What could be better than that? "Sports editor is a great job." I said.

She looked at me with considerable disappointment. I felt offended and sulked the rest of the drive that night.

So, you ask, what does all this have to do with my life as a newspaper man?

Everything.

We were more than husband and wife. We were a team. She went with me to whichever game I had been assigned. Even when she was nearly nine months pregnant, she carried a small overnight bag in case we had to go to the hospital for her delivery. Returning from road trips, she would drive while I sat with a typewriter in my lap, pounding out a story.

As I moved up to greater positions over the years, she was always by my side. As the editor's wife, she knew every member of the news staff, many of whom came to our home. She helped on recruiting trips and loved meeting young journalism hopefuls. As the publisher's wife, she was out in the community representing both me and my newspaper, serving on countless boards and making enormous personal sacrifices. The governors of both West Virginia and Arizona, struck by her intelligence and dedication, appointed her to special committees.

She was the first to convince me I could be something more than I had even dreamed, that I needed to grow and broaden and reach higher. She advised me, motivated me, and taught me, all the while raising three children, one of whom was profoundly handicapped. No matter what, she was always there for me.

It was never just my career. It was *our* career.

Ask anybody.

9
THE BIG STORY

Life at the newspaper continued to be interesting and enjoyable. One expected as much in the sports department, sometimes referred to as "the toy shop." But the city side of the newsroom was the real world. As police reporter, Jack Hardin knew that better than anyone. One day he found himself confronted with an odd request. He was accustomed to getting phone calls offering trips or asking questions. This one was different.

A woman from the west end of town asked him to go with her into wooded hills to meet with a relative who was hiding out from police. At first Hardin was skeptical. Why would a woman he did not know ask him to go into the woods with her? If there indeed were a man hiding from police, why would he be doing so? And what did they want of him? Then the woman revealed the man's name. Hardin knew it well. It was that of an escapee charged with murder.

Hardin said he would check with his editors and get back to her the next day. But first he came to me, told me the woman's name and asked if I, also being from the west end, knew her or anything about her. I made the mistake of saying I had known of a woman by her last name who was viewed as somewhat unreliable.

Hardin was reluctant to go with the woman. On the other hand, he could foresee a rare interview and a big story. What good reporter would turn down such an opportunity? The editors agreed. Hardin and the woman arranged to meet the following day. She told him that he should come alone, not bring his car, and above all, not bring the police. And then she warned Hardin that the man "hates newspapermen."

For whatever reason, Hardin asked me to drive him to the meeting place—a side road not far from town. I dropped him there, concerned about leaving him with no car, an escaped killer waiting for him somewhere. But he told me to go on.

What happened after that I only read about in my own newspaper—under Jack Hardin's byline, of course. The woman explained that the man wanted Hardin "to tell his story." She would take Hardin to him. What would happen after that was not clear.

She led Hardin into the woods where the man was waiting. They talked for some time, the man telling Hardin "his story." He was tired of running, he said, but fearful of being gunned down by police if he showed his face. Somehow Hardin convinced the man to surrender, saying he would talk with police, get their assurance that they would not shoot on sight, and personally accompany the man out of his hiding place to them.

And that is what happened, Hardin emerging from the woods, the killer close behind, police waiting below.

When Hardin wrote the story he mentioned his conversation with me and my saying that a woman by that name was considered unreliable—a fact he need not to have included. When the story was published the woman called to raise hell, not with the police or Hardin, but with me.

New lesson learned: Watch what you say to a reporter, even when he's a friend and co-worker.

Hardin later won the Pall Mall Big Story award for his act, and his story was depicted on television. I watched to see if I would be mentioned, for the conversation or the ride to the woods. But I was not. Ah well.

Reporting staffs changed often in those days. There were the loyal veterans like Hardin. But there also were often new faces—and not always those of rookies. There was an abundance of experienced reporters, some quite good, who for whatever reasons drifted from one newspaper to another. One such was a talented writer named Brooks Wells, obviously a veteran of some journalistic wars . He quickly became one of our very best, and fit right in with the staff, becoming close friends with other reporters. He had lived some time in Key West, claimed to have known Ernest Hemingway, and spoke fluent Spanish. He also wrote beautifully. I could not help but be impressed. He seemed cool—and tough.

But even the cool and the tough can be moved.

On February 28, 1958, a school bus carrying forty–eight students and their driver skidded on a slippery road in Floyd County, Kentucky, not far from Huntington, smashed into a truck and veered into the cold waters of the Big Sandy River below. The bus quickly sank. Some twenty-two students somehow managed to escape through an emergency door and survived. But the remaining twenty-six students, as well as the driver, perished.

Brooks Wells covered the story. His reports and his writing were superior. "This is too much," he wrote. "Too much." I was told he choked up and could hardly finish.

Again, this was something I had not experienced. The deaths of twenty-six children. A huge newspaper story. A veteran, hard-nosed reporter so affected. I had not expected that of him. He seemed so unfeeling. People are not always what they seem, I thought.

Another lesson.

Cruel postscript to the Brooks Wells story:

A few years later, having found the rustic camp he had sought, on the banks of Twelve Pole Creek in Wayne County, Brooks Wells had just learned that he had cancer. It was the Christmas season and his wife wanted to take their new daughter into town for Christmas shopping. He agreed to do so. On the way, their car was struck by a truck and he was seriously injured and transported to the hospital. While they were there that night, his cabin on the creek burned to the ground.

Three strikes, he said. Cancer, car wreck, house gone. "They've really got it in for me," he said.

Many newspapers carried his story. Life magazine sent a writer to interview him in the hospital. When the writer arrived and explained why he was there, Brooks looked up and said:

"Are you going to pay me?"

The writer said no, Life magazine didn't do that.

"Then F--- off." Wells said.

A fund was set up for those who wanted to contribute to Wells and his family. When he left the hospital he took the money in the account and went with his family to Florida. I never heard from him after that..

10
NO CHEERING IN THE PRESS BOX

It's the oldest rule in sports writing. Sports writers, like news reporters, must remain objective, must favor no side. And if deep down they do, they must never show it.

If you have only one college in town and if you have covered its teams for some time, that is difficult. You do care which team wins. You want your team, the local team, the team you've been covering, to win.

But you must not show it.

For that reason it follows that journalists should keep their distance from the people they cover so as not to be influenced by friendship or to be perceived as showing favoritism.

In my days as a sports writer, I had no trouble remaining silent in the press box. That is not to say I was not silently cheering. But I like to think no one knew it.

However, I proved to be a miserable failure in not making friends with a few of those I covered.

I told myself no one could tell that by reading my columns and stories. But in all honesty, I doubt that was the case.

Jim Lamb had been a star guard on the Marshall College basketball team and now was head coach at Huntington St. Joseph's, the city's Catholic high school. He was in his second year when I was in my first as a sportswriter. I cannot remember the day we met or quite how we became friends. It was just one of those special relationships that clicked from the beginning, in which one feels he has known the other forever.

Yet we could not have been more different. He grew up in Westerly, Rhode Island. He came to Huntington to attend Marshall because his aunt and uncle lived here and he could stay with them. He was not on a basketball scholarship. In fact, the Marshall coach, Cam Henderson, hardly knew of his existence. Having been a good high school player in Rhode Island, he tried out for the Marshall team anyway, but was quickly cut. So he played his freshman year in intramural games. One day Henderson came by and watched him, and the following year invited him to try out for the team again. Lamb turned out to be an outstanding guard especially in leading the Marshall fast break. He was tough, quick, had great hands and perhaps most of all, a good mind.

And now he was a new young coach and I a new younger sports writer.

I covered many of his high school games and

when I interviewed him afterward we usually ended up talking about subjects beyond that night's game. He confided that as a disciple of Henderson's zone defense, he began his high school coaching career by using it. It did not carry over as he had thought, and early on he was taken aside by the veteran Williamson High coach, Tony Gentile, who advised him, "Jim, you'll never get anywhere in high school running a zone defense. It just won't work with kids. You need to go man-to-man." He did.

One day he told me, "I can tell watching another team warm up whether it is well coached."

"How is that?"

"If all their players go in for layups the same way and shoot them the same way, no fancy stuff, they're disciplined and they're well coached."

I have tested that theory many times since and have generally found it to be true.

He was not a big man and he walked with a bounce. He seemed younger to me than he was, which was five or six years older than I. But he was clearly a man of conviction and great faith in his church. He loved history, which he taught at St. Joe. He was a strict disciplinarian in the classroom as well as on the court. There would be no foolishness in either of his worlds.

After I was married our friendship grew even stronger. Sandy and I had moved from our apartment over my parents' garage into a small house in the west end. We managed to buy it even though I had no money. What I did have was the nerve to ask administrators on the financial side of my newspaper for a $1,000 loan to be used for a down payment and repaid with small deductions out of my small check. And Lamb came by often, especially after his games, for beer and conversation. We talked about many things and argued about some, from religion to fiction to the role of journalists in the world, especially sportswriters, most of whom he considered suspect. Why he became my closest friend considering my "suspect" occupation, I do not know.

We played golf regularly. We played poker, we drank beer, we listened to music. He borrowed all my Four Freshman albums and I have not seen them since. My wife Sandy and his wife Nohad became friends. We spent considerable time in each others' homes. We traveled together to the Greenbrier Open golf tournament in White Sulphur Springs. And one summer Sandy and I accompanied the two of them back to his home in Westerly, R. I.

Each year the State Catholic High School Basketball tournament was held in Huntington, Catholic schools not being eligible at the time for the regular state tournament. St. Joe was always the host but never the favorite. But with Lamb as coach they became more competitive and soon he won the championship. Each year there was a party for all the schools' coaches and officials, and Sandy and I were always pleased to be invited.

A sportswriter is not supposed to be that close to someone he is covering. That is dangerous territory. In the years to come as an editor I would take sportswriters off their beats if I found them getting too close to the people they covered. But I plead guilty to having done it myself. However, not once did I resist asking Jim Lamb tough questions or reshape a story or cover up something he did not want in the newspaper if I thought it should be written about. He never complained . He might have argued with me about books and religion, but never about the job each of us had to do.

As time passed and I moved from Sports to the news side, we understandably did not see each other quite as much. But one night I received a call that his uncle had died. Sandy and I drove to a house where there was quite a wake in progress. And together, he and I "drank Unc over the bridge." Not long after that he accepted a position in New Jersey and I heard nothing from him for some time. Then one evening there was a knock on our door and there he stood. He had come to Huntington to see his aunt and was by himself. He came into the house and we had drinks and talked into the wee hours. The next day he returned to New Jersey. I never saw him again. Years later when I was living in Arizona I was notified of his death from cancer. Despite the passage of time, it was quite a shock, and I wept.

Jim Lamb was not the only source I became close to during my sportswriter days. John "Patsy" Jefferson was a junior high school coach and part owner of a small nine-hole golf course. I first met him when he was a student teacher at my high school, but he did not remember that. Now, as a sportswriter I was told to interview him about a new golf venture.

He told me was going to build a new nine-hole course along the Ohio River east of Huntington. He had a name picked out: Riviera Golf Club. But it wasn't going to be a club; it was going to be a public golf course. The land on which he would build his course belonged to his father-in-law, whose farm house still sat on the premises, overlooking the river. He suggested Sandy and I come by the following Sunday and we would "walk the course' even though there was no course as yet, only farm land. We said we would and looked forward to it.

The weather did not cooperate. The day was dark, cold and rainy. Still, my wife and I went. We pulled up in front of the farm house and were greeted at the door. We sat briefly by the fire while Jefferson spoke of his plans. His wife, Thelma, sat quietly, listening to his every word, which is the way I remember her almost every time we were together.

Suddenly he stood and said, "So let's go see it."

"In the rain?"

"Never rains on a golf course," he said. 'Didn't anyone ever tell you that?"

We went into the rain and walked his new course, from the point where the first tee would go to where he could envision a green, then onto the second tee, and so on.

"This one will be really tough," he said about an obviously short hole-to-be. "The green will be tucked right into the side of this little hill and you'll have to be accurate. Hit left and you're over the hill, hit right and you're down the hill and have to come back. Tough little par three." He was beaming, and we moved on.

Finally we came to No. 9, the finishing hole. And here, he said, would be a lake, which would pose a problem for long hitters on their drives and others on their second shots. "Do you lay up? Or go for the green?" He laughed. He was having a good time despite the rain.

We saw each other often after that, and I watched as the golf course came into reality. When it did he gave me a membership card and said, "You can play here any time with this." I thanked him but had a question.

"If it's a public course why do you call it a club and why do you have membership cards?"

"So I can restrict who plays," he said.

I looked at him, not sure what he meant.

"Any of those black boys show up here to play my course, I'll run 'em off."

"You're not serious."

"I'm dead serious. I don't want 'em on my course. They're not welcome here."

I tried talking with him. That's just not right, I said. If it's a public course, it should be open to all the public, without discrimination. Besides, I said, he was denying himself money-paying golfers. And he was buying himself trouble. But it was like talking to a stone wall.

"I know you like those people," he said. 'But we feel different about it. Let's just leave it at that."

I had already written about plans for the new course. Now I was writing about the grand opening. I reported the cost of green fees and cart fees and season membership. But I said nothing about the course being off   limits to anyone, blacks or otherwise,. I simply did a straight story on the opening of a new public golf course. "Public," after all, meant everybody, right? Let him deal with it.

In later years I would have written a different story: "New 'public' golf course excludes African-Americans." As an editor I would have been upset with my reporters if they had not done so. Why then did I not make this public then? In truth, it really didn't occur to me to write about it. I was young and this was the mid-1950's and such matters were not ordinarily written about unless someone made it an issue. I was disappointed in my new friend but I told myself he would "come around" and change his mind. Maybe, I thought, I can help him change.

Some time later I asked if any blacks had tried to play there.

"Yeah, we had a couple the other day."

"What did you do?"

"I told 'em we had no tee times. They weren't stupid. They knew what I was saying. so they just turned around and drove away."

I looked at him and he said, "I know, I know. We feel differently about this."

He wanted my boss, Ernie Salvatore, to see his new course and gave me a membership card for him. I convinced Ernie to go by the following week. To say that golf was not Ernie's game would be kind. But Patsy gave him a new set of clubs, hoping to get him involved. Ernie accepted and said he would return to try them out.

I looked at the irons. Wilson Staff Dynapower. Brand new, the best. I admired them greatly and Patsy must have noticed. A few days later he presented me with a set of my own.

In those days it was not uncommon for reporters and sportswriters to receive gifts from those they covered—just as I had been given a bottle of booze when I first met members of the police department. Salvatore, for example, had a watch from the Cincinnati Reds. As the years went by, accepting gifts—or free tickets or free travel or whatever—was considered unethical, which of course it was, and the practice ceased. But at that time I graciously accepted the Wilson Dynapower irons. I have them still, in my garage. They're antiques now and probably ought to be mounted on some wall.

After walking Patsy's course Salvatore had an idea. He thought it would be a great promotion for the course and for our newspaper if we were to stage an amateur public golf tournament there. Jefferson quickly bought in. Ernie said we would get together, form a committee and iron out details. Privately, I asked Jefferson what he would do if any blacks entered the tournament. As the co-sponsor, our paper can't very well turn them away, I said.

He hadn't thought about that. Finally he said, "Well, we'll see."

But none did.

The tournament was a success and so was Riviera Golf Club, despite Patsy's still unpublicized policy of not allowing black golfers to play there.

But time and fate have a way of bringing about great change.

The more successful Riviera Golf club and

Patsy Jefferson became, the broader his world became. He was able to give up his junior high school coaching job and do other things, including playing in tournaments as a club pro. He added a second nine holes to his layout, which meant more golfers could play. And gradually that included black golfers. Not everyone at the club got the message early on, and when one black golfer attempted to enter a tournament there he was told he could not. Two hours later that was discovered and the club called the golfer and told him a mistake had been made, to bring his money and come and get an entry form.

Impressed by a young black woman who worked as a bartender and server in a private dining club downtown, he managed to lure her away to head up his club's ' bar and food service. He later added another woman who also was black. He came to trust them and care for them.

Patsy had long been a fan of Marshall College sports. He especially supported the football team and as his fortunes grew he increased that support considerably. He got to know the players, many of whom were black. At that time it was considered acceptable for players to have individuals from the community as personal mentors or advisors. I do not know whether this involved financial support for the individual player; certainly it mean contributions to the football program. Whatever, in the late Sixties Patsy was assigned a star defensive back who happened to be black, and became very close to him. Tragically, in November 1970 that player was among those who perished in the terrible

Marshall plane crash. Patsy was devastated and seemed to withdraw for some time.

Patsy Jefferson had come a long way from the man who would not permit blacks to play his golf course. He would more than make up for that, as time would prove.

In 1971 a group of black golfers formed a golf tournament of their own, one to be organized and conducted by blacks but open to all. It was held at the small Forest Hills golf course across the Ohio River in Chesapeake. Some fifty-five golfers entered and the tournament was a success. The following year it was given a new name—the Ebony Classic—and moved to Sugarwood golf course south of Huntington. Participation grew.

Soon after, one of the tournament's founders, Joe Williams, was playing at Riviera when the young black woman at the bar asked him why he didn't bring his tournament to Riviera. Williams said he would be very interested in doing that. And Patsy Jefferson offered him the chance.

Joe Williams was the same golfer who had been sent home from Riviera when he tried to enter a tournament there years before. He had played Riviera often since and welcomed the opportunity to move the Ebony Classic there. And there it was held for the next fifteen years.

"Every year Patsy just turned the entire course over to us for our tournament," Williams remembered recently. "He was great."

What brought about such transformation?

"Times change, people change," Williams said. "I think it's a gradual thing. You know, often converts become your strongest supporters."

So it had been with Patsy Jefferson.

As an editor I have often editorialized against discrimination and assigned reporters to expose it. Yet as a young man I had not written that blacks were barred from the new Riviera Golf Club--not when it opened, not in my seven years as a sportswriter. Could this have been because Patsy was my good friend? Had I gotten so close to someone I was covering that I was trying to protect him from criticism?

In revisiting all this, the matter troubled me greatly. And so I talked about it with Joe Williams, who over the years has become my friend.

"I don't think that was it," Williams said. "Times were different then. People didn't write about those things. You were young, you probably never even thought about it."

There is no question I had gotten too close to Patsy Jefferson. As I had to Jim Lamb. As I had to others. Had that affected my performance as a journalist? I like to think not. But even now I am not so sure.

At least, I didn't cheer in the press box. Aloud.

11
MOVING ON

I believe it was Ernest Hemingway who said journalism is a good occupation if one gets out of it soon enough. After all, he had started as a reporter in Kansas City, and he became a Nobel Prize winner in literature. I do not know who said that sports is a great place to start in the newspaper business if one gets out of it soon enough. But I can vouch for it.

In 1960, after seven years in sports, I wanted out. That was quite surprising even to me because my dream had been to become a sportswriter, and that had happened. I had written an untold number of stories, had covered countless games, matches and events in every sport that existed in our town, on every level. I had become a sports columnist, risen to the position of assistant sports editor, had taught and supervised others, and like sports writers everywhere had suffered the proverbial slings and arrows of coaches, players, fans and parents. And I was tired of it, tired of the whole scene. I had even stopped being a sports fan.

I was also seven years older than the kid who had wandered into the newsroom in hopes of realizing a dream. I was married and the father of two—our son John Christopher had been born in late 1959. My priorities and my interests had changed. Now those included books, music of all kinds, theater. They always had been there, but now they took center stage. I now read The Saturday Review and Esquire and the Paris Review instead of sports publications.

And I wanted to write something other than sports. For some time I had worked on short stories and articles whenever I could find the time. I wanted to begin a novel, about what I had no idea. But the feeling grew that my job in sports was keeping me from doing that.

I thought about the day George Clark had mentioned my moving out of sports. Perhaps it was now time to do just that, to leave the "toy department."

My wife was not surprised. "I've seen you moving in this direction," she said. "I think it would be good. I know you'll miss sports."

"I don't think so," I said.

"It's a big decision for you. You know I'll support you whatever you decide."

As she would always.

I said nothing to Salvatore but after deadline the following Monday—his day off—I went into Clark's office. I did not intend to go behind Ernie's back. I would talk with him before anything actually happened. But for now I would talk with Clark.

"You once said you believed I could move beyond sports in this business."

"Yes, I did."

"Well, it may be time."

"Has anything happened? With Ernie?"

"No, it's all been great. I just….I feel I've…"

"Moved beyond sports?"

"I guess so."

"Have you talked to Ernie about this?"

"Not yet. I wanted to talk with you first."

"What would you like to do?"

"I don't know. I hate to go from being assistant sports editor to being a reporter or copy editor. At least now I have a title, even if it is in sports. I know that sounds arrogant."

"We could use some help on the news desk. Let me think about it."

The news desk was the key to the entire news operation, the production center of the news room, where local, national and world stories were edited, given headlines, dummied onto pages. The command center, I thought to myself. That wouldn't be too bad. But what would I do? What would I be? A copy editor? I could feel my ego getting in the way.

The following day George Clark motioned me to his office.

"How does 'assistant telegraph editor' sound?"

"Interesting. What's the job?"

The job was to "break down" the many wire reports pouring into The Advertiser newsroom: the "A" wire of The Associated Press, the general wire of International News Service (later to merge with United Press to form UPI), several AP state wires from West Virginia, Kentucky and Ohio, and a business news wire. Then, to sit on the rim of the news desk and edit stories and write headlines. I would be reporting to the telegraph editor, Bob Powers.

Salvatore was not surprised when I told him. "I could see it coming," he said. "I could see your interest in sports changing. You know I wish you the best."

I wasn't sure what to say. This man had hired me as an eighteen-year-old, trusted me, taught me, stayed with me. I knew and liked his wife and kids, I had helped him move from one house to another, we had taken trips together, we had had drinks. This man who had called me "Kid" for a long time, and then "Hattie," because he loved nicknames like that. I finally said. "I'll never forget what you've done for me."

"Hey, we're still on the same team," he said. "We'll still see each other."

And so I left the sports department, left my early dream, and moved on. I had learned a lot in sports, had enjoyed the time there very much. I appreciated what it had given me. And I was grateful, and would forever remain so, to Ernie Salvatore.

But I was right. It was time.

I knew life would be different for me, and I welcomed that. I recently had longed for change. I had lived in the city's west end most of my life. And I found myself still there, still in the city, with houses on either side. I began looking for a house more suitable for the writer I hoped to be, a house with space and trees and breathing room. In no time I found a fixer-upper in the woods east of the city that included an adjacent wooded acre. And I said farewell to the west end and farewell to sports and farewell to the boy I had been for too long.

So what did I learn in seven years as a sports writer—beyond the fundamentals of writing, interviewing, editing, and all the many other basics?

One learns a lot about human behavior in the wonderful world of sports. It is good training for dealing with every kind of news source—city and county government officials, holders of various offices, politicians. Especially politicians.

Readers of all sections of the paper have said forever that they want and expect "fair and objective" coverage. Not true. Very few actually want "objective" coverage. And just about everyone has his own definition of "fair." To most, "fair and objective" means coverage that favors their team or their candidate or their party or their school or their particular issue, that agrees with their own view of the world. To most, truly objective coverage is seen as being partial to the other side--"slanted," to use the age-old charge. This was true then and it is, unfortunately, even more true today. In fact, today it is a national epidemic.

That this was so for coaches, players, fans and parents came as a surprising and somewhat difficult lesson for me.

Take coaches. On any level--high school, college or professional--many coaches believe down deep that "you're with me or against me." They may deny it; often they are even unaware of it. But it is a fact.

"I know you have a job to do," some coaches

will say. That is usually followed by "But…" And it's what comes after the "but" that really matters to them.

Some coaches welcome the media—we said "press" in those days—with open arms. They realize that the more word gets out about their teams—"positive" words—the more fans will turn out and the more players will want to play there. Other coaches would be happier if members of the media never showed up. They view the media as a necessary evil, not to be trusted, not part of the "family."

Some coaches, especially on the college and professional level, have learned to take advantage of the media, to "use" the media. Not just to help build crowds or attract recruits, but to influence their own players or opposing players. They will speak of key injuries, then play the supposedly injured players. They will describe the opposition as if it were the greatest team in the history of the league. They will stonewall when they believe it best serves them. And some, if they feel wronged, will punish the guilty writer by not speaking to him or her or ban him or her from practice sessions and locker rooms.

On the other hand, they might become so friendly with a writer they believe they can influence that they will provide "inside" information and before the writer realizes it he or she has indeed become part of the "family."

One veteran sports writer, when asked about a report that two players had quit the local college football team, replied, "We're not ready to release that yet."

"We"? It was time to get that writer off the beat.

"Negative" was a very popular word among coaches and fans. Columnists were "negative" if they questioned a play or coaching decision. And many coaches were convinced that the press in general was negative and not to be trusted.

Once when I contacted a college coach about his outstanding recruiting class, he said he didn't want to talk about it. I was astonished. "I would think you'd want everyone to know what good success you've had," I said.

"Oh, you mean you want to write a *positive* story?" he said in all sincerity.

Once I quoted a high school coach saying his team had lost the game in the final minutes because "we got greedy." The next day his wife called our house to claim her entire family had been hurt by this terrible thing I had written and "Maybe someday something will happen in your family to hurt you too."

Fans can be worse and parents worse than that. A mother called one day to complain that our newspaper had published a story about the opposing team her son's school would be facing in the state playoffs. We had run at least three stories that week about her son's team and this was the first on the visiting team.

"Don't you want to know something about the opposition?" I said.

"No," she said.

"Deserve" was another popular word for fans and parents.

"Our team deserves more coverage than the other team…Our son deserves to have his picture in the paper…Our boys may have lost ten games this year but they worked hard and deserve better coverage…"

Not that this applies to all coaches, all fans and all parents. "Some of my best friends are coaches," I used to say, and it was true. Some of the people I most admire were and are coaches. I have named some of them in earlier chapters. Nobody is perfect after all (certainly not sportswriters or other members of the media). And most coaches work extremely hard and face a huge list of challenges and problems without worrying about whether writers are with them or against them. Still, dealing with them as well as the many other kinds of people who make up the sports world was a valuable lesson, well learned.

Lastly, and this did not come to me until later, I discovered that the sports department is the one place in the newsroom where one gets it all-- reporting and writing, editing local and wire copy, writing headlines, selecting stories, dummying up pages, going to the composing room to watch the pages being assembled. If you have worked in the sports department of a small- to medium-sized newspaper, you will be able to handle almost any job in the newsroom.

.

12
SLOTS AND RIMMERS

The news desk was a large horseshoe-shaped table in the center of which was the "slot," and there was a well-defined system to its operation. In the slot sat the news editor or "slot man." By the time of my move from sports, that title and responsibility had fallen to John R. Brown, who had been my city editor during that first summer. Local stories considered worthy of page one were passed to him by the city editor, who sat nearby, just as the most important national and world stories came to him from the telegraph editor, who sat beside him on the outside of the desk. The news editor determined which stories he would use on page one and which stories should go on inside pages, and also dummied up page one. The city editor made up the local page and the telegraph editor the inside wire pages. Stories were marked for pages with headline requirements assigned and were then distributed to the copy editors who sat on the outside rim of the desk—hence the nickname "rim man" or "rimmer."

There each story received another editing and a headline.

Once given headlines and dummied on specific pages the stories were sent through pneumatic tubes to the composing room one floor above the newsroom. There they were retyped either directly in a hot metal-producing Linotype machine or on a machine punching paper tape which was fed into other Linotypes. Out of the Linotypes came trays of hot lead type. Proofs were made of the type and passed onto a nest of proofreaders who read the stories yet again for typos, spelling and style. Corrections were marked and then recast and the final type was placed into steel frames the size of a newspaper page sitting atop steel tables on rollers. Smaller headlines were also set in hot metal machines, larger headlines were put together by hand, reminiscent of the old wooden block type. Photographs arrived from the engraving department in the form of zinc plates and were placed atop lead blocks. And the entire page was put together by printers or compositors following the paper dummies we editors had drawn up. By then the editors had come into the composing room to supervise the final lockup of the pages, which were then rolled toward "stereotype," or "stero" as the printers called it. There each page was covered with mats and shoved into a table-sized press with a roller so heavy that it created impressions of the lead type and zinc plates in the mats. The mats then went to the press room where they were bent into half-circles and cast—again in hot lead—into circular plates to be locked onto the huge rotary printing press. Webs of newsprint feeding from large rolls in a storage room below were threaded in seemingly impossible angles throughout the press, over and under the plates. And when the green button was pushed the giant press roared into action, the plates picking up ink and printing the plate images onto the newsprint. And voila! We had a newspaper.

Over the years proofreaders have at one time or another saved every newspaper, every editor and every reporter from mistakes and embarrassment. Alas, once "new technology" came to the newsroom in order to "capture the original keystroke," they went the way of the Linotype machines. And newspapers have not been as clean and mistake-free since.

But in those days stories got several readings—by the department editor, then a copy editor, and finally the proofreader.

I came in each morning at 5:30, turned on the newsroom lights and went first to the two teletype machines just a few feet from the news desk. A tangled stream of stories rested on the floor, having been printed and spat out during the night from each machine. I carried each pile to my place on the news desk, which consisted of one small drawer and a couple feet of surface space. Using a metal ruler I tore the stories apart, one from the other, and placed them into short stacks on the desk: budgeted stories (those deemed important enough to be listed on that day's wire news budget) in one stack, shorter, less important stories in another. Then I went into the wire room of the newsroom where hummed several other wire machines and gathered all those piles and took them to the news desk and went through the same procedure. West Virginia stories went into one pile, Ohio another, and so on.

Handling so many wire stories every day from so many points on earth, I became somewhat knowledgeable about national and world news. Naturally I wanted to see the stories I considered to be of major significance in the pages of our newspaper. But there was never enough space.

Most local copy produced by local editors and reporters did get used somewhere in the paper. Local editors had planned and assigned it and reporters had produced it, after all. Also, most afternoon papers emphasized local stories, whereas morning newspapers, at least in those days, tended to be more complete: world, national, state, regional and local. The Advertiser was very much an afternoon newspaper and very much a local newspaper.

So it was with some frustration that each day I went through interesting and readable stories that I felt were important enough to be included in our pages, only to have Bob Powers select a few and shove the rest aside. There just wasn't space for everything, he would explain.

I was new, of course, so I was hardly in position to debate which ones were chosen and which left out. And I understood that the number of news pages and the amount of news hole was limited each day, determined by the amount of advertising in that day's paper.

I learned that it was generally believed that to be profitable a newspaper should average about sixty percent advertising, forty percent news. When advertising was down, the number of pages was down. That's why the Monday and Saturday papers were slim. Few advertised on those days. Editors fought for more news hole so they could get in more news, local and otherwise, and so they would not have to cut a story. A reporter whose story has been dramatically cut is not a happy reporter. Photographers wanted to see their photos used. And telegraph editors and their assistants (like me) wanted to see more of their stories published. It occurred to me long ago that the newspaper profession is one of very few in which people want to do more work, not less.

Big newspapers in big cities didn't have such a problem, at least on the same scale. But we were not a big paper and Huntington was not a big city. And a newspaper's role varies. The New York Times had a far different function and responsibility than a small town daily.

The 60-40 advertising-news ratio changed over the years to 55-45, 50-50, and sometimes even 45-55 and 40-60, favoring news. One factor was that ad revenues could be found in the growing number of supplements. Mostly, I like to think, it was because responsible publishers and newspaper companies believed in the importance of presenting the news despite less ad revenue. That, as I said, is what I *like* to think.

In any case, in my early days on the desk, I told myself that eventually I would be in a position to choose the stories I thought should go into the newspaper, and until then I would keep quiet and learn as much as I could. Besides, I was right in thinking that my new job would demand much less time than my sports writing job, and that it would afford me far more time to get to my "serious" writing at home. Each day I left the office at 1:30 in the afternoon, spent some time with my family, and then went to the den to write.

In truth, however, the copy desk job soon became quite boring. Having no pages to make up, once I broke down the wires I had nothing more to do than edit stories handed to me, write headlines as assigned, and talk to others on the desk.

Fortunately, I was still writing a boating column for the Sunday paper. It had started in sports under the byline "Cap'n Davy"—Salvatore's idea— and somebody thought it would be a good idea to keep it going. So I did so, but under my own name. It helped break up the boredom.

Otherwise, it was the dullest time of my newspaper career, before or since. I started looking around. Most newspaper people read the classified section of Editor & Publisher magazine every week, to see what jobs were out there and what they were paying, although that was rarely published. I did as well. We had enjoyed going to Florida on vacation and I thought that might be the place for me. I did a bit of research and started sending letters to various newspapers, one of them the Miami News.

By coincidence, I heard from that paper just before we were leaving for a vacation in West Palm Beach. They wanted me to come in for a tryout. We registered at the apartment we had rented on Singer Island, and the next day I drove down to Miami. I spent a full day on the paper's news desk, editing copy and writing headlines. It was a factory. A break between editions, then back on the assembly line. At the end of the day, the managing editor, Jim Bellows, called me in and told me I had done quite well. He looked at my application and the money I was seeking--$125 a week. He smiled and said they could do better than that. He offered me the job at $145 a week. I told him I was very interested, but I wanted to think about it, and would rejoin my wife and call him later.

The more I thought about it, the worse I felt. I hesitated to call him back. We left West Palm and drove back to West Virginia, all the time my stomach sending me alerts. By the time we reached my wife's parents' home in Beckley, I had made up my mind not to go. I called the Miami News' editor and told him I just didn't feel right about it. He said he understood. And I returned to Huntington and forgot about a job in Florida. It was the best decision I ever made.

However, it might have been quite an experience working for Jim Bellows. He went on to become editor of the New York Herald-Tribune and the Los Angeles Herald-Examiner, became known as the father of "new journalism," and even headed television's "Entertainment Tonight." He was quite a name in the world of journalism.

Still, I have never regretted turning down that job. One can get lost on the news desks of large newspapers.

Besides, my boredom with my own desk job was not to last.

Bob Powers decided to take a job as news editor of the Athens, Ohio News Messenger. Clark wasted no time in choosing a successor. That would be me.

We talked about the position and how Clark hoped to expand it. "I try to look on every vacancy as an opportunity," he said, "an opportunity to take a look at what we're doing and how we can make things better." (I never forgot that and in years to come it would become my own policy.)

Change began with the title. Sitting in as acting news editor on Saturday mornings meant doing more than serving as telegraph editor or wire editor, outdated titles to begin with. So I became assistant news editor.

"Still an assistant," joked C. T. Mitchell, the assistant city editor, when my promotion was announced.

We both laughed but I welcomed the title.

It was Mitchell who in a sense came to my rescue early one weekday morning. I arrived before everyone else, as usual, turned on the lights, took the wire copy from the wire service machines, and settled in my chair on the rim, breaking apart the many wire stories. The night before a friend had visited our house and I had stayed up much too late, given that I had to get up at 4:30 a.m., and unfortunately I had drunk too much. So I sat, head down, looking at the stories in front of me, hardly my usually sharp self.

Suddenly I got the strange feeling that someone was staring at me, and looked up. And I saw a little man with white hair sitting atop a bicycle, in shorts and tank top.

I had heard nothing. How could an old man on a bike be two feet in front of me? This was the second floor; how would anybody get a bike up here? It was five-thirty in the morning; the building wasn't even open. I was alone.

"Hatfield," I thought, "this time you've gone too far."

Just then C. T. Mitchell came through the door and addressed the apparition. "Yessir, can I help you?" As if it were normal to see a little old man on a bike in the middle of the second floor newsroom.

"Hello," the man said. "I'm peddling two thousand miles for peace."

Mitchell ushered our bike-riding visitor over to his desk and started taking notes. And I sat there relieved to know the little man was real, muttering to myself, "Hatfield, you've got to stop this stuff."

On normal weekend days, I sat beside John R. Brown watching as he approached his open page one dummy as if it were a blank canvas. There were no ads to contend with on page one as there were on most inside pages. In those days the front page was considered holy and ads were not permitted there, no matter how much an advertiser was willing to pay (a policy that has faded into the green hills of advertising dollars today). He would take his metal ruler and draw sharp, even lines on the page, careful not to permit one line to escape beyond its vertical columnar boundary. He drew large diagonal lines, corner to corner, in the space where he wanted a picture to be placed. And when it came time to log in the first word or two of the headline, he would painstakingly print it there. No one would see this paper dummy other than the composing room printer. But he must have gained special satisfaction for himself once it was completed.

Strangely, he often drew up the page before knowing what was going to be there, without being informed as to what the city editor or I had for the front. That is not the way to do it, obviously. But that is the way he did it. The look of the page one dummy seemed more important to him than its content.

Once he had drawn up the page, indicating what size headlines he wanted where and which spaces were reserved for local stories, he would toss it to me and say, "You take the rest."

Sometimes I would say, "You want me to take the banner? But I don't have anything worth the banner."

One day he replied, "Don't you worry; the good Lord takes care of us newspaper boys."

Half an hour later the AP teletype machine bell began ringing. A large airliner had crashed in New York.

"See?" he said.

Gallows humor, distasteful and not to my liking. But John R. Brown was not your normal newspaper man.

However, I learned a lot about dummying up pages while sitting beside him. I also learned how not to do things. Foremost: Always know what you have for the page before drawing it up. Seems elementary. But it can keep one from overplaying or underplaying stories, just to put them in pretty spaces you've designed.

On Saturday mornings I did not have to do things John Brown's way. It was all mine. I drew up my own page one after checking with the city desk to see what it might have and going through all the wires. If there were no stories worthy of a page one banner, I went without one, using instead a three- or four-column head in smaller point size. I concentrated on giving each story what I thought it deserved in my own news judgment.

13
LOSS OF INNOCENCE

As the months passed into a year, another year, then another, I did things my way on Saturday mornings and John Brown's way the rest of the week. And when my work day was finished I returned home to my family and to my writing of short stories and magazine articles, hoping more than ever to become a "real" writer, comfortable in the knowledge that if that didn't work out, I still had a newspaper job.

Looking back, I should not have taken that for granted. The administration of the Huntington newspapers was changing. Walker Long, The Advertiser's publisher, had died, as had his brother Edward, the Huntington Publishing Company's finance chief. And in 1963, William Birke, The Herald-Dispatch's publisher, died of cancer. In a surprising turn of events, Edward Long's widow, Hilda, took over as publisher of The Advertiser and

Helen Birke, widow of William Birke, became publisher of the Herald-Dispatch. Neither had experience in the newspaper business. Both were intelligent and professional. Hilda Long was especially kind and warm but outwardly not what one would call forceful. Helen Birke was more business-like, well-educated, a lover of the arts. Both were approachable and apparently were working well together.

They made Raymond Brewster, editor in chief of the Herald-Dispatch, the top news executive over both newspapers. (Looking back, given today's joint operating requirements that newspapers remain separate, I am not sure quite how that happened, but it did). Now Brewster was over both news staffs, over George Clark, over everyone. He occupied the large corner office in the newsroom, overlooking Fifth Avenue and Tenth Street, and usually spent the entire day there with little time in the newsroom itself. Which is not to say he did not meet with editors and other news staffers; but he did so in his office, on his turf. He was an imposing figure, a large and serious man, and whether or not he intended to be so, an intimidating presence.

So I found myself working not just for John Brown, my immediate supervisor, and George Clark, my top newsroom boss, mentor and friend, but also this editor-in-chief who had been our competitor. My newspaper world was changing around me. I was not sure what that would mean— for the newspapers, for George Clark, or for me. I was quite removed from those at the top, after all. I told myself to just do my job and life would go on. Quietly. Peacefully.

It was November, 1963.

On the 22nd of the month, Brown had just finished his front page. Deadline had passed and I was doing what I did each day at this time-- checking all the wire machines for any last-minute news. I had hardly risen from my chair when the bell on the closest machine—that of the AP's main wire--began ringing in a manner I had not heard before. I thought the machine had malfunctioned. and went to it immediately. And there were these terrible words:

FLASH:
KENNEDY SHOT PERHAPS FATALLY

I had seen many breaking AP news stories slugged "URGENT" and "BULLETIN." I had not seen a "FLASH" before. President Kennedy shot? My stomach turned.

I held the paper curling off the top of the teletype and turned to Brown.

"John—better tell them to hold the press."

Brown stared at me. "What?"

"Kennedy's been shot."

He leaped to the machine where I was staring. Clark dashed out of his office.

John F. Kennedy, president of the United States, had been shot while riding in an open-topped limousine in Dallas. He had been rushed to the hospital and there were conflicting stories as to his condition.

And then it came.

FLASH: KENNEDY DEAD.

Clark and Brown called the press room and composing room to tell them we were holding for the story and would be starting over and going late. Clark moved into the slot and took over, which is the only time I saw him do that before or after. Brown sat in my chair and instructed me to keep funneling them every story moving on the wires on the Dallas shooting.

The entire newsroom came alive, reporters waiting for instructions from the city editor, copy editors waiting to handle stories. I suddenly was aware of our two new publishers standing behind me, looking over my shoulder as I ripped off copy from the wire machine. Raymond Brewster stood in the doorway of his office, glancing at the tv there, then at the newsroom scene. There was a lot to do in a very short time. It all did not seem real. In one explosive moment the world had changed.

I continued to take stories off the wire machines and pass them on to Clark and Brown and edited whatever they passed back to me and wrote the headlines they assigned. Our new publishers told us to do whatever needed to be done and they would stay out of our way. By this time the newsroom was crowded with employees from other departments and visitors from nearby office buildings and even people coming in from the streets. And their murmured comments and questions created a buzz. What happened? Who did it? Why? Do they have the killer? Was there more than one?

Finally our remade afternoon newspaper was finished and we went to press, considerably late. Circulation district managers and hawkers were waiting at the loading docks and rushed to downtown intersections and vending machines and other single copy outlets with the news. President John F. Kennedy had been assassinated.

Sandy was visiting her sister in Houston at the time, with our son Chris. We all had been Kennedy supporters since the day he announced his candidacy. I felt a great need to talk with her. But coworkers told me phones were tied up everywhere and I would not be able to get through, especially to Texas. Somehow, I managed to. Like me, Sandy could not believe what had happened. We talked only briefly, but I felt better sharing the moment with her.

For the next several days our front page did not lack for significant news stories. The world stopped with the assassination of John F. Kennedy, and in that there were many stories—national and world stories from the wires, and local stories as well. Jack Kennedy had come to West Virginia in his historic campaign of 1960. He had been in our city, had lunched in the restaurant next door. What did those who had seen him then remember about him?

How did they feel about his death?

I learned a lot in those few days. I learned about notifying the composing room and engraving department and press room and circulation about holding for a huge story. I learned about increasing the pages in the newspaper as well as the press run and getting fresh single copies in the hands of hawkers on every street corner. And I learned about localizing a national news story.

I also learned that if at all possible, one must put one's feelings aside and do the job at hand. And the job at hand was getting out the newspaper so that your town, your own small world could know as much as possible about what had happened. It was not easy in this case (nor would it ever be), for like many my age I had admired JFK enormously. And I was stunned and devastated by what had happened. But I told myself to save such feelings for my time at home, not here, in the office, with the teletype machines going into meltdown, and the reporters asking questions, and the page one dummies being drawn up, and the headlines written.

I was relieved when Sandy and Chris returned and our lives resumed. For Sandy, unfortunately, that meant the burden of caring for Lisa, our disabled daughter. But we tried to make life as normal as possible, for ourselves and especially for Chris. Perhaps we would take a vacation after the holidays.

Not long before Herald-Dispatch publisher Bill Birke died he had purchased a sizeable house, called the Blue Marlin, on the ocean in Fort

Lauderdale. He reportedly paid for it with company funds, put it in the company's name, and said it was for employees to use for vacations. I asked whether that extended to my level. Whether it was planned that way or not, I was given the approval to spend a few days there with my family. It was quite a new experience for us, a wonderful change.

In 1967 we were blessed with the birth of our second son, Joel. Our cottage in the woods was now too small, so we embarked on an expansion. I contracted professionals to erect the shell of a four-room addition, and I finished the interior. The expansion included a sizeable game room on the lower level, looking over a small creek. We had friends by—fellow writers, poets, teachers, musicians. There was folk music nearly every Friday night. I liked meeting new people, especially writers and musicians. Being a newspaper man helped.

One day Walt Tevis, author of "The Hustler," came to town for an appearance at Marshall. Written first as a short story, then expanded into a novel, "The Hustler" had been made into the classic movie starring Paul Newman, George C. Scott and Piper Laurie. I invited him to our house after his talk and he accepted. We sat up until the wee hours with a bottle of Scotch, talking about writing and the movie. He had spent considerable time on the set, watching the movie being made. I found his stories fascinating.

It was not the only time I brought new and successful artists to our house. Paul "Oz" Bach, a native of Huntington, was a member of the rock group "Spanky and Our Gang," which was enjoying a top ten hit with "Sundays Will Never Be the Same." He happened to be in town visiting family and the newspaper interviewed him. I contacted him, told him there would be a number of people playing music at our house that night, and invited him to join us. He came, borrowed a guitar from my son Chris, and sat in the corner playing and singing, Chris sitting on the floor beside him, watching intently. It was a fun evening.

But it was also the Sixties.

14
THE NIGHTMARES CONTINE

Over the next few years my job changed considerably. The Advertiser, under George Clark, took over publication of the Sunday Herald-Advertiser. Its editor, H. R. "Punk" Pinckard, moved to the Herald-Dispatch as editorial page editor. And I moved from the daily operation of the Advertiser to concentrate on putting out the Sunday paper and its Sunday magazine and TV section. No longer would I be working for John R. Brown on the Advertiser news desk.

I found a metal table in the Composing Room and moved it to a corner of the newsroom. I moved my chair and typewriter with its rolling stand to the corner as well and set up shop there, happy to be away from the Advertiser rim. Three days each week I worked on the magazine and entertainment sections. I made myself book editor and welcomed review copies of new books which found a home in our expanded house. On Friday, when the Sunday page dummies arrived in the newsroom, I planned the main part of the Sunday package and put together some of the pages. On Saturdays I came into the office in the afternoon and sat in the news desk slot, dummying up the front page and distributing stories to copy editors for editing and headlines. I worked through the final edition midnight press start and checked the pages in the composing room and the finished product as it came off the press.

One day Raymond Brewster called me into his office to advise me that a few more changes were being made. George Clark would become his special assistant and John R. Brown would be named managing editor of the Advertiser. Don Mayne, a veteran Herald-Dispatch editor, would becoming managing editor of that paper. And I would become managing editor of the Sunday Herald-Advertiser. *Managing Editor.* That was special.

I thanked Brewster for his confidence in me. He said there would be an announcement published in the papers and suggested that I should be identified as "C. Donald Hatfield," which was more formal than simply "Don," which I had always used.

"Also," he said, leaning back with his hands together, "you'll want to get new friends. You won't want to be mingling with the troops in the trenches anymore."

I was surprised by this, but should not have been. It was his philosophy of management: Observe the chain of command and govern from the corner office, not on the field. Officers ate with officers, not enlisted men. It had served him well.

I would not follow that advice, of course. Raymond Brewster came from a different time and that was just not me. But I understood that he was sincere in giving me advice and I appreciated his wanting to help me in my new position. I may not have been editor of either daily newspaper, but I was running the news operation of the company's largest publication, the 63,000 circulation Sunday Herald-advertiser. I would devote all my attention to that, and I welcomed the opportunity, whatever this new age brought.

The death of John F. Kennedy proved to be only the beginning of a decade of nightmares and heartbreak. Vietnam. Police turning water hoses on black Americans. Student protests. Riots across the country. And, unbelievably, more assassinations.

And in the hills and valleys of West Virginia, there was tragedy of another kind.

On December 15, 1967, a wintry Friday evening with snow flurries in the sky, traffic was heavy crossing the Silver Bridge spanning the Ohio River between Point Pleasant, West Virginia and Kanaugua, Ohio. A string of vehicles moved slowly on the bridge; others were lined up waiting to ease onto it. They carried Christmas shoppers, people returning home from work, children riding with parents.

Suddenly and without warning, an eye-bar snapped in the Ohio end of the bridge, and the forty-year-old structure collapsed into the river below. More than thirty vehicles fell into the deep cold water, seven others crashed onto the muddy bank on the Ohio side.

It took hardly more than a minute.

No one knew at the time how many vehicles had fallen. No one knew how many people they carried or how many were fighting for their lives or how many bodies there might be.

Rescuers hurried down the river banks, digging into the wreckage of cars still on land and climbing into boats to reach as many as they could in the dark river. Flash lights played over the water and automobile lights from both sides of the river pierced the night. There were shouts and cries and at the same time a strange and deathly silence.

Later it was learned that forty-six people had died. Nine others had been injured. An unknown number had survived.

There were many questions that night, and the next day, and for days and months to come. And there would be many stories.

Point Pleasant sat on the eastern fringe of the Huntington newspapers' circulation area, about forty miles away. Point Pleasant residents shopped in Huntington stores and some held jobs in Huntington. High school teams from the two cities played each other regularly. Friends and relatives were common between the two areas.

This was very much a local story as well as a national story.

On Saturday, the morning Herald-Dispatch and the afternoon Huntington Advertiser were full of stories and photographs of the disaster. By the time

I arrived in the newsroom Saturday afternoon to put out the Sunday paper, a wealth of material awaited-- interviews with survivors, more dramatic photos, news accounts, every inch capturing the terror, the sadness, the shock of this huge event which had occurred on our doorstop.

I examined the photos and stories before me, and I was moved. I did not know these people—the living or the dead. But I could not help thinking, What must it have been like to be sitting in one's car one minute and be trapped in that car in the cold river waters the next? I was very much on the outside. I had not been on the scene as had our reporters and photographers, nor had I been a part of producing either of the Saturday newspapers. Yet I felt a responsibility to do right by them in continuing and expanding their story in the Sunday paper. And this we did.

In just a few weeks a new year would begin. 1968. A new beginning, I thought. But I could not shake the feeling that something as yet unknown was lurking just around the corner.

Four months later, Dr. Martin Luther King Jr. was gunned down outside his hotel room in Memphis. I heard the news while talking with friends in my yard. I was stunned, angered, deeply saddened, and fearful. I had admired King greatly as a man of peace. What a terrible loss, not only for his followers, but for the nation. Already there was great unrest in the country, including Huntington, and I like others had great fears as to what might happen now.

There would be more violence—that much we knew. Ironic, given King's non-violent teachings. The man had won the Nobel Peace Prize, at the time the youngest ever to be so honored. How could this have happened? Yet given the climate in the country and the violent prejudices so many harbored, I should not have been surprised.

Stories streamed in from The Associated Press —news stories, reaction stories, stories seeking historical perspective. And we did our own local reaction pieces. I suggested to the city desk that we contact my friend Bill Congleton, a leader in the black community, for his comments. The city editor said he would add his name to the list.

Not all the comments were complimentary to King, even in our own building.

"Got what he had coming to him," said one composing room worker.

"No he didn't," I said, and walked away before I became even more angry.

The King story did not go away. There were the riots we knew would come. There were marches and protests nationally and locally. There was the search for the killer or killers.

Enough, I thought. Let there be no more killings in this country.

Only two months later, on June 5, Sen. Robert Kennedy was struck down, shot in the head close-range in the midst of a Los Angeles victory celebration during his own presidential campaign.

I heard the radio reports in the pre-dawn hours and went straight to the office. I asked John Brown if there were anything I could do, any help he might need, He was going through stacks of wire stories and arranging lines on his page one paper dummy. I told him I would clear all the AP wire machines for him.

Bobby Kennedy was still alive, the reports said, though critically wounded. I watched the wires for Brown and waited to be given something to do. The Sunday paper could wait. I thought of my son Chris, not quite nine years of age but an avid Bobby Kennedy supporter. He had written a paper on Kennedy and made RFK signs for school. I had left that morning before he woke. I called home to see how he was doing.

"He is devastated," Sandy said. "We're just praying that Bobby lives."

I went to a nearby snack shop to get coffee and donuts and ran into a friend who was a strong anti-Kennedy Republican.

"I never liked the s.o.b.," he said. "But if he pulls through, I swear I'll vote for him."

I returned to the office and told Brown I was available if needed and went to my Sunday desk in the corner. I knew there would be far more stories available for our Sunday package than we could ever find space for. I knew there would be updated reports on his condition, if he indeed lived. I knew there would be Kennedy family stories and political stories and reaction stories of all kinds. We of course would be doing our own. I tried jotting down some ideas I could share with the city desk. But mostly I just sat there. And I said a silent prayer that

Bobby Kennedy would pull through. Of all the Kennedys, he seemed the most socially conscious, the most sensitive even though to his detractors he was "ruthless."

Robert F. Kennedy died the next day. First Jack, then Martin Luther King, now Bobby. When would it end?

The unrest would not end. It would only grow, across the country, and in Huntington. Students marched to protest the Vietnam war. Blacks staged sit-ins at restaurants and other places where they were forbidden to go, including a few in Huntington.

The aptly named White Pantry became a prime target for such protests. (Some years later Bill Congleton would admit privately to me that he could not bring himself to participate because, he said, "I knew myself and I was afraid of what I might do when subjected to the treatment my brothers were receiving.") Another target was the popular Bailey's Cafeteria.

Marshall students and a few members of the Marshall faculty, mixed with other anti-war protesters, marched down the streets of Huntington and gathered outside our Fifth Avenue newspaper building beneath our newsroom windows.

"Hupco feeds the war machine," they chanted, referring to the shortened name of our Huntington Publishing Company. We were part of furthering the war, they shouted, and their signs repeated the message.

A number of us stood in the window watching

them below and I recognized several friends among them and tried to offer a smile and subtle wave and thumbs up without anyone noticing. I did not like being perceived as being part of the "war machine." I also opposed the Vietnam war.

In the midst of all this, the two publishers of the Huntington newspapers, apparently realizing they needed help in running the operation, brought in a new man to take on the responsibilities of general manager. His name was John L. Foy and he had been responsible for newspapers in Miami, Florida. He was a big Irishman, full of laughs, passionate, friendly yet stern. I did not report to him, as he handled the business side, leaving Raymond Brewster responsible for the news and editorial side. But I liked him immediately.

Taking note of the demonstrations across the country as well as outside our building, Foy called a meeting in Brewster's office and brought with him the city's police chief, Gil Klienknecht. Foy said he had received reports that demonstrators planned to enter our building and disrupt as much of our operation as they could. We would post a police officer at each entrance, he said. But he hesitated to restrict access to our building because we believed in the right of people to protest and we stood for freedom of speech. If they do get into our building, he said, we should not try to stop them. And if they do start to destroy something, we should step aside. "We can replace things," he said. "We can't replace people."

I was impressed by that.

The demonstrators did not enter the building, however. And they did not attempt to stop our delivery trucks or destroy anything. They marched, carrying their signs, they chanted, and they dispersed.

It was also about this time that H. R. Pinckard became ill. Editorials were needed for the Herald-Dispatch. It was hardly my responsibility and certainly not my newspaper, but always looking for a reason to write, I decided to offer a few to Brewster for the morning paper.

The first few were fairly innocuous and ran as written. Then I produced one criticizing downtown merchants for their anti-growth stance against early proposals seeking a downtown mall. He called me into his office. He was holding my editorial in his hands, sitting behind that large desk, and he looked up at me.

"We've got a nice little community here," he said. "Let's keep it that way." And he threw the editorial across the desk to me. "We're not running this."

Okay, I thought, no big deal.

In a few days I offered another. Real black power, I wrote, is green power: jobs, equal pay, money.

This time he did not call me into his office, nor did he mention the editorial. It simply disappeared. I never wrote another for him.

But I was becoming more aware of the need for action. Perhaps it was the protests, perhaps discussions I had with friends or in professional organizations. I became active in the local chapter of Sigma Delta Chi, which later changed its name to Society of Professional Journalists. I moved up to president of the chapter. And I learned that West Virginia was one of few states in the union without legislation calling for open meetings and open records. I assigned news stories to explore the issue. I wrote an editorial for the Advertiser calling for establishment of such legislation in our state. And I followed up with an editorial and personal column for the Sunday paper. I wrote the governor. I called legislative leaders and our local legislators. I discussed it in meetings of our journalists group, appealing to members to join in the fight. And I sent copies of our stories, columns and editorials to the governor. West Virginia needs legislation establishing open meetings and open records requirements for all government entities, I wrote in a cover letter. Let the sunshine in.

West Virginia Gov. Arch A. Moore Jr. must have been listening. On January 12, 1970, he issued "Executive Order No. 1-70." It stated:

"Whereas the Constitutional obligation of state government departments, agencies, boards and commissions is to provide for the general health, welfare and safety of the citizens of West Virginia, and

"Whereas in our democracy the elective process guarantees representation reflective of the wishes and mandates of the citizens by allowing them to select those who represent them in government, and

"Whereas the source of all government financing comes from the people themselves, and their government representatives determine the manner in which these funds are to be spent for the public's benefit, and

"Whereas the public's right to know is a sacred trust which is an historical and necessary part of our democratic way of life; and

"Whereas, fully realizing that government's business is the people's business:

"Now therefore I, Arch A. Moore Jr., governor of the state of West Virginia, by virtue of the authority vested in me by the Constitution and statutes of West Virginia do hereby order that all departments, agencies, boards and commissions under the jurisdiction of the Executive Department of Government conduct all meetings in a completely open manner whenever final decisions are made, or business transacted which enables government to fulfill its obligation providing for the health, welfare and safety to the citizens of West Virginia."

He sent a copy of the original order, signed by himself and Jay Rockefeller as Secretary of State, to me, with a note:

"You worked harder for this than anybody. So it's only right that you should have this."

My first major accomplishment as a newspaper man. I was thrilled—and humbled.

The decade of the Sixties was behind us. "Let's hope the Seventies prove to be better," I said to Sandy.

15

RESPITE

The Seventies started well enough. Billy Edd
Wheeler, a noted country music song writer and
performer and a second cousin of Sandy's, came to
our house to interview me about my Hatfield
relatives and whatever knowledge I might have of
the famous feud. I am not sure why he wanted to
talk with me or how he found me, other than I was a
local newspaperman named Hatfield. I had long
turned my back on the tales of Hatfields and
McCoys and the images of feuding mountaineers
and hillbillies. I wanted no part of those stereotypes.
I had never lived in the area where the feuding took
place and I knew little about the whole thing. But
Wheeler, a native of southern West Virginia and a
graduate of Yale, had been signed to write a musical
outdoor drama of the "Hatfields & McCoys" to be
presented at Grandview State Park in Beckley as a
companion piece to its successful "Honey in the
Rock" production. And now he wanted to ask me
some questions as he had dozens of Hatfields and
McCoys in his research.

When he contacted me, I told him that Sandy

was a cousin of his, which surprised him, and that we were having several friends in that night to play music. I invited him to join us. He said he would come by long enough to ask a few questions and then would leave.

When he arrived he immediately told me he was not my wife's cousin, to which I said, "Okay," and that he was not going to play or sing. I said "Fine" and we went inside.

We talked in my living room for some time and I told him what little I knew, having picked up some stories from a great aunt. Then I invited him to the game room to listen to some of the music being played. Reluctantly, he agreed.

The music was going well, highlighted by a talented young guitar player named Roger Samples. Billy Edd accepted a beer and picked up a cue stick and took a few shots. In a little while he stopped and looked at Samples and said, "You know, that boy's picking the ass off that thing."

He put away the cue stick and sat on the side of the pool table and listened some more. Finally he picked up someone's guitar—it was either my son Chris's or Sandy's—and started to strum. Before the evening was over, he was playing and singing songs he had written for Johnny Cash ("Jackson") and Judy Collins ("Coming of the Roads") and telling us how they came about. It was a great evening.

In June , Sandy and I were invited, with both our sons, to attend the premier of "Hatfields & McCoys" at Grandview. We were seated in the fourth row. And it occurred to me halfway through the show that on stage was an actor playing my great-great grandfather, Preacher Anse Hatfield. And my sons were there to see it. For the first time I realized I had ignored something important in my life, that I had rejected my own family history. What had made me think I was too "sophisticated" to recognize that and honor it? The event changed my attitude forever.

Later Billy Edd Wheeler sent us a copy of his new book of poems, "Song of a Woods Colt," with the inscription: "To my West Virginia cousins."

But the swift steel claws of tragedy are never far away in West Virginia. Even when all seems right and there is new hope in the land.

16
IN THE DARKNESS OF OUR DAY

Marshall University was growing and approaching a decade of university status. More than ever it served as the lifeblood of the community. And now, in autumn of 1970, there was new interest in its football team, with several outstanding players having moved up from the strong freshman team of the year before.

Not only were more fans coming to home games, but more were traveling to road games. With a big one coming up against East Carolina in Greenville, North Carolina, boosters were being offered a chance to fly on the team charter, for a price. Some would take their wives and make it a real pleasure trip.

That week I attended a panel discussion at Marshall where I ran into several friends. Among them were Ray Hagley and Murrill Ralston.

Hagley and I went back to childhood days. We both came from the west end of town and played in a summer youth baseball program held on a dirt infield park on property owned by the Owens-Illinois Glass Co. Our uniforms, common in those days, were jeans and tee shirts. But there was good competition and excellent instruction. It cost nothing to participate, which was a good thing because most of us came from families of very limited means. We competed against each other in junior high school basketball (I recall a tournament game which went into two overtimes) and high school baseball. Every game was competitive. Hagley, lean and of medium height, was nevertheless a good basketball player and an outstanding catcher, as well as a Golden gloves boxing champion. Now he was a successful doctor in town, a big supporter of Marshall athletics, and happily married with children.

Ralston was a former Sigma Phi Epsilon fraternity brother. He owned a clothing store one block from campus. I had not seen him in some time. He said he and his wife, known as "Flip," were going on the charter flight to the East Carolina game. Hagley said he and his wife, Shirley, would also be going. They urged me to go and take Sandy.

I told them I would like to but I had to work; I would be in the news slot Saturday night, putting out the Sunday paper as usual.

I mentioned the invitation to Sandy that evening and added, 'It's just as well. We probably couldn't afford it. It's a big game, though, and we might have a shot at winning."

Saturday, Nov. 14, 1970—game day—began as a normal fall day in Huntington. I listened to the first half of the game before driving to the office. By now it was raining and already the sky was getting dark. The game was close and the Thundering Herd did have a shot at winning, but lost late, 17-14. I went about the usual chores involved in getting the paper out. Our friend Keith Newman had invited us to dinner at his apartment. He would pick up Sandy and the kids and I would join them during my dinner break.

By shortly after 7 p.m. I had finished the first edition, including page one. There was still considerable time before deadline but it was a slow news night. Outside, the rain had become heavier and fog had settled in. I started to call Sandy and say I would be coming soon.

The police radio sat to my right where the city editor and I both could hear it. It was odd, but over the years I had somehow managed to hear only the things that were important and to hear none of the rest.

Now I heard something important. Something about a plane being down.

I froze.

A freelance photographer named Jim York called in saying there had been a plane crash at Tri-State Airport. He was on his way.

Police reporter Jack Hardin, enjoying the night off at his home in Ceredo, not far from the airport, checked in. He would soon be there and get back to us.

I looked at my watch. It would be about time for the Marshall plane to arrive.

Please. Not that.

I thought about the Wichita State plane going down just some weeks before, taking the lives of some of its players.

Don't let that happen here.

C. T. Mitchell, the Saturday night city editor, came in from dinner and I gave him the news: there had been a plane crash at Tri-Stat e Airport.

More calls came in and the police radio was barking out the terrible news. A large plane had crashed short of the runway and was burning. Only a portion of the tail section could be seen, bearing the letters "ERN."

"Eastern used to fly in here," I said. "Do they still?"

No. It was not Eastern. It was Southern. Southern Airways. The airline Marshall had chartered.

Hardin confirmed our worst fears. A wallet had been found bearing the name of a Marshall player.

The Marshall plane had crashed in the rain into the tree covered hillside, bursting into flames. It was carrying seventy-five people—players, coaches, townspeople. There were no survivors.

"There is nothing left," Hardin said. "It's terrible."

For a moment I did not move. I thought of Murrill and Flip Ralston. I thought of Ray Hagley and his wife Shirley, who had worked in the classified advertising department of our newspaper. I thought of their children. And I thought about the players. Kids, all of them. Kids with such high hopes.

It was almost more than one could bear.

I told the composing room not to roll any pages, to get page one and the jump page back, and to hold on.

I called Sandy and for a moment we could not speak to each other. She had heard the news on television. Then I managed to say, "I won't be coming to dinner."

"I know," she said. She was crying.

I told myself not to think about the players or about my friends. Do the job at hand. How many times had I said that?

I had learned. And I began to use what I had learned immediately.

Not long before, having experienced various kinds of disasters in the region and mindful of the skeleton staff that normally worked on Saturday nights, we had formed a task force of reporters, photographers and editors. We kept a chart containing their phone numbers and where they might be reached. It was now time to call out that task force, and Mitchell and a reporter contacted everyone.

Chief photographer Maurice Kaplan, who had been a combat photographer during World War II, was already speeding to the site of the crash. Fortunately, only a short time before he had installed a two-way radio in his car. There were no cell phones in those days, of course, and Kaplan's radio, and one borrowed from a state police officer, would prove to be the only method of communication we had from the scene.

We sent reporters to each of the main hospitals in town to speak with any possible survivors or families. We kept two reporters in the office to screen calls, man phones, check with state police in West Virginia and Kentucky, county sheriff's departments, and police departments in the small towns of Kenova and Ceredo and as well as in Huntington. Sports staffers meanwhile were trying to put together game travel lists. Every person in the newsroom was occupied with chores too numerous to be aware of at the time or to remember later.

George Clark arrived from his home in the country and said, "What do you need?" I remember saying, "Beer." Rex Baumgardner, production director, showed up at the news desk, having hurried in from home. "What can we do?" he asked.

"Color on page one—red," I said.

"You got it," he said.

"And we'll go up four pages. And we're going to be late."

He disappeared up the steps linking the newsroom to the composing room.

I asked Clark to notify the press room about the hold on press start and the circulation department about the delay in getting papers to district managers and single copy hawkers. I also asked that he call Editor in Chief Raymond Brewster and our two publishers and general manager to alert them. Before he could do so, John Foy called from Florida where he and the publishers were attending a newspaper convention. They had heard the news.

Clark filled them in as well as he could at that early point.

We would need a list of all those aboard—players, coaches, university officials and local boosters. There was confusion as to which players had made the trip. Some with injuries had stayed behind. We also weren't sure about media aboard. Our own football writer, Mike Brown, had covered the game. Was he on the flight?

We would want photos of everyone on board if at all 1 possible. The sports staff was feverishly working on that.

Mitchell, the only editor on the city desk, would be putting together the main story, collecting bits and pieces from all the reporters involved. Reports streamed in via Kaplan's radio. Reporters in the office were churning out sidebars about the team, the airline, the airport, touching all the usual bases. All of the stories and reports would go through Mitchell. And somehow he was bringing it all together.

When the stories reached me I determined where they would go in the paper and passed them on to copy editors around the rim for editing and headlines. Even Clark joined in, wanting very much to help but not wanting to take over the job I had begun. I was grateful.

We assumed all the Marshall coaches were aboard and produced their photos with an all-inclusive headline saying they had died in the crash. The athletic director, Charlie Kautz, was also aboard, as was the sports editor of the Marshall student newspaper. And we learned that Ken Jones, a local radio personality who had worked part-time in our circulation department, was also aboard. It hit me that I had talked to him just the day before.

I edited the main story, a masterful piece by Mitchell, and wrote the page one headline, which would appear in red:

Marshall Team, Coaches, Fans Die in Plane Crash

Below that there was a deck headline:

75 Believed Aboard Plane; Airline Silent

And somehow the first edition went to press.

Now there was even more to do for the final edition. The press had already been webbed—the newsprint threaded through the giant piece of machinery—so there was not time to add four pages to the first edition. That actually gave the city and sports desks more time to produce stories for the final edition, and the four pages were added for that press run. Bringing out a second edition also gave us an opportunity to update the information we had and to correct any mistake we might have made in the first edition.

Chief among them: Assistant coach Red Dawson was not on the plane after all. He had given up his seat on the return flight and driven back to check on a couple of recruits. He was still alive. Our first edition had listed him, with photo, as being among the dead.

(Red Dawson left coaching after one more year to enter the construction business, where he became quite successful. He still lives in Huntington and is a friend whom I see at a monthly men's club dinner. I do not know if he was ever made aware that the first edition of the newspaper had him pictured as being among those who had perished. We have never discussed the crash and I am reluctant to do so unless he mentions it.)

We also learned that our own writer, Mike Brown, was driving rather than flying because he intended to visit family in Beckley, so he was safe as well.

The long night stretched on interminably. I had somehow managed to put aside thoughts of what really had happened while doing my job. When the final edition was finished and there was no more to do, and the lights in the old building on Fifth Avenue were being turned off, and news staffers were gradually leaving the suddenly silent newsroom, I sat at my desk and put away papers, dummies, straight-edges, scissors, pencils, the tools of the trade in those days. And then I sat back and stared into space and permitted myself to quietly say the words.

Seventy-five people were dead. Players, coaches, doctors, dentists, car dealers. My friends, their wives. A number of children had suddenly been orphaned, including one of the Marshall cheerleaders. An entire football team was gone. Our town had lost some of its key leaders. Nothing would ever be the same.

I left the building and walked to my car and drove through the rainy and foggy night to my home. It was past three in the morning. Sandy and the children were asleep, as I hoped they would be. I really did not want to see anyone or say anything. I went into the kitchen and took two beers from the refrigerator and walked into the living room and sat on the couch in the dark and opened one of the beers and took a long drink. And then I started shaking.

17
GANNETT COMES TO TOWN

First it was a man named Chinn Ho, owner of the Honolulu Star-Bulletin. He and his company had just purchased the Huntington newspapers. It was January 1971.

Why would a newspaper owner in Hawaii be interested in newspapers in Huntington, West Virginia? Chinn Ho was an extraordinarily forward-thinking man who saw on the horizon what new technology would mean to newspapers. John L Foy, our general manager, did as well, and had leased a new machine called a "Hendrix CRT" (for "cathode ray tube"). It looked like a medium-size television set with a typewriter keyboard. The wire services, United Press International first among them, had already moved them into their newsrooms. When ours arrived Foy had it delivered to the newsroom and told George Clark to do something with it. There was at the time not even a manual. What Foy wanted more than anything was to say that we were the first newspapers in the country to have one. (Whether we were is probably open to debate, but he felt comfortable with the claim.)

Foy announced his acquisition in the proper publications and Chinn Ho took notice and was impressed. Then he learned that our newspapers were for sale. Our two publishers had determined that no one in their families wanted to take them over and devote their lives to newspapering.So here we were, under new ownership.

Not long after the purchase, a chartered plane touched down at Tri-State Airport loaded with Honolulu Star-Bulletin officials and what appeared to be tons of flowers. A reception was held at Guyan Country Club and every woman present was given an orchid lei.

Sale of the Huntington papers had been reported in all the media, and it seemed the entire town knew of the visit by our new owner. Among those waiting for him were several black leaders in the community, including Bill Congleton and a woman named "Bunche" Gray. They drafted a special message outlining the problems black Huntingtonians had experienced with the Huntington newspapers over the years and requested a meeting with him. The letter was delivered by messenger to Chin Ho on the Guyan Country Club golf course as he was enjoying a round of golf. He responded that he would be pleased to see the group and a meeting was arranged for the following day. Congleton, unfortunately, could not attend because of work. Little is known about the informal meeting—only that the others were encouraged by Chin Ho's response to their concerns.

Chinn Ho and his team returned to Honolulu, leaving Foy in charge of the Huntington operation now that our two publishers were no longer on the scene. He also left an impression on a number of employees and citizens who were looking forward to a new day for the Huntington papers.

Not long after that George Clark called me to his office to talk about our new Hendrix CRT, which I had nicknamed "Cyclops" and which had been sitting in part of our photo studio just off the newsroom, untouched by anyone other than Clark. He had been going to it every day and had even written a kind of manual for it. He told me that soon all newsrooms would be equipped with these machines instead of typewriters. They would revolutionize the newspaper business, he said. Editors would have to change to accommodate them and all the wonderful things they could bring about. He said such editors for the future would be young and energetic and intelligent. He wanted someone to take this crude new CRT in our newsroom and see what could be done with it and eventually be the key newsroom person to move into the new era. He said he was thinking of me for that assignment.

I knew nothing about computers. To me, a computer was one of those seven-foot tall black cabinets in the business office. I told him I really didn't know anything about such matters. He said no one did.

He gave me a few brief lessons on the Hendrix —how to turn it on, how to use the keyboard, how to close out and save what one had written, and how to call it back onto the screen.

I practiced daily.

About this time plans were made to produce a sesquicentennial edition celebrating the birth and growth of the city of Huntington. Clark assigned that project also to me. When I told him I would need a special writer sprung free from daily assignment, he asked if I had anyone in mind. I asked for Dave Peyton, a young reporter with good writing talent. Granted.

Peyton would research the past and write stories to be used in the edition. I would edit them and produce the section. Then I got an idea. Why not have Peyton compose them on the CRT instead of a typewriter? Then I could call them up and edit them on the screen. But, what to do with them once written and edited? We could save them but there was no way to print them out or to output them.

I had a second idea. I went to the composing room where paper tape was punched by teletype setters to be fed into linotype machines. Could a paper tape punch be attached somehow to the CRT? If so, we could write and edit the stories on the screen, punch them out on paper tape, carry the tapes to the composing room and feed them into the linotype machines.

It worked.

The special section was published in July 1971. To my knowledge it was among the very first sections of a newspaper produced on a CRT, or newsroom computer, if not the very first.

Clark was proud of the effort, and so was Foy. It gave him something else to brag about. They decided to send me to the American Newspaper Publishing Association/s Research Institute, an annual meeting focusing on new technology, to be held that year in Cincinnati. Jim Hoffman, our controller, would go along. It was a good trip. Hoffman and I got to know each other better, and I learned a great deal about what we then called "new technology" in the newsroom.

Even with new ownership which left Foy in charge of the Huntington operation, his control still did not appear to extend to the newsrooms where Raymond Brewster continued to rule. Each Saturday night as I sat in the slot preparing to put out the front page for Sunday's paper, Brewster would call to see how things were going and to ask what the news was and what we were going to lead the page with. Most Saturday nights I would respond truthfully that it had been a slow news day, and tell him what I had chosen for the lead story. He always seemed a bit disappointed there was not something big. I mentioned this to Sandy and she suggested that perhaps I might be a bit more enthusiastic about the news and our lead story. It made sense.

So the next Saturday night when Brewster called, although it had been an even slower news day, I told him the Weather Bureau had issued a prediction that during the night our city would be hit with a snowstorm. "They say we're really going to get it," I said, with some excitement in my voice. "Put two exclamation points on it and go with it," Brewster said.

What should I do now? We had only a small story prepared; readers would know by the time our paper arrived whether there had been a snowstorm or not.

I turned to C.T. Mitchell, sitting in as always as the Saturday night city editor, and told him what Brewster had said.

"I guess I could put together a little longer story," he said.

"Well, I may lead the page with it but I'm sure as hell not going to put two exclamation points on it," I said, having had a lifelong aversion to exclamation points.

Mitchell prepared a story, padded enough to stretch into the banner, and we did indeed go with it.

"You better pray it snows," Mitchell said, "or we'll look pretty damn stupid."

The following morning he called, awakening me.

"Have you looked out the window?" he said.

"No."

"Don't."

Not one sign of the white stuff.

Neither Raymond Brewster nor I mentioned it the following week. But I promised myself I would not be quite so enthusiastic about our lead story next time unless we did indeed have one that deserved it.

During the week I worked back at my metal table in the corner, producing our Sunday magazine. I was involved in that one day when I noticed two men come into the newsroom and stop at our receptionist's desk. One had long blond hair and was wearing bell bottoms, a flowered shirt with big collar and bell sleeves, and a leather vest. The other had long hair and a beard and was in jeans. My phone rang, and it was C. T. Mitchell from across the room. He too was looking at the men who had just come in.

"Ten to one they're looking for you," C. T. said, and hung up.

Sure enough they started walking my way, and I stood.

The golden-haired one in the leather vest introduced himself as Clyde Ware, a Hollywood writer, producer and director. He introduced the man with him as Martin Sheen, an actor. Sheen nodded and muttered hello. He seemed almost shy to be in the newsroom. Ware did all the talking; I do not remember Sheen saying another word.

Ware explained that he was a native of West Virginia and that he had just completed a movie set in the state with Sheen as its star. He said he wrote scripts for many of television's biggest shows, and that he had just signed a contract to write a screenplay for an ABC made-for-tv movie on the Hatfields and McCoys, to star Jack Palance as Devil

Anse Hatfield. He had heard that our newspaper had published many stories on the feud over the years and wondered if he could take a look at them. So I took him to the morgue.

He had come to the right place. Our files contained possibly the most clippings on the feud that existed anywhere. When he saw how many there were, he said he didn't have time to examine them there, and asked if we could make copies and send them to him at his Hollywood Hills home. He said he would gladly pay whatever that would cost.

In those days, of course, there were no digital data banks, only the paper clippings, many of them yellowed, all residing in manila envelopes. Nonetheless, our librarian set about making copies, which took more than a week. And then we shipped them off to Ware. He did indeed use them in writing his screenplay, and the movie hit America's television screens as planned.

I never saw Ware again, although I heard from him when he published a novel. Nor did I ever run into Martin Sheen again or think about his visit to our newsroom until years later when he had become a huge movie and television star.

My working world changed again, and quite suddenly, when Brewster suffered a stroke. Foy immediately assumed control over the newsroom as well. And now he was the one who called on Saturday nights. The difference was that Foy was always in a talking mood, and that grew each week. First we talked about the night's news, and then gradually about many things. We talked far more than we ever had at the office. Sometimes I had the feeling he was sitting alone in an easy chair, or perhaps lying in bed, sharing with me whatever was on his mind. He talked about the Huntington operation, about his small farm in Ohio, even about personnel. Sometimes he talked for such a long time I had to interrupt so that I could go to the composing room and close out the paper.

When it was determined that Brewster would recover and eventually return to work, Foy came into the newsroom and motioned me to join him across the hall, where the two vacant publishers' offices and a small conference room were located. He said he was turning the largest of the offices into a larger conference room and he wanted me to take the present small conference room for my office. "We've got to hurry," he said.

I took that to mean he wanted to complete the move before Brewster returned. And I had mixed emotions. I had longed for my own office since coming to work as a teenager. I had put together my own Sunday area in a corner of the newsroom. Now I had my own office, with a window looking out over part of the city. But it had not come from Brewster, the editor in chief and my boss, who in fact knew nothing about it. I did not know quite what to do. I could hardly tell Foy I didn't want the office. So I followed his orders and moved in.

By the next morning my name had been painted on the glass door leading to the area, in letters much too large.

Each day Foy was in contact with the Chinn Ho

company and each week he held meetings of all department heads in the new conference room. He shared news about the Star-Bulletin company and urged those present to report on their departments. One day he asked me to stick around to talk.

Privately, he told me that the Honolulu Star-Bulletin company would be needing him, not only in the Huntington operation, but for other matters as well. He expected to be traveling a great deal. He was putting Jim Hoffman in position to step in for him during his absences. Hoffman would need a second man he could depend upon in his function as controller. Both Foy and Hoffman, for whatever reason, had chosen me. He said I should meet with Hoffman.

Now here I was, a guy who could not balance his own checkbook, who had never studied finance or accounting in college, who had for years boasted about the newsroom being pure and far removed from the "bean counters."

Hoffman said I was his choice and he hoped I would leave the newsroom and join him. It would be immediately more rewarding financially, he said, and open all kinds of new doors for me. He could see himself becoming publisher or general manager in the near future, he said, and who knows? That might even happen to me.

I talked to Sandy that evening about the offer. She understood, as she always did, my feelings. It wasn't just that we thought journalists were "pure," a term I frequently used somewhat in jest, but that bringing the news and the truth to people was a special, enormously important thing to do. We took that responsibility very seriously. And Sandy said she had always been proud of what I did. Neither of us could imagine I would leave that to become involved on the business side.

Nevertheless, I was leaning that way because of the money. I was tired of always worrying about paying bills. Few newsroom staffers made much money and I was no different.

As it turned out I did not have to make that decision.

The top news person in the Honolulu Star-Bulletin organization suffered a fatal heart attack and not long after, the company decided to sell all its newspaper holdings.

John Foy would not be traveling, Jim Hoffman would not be filling in for him, and I would not be needed in the business department. I was somewhat disappointed, yet at the same time greatly relieved.

In October, The Star-Bulletin company sold its newspapers to Gannett, a growing organization which owned several newspaper properties, the largest of which was in Rochester, New York, also the site of its headquarters. Included were the Star-Bulletin, a paper on the island of Guam, a small paper in Idaho, and the Huntington papers. Whether that had been in the works and Gannett had planned to acquire the Huntington papers all along, I do not know. Whatever, it happened quickly.

Once again we were under new ownership. And nobody knew what to expect. Not even John Foy.

By coincidence there was an Associated Press

Managing Editors   meeting coming up in Philadelphia and Gannett had scheduled a session for all its editors. Foy thought three of us should go--George Clark, representing The Advertiser, Don Mayne of the Herald-Dispatch and myself--should attend. We traveled together, and as soon as our plane was airborne out of Tri-State, Clark ordered drinks for the three of us, even though it was early afternoon, and toasted to our future with the new company.

The Gannett session was lead by its chief of news operations, John Quinn. I was immediately impressed with him and felt if Gannett had such people as this it must be a pretty good company. There also was in the room a bright young editor named John Curley, who also had good things to say.

Going into a reception that night another Gannett editor introduced himself to me as Jim Geehan, from Binghamton, New York. When I told him I was from Huntington and we had just been purchased by Gannett, he smiled. "I think I know what you're feeling," he said. "You're probably a bit uneasy wondering what this company is all about. Well, I was in your position once, and I can tell you it was the best thing that ever happened to my newspaper and to me." That was reassuring.

Dinner that night featured the CEO of Gannett, Paul Miller, who also happened to be president of The Associated Press board of directors. Again, very impressive. I returned to Huntington excited.

On the day Raymond Brewster returned to

work, I was in the newsroom on my way back to my new office across the hall and by coincidence Brewster emerged from his office to go in the same direction. Before us stood the glass door which previously had held the names of our two publishers and which now offered my name in signage much too large. He looked at it—I am sure he had seen it when he came in that morning—and then he looked at me. I wanted to say none of this had been my idea. I wanted to tell him I had not done anything behind his back. But even though those things were true, I still felt guilty, as if somehow I had betrayed him. He said nothing and we both walked through the door and into the hallway. He never mentioned it.

18
BUFFALO CREEK

And Death and Disaster came riding in once again.

On February 26, 1972, a coal slurry impoundment dam on a hillside in Logan County, West Virginia, burst, unleashing more than a hundred thousand gallons of black waste water into the Buffalo Creek Valley below, tearing through unsuspecting hamlets and communities before thousands who lived there had any warning, any idea of what was happening. Many were swamped while sleeping, others ran and swam and waded or crawled up the back hillsides behind their homes.

Only days before, a federal mine inspector had declared the Pittston Coal Company dam was "satisfactory."

In the offices of the Huntington newspapers editors, reporters and photographers quickly assembled and prepared to go into the area. Reporters were advised what to expect. John Foy and George Clark sent runners to nearby liquor stores to purchase all the half pints of liquor they could find. These were distributed to the reporters and photographers, to be used in exchange for information or rides into flooded areas or as antiseptic to be poured on any open wound in what could quickly become a land of infection. All were also given money in small denominations for whatever might be required.

The experienced reporters and photographers arrived prepared for the assignment—boots, jeans, rain gear, hats. But one young reporter showed up in an off-white trench coat, sports coat and tie. He was quickly sent home to change.

They boarded trucks and cars and left not knowing what they would find.

What they found was chaos and tragedy beyond imagination. Floating houses and vehicles. Railroad tracks buried, roads gone, mud and water everywhere. Stone foundations where houses once sat. Here and there a few faces in shock staring over the rubble.

"I have never seen anything like it," one reporter said.

Some sixteen villages and settlements were all but wiped out. Of a population of five thousand people in the Buffalo Creek valley, more than four thousand were left homeless.

One hundred twenty-five people lost their lives. Another 1,121 were injured.

More than five hundred houses and fifty mobile homes were destroyed, along with more than thirty businesses.

All this from a coal slurry dam declared "satisfactory."

"Tell that to the victims," an editor said, once that declaration had surfaced.

It was only the latest in this region's recent history of extraordinary deaths and disasters. The Floyd County school bus mass drownings in 1958. The Silver Bridge in 1968. The Marshall plane crash in 1970. And now this. When does it end? an editor asked aloud. It doesn't, another answered. Not here.

Survivors were interviewed, their stories published. Photographs piled high atop newsroom desks. The national media swarmed in. Nothing new there.

Death and disaster were no strangers to West Virginia.

Later, Pittston Coal officials would say in court that the dam collapse was "an act of God."

They did not say what God had against the unfortunate people who lived in Buffalo Creek.

And certainly the dam's collapse could not be the fault of the coal company which put it there. Right? Or the inspector who called it safe.

But West Virginians have a way of moving on. Always have. What else does one do?

In the days and months and years to come, newspapers published accounts of legal battles, investigations, special committee reports, and the words of countless politicians and coal company execs. All had something to say.

But the voices of one hundred twenty-five

residents of Buffalo Creek Valley were stilled.

19
BUDDY

N. S. "Buddy" Hayden arrived on a Gannett corporate jet in early March, 1972. He came with several Gannett executives.

John Foy had been notified of the corporate visit and had scheduled a meeting of Huntington newspaper department heads and editors to hear from our new owners. He expected some kind of special announcement and he felt sure it would involve himself. He was excited.

We were seated in the conference room, which had been the office of Helen Birke when she had been publisher of The Herald-Dispatch, awaiting our visitors. Foy himself had not yet arrived and our assumption was that he was meeting with them first, and then would bring them to the conference room.

And that is what happened.

But when they entered the room, Foy looked strange. He was smiling broadly, but it was a smile I had never seen on his face. He did not sit down and stood off to the side. The visitors from corporate also remained standing. One of them cleared his throat to speak.

John L. Foy, he said, had decided to retire. Thus Gannett had brought in a new publisher, N. S. "Buddy" Hayden.

The speaker gestured to Hayden who was standing at the opposite end of the group. Hayden smiled and waved.

Foy's forced smile widened. Retiring? His eyes told a different story.

The Gannett exec went on to say Foy had done an outstanding job and now deserved to take things easier and enjoy the rest of his life (I don't think he went so far as to add "and the fruits of his labors," though perhaps he did.) Foy, he said, would stay on for a while as president, and would retire "later in the year."

He asked Hayden if he wanted to say anything.

Buddy Hayden stepped forward. He was a short, stocky man with slick dark hair and a ready smile. He was young, just thirty-four, and clearly eager to get started.

He said he was pleased to be here and looked forward to getting to know all of us and to working with us to make the two Huntington newspapers "better than ever."

The Gannett team began leaving the room except for Hayden and Foy. We all stood and shook Hayden's hand and introduced ourselves and welcomed him. And we shook Foy's hand and wished him luck. I wanted to say more but did not.

Each of us returned to our offices and I sat

wondering what was going on. Not once had Foy mentioned to me any thoughts about retiring. Not that he necessarily would with someone at my level. Then again, he had shared a number of things with me, including his enthusiasm for his job. This was quiet a surprise to everyone.

In less than an hour Foy and Hayden came into my office.

"We need your office," said our new publisher. "I'm moving into John's office and we need this space for him."

Foy was still smiling in that vacant way.

"Okay," I said.

"I'll build you a new office," Hayden said, which surprised me.

"Okay," I said again. "Where do I go for now?"

It would be a small vacant office off the newsroom, formerly used by H. R. Pinckard.

"When do you want me out of here?"

Hayden smiled a smile that I would see a lot for some time to come. "Immediately. We'll send somebody up with a box for your things."

In a short while I walked through the newsroom with a box full of stuff and a maintenance employee trailing behind me with two boxes of books on a cart. The rest of the newsroom employees watched as I quietly approached Pinckard's old office and entered and I could not help but be embarrassed. I knew at that point nothing had been explained to any of them. The maintenance man set the boxes down and left.

I looked around. Not much room. An old desk.

A small bookcase. A window looking onto the roof of an adjacent building. I set about moving in, putting things away.

Shortly after five o'clock John Foy entered my office, alone. The phony smile was gone from his face. He closed the door behind him.

"Let me give you some advice," he said. "Always put yourself first. What's best for you and your family, not anybody else."

I nodded, not knowing what to say.

"Protect yourself. Otherwise you'll get screwed."

"I'm sorry," I said.

"Yeah."

He turned and left the office.

The rest of that day and the next Buddy Hayden toured the building and introduced himself to every employee he could find. He was friendly, conversational. He took time to ask each person what he or she did and how long he or she had been there. In the newsroom, he asked each reporter what he or she covered. He listened, he nodded, he joked.

"He's certainly personable," said one staffer.

Over the next several days Buddy Hayden took a different department head or editor to dinner each night. That included George Clark, then assistant to the ailing Raymond Brewster, Don Mayne, and myself. He did not invite John R. Brown, The Advertiser's managing editor. I realized that my position handling just the Sunday publication hardly matched their positions. All the more reason I looked forward to talking with him.

He took each of us separately to the Rebels & Redcoats, at that time perhaps the best restaurant in Huntington. He was waiting at the bar when I arrived, and we quickly moved to a table where a young woman took our drink order. When I ordered scotch he smiled and said, "That's my drink too."

There were many scotches that night, and the finest steaks, and good conversation. I did not feel that I was being interviewed, which, of course, I was. I was not quite sure for what.

We talked about newspapers in general and the Huntington papers in particular. He could not understand why there was a separate Sunday operation, which concerned me immediately. He said he was thinking about abolishing that and making The Herald-Dispatch a seven-day morning paper and The Advertiser a six-day—"maybe five-day"—afternoon paper.

He intended, he revealed as the scotches kept coming, to name an executive editor over all newsroom operations and a managing editor for each of the two daily papers. Bolstered by the scotch, I assured Buddy Hayden I could handle whichever of those three positions he might consider me for, including executive editor.

Two days later he sent for me and when I entered his office he told me to have a seat and closed the door.

He said he was following through with his plan to abolish the separate Sunday operation and make the morning Herald-Dispatch a seven-day publication. It would become the complete newspaper—world, national, state, regional and local news. The afternoon Advertiser would be a local emphasis newspaper, he said. He wanted me to take over as its managing editor. "I think you have the right feel for it," he said.

Mayne would continue as managing editor of the morning paper and Clark would become executive editor over the entire news operation. "He's a fatherly type, very experienced," he said.

"George is a good man," I said.

I did not ask what he had planned for Raymond Brewster, who had become ill again and was recuperating at home. There were rumors that he would not return, that he would take retirement.

There was one other person he had not mentioned. What would become of John Brown, who still had the title of managing editor of The Advertiser?

"That's up to you and George Clark," he said. 'You're the managing editor of that paper now. Do anything you want with it, but do something. Because it's terrible."

I met later that day with Clark, who was his old optimistic self, more energized than I had seen him since his becoming Brewster's assistant. I welcomed that. This man had meant so much to me. Since Brewster had assumed control of the newsroom and I had been given the Sunday news operation, he and I had not worked together quite as closely as we once had.

Clark moved into the office of the Advertiser's

former publisher, Hilda Long. There were sconces and expensive wallpaper on the walls and a small French Provincial desk and he almost seemed out of place there. I sat by his desk and said, "I am really happy for you, George. And I really look forward to working for you. Buddy Hayden couldn't have made a better choice."

"We're going to have some fun," he said.

Then I asked about John Brown, now that I had been given his title. Brown was at this point unaware of that.

"We'll have to find him another job," George said.

I had already decided on C.T. Mitchell, my long-time Saturday night partner, as my news editor. The only job open was city editor.

"John Brown was once a very good city editor for The Advertiser," I said. "Do you think he would go for that?"

We brought Brown in and I sat silently while Clark explained to him what was happening. Brown was stunned. Then he looked at me, a look that seemed to say, "Are you kidding me?" I am sure Brown still thought of me as that young boy who had come into the newsroom at the age of eighteen. Then he looked back at Clark.

"So what does that mean for me?" Brown said.

George looked over to me.

"John, you were a great city editor for this newspaper," I said. "I would love to have you as our city editor once again."

Brown looked down in disbelief. Then he

looked up. "And if I don't?"

Clark sighed. "We're hoping you will."

Brown shook his head. "I don't know. I'll have to think about this."

"Of course," Clark said.

"I hope you'll do this, John," I said. "The Advertiser needs you."

He gave me a look that said "Don't B.S. me," then stood and left the room.

Clark and I looked at each other. "What do you think?" I said.

"I don't know what choice he has," Clark said. "If he takes the job, it isn't going to be easy for you."

"I wouldn't expect it to be," I said.

Brown took the job. And I set about putting together a staff. My two Sunday staffers were absorbed by The Herald-Dispatch. I inherited Brown's Advertiser staff, and immediately started looking for others.

I wanted to make sure I had a good mix of experience and young blood—experience in the key editing slots, youth and energy on the reporting staff. There was good experience with Mitchell as news editor and Brown as city editor, though he clearly harbored great resentment. Charlie Tucker, who had been The Advertiser's city editor and before that its telegraph editor, was asked to become our Lifestyles editor. He wasn't happy about that, but given his experience and the kindness with which he treated others as well as his knowledge of the community, I thought it would be a good assignment for him. Dez Reynolds would continue as editorial page editor, though he was nearing retirement. And among those I inherited was the veteran and "award-winning" police reporter, Jack Hardin. Now for the young reporting staff.

On the Herald-Dispatch was a bright young reporter named Charlie Bowen, whose wife Pamela was already on The Advertiser staff. One of Raymond Brewster's policies had forbidden husband and wife working on the same paper, hence Charlie on the morning paper and Pamela on ours. I was able to bring Charlie to our paper as well, which turned out to be one of the best moves I ever made. The Bowens were exactly what I was looking for as a foundation on which to build a new kind of Advertiser staff. They were clearly special, and over the years I learned a great deal from them.

Meantime, Buddy Hayden had me working on a re-design of The Advertiser. Each day I brought him a proof of a new front page design and each day he found some minor detail to change or correct.

Hayden loved the color orange. He wrote only with orange pens. His two-way radio moniker was "Orange One." I once asked him about all this and he said, 'Nobody ever uses orange; everybody uses red or blue. Anybody can use red or blue."

But I came to hate those tiny orange marks on the proofs of my proposed new front pages. I took great pride in my page designs and here was a man not as skilled in the matter as I who somehow always found some ridiculously small thing to mark up.

Which is not to say he was necessarily wrong in what he found.

Away from the office, it was often a different matter. We sometimes met in Ritter Park for an early morning game of tennis before going to the office. We would play a set or two under the most friendly yet competitive (he was very competitive) circumstances, and then as we walked to our cars he might turn on me, as he did one morning, and complain about something we had done in the paper the evening before.

Even so, he was good at making a distinction between our work relationship and that away from work. One evening he called to ask my wife and me to drive over to his house within the hour to join him and his wife, Elaine, for drinks and to listen to some new LP albums he had bought. He had purchased a large house high atop a hill overlooking the city. It was an older home and he wanted us to see a new room he had created by enclosing a porch. He led me to a balcony where we stood, scotches in hand, looking over Huntington.

"Someday, son, this will all be yours," he said, toasting the sky, laughing.

On a Sunday afternoon he called to ask that we meet them at the country club for dinner in an hour. I never felt I could turn those invitations down, although they sometimes did create a problem for my wife and me, given that we had three children, one of them severely handicapped.

It would be business as usual the next day at the

office and I would be treated like other department heads. He had brought in two new directors and was close to one of them. But I realized he turned to Sandy and me for a different kind of relationship. I wasn't sure what it was. Elaine and Sandy became friends and their son Alex and our son Joel, about the same age, often played together. I wasn't sure what all this meant, or how long it would last.

20
A NEW HUNTINGTON ADVERTISER

There was a pulse in The Advertiser newsroom I had not felt before. The small Advertiser staff, perhaps half the size of the morning Herald-Dispatch staff, was energized and committed to becoming *the* source for local news and to beating The Dispatch on every local story.

My personal writing at home--short stories, attempts at a novel and magazine articles-- came to a standstill as my work as managing editor of the afternoon newspaper took up most of my time and energy. I had sold several articles, which brought in money at a time when it was needed, published a few short stories for practically no money, and had come to the realization that being a writer was not quite as glamorous and romantic as I had imagined as a young man. It appeared I was destined to enjoy more success as a newspaper man. I figured it was no great loss to the world of letters.

The myth that big absentee corporate owners dictated the news and editorials and limited local news coverage proved to be just that—myth. We enjoyed far more freedom under Gannett than we had under local ownership. There were no favors owed country club members. We did not have to worry about pressure from advertisers. Our editorial pages could be whatever we decided— liberal, conservative, whatever, although Hayden thought it would be good if the two papers were as different from each other as possible. Given the histories of the two, there was not much danger of them being the same in any way, especially on the editorial page. Handling the news was left up to local editors—but that carried the responsibility of local editors knowing the needs and interests of the community.

(I must say that in my entire Gannett career, not once was I ever told what candidates to endorse, what measures to support, what news to publish.)

Early on Gannett's chief news executive, John Quinn, came to town to meet with editors and other members of the news staff. At the end of his first day Sandy and I took him to dinner. We talked past the restaurant's closing time. I had been impressed listening to Quinn during Gannett sessions in Philadelphia. Now I was even more so. He was a man of class and intelligence, friendly and warm and unassuming. I felt that although I had local bosses—an executive editor and a publisher--he was my ultimate news boss. I was excited.

"What do you like better, news or features?" he asked.

I struggled for an answer. Finally I said, "Both. A good news feature is still news. I like to see good, hard investigative stories. But I also like to see features and profiles that enable one to see into a person or situation."

In years to come Sandy and I would become good friends with Quinn and his wife, Loie. We drank and dined in fine restaurants and at editors' meetings. I felt he was in my corner from the start, and that never changed.

Gannett may not have had policies affecting news coverage or editorials. But it did have an ethics code. There would be no accepting gifts of any kind. Salvatore's and my golf clubs from the Riviera in those early years, Salvatore's watches from the Cincinnati Reds and sweaters from golf clubs, my bottle of booze from the cops in my rookie year--all forbidden. No free movie passes, no free tickets to any sports event unless you were covering it, no free trips, and no free meals. It was plain and simple. We pay our own way. We do not accept gifts. And we will not become vulnerable to charges that we were "bought off" or that someone "bought" his way into our pages. No newsroom staffers, including editors, could serve on boards or committees or groups they might be called on to cover. And at no time could anyone become part of a governmental entity, as Brewster had in being president of the State Board of Education while he was editor-in-chief.

Meanwhile, I concentrated on running my newspaper and to building a better staff whenever the opportunity came.

Among my new hires was a Vietnam veteran and graduate of the University of Maryland named

Dick Stanley, who would become our "investigative reporter," an increasingly important position on newspapers at the time. (Some argued that all good reporters were investigative reporters, and there was some truth to that. Basically, the title referred to a special reporter who had no specific beat and who was given time to work on just one in-depth story.)

Stanley made up in guts what he lacked in reporting experience. Tipped that we should look into strange doings inside the county jail, he did just that. What he found was that the jailor operated a jail cart which was taken around all the cells as well as the "bullpen," a large cell that held several temporary prisoners. The jailer sold the prisoners cigarettes and candy bars, chips and sodas at exorbitant prices and pocketed the money.

Stanley also discovered that on certain mornings the jailer backed his truck up to the jail and loaded it with prisoners, drove them to his personal farm in the country, had them work on the farm, then drove them back. Stanley even managed to get photos of the act taking place.

He also learned that drugs were considered easier to get inside the jail than on the street, and that some prisoners got themselves arrested for petty crimes just to go there.

And incredibly, he uncovered the story of a former Marshall University football player who managed to escape from jail in order to play in the annual Marshall alumni football game, then slip back into jail once the game was over. No one would have known except that he scored a touchdown and his name was in the paper the next morning.

Stanley also looked into suspicious pinball machine operations rumored to have links to crime, and many other stories. Asked one day how he liked his job, he replied: "Beats working."

And there was Angela.

Even before taking over The Advertiser I had promised myself that if I was ever in position to do so, I would hire a black reporter. That had never been done on either Huntington newspaper. There had been a black female intern for a short time (I do not know if she was paid) but when her internship was up she was not offered a full-time job. That just wasn't done.

Now I was in position to do something about that. Hiring what was then called a "minority staffer" became my primary goal.

I started my search with the Journalism Department at Marshall. In reading the school's newspaper, The Parthenon, I discovered the work of a young woman who occasionally wrote a column that included her photograph. Her name was Angela Dodson. She was black. I liked her work. And I liked her face.

I called the department chairman asking if he would tell her that I would like to talk with her about employment. After a few days he called to say she was not interested. I pressed the issue. Why was that? Well, he said, she doesn't want to work for the "honky press."

Where else to turn but my old friend, Bill

Congleton.

I told him I had been named managing editor of The Advertiser and wanted to hire a black reporter. I had discovered this young woman at Marshall who interested me, but she wanted nothing to do with the white press. I can understand that, I said, given our newspapers' history and what was going on in the country these days. But how can we change things if talented young black people turn their backs on us?

I told Bill my prospect's name, doubting that he would know of her. But of course, being Bill Congleton, he did. He knew better than anyone what was going on in the black community and apparently that carried over to the campus.

"I'll talk to her," he said.

In two days he called back to tell me Angela Dodson would be contacting me to set up an interview. "I'll be honest with you," he said. "She doesn't want to. But she will."

(Years later I asked him what he had said to her. "I just told her that she was *the one,*" he said.)

When Angela Dodson came to my office she did so in her own way and on her own terms--hair in a huge Afro and wearing a bright orange dashiki flowing from neck to ankle, bare feet in sandals. Clearly an African effect. She was not smiling.

I welcomed her to my office and thanked her for coming. I told her I wanted to talk with her about working for The Advertiser. She was not impressed. I told her I had read her work in The Parthenon. I thought she might be a good addition to our staff. We had no minority reporters, I said. In fact, I added, smiling, there has never been a minority reporter of any kind on either Huntington newspaper.

"So why start now?" she said.

I told her I believed a good newspaper should reflect the community it served, and as long as we were an all-white staff we weren't doing that. Also, I said, how can we write editorials urging others to hire minorities if we don't practice what we preach?

Her face seemed to soften a little. Or was it my imagination?

"So," she said, "you want me to be your 'black reporter.'"

I knew what she meant—a token job in which she would be assigned strictly to the black community and write minor stories for a small population.

"No," I said. "We already have a 'black reporter' and he's white. His name is Charlie Bowen. He has a lot of contacts in the black community and he does a great job. No, what I need is an education reporter. Are you interested?"

Clearly she was surprised. She wanted to know what the job entailed.

"Covering two county school boards and Marshall University. Going to board meetings, interviewing superintendents and the university president, doing occasional features on schools, students, whatever comes up. It's a big job. It should be two jobs really but I can only afford to hire one education reporter."

She nodded. This was not what she had expected.

"What would you do with me? Where would I work?"

Now here I gambled and took a big chance, and I am not sure why. It was not terribly smart, looking back. But—

"I'm going to build a glass cage out over the sidewalk on Fifth Avenue and put you in it with a sign that says 'See, we've got one.'"

She started to smile—first time since she had arrived—but quickly put her hand to her face to cover it. But it would not go away. And then she laughed.

"I'm kidding, obviously," I said. "If you come here you will not be a token. You'll have a desk in the newsroom and you'll work your tail off like everybody else on this staff because the morning paper has a much larger staff and we aim to beat them on every story every day. There's a lot going on in this town that nobody's writing about and we're going to do that. If you come here, you'll be a part of that. I think we can do good things together and have some fun."

She accepted the job.

Congleton called the next day. "Well, I hear Miss Angela Dodson is going to become a member of The Huntington Advertiser news staff." And he laughed that gentle laugh of his.

"Yes," I said. "And I have you to thank for that. You made it happen."

"I didn't do anything," he said, as he always

did. "You made it happen."

We both knew better than that, but you don't argue with William.

So Angela Dodson became the first black news staffer at the Huntington newspapers.

I know she learned a great deal in her time on The Advertiser. But I learned more from her. Some time later she was working on a story in which she used the word "ghetto" in referring to an area south of Sixteenth Street and Eighth Avenue. For some reason I cannot remember I had asked to see the story before it was published. When I came upon that word, I felt it simply didn't apply. "Ghetto" to me at that time meant slums and in my ignorance I thought Huntington had "no real slums." I called her in and said as much.

She looked at me in disbelief. Then she sighed, leaned back in her chair and for the first time since I had known her started to tear up. And with that came anger.

"It is very definitely a ghetto," she said pointedly. "It doesn't have to be a slum to be a ghetto."

And she proceeded to give me a lesson on what the word actually means, how it refers to a defined area with specific boundaries inside of which are people who feel bound and trapped there by various social and economic factors including race.

"I'm sorry," I said. "I should know that."

She paused and added, "You don't know what it's like, working here and then going into the community. 'What you doin' workin' for the honky press?' they say. You don't know how they look at me because I work here."

I apologized again. I told her I realized it must be tough at times. She just shook her head. "You don't know," she said.

"That's why I want to change things," I said. "With your help, we will."

I felt like an ignorant man. Which, of course, I was.

She helped me many times after that and at one point provided an enormous assist with what became a significant national report.

I was serving as Minorities Committee chairman of the Associated Press Managing Editors Association. As such I was to produce a special report on minorities in the media. I had seen countless reports from various groups citing statistics on the number of minorities in the media. They told me nothing. I wanted to go in a different direction and get beyond the numbers.

I called Angela in and told her about my assignment and my thinking. "What is your greatest concern as a minority journalist?" I asked.

"How I am perceived," she replied without hesitation. "How I am perceived by my co-workers, by the people I cover, and by the readers."

Dynamite.

We shaped a questionnaire to be sent to newspapers across the country to be distributed to their minority journalists, asking those questions and seeking their responses. My vice committee chair was Mike Davies, then managing editor of the

Louisville Times. He took the responses and with help from the Times staff produced a special report. It was bound and printed and made available to all newspapers. Time magazine even wrote about it. All because of Angela Dodson's response to my simple question: What concerns you most as a minority journalist?

But all that, as I say, came later. For now I was pleased to have added her to the staff, pleased for the community, and frankly, pleased for myself.

21
A TIME OF GAINS ... AND LOSSES

While I was building a new news staff for The Advertiser, Buddy Hayden was putting together an almost entirely new group of department heads. Over the next several months he hired a new circulation director, production director, promotions director, and advertising director, all from outside. He retained Jim Hoffman as controller, and, of course, had gone with Clark, Mayne and myself in the top three editing positions rather than—at this point, at least—bringing in a new editor.

Only a few months after Hayden's arrival we were having our weekly department head meeting in his office when his phone was buzzed by his secretary, which meant he should take the call which had just come in. He did so, then looked up to all of us.

"Raymond Brewster just died," he said.

The news jarred me for several reasons. This was a man who had ruled over the newspapers for some time. Although I sometimes disagreed with him, he had been the man who named me managing editor of the Sunday operation. He had given me my identity as "C. Donald Hatfield," which has remained to this day. While he had been viewed by many as a stern man, he had never treated me badly. He was known throughout the state, and he was a good family man. His wife, Esther, was a kind and lovely woman. And his son John and I were good friends and played tennis regularly.

I thought of all this that morning and especially later at the funeral. I worried for Esther because her family had been her life, and she loved and admired her husband greatly.

Not long after the funeral John Brewster called to ask a favor. His mother wanted to visit his father's office, which had remained closed, to go through whatever personal things might be there. He asked if I could arrange that and prepare the office for their visit. I was of course pleased to do so.

I left them in the office with the door closed and when they were finished they thanked me and left. An era had ended, I thought, and as I watched them leaving I had a strange feeling of loss.

In a few weeks John Brewster stopped by the Ritter Park tennis courts where Sandy and I were playing. He called me to the fence and handed me a small box.

"Mother wanted you to have these," he said. "They were Father's. He wore them to the American Society of Newspaper Editors convention in Washington."

In the box were expensive cufflinks and studs. I told John I was honored and would think of his father whenever I wore them. If someday I was chosen to attend that convention, I would wear them there proudly, I said. And I did.

Raymond Brewster was not the only one to leave us that year. Now fully retired, John Foy was working on his farm in Ohio, clearing land and cutting wood. He felt a sharp pain in his back. He thought he had strained a muscle and did little about it. Later, it returned in the form of a major heart attack. He did not survive.

When I heard of his death I immediately thought of the talks we had enjoyed and all he had done for me. And I thought of the day he had been relieved of his duties and came by my office to advise me to always put myself first. Now he was gone.

My wife and I went to the visitation on a bright autumn afternoon and found Buddy Hayden there. After a few minutes Hayden eased over to me and whispered. I thought he was going to say something about John Foy's passing. Instead, he said, "It's a beautiful day. Let's get out of here and go play tennis at the country club."

The year also proved to be difficult for George Clark. His migraines grew worse, the medication he was forced to take left him all but incapacitated, and he spent more and more time at home.

Hayden kept his promise of building new offices for his two managing editors. They were small and sat side by side just outside the office that had belonged to Raymond Brewster. They looked through large windows over Fifth Avenue and despite their small size worked out well, providing room for daily news meetings.

In fact, Hayden had the entire combined newsroom done over, with carpeting and wood paneling (then much in vogue). Everything was changing.

There was also a major change on The Advertiser's news staff. My news editor, C. T. Mitchell, decided to leave the world of newspapering in exchange for Academia, becoming director of communications at Marshall. We had worked together a long time and I was sorry to see him go. But there are always changes in newspaper staffs, and I set out to find a replacement.

I found him at the Charleston Gazette, the state's largest newspaper. His name was Chuck Carpenter and he was the Gazette's assistant news editor. Somehow I managed to convince him to join The Advertiser even though we were a much smaller newspaper with a smaller staff. He would be news editor, second in command, I stressed. And he would be joining Gannett, destined to become the nation's largest newspaper group, where there would be many opportunities for advancement. It worked.

Chuck Carpenter proved to be a joy in the newsroom. He would arrive early in the morning, go to the news desk slot, face the copy editors and city desk, rub his hands together and exclaim: "All right, Gang, let's have some fun."

As 1973 loomed, Hayden informed all department heads they would be expected to put together a budget for the coming year. That was old stuff for those on the revenue side. For those "purists" in the newsroom, we suddenly had the challenge—and the opportunity—to budget our expenses. Little did we know that after doing so, they would be tossed back to us with the order that they be cut a certain percentage or dollar amount. It was my first view of this side of Gannett. It was not fun.

In the spring of '73, I was chosen to attend an American Press Institute seminar for managing editors at Columbia University in New York City. Actually, Don Mayne, managing editor of the morning paper, was to attend this session, for newspapers of more than 50,000 circulation, and I was to attend a later seminar for papers below that. As it turned out Mayne was unable to attend and I took his place. This threw me in with America's largest newspapers. Other editors there represented the New York Times, Wall Street Journal, Washington Post, and even the Associated Press.

This proved to be a life-altering event for me. I had not been to New York before. After this trip and the two-week seminar at Columbia, I would be a changed person in many ways.

We were quartered in the King's Crown hotel, an antiquated structure in a high-crime area near the university. Upon our arrival, we were warned about walking alone, catching the right trains from the city to the university area, and watching our wallets. As if planned as an exclamation point to that, on the first night one of our members was robbed at gunpoint in the basement of the hotel where he had gone to get a soda from a machine.

Before I had unpacked my bags in my tiny room, the phone rang and a voice asked jokingly, "Is Sandy there?" It belonged to Burl Osborne, then managing editor of the Associated Press, a fellow Marshall University alum and a friend who had attended a party at our house not long before. It was good to know I had a friend there.

Each day was filled with panel discussions, speakers, exercises having to do with newsroom management. I was impressed to know that some of the problems which faced these huge newspapers were not that far removed from some I had experienced with our small paper. At first I said little, but as the days went by I gained confidence to take part as if I belonged.

We were taken to receptions at the New York Times and the Associated Press building overlooking Rockefeller Center. We met senior executives of both organizations. We walked the streets of New York. We went to Broadway plays.

I had arranged for Sandy to join me for the weekend, but not at the King's Crown. Instead, I reserved a room at the St. Moritz, on Central Park. As soon as we finished with Friday's sessions I caught the subway to the hotel to join her. She had arrived earlier that day.

I was astonished to discover that she had been given not a room, but a two-room corner suite overlooking Central Park. Obviously, there must have been a mistake. I couldn't possibly afford this.

I called the front desk and was assured the cost would be the same as the room I had reserved. Why had they done this for her? She wasn't sure. She remembered that another person checking in at the same time gave the desk clerk a tough time while she did not. "I suppose they thought I was nice," she said.

We had a wonderful weekend of theater and fine dining, almost as if we had money.

The second week of the seminar was even better than the first, although it involved a meeting with Buddy Hayden and two representatives from United Press International. The Huntington papers had dropped UPI some time before, opting to use only the AP. UPI had approached Hayden in an attempt to regain our business. Hayden thought about going with UPI in The Advertiser and the AP in the Herald-Dispatch. That would make the two newspapers even more different from each other—and it would be cheaper, because wire services charged according to a newspaper's circulation, and the AP cost much more than UPI.

I was against the move from the start because of my long respect for the AP and its great writers, and my growing involvement in the Associated Press Managing Editors Association. Buddy said he would come to New York while I was there and he and I would meet with UPI executives over dinner.

I took a cab to Hayden's hotel, where the UPI execs were waiting. We had a drink and then walked to a nice seafood restaurant. It was a long and wet evening and we listened to their proposals and I asked several questions about news coverage and we agreed to meet again in Huntington. Again, all this was quite new to me. (As it turned out, I won—we did not change from AP to UPI. In fact, we ended up with both.)

I left New York with a certificate from Columbia and a lot more knowledge about newspapering. I couldn't wait to get back and resume putting out The Advertiser.

Not long after, Buddy Hayden called me into his office. He said George Clark would be taking early retirement, which did not come as a shock to me but saddened me greatly. He had been so important to my life and my career. He would be replaced by an editor from outside, rather than from within, he said, meaning I would not be moving up. He had someone in mind who would be visiting to check out the operation and talk with several of us. His name was John McMillan and he was managing editor in Worcester, Massachusetts.

I had met McMillan while attending the ANPA/RI sessions in Cincinnati. We had talked about the future directions of computers in the news room. I mentioned that to Hayden and said McMillan was a respected editor.

He was pleased to hear that and told me if McMillan indeed became executive editor in Huntington, it undoubtedly would not be a permanent move for him. While he was here, I would have the opportunity to learn from him and when he moved on, I would move into his position.

When McMillan and I met during his visit to

Huntington he asked how I viewed the relationship between the executive editor and the managing editor, should he take the job. I responded that while he would be in charge of the overall newsroom operation and obviously my boss, I as managing editor would be in charge of the daily operation of my paper.

"I would agree with that," he said.

He accepted the job that day and returned to Massachusetts to finalize things at that end. While he did so his wife Carolyn came to Huntington to look for a house. Hayden asked if Sandy and I would take her to dinner, which we were pleased to do. When we called her to set a time, she said that a simple hamburger place would do. But we weren't about to do that; we wanted her to have a good feeling about Huntington. We took her to the Rebels & Redcoats Tavern. We ordered wine and good food and there was live music. We knew the musicians and during a break one came to our table, sat down, and started talking. I introduced him to Mrs. McMillan, but he kept on talking, clearing interrupting our time with her. She seemed uncomfortable and the evening ended early. I felt I had made a mistake in bringing her here.

McMillan would move into the corner office previously occupied by Raymond Brewster, which meant that we would share a common wall and our office doors would be literally a few feet apart. I felt good about that. If I were going to learn from him, being close was a good thing.

But first, Sandy and I would realize a dream of

ours for many years—our first trip to Europe. We took our son Chris and were joined by our bachelor friend, Keith Newman, who had become very much a part of our family and, in fact, our sons' godfather. We went to London, Paris, Rome and Madrid, on one of those tours that packs a lot into sixteen or seventeen days. It was wonderful, and I returned to work with what can only be described as great expectations.

Life with John McMillan turned out to be quite different from what I had expected. I had sent post cards to the staff from Europe, signing them "The Boss." They had been pinned to the staff bulletin board. When I returned to the office, McMillan called me in and said I should not have signed them "The Boss." Newsroom people object to that, he said. I tried to explain I used it in fun, targeting myself. He did not understand that.

His New England manner was more formal than we were accustomed to in this West Virginia city. He called everyone "Mr., Mrs. or Miss," rarely using first names When he wrote memos to me he carried them from his office past my open office door across the newsroom to the mail boxes against the wall and inserted them into my mail slot. "Mr. Hatfield," they began.

We clearly came from different worlds. In his, people were to be addressed as "Mr." and "Mrs., " even if they were co-workers. In mine, everyone was on a first-name basis, especially those one worked with every day.

One day he called me into his office and closed

the door and spoke almost in a whisper. He said he had heard me call a black member of our staff who had just transferred to the newsroom from Production, by her first name.

"Well, yes," I said, "Why?"

"Black women are offended when addressed by their first names," he said. "They want to be addressed as Mrs. So-and-so."

"Really," I said.

"You might keep that in mind."

"Okay. But if we call her Mrs., she'll be the only one in the newsroom addressed that way, the only one not called by her first name. That will set her quite apart, seems to me. Is that what you want?"

He looked at me and then said, "Whatever you think."

Still, I was eager to get to know McMillan better and, perhaps more importantly, for him to know me. Not long after he and his wife had settled into their new home on the Southside, Sandy and I invited them to our house in the woods of Pea Ridge for dinner. She prepared beef Stroganoff, and it was not easy given that we had three children, one of them severely handicapped. But she was willing to do it because this was her husband's new boss.

We talked that evening about the community, so new to them, and about our own lives here, and about family, theirs and ours. He seemed surprised that Sandy was the total caregiver for our daughter, who could not walk or talk or even sit up, and that we had not placed her in an institution. The two of them sympathized. And we talked about newspapers in general and the Huntington papers in particular. But when they left I did not feel that either McMillan nor I understood the other any better.

There was no question that I was learning from him. He was an excellent newsman and could find holes in a story better than anyone I had known. He could spot questions that should have been asked, detect areas that should be broadened, find opportunities to expand a story and make it more significant. He made every story better, the mark of an outstanding editor, and I learned what to look for in a story before it was published.

He also was something of a psychoanalyst. He said to me early on, "I've got the other guy (the morning managing editor) figured out, but I don't know what niche to put you in."

"Why would you want to put me in a niche?" I said.

One day when I returned to the office after speaking during a special journalism program at Marshall, he summoned me, wanting to know where I'd been, and I told him

"You didn't get my permission," he said.

I was stunned. I had been speaking at this annual program for years. Why would I need his permission? I told him all this and added, perhaps unwisely, "This is my town. I grew up here, I went to Marshall. You just got here."

He stared at me and then said, "Well, that's true. But when you do these things you're representing the newspaper and I just think it's good if we're all aware of it."

I thought it might be good if the two of us could have a conversation outside the office, hoping that would present an opportunity for him to know me better. I had heard that he had invited another news staffer to his house and they had enjoyed a private talk there. He agreed to meet, but instead of inviting me to his home as he had others he suggested we go to a restaurant, the Rebels & Redcoats, as it turned out. We ordered scotches and steaks and talked. At least I talked. I told him about growing up in the west end of town in a small house where there was little money but much love. I spoke of wanting to "be somebody" as a boy, and of always wanting to be a newspaper man and writer. He nodded knowingly, then said, "Well, you've made it, so relax."

When I sat in silence, he added that it was obvious I thought of myself as "the best writer in the newsroom," which, he said, made me jealous of other news staffers such as Dave Peyton. Again, I was stunned. Where had that come from? I had never been jealous of anyone at the newspaper, much less someone who worked for me. I realized then that not only did he not know me; he never would.

Nor did he understand Sandy and how and why she took such care of our handicapped daughter. "I tend to think Mrs. Hatfield sees herself in a martyr's role," he told me one day.

I was hurt and angered but I said quietly, "That isn't true at all," and walked out.

Clearly, McMillan was not impressed with me as a newsman. In fact, he told me bluntly one day that he had decided I did not really belong in a newsroom. "You don't seem to have a hunger for the news," he said, which surprised me given the types of stories my paper had done and was doing.

"In truth," he said, using his favorite phrase, "you like people too much. You probably should be in public relations."

When our promotions director left, McMillan urged me to apply for the job. I told him I didn't want to be in promotions. Similarly, when our production director's job became open, he suggested I apply for that job. Again, I told him I did not want to be a production director.

"You know I'm saying these things out of love, don't you?" he said.

I couldn't think of a thing to say to that.

Fortunately Gannett VP/News John Quinn came to town on one of the many visits he made to Gannett newspapers. At the end of the day he asked if I would drive him to the airport where the corporate jet was waiting. As he grabbed his briefcase from my car he turned to me and asked how things were going with McMillan.

I paused, wondering what to say. In the brief time I had known Quinn I had come to feel that I could be honest with him.

"To tell the truth," I said, "not all that great. He says I don't belong in a newsroom, that I don't have a 'hunger for news.' He says I should go into public relations."

"Really." Quinn said. It was more a comment than a question. Then he added:

"Well, I would disagree with all that. You hang in there."

I felt considerably better.

I told myself to stop whining, that it was not important whether McMillan gave a damn about me. He was a good editor and had the respect of the staff. What was important was to learn from him and do my job.   I never mentioned him again to anyone, not Quinn, not Buddy Hayden. In fact, Hayden and I saw very little of each other now that McMillan was here. There were no more calls for tennis or drinks or dinner. I could understand that. And I was okay with that too.

Meanwhile, on the national front, there was great change if not crisis in the air. The Vietnam War was winding down. Thousands of troops were being brought home, a shaky truce was being put in place. There was even some progress seen in the desegregation of schools in the Deep South. But a new word had found its way onto the front pages of the nation's newspapers.

Watergate.

22
"I AM NOT A CROOK"

It was not unusual for the President of the United States to speak at conventions of the nation's premier newspaper organizations, the American Newspaper Publishers Association, the American Society of Newspaper Editors, and The Associated Press Managing Editors Association.

I was active in APME, which was viewed as a hard-working group of editors whose charge was to monitor the work of the AP and to dig into other newsroom issues. I had served on various committees and would eventually do much more.

Gannett chose the APME convention each year for a gathering of its editors. In fact, as Gannett grew there were even complaints that the Gannett meeting held at APME was becoming larger than the APME convention itself. Not true, of course, but non-Gannett editors were well aware of the Gannett meetings going on, and some were not terribly pleased about it, believing the Gannett receptions and meetings caused a distraction.

On the other hand, Gannett's Vice President

News, John Quinn, also happened to be president of APME, so complaints were few.

This year the APME convention was to be held in Orlando, Florida, at Disney World. Many editors brought their families, and Sandy and I were accompanied by our sons, Chris, then fourteen, and Joel, six.

The key speaker was none other than President Richard M. Nixon.

It was November, 1973.

The ugly cloud of Watergate hung heavily over Nixon's head. What had begun as a seemingly minor burglary of the Democrat headquarters at the Watergate complex in Washington, D. C. had turned out to involve the Committee to Re-Elect the President. A couple of reporters for the Washington Post named Bob Woodward and Carl Bernstein kept digging into the story, aided by a key source they referred to as "Deep Throat." And each story they produced moved closer and closer to the White House. Nixon insisted he did not sanction the burglary and knew nothing about it. Then it was discovered that there existed a number of White House tapes that would prove otherwise. The tapes were the subject of subpoena, but Nixon fought that, saying as President he enjoyed the executive privilege of keeping them to himself. Charges grew that the President had ordered a cover-up of the crime and there were calls for his impeachment. Whatever credibility he may have had was fading, and support even among members of his own party was dwindling.

Such was the setting the evening of November 17, 1973, as some four hundred editors and many members of their families entered the grand hall to hear the President.

We were fortunate in finding seats up front, in the fourth row. We sat directly facing the podium at which the President would speak. And we awaited his arrival. I was excited for my sons to be present.

After several minutes John Quinn and a couple of other APME officers entered and stood near the podium. Then came "Hail to the Chief" and President Nixon entered with his Secret Service agents, who always blend into the background.

Quinn opened the session and explained that more than four hundred managing editors of AP newspapers were present and that the President had agreed to take questions from them for one hour, without restrictions. Then he said simply: "Ladies and gentlemen, the President of the United States."

Richard Nixon appeared to be quite nervous. He presented the forced smile we had seen so many times before and he clutched both sides of the podium tightly. He was obviously tense. There were beads of perspiration on his forehead, perhaps partly because of the camera lights. He hesitated and cleared his throat and began.

He said he welcomed the chance to speak to the nation's managing editors, and since there were so many he would have no opening statement. It will be hard enough to get to all the questions in just an hour, he said. Then he offered Quinn the opportunity to ask the first.

Quinn recalled the words of Benjamin Franklin when asked whether the constitutional convention had given the new country a monarchy or a republic. Franklin responded: "A republic, sir, if you can keep it." Quinn then asked, "In the prevailing pessimism of the larger matter we call Watergate, can we keep that republic, and how?"

Nixon responded immediately. "I would certainly not be standing here answering these questions unless I had a firm belief that we could keep the republic; that we must keep it...I recognize that because of mistakes that were made, and I must take responsibility for those mistakes...that there are those who wonder whether this republic can survive. But I also know that the hopes of the whole world for peace, not only now but in the years to come, rests on the United States of America. I can assure you that as long as I am physically able to handle the position...I am going to work for the cause of peace...and to the best of my ability to restore confidence in the White House and the President."

The podium seemed to tremble in his clutches. This was the President of the United States. And he was afraid. The world was watching. My sons were here, only a few feet from him. I had wanted them to be proud of the President. Instead I was embarrassed for the President.

For more than an hour he responded to questions, apparently without notes. He was obviously well prepared and seemed to speak with total recall. But he sometimes stammered and at least once misspoke. He defended his actions, spent considerable time answering questions about Watergate, repeated that he had no knowledge of the break-in and certain missing White House tapes, and denied several charges that had been making headlines.

Then he was given what some journalists might describe as a "softball" question which would provide him the opportunity to respond in a very positive manner. An editor mentioned that we Americans expect our President to play so many roles he cannot possibly take care of them all, and asked whether that made possible something like Watergate. But instead of seizing the opportunity, Nixon went to great lengths to discuss his personal finances including his tax returns and how he had made money in his professional life, although those matters had not been brought up. And then after all that, he suddenly said:

"People have got to know whether or not their president is a crook. Well, I'm not a crook. I've earned everything I got."

It was a historic moment. What a sad thing that the President felt he had to utter those words. And, that the world had to hear them.

At the time, and in years to come, most would tie the "I'm not a crook" comment to Watergate, as I always have and I was there. In re-examination, he was not referring to Watergate, but rather to his personal income. Consciously, at least.

In any case, history has tied the comment to Watergate and Nixon's 1973 APME speech has become known as the "I'm not a crook" speech. And as we all know by now, he did not survive as President, choosing to resign in August, 1974, as impeachment charges mounted.

However, the Republic did survive.

The work of Woodward and Bernstein in exposing the President's Watergate role had an enormous effect on news reporters everywhere and especially on young college students hopeful of following their example.   At the time I was interviewing students for Gannett, specifically at the University of Kentucky, Ohio University and Marshall which were nearby. We evaluated them and sent our remarks and their resumes to Gannett Corporate for its "Talent Tank," a very good thing for the students because it gave them far more exposure than interviewing with just one newspaper.

Normally, students were simply looking for entry-level jobs, Now I was facing students who did not want to be just beginning beat reporters, but rather "investigative reporters" like Woodward and Bernstein. They overlooked the fact that neither Woodward nor Bernstein was an investigative reporter when they stumbled on to Watergate. Both were beat reporters assigned to pretty routine beats, which is how they found the story. But they were talented, intelligent and relentless and turned what appeared to be a routine story into one so big that it would bring down a president.

I was asked several times, in a quite derogatory way, "Does your newspaper still rely on the beat system? Or do you allow your reporters to do real reporting?"

To which I always responded, "It's all real reporting."

Journalism schools became crowded and so in a matter of time did the journalism job market. Still, it was clear that these graduating journalism students would be a bit more idealistic and demanding than most we had seen before.

There is no question that Watergate became a watershed in terms of newspaper reporting. To a great extent that was also true in the way many in the media felt about covering politicians and officials including the president.

I remember being present during another Nixon address when CBS News' Dan Rather stood to ask a question and received a smattering of applause because of his celebrity and his perceived toughness (Rather took that a long way). Noticing the applause, Nixon smiled and asked jokingly, "Are you running for office?"

Instead of moving on with his question, Rather replied: "No, Mr. President—are you?"

It was a sarcastic, nasty, ill-mannered comment to make to anyone, especially the President of the United States, no matter who he is.

I have heard many times from those outside the media that in their opinion, the media have always treated Democrats, particularly presidents, much kinder than Republicans. They point to the treatment John F. Kennedy received compared to that Richard Nixon received.

My own opinion is that, yes, Kennedy was treated very well and Nixon not so well. However, I would point out that President Ronald Reagan, a Republican, was also treated very well and President Lyndon Johnson, a Democrat, not so well. The media ignored JFK's sexual pursuits and Reagan's nodding off and what turned out to be his early stages of Alzheimer's, and they were soft on his handling of the Iran Contra affair. Many in the media, especially in the print media, were won over by JFK's sense of humor and his seeming to be "one of them." And many both inside and outside the media were charmed by Reagan, who seemed like such a decent, down-to-earth guy even though he had been a movie star. How could anyone with a smile like that not be sincere? I have been in his presence several times and can say first-hand, that is the way he came across.

I also think media treatment can change involving the same president. Democrat Bill Clinton was treated well by the media in his first term, not so in his second, when sexual misconduct in his office came to light. And Republican George W. Bush was treated well in his first term, in which the September 11, 2001 World Trade center attacks occurred, and not so well in his second, when all sorts of distortions of fact involving this country's invasion of Iraq became obvious.

I also have heard time and again the phrase the "liberal press" almost as if it were one word. That is painting with a pretty broad brush. At a time when Gannett Company Inc. owned more than one hundred newspapers, about half of its newspapers editorially endorsed the Democratic presidential candidate, the other half the Republican. And that occurred strictly by coincidence as endorsements were a local, not a corporate, matter.

I can say from my own experience that you cannot find consensus on political matters even in one newsroom, much less all the newsrooms in the land.

As I said earlier in writing about sports, most readers and viewers do not really want "fair and objective" reporting. They want reporting that agrees with their views and favors their candidates and teams and schools. When it does, they view that as objective. When it does not, they view it as biased. It is true in politics, sports, and in the community, from PTAs to city councils.

Years ago, a common belief about newspapers was that most publishers and top editors were Republicans and most lesser editors and reporters were Democrats. I have found that not to be true. One finds a mix among all categories—reporters, editors, publishers--from one coast to another. But then, I speak only about my experience with newspapers, not the electronic media where I have no experience.

Whatever, I do not remember much real joy from the resignation of Richard Nixon, in newsrooms or front offices or, for that matter, on the street. I remember mostly regret and relief.

23
WORLD OF WONDERS

There would be magic in the newsroom accommodating both newspapers in Huntington. And I was assigned to put it there. "Magic," in that it was time for the wonderful world of new technology to take over.

"New technology" had come to many of the nation's newsrooms. Small terminals wired to computers were replacing typewriters. The "original keystroke" was being captured, as once a story was written it could be zapped to an editor's computer and then on to typesetting. No longer did it have to be retyped on a Linotype machine or on paper tape. Now it was being captured on film and paper to be cut apart and pasted onto pages and then photographed again for plates to be put on a press.

The Huntington papers had fallen behind. Ironic, because we had been among the first newspapers to have what was then called a CRT and among the first to produce a news section on one. But once Gannett arrived the CRT which John Foy had leased had been sent back to its owner, and we continued with typewriters and pencils.

But now, clearly, it was time to move on, time

to leave the antiquated method of producing newspapers, time for the newsroom staffs of both papers to enter the new world. Someone would have to get us there.

I am not sure why I got the assignment. Was it because I had been involved with the leased CRT that sat blinking in our photo studio? Because I had figured out how to produce a special section with it? Was it because McMillan wanted to get me out of the daily news operation, feeling I really didn't belong there?   Or, had he developed a new confidence in me for this obviously important task?

Whatever, I was to handle the newsroom part of the transition, to come up with a plan and carry it out. And I was given considerable freedom.

Hayden, with help from the Gannett corporate staff, had already chosen which way we would go. We would use three different companies to get us into the world of wonders. Our computers would come from Digital Electronics Corp. of Massachusetts, our software from Datalogics of Chicago. And our terminals—dumb monitors with keyboards—would come from the Beehive Corp. of Salt Lake City, Utah, and were called "Super Bees."

It was almost as if they had said, "Here's the stuff, make it work."

The challenge was that we had two newspapers sharing one newsroom. I was to make it work for both.

I told Hayden and McMillan the same thing I had told George Clark and John Foy, that I knew nothing about computers. I did not know the terminology. All I knew was how to put out a daily newspaper and what editors and reporters needed in order to do that.

That was a good start, they said.

I met with representatives of all three companies. I felt lost in the conversation, although I was somewhat comforted when the representative from Digital said, "It's all about getting this guy to talk with this guy," referring to computers, not people. I could understand terminology like that.

I next met with newsroom staff members of both Huntington papers, which was quite a change in itself because I had urged my staff to "kick hell out of the Herald."

I asked all what they would like computers to do for them. I took hundreds of notes.

"I've love it if a computer could count headlines so I don't have to count them," said one copy editor.

"Better if they could just make them fit," said another.

"I want the computer to measure the length of stories," said a city desk editor.

"If only one could teach me how to spell," said a reporter.

"If I could save what I've written so I don't have to keep starting over when I want to change something, that would be great," said another.

Armed with this information and more, still lacking even basic knowledge about computers and computer terminology, I flew to Chicago and met with Datalogics.

"I don't know the proper terminology," I said, "but here are the things our people want a computer system to do."

They made notes and copies of my lists and assured me not one of these requests presented a problem, In fact, they said, their software would do all this and a lot more.

When I returned to Huntington two Super Bee terminals awaited in our newsroom library. They were not connected to a computer, but we could use them to familiarize ourselves with the key boards and certain functions. George Clark already had been working with them, and now he would teach me. We then set up individual training sessions for every member of each news staff.

Another challenge was one of resources. We would have a limited number of terminals to serve two separate and competing news staffs in one newsroom. The terminals would have to be shared. How to do that? Also, I was told to watch costs in making physical newsroom changes.

I found an old cork dart board in my garage at home. I went to a school supply store and bought several pieces of balsa wood and a box of colored pin-heads. And with the help of my sons, I fashioned the balsa into inch-long pieces, each one representing a reporter's desk, and painted them different colors to distinguish not only the different papers, but also different departments on those papers. I put tiny nails through the balsa "desks" and attached them to the back of the dart board. I cut longer pieces to be used as counter tops to hold terminals. Lastly, I placed the colored stick-pins where terminals would go.

My thinking was this: Place the countertops between rows of desks. Put the terminals on turn-tables fastened to the counter tops. The evening paper staff would come in, sit at their desks, and simply turn in their chairs and spin the terminals to face them. At the end of their shift, the morning staff would come in, spin the terminals back to face them, and use the same terminals.

I brought my cork board with balsa cutouts and pin-heads to the newsroom and set it up. I asked every newsroom staffer to examine it, shoot holes through the entire idea, and tell me what they thought would work and, more importantly, not work.

There was a lot of movement of the painted blocks of balsa.

Finally we reached agreement on the crude model I had created, and we proceeded.

I drew up a floor plan showing where the various departments, desks and counter tops would be placed, where the cables would be located, the terminals, the pneumatic tubes for page dummies and photos, and the circular news desks. I measured cabling for the counter tops and the news desks. I would use kitchen counter tops placed atop short metal file cabinets. The two circular news desks would remain, as would the reporters' desks, the latter with new coats of paint.

I went to an office supply firm and specified the size file cabinets I wanted. Even those with two drawers were too high, but when the pedestals were removed were perfect. I went to Chandler's Plywood Products in the Westmoreland section of Huntington and ordered kitchen counter tops which would hold our banks of terminals. Each top would need several turn tables, one for each terminal, and some mechanical piece to allow each to turn. We used sink cut-outs for the turn-table tops and Lazy Susan hardware for the mechanics.

Of course, staffers on both papers thought I was crazy. Well, I told myself, people probably thought the same about Thomas Edison.

I did not want a newsroom full of cables, so I positioned the counter tops to butt up against pillars in the newsroom—originally octagon-shaped concrete but later boxed in with paneling. We placed the cables over the false ceiling, brought them down inside the boxed-in pillars, and then under the counter tops. On the news desks we built small boxed-in power poles.

When all this was completed, we had a newsroom of differently painted desks and chairs separated by rows of terminals sitting on Formica-covered counters. Nowhere was a cable to be seen. Surprisingly, it looked pretty good.

But would it work?

The system—computers, Beehive terminals and software—worked fine. The human element was something else.

New technology "experts" at the time liked to say computers would eliminate the need for paper. How, then, would a reporter notify an editor that his story was finished and could be called up for editing? How would one pass the story from city desk or news editor to copy editors and headline writers? How, in short, was one to communicate?

Nobody was about to give up paper just yet no matter that the experts said. Notes were scribbled on paper and passed. Paper lists were kept. Vocal calls were made across the newsroom.

"City Council story's done, here it comes."

"Give me a 3-column 36-point head on that."

And so it went.

In time, of course, methods of electronic communication were developed and there was no longer a need for paper—not even for paper dummies a few years later, once pagination came to newsrooms and all page makeup was done on the computer. But in those early years, it was something of an adventure.

What I noticed from the start was that the quality of editing went down the tube—and I don't mean cathode ray tube. My theory, then and now, was that on a computer screen a story appears to be more correct—in typos, spelling, whatever--than on paper. Those editing stories on terminals flew past mistakes they would have caught when editing with pencil on paper. Understandably, they were accustomed to paper. Still, I find even now it is easy to breeze right by an error on the screen. It just looks so right.

In any case, my newsroom technology assignment was complete. Now it was up to those who used it to make it work. And it was time for me to become a managing editor again and get back to running The Advertiser.

It had become clear to me that John R. Brown was not doing the job of city editor as I had hoped. He was still a good judge of the news and an excellent editor of copy. But he did not work with reporters as he once had, nor did he plan and assign stories as he should. When he went on vacation I moved reporter Charlie Bowen into the city editor's slot on a temporary basis. Bowen performed extremely well, especially in dealing with staff. When Brown returned I approached him about becoming a fulltime columnist. He would have his own office—my old one was still vacant—and he would no longer have to worry about running a staff. He liked the idea. And Charlie Bowen became our permanent city editor. Both were good moves.

Sadly, Brown became ill not long after. The diagnosis: cancer. "What the hell," he told me. "I've had a good life." He took weeks off for treatment, and returned to the office. But the cancer worsened, and he died. He was only fifty-two. It occurred to me I had not thanked him for what he had done for me years before as my boss and later as one of my staff. I regret that.

And in the midst of all that had been going in my life of new technology and staffing changes, there came the sad news that George Clark, our retired editor, my friend and mentor, left us. Struggling from his almost constant migraines and physically ill from the medicines given him, he took his own life.   I remember his stories about

Washington politicians, his having worked there, and how they can never be fully believed. Mostly, I remember his words to me that day in his office:

"Life is so goddam beautiful."

As it turned out, Hayden and McMillan were waiting with another assignment for me.

Afternoon papers around the country were losing circulation and readership (they are not necessarily the same thing). That included the Huntington Advertiser. In years past afternoon papers had dominated because our society was mostly blue-collar. Workers went to their jobs before morning papers arrived and got home in time to read that evening's paper. Now we had long since turned into a white-collar society and most people read newspapers in the morning before going to work. They had less time to read in the evening with so many family activities taking place. There also was the lure of that magic TV box in the evening. The time had come and all but gone for afternoon newspapers.

What to do? If you were the only paper in town, the answer was obvious: you switched to morning. But if you were the p.m. paper in a two-newspaper town, you had a problem: how to maintain your readership, how to continue as a necessary part of every family's day when another paper had arrived hours before yours. The blunt realization was, you were no longer necessary and never would be again.

Okay, some said, if you can't be the newspaper people need, perhaps you should try to be the one people want. How to do that? My own idea was to produce important and readable stories the other paper was not doing. But would that be enough? And what if the other newspaper started doing those stories, as it should have been?

Various newspaper organizations were studying the problem, including the Associated Press Managing Editors Association. In Huntington, John McMillan and Buddy Hayden decided that the best thing for the Advertiser was to become a totally different kind of newspaper, a sort of daily magazine, changed in appearance as well as content. More soft features, how-to articles, life improvement tips. More of what readers want than what we editors think they need.

I went kicking and screaming into this. We're dumbing down the paper, I thought. They want the morning paper to be a good newspaper and my paper to be a daily Better Homes & Gardens. That is not the kind of newspaper I want to produce, I said.

"You've got to face reality," McMillan said.

I have never been very good at that.

They suggested I hire a graphics person for the Advertiser. No editor ever turns down the opportunity to hire an additional staffer. I readily agreed and began the search. I found the perfect person for the job of overhauling the look of the Advertiser and creating the pages of a new, non-traditional newspaper. He was straight out of the University of Missouri, one of the top journalism schools in the country. His name was Rick

Baumgartner. I gave him John R. Brown's old office for his studio.

Our new Huntington Advertiser—this would be the second new Advertiser since Gannett came in the beginning of 1972—would be heavily themed. Each day would focus on one major subject, offer features on one specific part of town, etc. After a while it became obvious that the easy way out for our editors was to combine the two. We soon themed ourselves to death.

The worst blow of all to me was tossing out our time-honored page one nameplate and replacing it with the day of the week. Instead of "The Huntington Advertiser" as it had been for nearly a century, now the top of the front page stated in strange, flowery script-like type, "Monday evening" and "Tuesday evening" and so on. That, of course, made it incumbent on the composing room printers to be certain to change the nameplate each day. We did retain "The Huntington Advertiser" in very small type but I still gnashed my teeth.

Our young staff did not seem nearly as bothered by all this as I was. And Baumgartner was having a ball. I did have to admit that the pages were refreshing and downright unique. But none had the Hatfield look (which may have been a good thing if you are not Hatfield.).

Actually, we were not alone. The afternoon Louisville Times, just a couple of hours west on the Interstate, was also undergoing great change. So were many other p.m. papers in the country. When APME put together the program for its 1975 convention, to be held that fall in Williamsburg, Va., it scheduled a panel on the changing afternoon newspaper and invited me to make a presentation on the new Huntington Advertiser and Mike Davies, managing editor of the Louisville Times, to talk about changes on his paper. McMillan suggested I visit Davies since we were going to be appearing on the same panel. Good idea.

Davies and I spent an afternoon in his office complaining about the winds of fate bringing us to this. Neither of us wanted to produce the kind of paper being envisioned. We eventually got around to discussing what we would do and I drove back to Huntington. Davies and I would remain friends for the rest of our careers.

By coincidence, APME had also asked me to make a short presentation on our new computerized newsroom, with photos and drawings. Apparently word had gotten out that we had done it on the cheap. In any event, I found myself working on two separate APME presentations.

To my surprise, both were well attended. Most newspapers were going into new technology and every afternoon newspaper in America was worried about its future. Both sessions went well, with that on afternoon newspapers especially capturing attention.. More than one editor wanted copies of the slides showing our new look, primarily because of the graphics and designs of Rick Baumgartner.

When I returned to Huntington, McMillan asked how things had gone. I told him they had gone quite well, and that I had to admit that the new look of the Advertiser was especially well received.

"That's why I wanted you to go there and do these sessions," he said. "Such things can turn into job offers."

First time in months he had mentioned my going elsewhere.

24
GOODBYE AND GOOD LUCK

As it turned out, I was not the one to go. First it was John McMillan. After the good job he had done as executive editor in Huntington, Gannett transferred him to its newspaper in Salem, Oregon. Huntington publisher Buddy Hayden made the announcement in a specially-called meeting of his Operating Group, the name he had given to his directors and top editors. He added that McMillan would not be replaced. "The two Dons," he said, referring to Herald-Dispatch Managing Editor Don Mayne and me, will continue to run their respective newspapers, reporting directly to the publisher.

That jarred me. When Hayden had brought McMillan to Huntington, he told me I would learn from him for a couple of years or so and when he left I would succeed him. Sometimes that promise had kept me going. It also had kept me from seriously considering a move to another Gannett newspaper when Corporate brought up the subject. Now Hayden, my boss, one-time tennis partner and friend, was reneging on that promise. What had happened? Did Hayden change his mind because I had not measured up? Had McMillan influenced him? Was Hayden simply trying to save money, as was the Gannett way? Did this mean I would never move into the top editor's job under him? Or was there something else going on? I was full of questions.

When the meeting ended I followed him to his office and said, "Got a minute?" and walked in, closing the door.

"You're not replacing McMillan?" I said.

"That's right" He frowned and sat down and looked at me.

"I think you owe me an explanation."

"Why is that?"

"You said when you brought him here that I would succeed him when he left."

"Well, you're not," he said testily. Then he sighed and seemed to soften for a moment. "I don't have time to talk about it right now. Let's have lunch and we'll talk then."

I returned to my office and took from a file folder the note I had made the day Hayden told me that with George Clark retiring, he was bringing in a new executive editor from outside. I would learn from that editor over a period of two or three years, and when he left—said Hayden--I would succeed him. I had dated the note and put it away.

I took the note with me to our lunch a few days later. I slipped it from my coat pocket, unfolded it and began to read it to him.

"I don't care what that says," he said abruptly. "You're not going to get that job, at least for now.

210

Now get over it."

He started talking about the two Huntington papers then, commending me for the job I had done with The Advertiser. I did not mention the executive editor's job again.

Before our lunch was over, a prominent member of the community stopped by our table to speak with Hayden and mentioned a new venture of his. I asked him what it was, where it was, and had a couple of follow-up questions, as any decent reporter would. When he left Hayden looked at me and smiled. "I'm glad you did that," he said. "That's the Hatfield I know."

There was a going-away party for John McMillan. Members of the Operating Group chipped in to purchase a handsome piece of luggage as a gift—a two-suiter. "We know this will be a challenge for you," Mayne joked, in reference to McMillan seemingly wearing the same grey suit every day. My wife Sandy gave him a miniature bottle of Beefeaters gin for a martini on the road. Everyone had a few good things to say, everyone wished him well, everyone had a good time.

I had mixed feelings about McMillan's leaving and even more about his having been here the past two years or so. There was no doubt he had raised the bar in the newsroom. He was a professional, a solid newsman, and had set high standards for editing and coverage of the day's news. The news staff respected him, and most of its members genuinely liked him. I regretted that from the beginning of our relationship he had found me wanting as a newsman. But I had put that behind me and moved on. I had hoped that by the time he left, he would have a different opinion of me, and I was sorry to see him go without that having occurred— if indeed it had not. But, the world is not a perfect place and I had been very fortunate to be where I was.

I felt a new freedom after that. The Advertiser continued to do the kinds of hard news it had done before, despite the switch to the "new" Advertiser and its weird format and soft features. Not that McMillan had discouraged hard news reporting. He was all for that. But we moved away from the daily themes and cut back on the how-to stuff. And I went back to having fun in my job.

One morning we learned that the executive committee of the Chamber of Commerce, `which included Hayden, was meeting in private at an undisclosed location away from its offices, and that the meeting would be closed to the press. Those are fighting words for editors and reporters, who believe strongly in "the people's right to know" and that "the people's business is the people's business." Hayden agreed with that, except when it came to private business. His oft-stated view was, "Private business is private until private business wants to make it public." To which I would respond that when private business affects the public, it was the public's business.

Hayden wore his two hats of newspaper publisher and community leader quite well. He distinguished, at least in his own mind, what should be public and what private. Apparently he placed the Chamber of Commerce in the latter category.

At first we couldn't find where the meeting was taking place. Then we discovered it was going on in a motel outside the city limits. We sent a reporter and a photographer. They knocked on the door of the room in which the meeting was being held, but could not get in. They waited outside until finally the door opened and the Chamber brass, including Hayden, emerged, straight into the eye of the camera. Our reporter asked several questions and later wrote about the meeting, accompanied by a photo. The chamber group had been discussing candidates and issues in an upcoming election for its endorsement slate. Not exactly big news. But we had interrupted a private meeting of public people and reported it, and we felt good about that.

Was Hayden upset that we had barged into his closed door meeting? He was beaming. His newspapers had made him proud. And we in the newsroom took pride in our independence from the power brokers in town—local officials, the country club set, our advertisers.

It was our biggest advertiser who called one morning with this cryptic message: "If you print the story about my wife, I will cancel all my advertising."

Now, in spite of popular belief, advertisers who attempt to influence the newsroom are pushing a hot button. News people are super-sensitive to charges that big advertisers can affect the handling of news. They go the other way to prove the point.

The funny thing was that we had no idea what he was talking about—we had no story about his wife, no idea who his wife was. But the newsroom immediately went into high gear to find out. What we discovered was that the night before his wife had been drunk, had driven up Fifth Avenue and sideswiped a number of parked cars, and had fled—a clear DUI hit-and-run, with several thousand dollars in damages left behind. Normally we would not have bothered with such a small matter. But we certainly did that one, having been threatened. So we printed the story in the next edition, with his wife's name.

Having been told numerous times by Buddy Hayden that "publishers don't like surprises," I called to tell him what we were doing. It would be in that day's final edition, I said. He said nothing for a moment. Then he said, "Okay." The next day he called me into his office. He was holding the paper with the story.

"Do you know what this cost us?" he said. "Sixty-two thousand dollars."

"So he went through with his threat."

"He did. He canceled all the ads he had scheduled."

"I'm sorry to hear that," I said. "But we can't allow an advertiser to think he can keep something out of the newspaper. Not even Presidents can do that."

"Still…"

"That story deserved to be in the paper. Somebody may have seen it happening and wondered what was going on and why it wasn't in their newspaper. People have a right to know what's happening."

I felt very righteous.

Hayden looked at me, and then sighed that sigh of his and shrugged his shoulders. "Well," he said, "he'll come back."

And so our advertiser did, after talking with his corporate boss. That was one more thing I liked about Buddy Hayden: He backed up his newsroom.

Not long after that he called me into his office to say it was review time. That also meant salary review time. He said he was increasing my salary to $20,000 per year. I could not hide my pleasure.

"Twenty thousand; you finally made it," he said. Then he added: "DH, one of these days you'll be making twice that much in this business."

I couldn't imagine that. Forty thousand a year? No way. But the thought made me happy.

Before that year, 1976, was out, Buddy too was gone—transferred to, of all places, Salem, Oregon, where he would join his former editor, John McMillan. Apparently the Salem operation was in such shape that it required not only a new editor, but a new publisher as well. Gannett insiders said while publishers who were transferred may often send for their former editors, this was the first time a transferred editor had sent for his former publisher.

Buddy Hayden had done good things in Huntington—for the newspapers, and for the community. He established a Christmas tree lighting ceremony, insisting on having a huge tree lashed atop the roof of our building. No one was sure whether it would hold. Thousands came out to watch the ceremony and sing Christmas carols from below on Fifth Avenue. He also held July 4 community celebrations in Ritter Park, invited the entire city, and set up all kinds of games for families, free of charge. Nearly ten thousand people showed up. He gave away popcorn and sodas, and held a mixed doubles tennis tournament which he asked me to handle.

Hayden was a unique individual. He certainly had his detractors and I am not sure just how much he could be believed or trusted. He had a huge ego. There were those who called him a "phony." But I liked him. I liked him as publisher and as a friend. I endured his excuses, on the tennis court and elsewhere, and his excesses, and his affectations. He was fun, especially away from the office. He listened to me and respected me. He also argued with me. Then we could play tennis and have a drink.

After going to Salem he became publisher of the Philadelphia Bulletin. He later went to the Trenton Times, and in between ran an online advertising company. Along the way, after a diet of Scotch and popcorn, he suffered a heart attack. After recuperating he returned to the tennis courts and the life he always had. One year Sandy and I ran into him during a newspaper convention in New Orleans. We shared a few drinks and a few laughs. I never saw him again. Sadly, he died some years later from a second heart attack. I do not know whether he had returned to that diet of Scotch and popcorn.

His leaving Huntington meant that we were once again in for change, with a new publisher coming in. His name was Hal Burdick, and he came to us from the Gannett newspaper in Chambersburg, Pa. Burdick had been in Huntington not long before to attend a Gannett subsidiary meeting. Dinner that evening was held at Guyan Country Club and with Burdick was his editor in Chambersburg, a young man named Bob Collins, who sat at a table with my wife and me. Little did I know then the role Bob Collins would play in my life in the years to come.

Burdick came in to my office his first day as publisher and said he believed in editors running the newsroom and publishers running the business side. I should go on running the afternoon newspaper the way I had been, he said. That was great news. Not all publishers share that philosophy. He kept his word, too--unusual for some publishers, including many in Gannett. He never questioned any story we did nor any endorsement we made.

A former World War II Army Air Force veteran who had been shot down in Sicily, he had a certain style from that era. He had a lovely wife named Lillian, he liked golf, he was a good businessman, and he was one of those rare publishers from the business side who appreciate the importance of the news side.

He had the great practice of walking all over

the building once each day. He would drop in on every department, starting in the basement pressroom, and speak to everyone in sight. It meant a lot to the employees. Most of the time he ended his tour in my office, and we would talk briefly about a number of things--what was going on in the community and in the world, occasional staff problems, his golf game, his family.

Very much a traditional type, he was bothered when he saw a reporter-columnist often stretched out with his feet on the desk reading magazines. He decided the reporter could not possibly be productive, and asked me to check on him. First, I assured him that this particular reporter was, like some, a bit weird in his work routine, and that he often worked far into the night when no one else was around. He might be writing at 4 a.m. if he felt like it, or resting at 2 p.m., I said. This was beyond Hal and his business sense. He was sure I was wrong, that I was protecting a staffer who was loafing while being paid to work. So we ran a story count on all the reporters and, as I expected, this particular reporter came out considerably on top. He was our most productive writer. When I presented the evidence to Burdick, he was astonished, and then he just put it aside. He never mentioned it again.

The reporter's name was Dave Peyton, who went on to become a highly respected columnist. He probably wrote his columns in the wee hours, too.

Hal Burdick did not always understand newsroom people. But he was smart enough to accept them. They're a different breed, I told him one day.

"I believe it," he said.

As time passed Hal Burdick was approached by the Ford Foundation which was then involved in a series of media-law seminars throughout the country. The head of the effort was retired CBS News president Fred Friendly, and the lawyers who took part were among the top names in media law— Arthur Miller, who later had his own national television show, and Charles R. Nesson of Harvard.

They discussed a possible seminar in West Virginia with our newspapers acting as host. . That year's seminar was being held at a resort in Lake of the Ozarks, Missouri. Hal asked that I attend so that if we did host such a seminar in West Virginia, I could organize it. He said it would be fine for me to take my wife.

Sandy and I went, notebooks in hand, to Lake of the Ozarks. We met with Fred Friendly and Arthur Miller and Charles Nesson. We observed every session and took notes. And when we were ready to leave we were astonished to discover at the small airport that our travel agency had slipped up, booking us on a flight that did not exist on Sundays. We had a connecting flight in St. Louis. But how were we to get there?

When I could find no other flights I chartered a small plane, paid the owner-pilot his outlandish fee by credit card, and we flew to St. Louis where we made our connection. The next day I gave glowing reports about this most important seminar to

Burdick, and he agreed on the spot to seek the seminar for West Virginia.

It would be held at the Greenbrier, that magnificent resort in Greenbrier County. It was up to me to select the participants, from the media and from the legal side. Fred Friendly would bring his usual team of Arthur Miller and Charles Nesson.

The Ford Foundation media-law seminars were done in the Socratic style, with long tables arranged in a circle at which were seated journalists, lawyers, prosecutors, a couple of judges and one or two law enforcement officers. In the center were the Fred Friendly troops, Miller and Nesson. It was all about role-playing, pitting the two sides—media and law —against each other in a theoretical enactment.

The night before the sessions were to begin Friendly, Miller and Nesson met with Burdick and me to discuss procedures. Miller and Nesson wanted to know what I could tell them about the participants—who might be good targets to call upon, who might make the day interesting. We discussed the tendencies and personalities of each one, and they made many notes. By the end of the meeting, both Miller and Nesson felt fairly good about the next day. I later learned that in spite of Miller's huge national reputation, his broad experience and his enormous abilities, he often was so worried about the upcoming session that he could not sleep and in fact sometimes became physically ill. But in the round, he was a genius and razor sharp.

One moment stands out for me concerning the

sessions. As the game played out, the matter of evidence--destroyed, subpoenaed and otherwise-- came up. A prosecuting attorney said he would subpoena a reporter's notes. Hearing that, Nesson wheeled to face me.

"All right, Mr. Editor, what do you say about that?" he demanded.

"What notes?" I said.

Nesson seized the opportunity. "Aha! 'What notes,' the editor says. So, you destroyed them. Burned them, no doubt. Torched them to keep from giving them up."

Our own newspaper lawyer, Bill Beatty of Huntington, was at the table that day. And forever after, he referred to me as "Torch." When I would call, he would respond, "Hello, Torch, what's up?"

Bill Beatty was the best media lawyer I ever worked with, in West Virginia and in Arizona. He worked with editors and reporters to find a way to get a story into the paper, not for reasons to keep it out.

Before the seminar ended, Sandy and I had lunch with Fred Friendly and his wife. We didn't talk about the seminar. They wanted to know about us, about life in West Virginia, about our family. When they heard we had a bright young son graduating from high school, Friendly suggested he consider Columbia, his school, and offered to help shepherd my son's admission application. Whatever may be said about Fred Friendly as the greatest of all CBS news presidents, I can say more about him as a person. Unassuming, kind, a listener. Some time

after the seminar, he sent me tapes of all the
sessions with this note: "Look at what we did!"

25
KEVINNE AND THE GANG

From 1972, when Buddy Hayden changed the structure of the Huntington newspapers, until 1979, The Huntington Advertiser was the local-emphasis news source in the city. The larger morning Herald-Dispatch placed a high priority on tri-state and regional news, with zoned editions in Ohio, Kentucky and southern West Virginia. Local television stations did pretty much the same, with viewers spread over several miles. But the Advertiser focused on Greater Huntington. More importantly, the paper was not merely local, but readable and often hard-hitting. And we did all this with a limited news budget and a small staff.

How was this possible? We hired good people —young, intelligent, well-educated, idealistic, willing to work for less money than they might get elsewhere. And they believed in what we were doing.

They came from various places and noted universities—Northwestern, Michigan, Southern California, Ohio University, Ohio State, Penn State, Illinois, Missouri, and Connecticut. And as one would expect, Marshall and West Virginia Universities. Most were beginning their newspaper careers; a couple had worked for even smaller papers than ours. Some had master's degrees, one had no degree. And they came to work for a newspaper of less than 20,000 circulation.

Looking back over those seven years, they comprised quite a diverse group. Dick Stanley, Angela Dodson and Rick Baumgartner early on. And then Jackie Jadrnak, John Koenig, Jeff Day, Jim Hunyadi, Lin Chaff, Sara Berkeley, Joe Cosco, Bob Hall, Kathy Legg, Jim Leunk, Deborah Higgins, Bruce Ebert, Patty Rhule. And there was Kevinne Moran.

They joined strong, experienced Advertiser staffers like Jack Hardin, Charlie and Pamela Bowen, Dave Peyton, C. T. Mitchell, Chuck Carpenter, Bob Withers, Lowell Cade.

And it worked.

We had a connection with Northwestern University's Medill School of Journalism, one of the best journalism schools in the country. Thanks to John McMillan, we were one of the professional sites for its Teaching Newspapers Program.

Jadrnak came to us as an intern in the Northwestern program. We liked her so much we asked her to return for a paid summer internship, and later to join our staff fulltime.

I once asked Jadrnak why the Northwestern students seemed so far ahead of many other students we interviewed. What was it about that school that made them what they were?

Said Jadrnak: "Did it occur to you that maybe we were advanced when we got there?"

Actually, it had not. Good answer.

I cannot remember how I heard about John Koenig until he arrived in Huntington, but I was impressed and asked him to have dinner with Sandy and me at the Rebels & Redcoats. The evening went well and I offered him a reporting position. He said he was considering a few other places. I pressed the issue until he gave up. "All right," he said. "I'll work for you."

Jeff Day called out of the blue, asking for an interview. He was working on a newspaper in Steubenville, Ohio. I invited him to Huntington, interviewed him and learned that he was an economics major. Economics? What did that have to do with journalism and writing? He stayed that night in the local Holiday Inn. The next morning I sat him at a typewriter and told him to write anything that came into his mind. I just wanted to see how he put words on paper. He turned out a beautiful mood piece about sitting in the window of his room at the Holiday Inn watching scrap paper blow down the alley. I offered him a job and he accepted. We used him in many ways, but mostly as a feature writer with special assignments such as spending a weekend with the National Guard on maneuvers and then describing it for our readers.

Day was always looking for a different angle. Once he went too far. Assigned to write about skiing, which had recently become the hot thing to do in West Virginia, he turned in a story that City

Editor Charlie Bowen brought to me, saying, "You better read this one." It began like this: "Listen to me, brothers and sisters," and continued in what seemed to me a parody of a southern black church.

I called Day in and said, "First, this isn't going to run. It seems to me you're making fun of people in a church and maybe a black church at that, and we're not going to make fun of anyone. But I am curious. What the hell has this got to do with skiing?"

Day replied that he had not wanted to write the usual soft story about skiing; he wanted to take a different approach. What, he asked himself, has skiing become in this state? To some, he answered himself, it has become a religion

A religion. Right. But it's still not going to run.

He became one of our strongest writers, one who cared deeply about his job and more importantly, about people.

I learned a lot from all of them. I have mentioned the things I learned from Angela Dodson, not only about the word "ghetto," but also about the sensitivities and concerns of those we then called "minority journalists."

I was educated similarly in matters of gender and what might be called "unconscious sexism" by Jackie Jadrnak and Lin Chaff.

We received reports of heavy flooding in southern West Virginia. Already many roads were blocked and authorities and members of the media were having difficulty reaching the flooded areas. We hurried to get photographers and reporters to the scene. It did not occur to me that all were male. In my outdated and old world thinking, that was logical. After all, this was a physically difficult and perhaps even dangerous assignment. Men were given such assignments. Women were to be "protected," even if they were reporters.

Into my office came Jadrnak and Chaff, wanting to know why only male reporters were being sent on this story. Quite surprised, I found myself trying to explain and then realized how stupid I sounded. Finally I said, "You're right. You'll both go."

We chartered a small plane and put Jadrnak aboard with photographer Jack Burnett. We were not sure if it could land in the flooded area; if not, they were to shoot and take notes describing the scene from the air. Chaff was sent by car on a back road.

Jadrnak's plane put down on a small field near Williamson where she, in her own words, "sweet-talked" a local resident into giving her a lift into the flooded town. She got interviews, "sweet-talked" someone else into a lift back to the airport, and dashed into the Advertiser newsroom a half-hour before deadline. The following day she took another plane into the area, again "sweet-talked" a local into letting her use one of only three working telephones to call in her story.

Chaff meanwhile also got into the area and scored interviews with victims of the flood. Their stories led The Advertiser's coverage. And Jadrnak was later honored with a "Gannett Well Done" award for her work.

Thankfully they had complained to a once-old-fashioned editor and educated   him. And the Advertiser and its readers and that editor benefitted greatly.

Kevinne Moran was, like Jadrnak, a product of Northwestern's Medill School of Journalism. I had visited Northwestern before to speak to a class and to meet with our interns and was about to do it again. Shortly before leaving Huntington I received a call from Moran, a new name to me, who said she had heard I was coming to Evanston and hoped to have some time with me. I told her I had no time in my schedule. I would be arriving in the afternoon, meeting people for dinner, speaking the next day and then flying out. Besides, I had no openings. She said she wanted to see me anyway. I repeated that I would have only a few moments in my hotel room to freshen up. She said that would do. Who was this person?

Shortly after my arrival in Evanston there was a knock on my hotel room door and when I opened it there stood this young woman with scrapbooks under her arm. She said, "Hi. I'm Kevinne," came right into the room, and promised she would not take much time.

Why was she so interested in a small newspaper in West Virginia? She was from the South Side of Chicago. A graduate of Medill. An MA.

She said she had heard good things about us.

I told her again I had no openings and if I did, I

wasn't sure our small newspaper could afford someone with an MA from Medill.

She said that was okay.

We talked about newspapers and books and writers and life and when finally she left I thought, here is a young woman who practically kicked down the door to my hotel room for an interview. What would she do to get a story from city officials?

When I returned to Huntington she called and repeated her desire to work for our newspaper. Later, when a job did come up, I gave her a quick call, hoping she was still available. She was. Little did I know that she would become not only a great reporter, but a central part of our personal lives, that someday she would work for me in Arizona as well, and that I would stand up at her wedding and be there when her first child was born.

Before all that happened, Moran became the most talked about reporter in town, especially by city officials. Assigned to cover city government, she took that responsibility further than anyone had. She dug into every city government office and department. She developed sources, made contacts, followed up tips. One told her that the city's housing inspector was linked in some way to slum landlords and was overlooking their violations. Moran went to his office and asked for the records. She was told they were not available to the public.

"Really?" she said. "My editor will be interested to hear that."

On second thought, the staffer there said, they

would be made available to her the next day. "It will take a while to get them together," she explained. Moran agreed to wait.

When she went to City Hall the following day she was stunned to learn that there had been a "robbery" in the housing inspector's office and that all the records—surprise--had been stolen. What's more, she was told, she was the prime suspect.

Why, Moran said, would I steal them when they were promised to me today?

She returned to the newspaper offices to fill me in and then wrote the story of the reported "robbery" of the records, including the fact that it had occurred hours after our paper had requested them.

That evening I was at home having a drink before dinner with our friend, Keith Newman, who just happened to be a defense lawyer and former assistant prosecutor, when Moran called to inform me that the police had just come to her apartment. She asked what she should do. I told her to hold on and I would be right there—with, coincidentally, a lawyer.

Newman and I were there in five minutes. The police were surprised to see us both. I asked what they were doing there. They stammered that they were just talking with Moran about what she might know regarding the "robbery" at City Hall. I told them to buy that evening's newspaper and they could read what she knew. I also told them we at the Advertiser did not take lightly what appeared to be attempted intimidation of one of our reporters.

They left.

The next day—surprise No. 2—the missing records showed up, the result of a "mix-up" in that a staffer "had taken them home to sort them out." It was no surprise that the records that suddenly turned up contained nothing to indicate the city's housing inspector had ever been involved in any unethical or illegal practice involving slum landlords. There was even a plan for him to inspect those very properties we had on our list, we were told.

Moran became quite a name at City Hall. One morning I was summoned to publisher Hal Burdick's office to find several members of City Council there. They had come to complain to Burdick that they had good evidence that Moran "is a Communist." To their surprise, Burdick called me in immediately and told them to share that with me as Moran's editor and boss. When they did, I showed shock and dismay.

"Do you know what you're saying?" I said. "You're accusing this woman of being a Communist and you're doing it in front of us. Do you realize what a serious charge that is? Do you know you could be guilty of slander? Who told you this? What evidence do you have?"

The Councilmen shuffled uneasily. "Well, she didn't stand up and put her hand over her heart at the Pledge of Allegiance at the Council meeting," one said.

"So that makes her a Communist?" I said. "That's all you've got?"

"We just…" began another.

"We just wanted you to know what we've heard," said another, "in case you wanted to do something about it."

"We really don't know," admitted still another.

"If I were you I would be very careful about spreading such things around," I said.

After a few more minutes they were gone.

Burdick had not stirred from his leather chair. He had sat there watching, hands clasped. He smiled.

"Thanks," I said.

He just nodded.

Moran fit right in at the Advertiser. Although very serious about her work, she was at the center of fun in the newsroom. So was a big, burly, long-haired, mustached guy named Jim Hunyadi, whom I found during a recruiting trip for Gannett to the University of Kentucky. It was one of several such recruiting trips Gannett editors made around the country for candidates for the many Gannett newspapers.

Dwight Teeter, whom I knew, was director of the UK Journalism Department at the time. And Nancy Green, who once had been a copy editor on the Advertiser news desk, was in charge of the UK student newspaper. So I was among friends. They introduced me to Hunyadi, a graduate assistant who had put together my recruiting visit. At the end of the day he asked if he too could be interviewed and I agreed. After half an hour I thought, I've got to take this guy home with me. Having no openings, I convinced him to accept a summer internship. And when an opening occurred later, the job was his.

Hunyadi proved to be one of those staffers who make life interesting and fun. He drove a red pickup truck on the side of which he had painted, "Copy editing, five cents a word." He once posed for a fashion layout in a rain coat and high top boots, holding a pitchfork. He contributed to the page one weather box by referencing "the people along the river."

Bob Hall came into the newsroom one day totally unannounced, saying he was looking for a job. He ended up in my office. He had long hair and a beard but wore a three-piece suit and tie. He sat in the chair beside my desk. I asked about his experience. He had almost none, just a few part-time stints on alternative newspapers in California, I asked him where he had obtained his degree. He had none. After a few more questions, I finally asked why I should hire him.

"Because I'm good," he said.

I can't remember how he managed to get on my staff, but before long he was our editorial page editor. A talented writer, an easy-going—make that California mellow—guy who was intelligent and witty and whom everyone liked.

And there was Joe Cosco, a highly intelligent young reporter and another gifted writer who had three degrees, one of them from Trinity College in Dublin. Instead of calling him Joe, Jack Hardin called him "Three Degrees."

I cannot name all the staffers who worked for

The Advertiser in those years. Already I have made the fatal error of naming just a few. Suffice to say that it was an unusual blend of hard-working, intelligent people on a small newspaper and it was special. And that we had fun.

But newspapering is not always fun, not when tragedy occurs.

In April 1978, Death came once again to West Virginia.

Fifty-one men were working on a scaffolding high atop a new cooling tower at the Monongahela Power Company's Pleasants County station at Willow Island, down the Ohio River from St. Mary's, West Virginia. They were preparing a new layer of concrete when suddenly the scaffolding broke, sending all fifty-one plunging to the ground one hundred sixty feet below. Reports indicated there were several fatalities.

The Associated Press was already on the scene and other reporters and photographers were rushing in. We sent Kevinne Moran and a photographer. I told Moran to interview survivors and relatives and we would rely on the AP for the main story.

By the time she reached the scene, we had learned that all fifty-one men were dead. Family members arrived, praying that their husbands, sons, brothers had survived. But none had.

Moran called on my direct line. She was shaken.

"Hatfield, I can't do this," she said in a breaking voice. "They're all dead. This is too much. The families...they're in shock, they're crying. I just can't talk to them, I just can't."

She kept apologizing. "I'm sorry. I'm sorry."

I told her to pull herself together. I knew it must be a terrible scene; I knew it was tough. I told her anyone would find it difficult to talk with surviving family members so soon after the tragedy. If she could not face them, I said, she should talk with authorities, get what she could from them. I was sure the AP would have comments from families and we would go with that.

But I was thinking, that's part of the job, Kevinne. And I was surprised. This was a different Kevinne Moran from the tough young woman out of the South Side of Chicago who had been giving City Hall a rough time.

After talking with officials and getting more information on the accident, Moran was able to approach a few of the family members. And her reports, combined with stories from the AP, enabled us to publish a solid package the following day. I commended her for composing herself and toughing it out.

Kevinne Moran went on to do good things for us in Huntington, to work for newspapers in Rochester, New York, for the Asian Wall Street Journal in Hong Kong, the China Daily in Beijing (wouldn't the Huntington City Council have loved hearing that?), for newspapers and universities in Shanghai, China, and Portland, Oregon, and again for me, in Tucson, Arizona. I doubt she ever said "I can't do this" again.

The Willow Island scaffolding collapse was a

huge national story, another on the long list of tragedies that had struck our region without warning. One never got used to them; but in these mountains and valleys, neither was one as shocked as might be expected.

26
DEATH OF A NEWSPAPER

In October, 1978, another life-changing event came my way. Having been active in the Associated Press Managing Editors for a number of years, I was nominated for its Board of Directors to represent the nation's under-25,000 circulation newspapers. The voting would take place at the organization's convention to be held that year in Portland, Oregon. Sandy and I attended with high hopes. And she became my major campaigner, telling friends and associates at receptions and dinners that they should vote for me. I also received great support from John Quinn, Gannett's top news exec and a former APME president. During a meeting of Gannett editors attending the convention, Quinn urged all present to "vote early and vote often" for Gannett nominees, including me.

At the closing dinner the names of the new APME board members were announced, and mine was among them. I was thrilled and so was Sandy. The votes of the Gannett editors present had no doubt been a big factor in my being elected, but I think it was really Sandy's campaigning. Who could say no to her?

When we went to our room that night, there was a message of congratulations from Kevinne Moran who was back in Huntington. How did she find out these things so quickly?

A few months later the new APME board gathered in the large conference room of The Associated Press in New York. I arrived earlier than anyone else, and looked around the room and then stood at the window looking down on Rockefeller Center. And I thought, "Hatfield, you've come a long way."

I refer to my being elected to the APME board as "life-changing" because for me—not for most other board members, I'm sure—it truly proved to be that, just as my attending the American Press Institute at Columbia University had been some years before. As an APME board member, I had the opportunity to know editors from all over the country as well as the top writers and editors of The Associated Press, several of whom became close personal friends. APME served as a monitor for the AP's news coverage. I took that responsibility seriously, and still consider my time on its board as one of the true honors of my newspaper career.

On my own newspaper, meanwhile, there was about to be change once again. A paper our size expects turnover. Young, talented reporters learn and then move on. In this case, it was a veteran editor. Chuck Carpenter, my news editor, received a call from the publisher of Gannett's newspaper in Danville, Illinois. She needed a managing editor, the top job in her newsroom, and Corporate had recommended him. It was quite a promotion, and he accepted. Fortunately, Pamela Bowen was ready to step into his slot. And the Advertiser rolled on.

But the elephant in the room was that across the country evening newspapers were dwindling and dying, even those that had made major changes as we had. Like the others, our circulation continued to go down. Hal Burdick was hardly oblivious to the facts. And certainly he paid far more attention to advertising and circulation numbers than I did.

Looking back, I was either blind or in refusal mode.

Burdick suggested it might be time to combine the two Huntington newspapers. To his credit, he discussed it with me before taking it further. Of course I tried to find every possible reason to illustrate that this was a bad idea. Then he mentioned it to a Gannett regional officer on one of his visits to Huntington.

I am not aware of whether all this began at Gannett Corporate or with Burdick. Whatever, he summoned Bill Southerland, who had replaced Don Mayne as the Herald-Dispatch's managing editor, and me to a meeting and laid out an almost impossible task for the two of us. It was also an unfair one, which he admitted.

He wanted us to work together on a plan to merge the two newspaper staffs, should the two newspapers be combined. We were not told where either of us would fit in. We were to ignore the positions of executive editor and managing editor, he said, and work together to agree on the remaining structure, with names, of a newly combined news staff. And we were not to discuss it with anyone. After all, a final decision to combine the papers had not yet been made. Only Corporate could do that.

So that is what we did. Oddly enough, neither of us was bitter or questioning or jealous. Southerland was good to work with. Early on, as we reviewed our two staffs, he said, "You know, Don; it just occurs to me. I hire all the straights and you hire all the freaks."

I took that as a compliment.

There was good discussion between Bill and me on who should be the combined paper's top editors—news, city, sports, regional, lifestyles, editorial—and which reporters should be assigned which beats. There was the obvious fact that Southerland's newspaper was much larger than mine and his editors were already in place while mine were suddenly being brought in. Still, a couple of mine were better. In the end, I thought it was better to leave his editors in place and let mine be their assistants—for the time being.

We met with Burdick to show him the plan. He

said the timing was good. Gannett corporate visitors would be coming in the following week, including VP/News John Quinn. He said nothing about whether Southerland or I would survive or if so, which positions we might hold. Each of us now had the title of managing editor. But I was older and more experienced. Would Burdick keep both of us? With what titles? Since the departure of John McMillan, no one had held the title of executive editor, even with two newspapers on site. Now, with only one, why would we resurrect that title?

We gathered off site to discuss the pending merger and I was heartened when Quinn walked in and slammed his briefcase on the table and asked what was going on. Burdick said we had been working toward combining the two newspapers.

"That is not a done deal," Quinn said. "I need to hear more about this."

We met throughout the day and, unfortunately, the bean counters and Burdick convinced Quinn this made sense. And the decision was made. The Advertiser would be combined with the Herald-Dispatch into one seven-day morning operation. I was defeated soundly when I suggested the name of the new combined paper should be "The Herald-Advertiser," which had been the name of our Sunday paper prior to Gannett's arrival. The name, they said, would continue to be "The Herald-Dispatch." "The Huntington Advertiser" would fade away.

The subject of an executive editor, if there were to be one, was not mentioned, nor what was to happen to Southerland and me.

Only a couple of nights before I had received a call at my home from Bill Cole, dean of Northwestern's Medill School of Journalism, I knew him personally for two reasons. First, because of our involvement with his Teaching Newspaper Program and my visits to Evanston. Second, because of the close friendship between his daughter Molly and my reporter Kevinne Moran. They had been classmates and close friends at Medill. In fact, during a visit to Huntington, Molly Cole and Kevinne had not only been to our house one weekend but had helped paint the "cabana," a converted garage in our back yard.

"I know what's being discussed in Huntington regarding your paper," Bill Cole said, which surprised me. "I know you're facing some uncertainty. I hope it turns out well for you. But if it isn't to your liking, I want you to know there is a place for you here at Medill."

I could hardly believe my ears. For a moment I could not speak.

Finally I said, "I can't tell you how much I appreciate that, Bill."

"We'll keep in touch," he said.

When I told Sandy, she suggested that being on the staff at Northwestern might be better than staying in Huntington on the newly combined newspaper.

However…

At the end of our lengthy sessions that day it was time to take Quinn and other Corporate visitors back to the great Gannett bird at the airport. Quinn said he would ride with me.

When we arrived at the airport he got out of the car, picked up his briefcase and said, "I've told Burdick you're to be the executive editor. Okay?"

I was thrilled and greatly relieved. "That's great, John. Thank you. I won't let you down."

"I know that," he said. He shook my hand, said "Good luck," climbed aboard the sleek private jet and left Huntington.

When I returned to the newspaper, Burdick called me to his office.

"I've made a decision," he said. "I've decided you will be my executive editor."

I thanked him and told him I appreciated his faith in me and that I would do my best.

"Now call your wife and tell her," he said. "You and Sandy and Lillian and I are going to dinner at the Rebels & Redcoats to celebrate."

And that's the way it happened. Let Hal Burdick take credit for choosing me. He may have anyway. But it was John Quinn.

Bill Southerland was named managing editor, but we both knew that would be temporary. Just a few months later he would be named executive editor of Gannett's newspaper in Chillicothe, Ohio.

The date of the final edition of the Advertiser was set. The details of the merger were ironed out. The only thing left was to inform the staff.

I held a staff meeting, this time without pizzas and Pepsis. I outlined the decision that had been made. There was great disappointment, a few tears, a few words of anger directed at Gannett. For years I had told our staff to "kick hell out of the Herald." Now I was telling them they were a part of it. It was not easy.

In the days to come some of the staff came to me and said they wanted no part of this, that they preferred to transfer to another Gannett newspaper or simply to leave and look elsewhere. Kevinne Moran was among the former and the Rochester newspapers quickly said they would take her. Bob Hall was among the latter, and on the final day of Advertiser publication still had no idea where he was going. I think he expected that something would come along to stop this train. But nothing did.

There was one more staff meeting right before The Advertiser's date of execution. I wondered what I could say.

Finally I said basically this: We have had a very special thing here. Don't expect to find it again. Not that the next paper you work for won't be larger and maybe better, or that your coming years won't be far beyond what we've had here. But it will be different. We've been a small team, a bunch of people who've cared about each other. We've worked hard. We've had fun. And what we've had is a special thing that you will not find on a larger paper. I cannot begin to thank you enough for what you did for this newspaper and for me.

The final day's Advertiser, on Aug. 24, 1979, carried this banner: "The Final Edition." A headline I wrote myself.

The paper contained memories and old photographs and a recounting of our history.

As the presses were rolling, a news staffer from one of the Charleston newspapers, a former intern on our own paper, called to talk about the death of The Huntington Advertiser. I took the call in the newsroom. He asked several pressing questions about circulation and revenues that I tried to fend off. And then he asked to speak to some of our staff about how they felt. His tone was almost accusatory, as if we had brought this on ourselves, and he clearly was enjoying the assignment.

I blew up. I had contained all this for some time, had tried to say and do things with rational thought and to protect the staff. But this was too much and I lost it. I shouted at him to get the hell out of our business, called him a "vulture come to pick our bones," said he wasn't going to bother our people at a time like this, and slammed the phone down.

I turned to find the entire Advertiser news staff standing and applauding. I was shaking with anger and frustration and the huge sense of loss and the sudden realization of the heavy finality of the moment.

That night the staff gathered at Charlie and Pamela Bowen's house for a "Farewell to the Advertiser" party. Far too much beer and wine and booze flowed and I had far more than my share of Scotch. I wandered from the porch through the house telling members of the staff that I loved them and hearing in return "I love you too, Hatfield."

There was laughter at the retelling of old stories and there were tears and there were promises made to stay in touch forever.   And eventually the night came to an end.

The following morning I awakened hung-over but determined to move on. I dressed and went to the newsroom and then into the office that would be mine, the office once held by the editor-in-chief, Raymond Brewster, and then by John McMillan, and more recently shared by two Herald-Dispatch editors. It would no longer be shared. It would be the office of the executive editor.   That would be me.

I moved a few of my things from my small Advertiser office. Then I went across the street and picked up a burger and an extra-large Coke and brought them back to the office and sat there and ate and thought.

Okay. The world had changed. Damn the torpedoes. Full speed ahead.

27
BIGGER, BETTER, BRIGHTER

That's what we told readers of the newly merged Herald-Dispatch and Advertiser. More pages, more news stories, a dazzling new product the result of additional reporters and editors and photographers all working for one newspaper instead of two.

Think about it for a moment. If the number of news columns and news pages is based on the amount of advertising in the newspaper—and it is—and if the same advertisers advertised in both newspapers but now had just one, where would additional advertising come from?

Obviously, it would have to come from new advertisers. But if there were no new businesses in town, and if the present advertisers were already maxed out, what then?

And where would "more pages with more stories" come from?

For a while we made sure there were more pages in the new Herald-Dispatch than in the old even though that meant lowering the percentage of advertising and expanding the percentage of news hole. That would mean higher newsprint costs. And that would not be permitted by Corporate to last very long. And so it didn't.

As for "better and brighter," that was another matter. More news staffers are always better than fewer news staffers. And some of the Advertiser staff now on the Herald-Dispatch definitely brought a new style to the paper. But they found themselves reporting to different supervisors because we had kept Herald-Dispatch editors in their positions and made Advertiser editors their assistants. The Advertiser was, after all, the newspaper that had closed.

The combined paper was not what I, as its executive editor, had envisioned. We were not yet doing the kinds of stories I wanted to see in our pages. The staff did not seem comfortable with itself. We lacked energy. The place seemed too quiet. I was accustomed to the craziness we had on The Advertiser. It felt as if we were playing it safe. Clearly we could do better.

It quickly became obvious to me that we needed a change at the top of the city reporting staff. The Advertiser's city editor, Charlie Bowen, clearly was the superior editor and, in my mind, just what the staff needed. That did not come as a surprise to me, but I had been reluctant to replace current Herald-Dispatch editors with my Advertiser editors. Now it had to be done, at least on the city desk. Even Bill Southerland agreed. So we moved

Bowen into the city editor's job and the H-D's city editor   to regional editor, where he had been outstanding in previous years. Both proved to be good moves.

When Southerland was transferred and his managing editor's job opened, I resisted promoting the assistant managing editor into the slot as was expected, even though he was a dedicated, hard-working, detail-oriented and deserving person. But he was also a worrisome sort, who walked across the newsroom with a very serious look on his face. Some of the staff also complained that he was "picky" and made too much of small things. I recalled what Charlie Bowen had once told me about the staff picking up on my expressions when I sometimes walked through the newsroom with a worried look on my face. What we needed was someone to "fire up the troops," get them back to having fun again. So I turned to the features editor, Fran Allred, an experienced editor with a good sense of humor. But first I called John Quinn at Corporate and shared my thinking with him. He agreed. And Fran Allred became managing editor.

We started doing out-of-the box stories. Tipped that the local state hospital, which housed mentally challenged patients, was a hotbed of abuse, we assigned a new young reporter, Doug Imbrogno, to apply there as an unpaid volunteer. Concerned that administrators might recognize his name from his byline, we asked him to use his middle name instead of his first name. We did not tell him to give a phony name or to lie, because I have always believed that we should not lie to get at the truth. However, to fool someone was another matter. So Imbrogno applied and was accepted.

Surprisingly, he found that the rumors were false, that the hospital staff was terribly understaffed and doing its very best to care for the patients. And what was expected to be a story about wrong-doing turned out to be one of good service but limited resources and great need.

We urged our reporters to challenge sources and to be "real reporters, not mere stenographers" jotting down whatever they were told. One day the vice president of communications of Ashland Oil, then the nation's fourteenth largest oil company and located just across the river in Kentucky, called me with a complaint.

"Your reporter is driving me nuts," he said. "What do you call a reporter who won't take no for an answer?"

"A damn good reporter," I said.

My new job reunited me with Ernie Salvatore, the man who had hired me as an eighteen-year-old straight out of high school. He had become the Herald-Dispatch sports columnist. And now I was his boss. I wondered how that would go, and was pleased and relieved when early on he came into my office and said, "What the hell is this? I take you in, I teach you all I know, and now you're my boss? You'd better not be giving me any crap." And then he broke into that big grin of his, stuck out that Italian hand which always seemed bigger than his body should have allowed, and said,

"Congratulations, kid. I'm proud of you."

Still calling me "kid," I thought. It was great.

It also reunited me with Tom Miller, with whom I had worked in the Advertiser's sports department. He had moved to the Herald-Dispatch sometime before where he became a tough-minded special reporter who had been featured in a book on investigative reporting. He had produced a superb report called "Who Owns West Virginia?" which won a number of national awards. Now he was the newspaper's political and legislative writer. It was good to be on his side again.

And we continued to hire good young people. On a Gannett recruiting trip to Ohio University, among the students I interviewed was a bright, bubbly, energetic young woman named Mara Rose. The more we talked the more I wanted to bring her back to my newspaper. And when she graduated, I did just that. She proved to be not only a productive reporter, but a tonic for the newsroom, always laughing, helping to provide that spark we needed.

And there were others. Margaret Bernstein, a graduate of the University of Southern California, a sensitive and intelligent young woman who would later work for me in Arizona, become a close family friend. She had applied for a job with Gannett and had met with Mary Kay Blake, who handled newsroom recruiting for Gannett and happened to be a friend of Sandy's and mine. Mary Kay told her she had just the place—and the editor-- for her. And Bernstein came to Huntington.

And there was Elizabeth Skewes, a UCLA

alum and another bright and talented reporter who preferred spending all her time in the newsroom instead of in her apartment. When I tried to get her out of the office, she said it was more fun here "than staring at four walls in my apartment."

As the staff got better, the newspaper improved, and so did my world.

Each day Hal Burdick made a brief visit to my office. It was the last stop on his daily tour of the building, or "plant" as he called it, with appearances made in every department, from press room to photo lab to newsroom. He would ask how things were going, talk about community matters, his golf game, and Corporate. He would relay Corporate news and gossip, sometimes rolling his eyes. Occasionally, speaking about a Corporate officer, he would say, "Well, what does he know?"

One day he told me he had accepted a directorship at the city's largest bank. "I don't want you to let that affect in any way how you cover this bank or all the other banks in this town," he said. I knew he meant it. Others might not have.

"I won't," I said.

"I didn't expect you would," he said.

Among the good practices John McMillan had initiated during his time as executive editor was a regular written critique of the work done in the two newsrooms. It was a "winners and sinners" kind of written report, an idea stolen years before from the New York Times, and commented on things well done and things not so well done by the news staff. I resumed that practice, each month going over all the papers we had published, clipping stories, marking up pages, and then producing a two- to-three-page report. I then turned it over to be checked and edited by Pamela Bowen, the newsroom's best at style, grammar and punctuation. She produced it and distributed it to the news staff. She had replaced Allred as features editor, but somehow found time to be my right hand in such matters.

As managing editor of the Advertiser I always ran our daily news meetings. Now, as executive editor, I turned that over to Fran Allred. In retrospect, that probably was not the best thing to do —not because Allred was deficient in any way, but because I should have remained closer to the daily news product. Allred came to my office at the close of each news meeting to fill me in on plans for the next day's paper. And when I had ideas for stories and assignments, she would act on them or, if she felt I was off base, tell me so. Which is what a good managing editor should do. No top editor should ever be surrounded by "yes" men and women, and fortunately I was not.

At that time the world of Gannett was divided into regions. We were a part of Gannett Central and were overseen by the publisher of the Cincinnati Enquirer, Bill Keating. He was a true gentleman, soft-spoken and exuding class. He visited Huntington often and each time spent some time in my office. It was always a pleasure.

His editor in Cincinnati was a good friend named George Blake, whose wife, Mary Kay, worked on the corporate news staff with Phil Currie, another good friend, in the discovery and development of young journalists for Gannett papers. It was Mary Kay who had sent me Margaret Bernstein. She spent weekdays in Washington and weekends in Cincinnati with her husband. On a couple of occasions she and George drove to Huntington to spend the weekend with us. And we returned the visit to their home in Cincinnati. Once, while there, we had an enjoyable dinner with Bill Keating and his wife Nancy. I was somewhat surprised that Bill Keating seemed to have a more than passing interest in me. Ordinarily, as regional president, he would be involved with a newspaper's publisher, not its editor. I considered it a compliment and was grateful for it.

Nancy Keating even took part that evening in a somewhat silly tradition my wife and I and a couple of other Gannett editors had established in special honor of Phil Currie. Some time before, late in the evening following a Gannett (or perhaps APME convention) dinner in some city or other, Currie had picked up spoons from the table and had begun to play them, as if they were drumsticks. After that, whenever we found ourselves at an out-of-town restaurant, if Currie were not present, we would smuggle out a spoon and mail it to him with no message and no return address. I have no idea how many spoons we sent his way, but it must have been maddening at his end to receive them and have no idea who sent them (although in time I'm sure he knew exactly who the criminals were).

But this night in Cincinnati, sitting with the Gannett Central president and his wife, Sandy and I started to steal a spoon just as the server took it away. Having no spoon to steal, we asked Nancy Keating for hers, and I felt obligated to explain what we were up to. She loved the idea and smuggled it under the table to us and we escaped with it. Neat lady.

In 1981, my three-year term on the Associated Press Managing Editors board expired. I had been elected while managing editor of The Advertiser, a newspaper of less than 25,000, to represent newspapers of that size. Now I was executive editor of The Herald-Dispatch, a newspaper of more than 50,000 circulation. If I hoped to serve a second term on the board, I would have to run against editors from the largest newspapers in the land. I wanted very much to continue. Once again Sandy turned out to be a great campaign manager. Once again John Quinn told Gannett editors to vote for Gannett editors. And once again I was elected.

Serving on the APME board meant far more than an ego trip for me. It was the highlight of my newspaper career, my door into the greatest news-gathering organization in the world. It enabled me to meet editors from other papers, such as Ed Cony of the Wall Street Journal and Bob Haimon of the St. Petersburg Times. Sandy and I occasionally played tennis with Coney and his wife during APME conventions.

And there was the chance to know the great AP writers, from Saul Pett to Hugh Mulligan, Jules Loh to George Esper, Walter Mears to Peter Arnett, and great AP editors such as Jack Cappon and Burl Osborne and the man himself, Lou Boccardi, who went from executive editor of the AP to become its general manager and CEO.

We were able to bring Mulligan, Loh, Esper and Arnett to Huntington to speak to varied newspaper groups. And more than once Cappon, the AP's reigning wordsmith, came to town to critique our newspaper and meet with staff. He would go over several weeks' papers before arriving and was superbly prepared when he got here. All at no expense.

Sandy and I became close to Cappon, a fellow tennis player. On one of his visits we arranged for a very good female tennis player on the athletic staff at Marshall University to play as his partner. We had a fun match but he later confessed that he could not keep up with her.

On his last visit he brought along Esper, the last AP reporter out of Saigon before it fell. I asked him why he had chosen to stay in Saigon while others left. He replied simply: "I felt that we needed an AP presence there." We went to dinner at a fine restaurant that night, had far too much to drink, and returned to our house for a night cap. I mentioned to Cappon that I had been working on a few short stories and he said he wanted to see them. So we went upstairs to my den, leaving George and Sandy to talk. I pulled out the short stories and began to read one of them, and Cappon, clearly in his cups, said, "God, that's beautiful."

Esper, a fellow West Virginian and for years a professor of journalism at West Virginia University, later sent us a lovely set of pewter wine goblets in thanks for the evening. Sadly, he passed away in 2012. As many observed, he was a true gentleman as well as a great newsman.

Now holding the title of executive editor, I also became a member of the American Society of Newspaper Editors. Its convention included a black tie dinner, and I wore the studs and cufflinks which had belonged to my old boss, Raymond Brewster, just as I had promised his son John when he gave them to me.

It was during the 1981 ASNE convention in Washington that we were invited to a reception in the White House. President Reagan was to have been there, and we looked forward to the opportunity to meet him. Unfortunately, in March, he was the victim of an attempted assassination, and his wounds required considerable recuperation. But the reception went on without him. First Lady Nancy Reagan welcomed us in the Rose Garden, apologized for "Ronnie" not being there. She was most gracious, and even pointed to an upstairs window where, she said, he was resting and aware that we were all here. He sends his best wishes, she said, and hopes all of you have a good time. We then were ushered into the White House where food and drink awaited.

It was at this same convention that we met actress Elizabeth Taylor, who was starring in the Lillian Hellman play, "The Little Foxes." There was a post-theater reception for editors and spouses with the actress as the featured guest. I went to the bar as everyone waited patiently for her. What none of us realized was that she had arrived a few minutes before and was standing in a corner, talking with Sandy about the play and her role. Sandy had told her that she was perfect for the role, and Taylor had smiled and responded, "Why? Because I'm such a bitch?"

"No," Sandy answered, "because you're such a good actress."

I always said Sandy would have made a good reporter. She has always been very good at getting people to talk.

Meanwhile, a terrible sadness had come over the home of my publisher, Hal Burdick. His lovely wife Lillian had been diagnosed with cancer. She underwent both chemo and radiation and lost her hair, but continued to go into the community and out to dinner with us, donning wigs and hats, and always wearing her gracious smile. We had every confidence that she would defeat the cancer. However, she did not, and Hal lost his best friend, his favorite golf partner and his partner in life. He was a tough man and seemed to be standing up relatively well. But when he came into my office one day and I asked him how he was doing, he suddenly teared up and said simply, "I am very, very lonely."

And there was nothing I could do or say.

28
PUBLISHER

By the summer of 1982, I had grown quite comfortable in my job as executive editor. I was comfortable with my publisher, Hal Burdick, who allowed me free reign in the newsroom. I held my dream job. From a personal standpoint, I had achieved more than I had ever thought possible. It was all so comfortable that it was downright cozy.

One lovely spring morning Burdick came into my office, sat in front of my desk, and told me I had been selected to attend an elite Gannett management seminar in Rochester, N.Y., where the company had its headquarters. It would be conducted later that summer and would last a full week. Only certain people had been selected by Corporate, he said.

The date conflicted with my scheduled family vacation in Cape Cod. No way, I thought. And what would I get out of a management seminar, anyway? I was doing fine in my job as executive editor, wasn't I?

I told him my family and I had plans for a vacation at that time and I had already sent a deposit for the cottage we would be renting, as we did for two weeks every summer.

He said nothing for a moment and a frown came over his usually pleasant face.

"What if I just don't go?" I said.

He leaned his forearms on my desk and looked at me. "You'll be making the biggest mistake of your life," he said.

That was a pretty serious comment and stopped me cold. Why would he say that?

"How can I find out more about it?" I said.

He stood. "You'll be getting a package of materials. It's on its way."

I told my wife the news that evening. We could not change our vacation dates because the cottage would not be available at another time. I was trying to think of a way to get out of going to the seminar, I said.

"I don't think you can turn it down," she said. "It's only a week and we'll be on the Cape for two weeks. The kids and I will go to the Cape and you can join us when the seminar in Rochester is over."

I told Burdick the next day I would be pleased to go, and I looked forward to receiving the corporate package and whatever else might help.

The package contained reading materials and one very large black loose-leaf notebook filled with questions and exercises. I was to study the materials, respond to the questions, participate in the exercises. They were filled with financial matters, challenges for many but especially for me, a somewhat arrogant newsman who had boasted for years about working in the "pure" part of the business.

I went to our controller, Ed Burns, explained what was going on, showed him the big notebook, and said I would probably need his help in preparing for the seminar.

"Sounds like they're sending you to publisher's school," he said.

I literally shuddered. I had never wanted to be publisher. I was not prepared, not qualified, not educated properly for that job.

"I'll be happy to help," he said. "Just study this stuff and work these things out and we'll go over them whenever you're ready."

It was the first time I was saved by a controller, but certainly not the last. A controller can make or break a publisher. Like most news types, I had never regarded the finance people, the "bean counters," as really being "newspaper people." They were always trying to put financial matters ahead of more important matters, such as the news.

I studied the materials—budgets and balance sheets and revenue and cost projection charts, and all the other strange stuff in the package, and I filled out the work sheets and completed the tests and took it all back to Ed Burns.

Burns' office was piled high with papers and reports stacked up on the floor on each side of his desk and atop the desk and on a table behind it. Not unlike many controller offices I would later see.

I sat while he looked over my work. Then he looked up and smiled and said, "Not bad."

I had several questions for him and he answered them with patience. And I returned to my own office feeling a little more at ease.

Later that summer I drove my family to Cape Cod, then took a plane to Rochester. There I saw several familiar faces, all having been identified as having "publisher potential," as had I, much to my surprise. Amazing.

At the opening reception that evening I talked with George Blake, my editor friend in Cincinnati.

'I have no idea what I'm doing here," I told him.

"Keating thinks you can be a publisher," Blake said, referring to his publisher and Gannett Central's president, Bill Keating.

"You're kidding," I said.

I admired Bill Keating a great deal and in my three years as executive editor had talked with him many times. He had visited my personal office each time he came to Huntington to meet with Burdick.

The seminar proved to be a high-intensity conference of speakers and various studies and exercises from early in the morning until dinner. The week flew by and on the last night every participant and every Gannett corporate staffer celebrated together. The wine and beer and booze flowed freely.

I caught a flight back to the Cape the following day, and have since been told by my wife and sons that when I arrived they found themselves dealing with a different man.

"He was buzzed," Sandy remembered to friends recently. "Uptight, rushed, full of Gannett, and totally unable to relax. We had made arrangements to take the ferry to Martha's Vineyard and he was wrapped so tight the kids and I couldn't wait to get him a beer. We rented a car and drove to this small town and walked into this restaurant and as soon as the waiter came, he ordered a beer. Our hearts sank when the waiter informed him we were in a dry town; there was no beer."

Oddly, she continued, once that happened instead of exploding as my dear family expected, I appeared to accept my fate and actually seemed to relax.

Two hours later, of course, we were in Edgartown, where I found plenty of beer.

My one week on the Cape was wonderful, and probably more appreciated than had I been there for both weeks. I shared with Sandy the activities of the week in Rochester and told her that Gannett might actually be considering me for a publisher spot somewhere. "Probably one of our smaller properties," I said. "A place like Huntington would be the second or third stop for a publisher, not the first."

It was only a matter of weeks until I got the call. It came from the office of Jack Heselden, deputy chairman of Gannett. He asked me to come to Rochester the following week and to "buy a one-way plane ticket."

That puzzled me. How was I to get home? Did

they plan to keep me for a while?

I asked if I needed to pack for a few days. No, he said. Don't bring a thing.

I shared the news with Sandy and told her, "I have a feeling they're going to make me a publisher —somewhere. I have no idea where."

On the morning of departure I kissed her, told her I had no idea when I would see her or be able to speak with her, but I would contact her as soon as possible. She wished me good luck and smiled that wonderful smile I had seen since that first night I had given her a ride back to her dorm room following church.

By coincidence I had just bought a three-piece pin-stripe suit, and I wore it so that I would appear to be business-like and serious about what was to happen. Whatever that might be. I drove to the airport and as we took off I looked down at my world and wondered how it would be changed by the time I returned. Whenever that would be.

A driver met me at the Rochester airport and drove me straight to the Gannett building. There I was ushered to a top floor office occupied by Jack Heselden.

Heselden got up from his desk, smiled and shook my hand and guided me to a table. He said he had ordered lunch for the two of us and it would be arriving soon.

He asked about my flight and the weather and how things were in Huntington, and then the food arrived, with napkins and silver. And as he ate, he paused and said, "I want to talk to you about becoming publisher."

Okay, I thought. Where?

"We have a new assignment for Hal and we want you to take over in Huntington."

I sat stunned.

"Well, what do you think?" he said.

"I…thank you. That's great."

"Think you can handle it?"

"Yes. Yes. I'll have a lot to learn. I know production pretty well, and circulation and advertising some. I have to admit I am a little concerned about the financial side."

"That's why you have department heads," he said.

We spent a few minutes talking about each one —the advertising director, circulation director, head of production, and our controller, Ed Burns.

"I'm glad he's there," I said.

"Ed is a good man," Heselden said.

The change in publishers would take place the first week in September, he said. He and other corporate executives would come to Huntington, call all employees together, make the announcement, then take Hal Burdick on to his next assignment. He would not tell me where that would be. Also, he said, I was not to tell anyone anything about the change until that announcement was made. I could, of course, tell my wife, he said. But no one else.

Then he abruptly stood. "We're going to fly you to Cincinnati to meet with Bill Keating. He'll be waiting at the airport."

"All right. Fine."

He went to his desk and picked up the phone and said a few words, then turned back to me. "Our corporate jets are tied up. All we have available right now is the prop plane."

I actually heard myself saying, "Oh, that's all right." As if this sort of thing happened to me every day.

He shook my hand and said, "We'll be in touch," and his secretary appeared and walked me to the driver waiting in the hall. And we went to the car in which I was whisked to the airport where awaited a twin-engine prop-driven plane large enough for pilot, co-pilot, steward, and a few passengers.

Except that I was the lone passenger. I climbed aboard and before I sat the steward showed me a tray of fruit and cheese and apologized for not having a warm meal. "Oh, that's all right," I once again heard myself saying. "I've already had lunch."

And we took off toward Cincinnati where Bill Keating would be waiting, I in my own (for the moment) private plane, being offered newspapers, magazines, something to drink.

And oddly, I thought of my father. *If only he could see me now. How proud he will be when I tell him. I'll have to take in everything because he'll want to know every detail.*

When we landed in Cincinnati we taxied to a small brick commercial terminal building and a small man ran out carrying something under his arm. When the plane came to a halt and the steps were put in place, he unrolled a red carpet and spread it on the tarmac between the building and the steps of my plane. A red carpet. I couldn't believe it.

Bill Keating sat in a small room by himself, and rose when I entered. He was smiling broadly and shook my hand and said, "Congratulations."

I thanked him and we sat. "Well," he said, "You don't seem very excited."

"To tell you the truth, I'm a bit overwhelmed."

He laughed and told me not to be.

"I guess I'm thinking about all the departments and the things I don't know."

"You don't have to know everything," he said. "You just have to know what questions to ask."

I never forgot that.

As with Heselden we talked about the department heads, with whom he was quite familiar. He saw some strengths there, and some weaknesses. He told me that my salary would be fifty thousand dollars. I thought of the day Buddy Hayden had raised my salary to twenty thousand, saying someday I would make twice that—a prediction I could not grasp at the time. Keating went on: I would receive stock options and additional stock incentive rights and an annual bonus based on performance and a new car.

My head was swimming.

I thanked him again and told him he could count on me and that I looked forward to working for him.

He stood, held out his hand and said, "Well,

your plane is waiting to take you back to Huntington. Good luck."

The red carpet had been taken away when I walked back to the plane. The engines were already humming and I climbed aboard and fastened my seat belt and looked at my watch. It was still only late afternoon. A lot had happened in these few hours. I hadn't even had time or opportunity to call Sandy and tell her what was going on.

We landed in Huntington in no time and I thanked my crew of three and got in my car and drove home.

It was still light when I parked in the driveway and walked to the front door. Sandy had heard the car and was standing in the door.

"Back so soon?"

"Yeah."

"Well?"

"They're going to make me a publisher."

"Where?"

"Here. Huntington."

She gave me a hug and then stood back. "Well, you're still going to get peanut butter sandwiches in your lunch."

And we went inside.

29
CHANGING OF THE GUARD

The following morning I went straight to Hal Burdick's office and closed the door. He stood and, grinning, said, "Well? Glad you went to that seminar now?" And then he shook my hand and said, "Congratulations."

I shared with him my surprise and my hopes and some of my fears as to being able to do the job.

"You'll be fine," he said. "You'll have a good team to work with."

I thanked him for all he had done for me, and asked where he would be going. He would not tell me.

"You know Gannett. They like to keep these things secret. Usually these moves create a domino effect—this publisher goes here, another comes in, another replaces him."

The announcement would be made in the newsroom the first week of September. Until then we would say nothing to anyone about the coming change in publishers, not even to members of his—

soon to be my—Operating Group. All employees would be asked to attend an early morning special meeting. No one would be told why. The corporate jet would swoop in, spill out Gannett execs. Hal Burdick and I would meet them at the airport and bring them to our building where they would go immediately to the newsroom to speak with all those assembled.

And soon it was time.

The Corporate jet arrived at the exact time we were told. Jack Heselden and a couple of others emerged from the plane and walked briskly toward us, shook our hands, and then we went to Burdick's waiting car.

"Everything is set?" asked Heselden.

"All employees are waiting in the newsroom," Burdick said.

"We won't take very long," said Heselden.

I can't remember saying anything during the short drive. My stomach was churning.

Burdick entered the crowded newsroom first, followed by Heselden and the others from Corporate, and then me. Everyone in the room was watching closely and waiting. I could feel the surprised looks on the faces of my colleagues on the Operating Group. They must have been wondering why I wasn't standing with them waiting on whatever was about to take place.

Heselden spoke directly and briefly. Hal Burdick had done a good job as publisher in Huntington, he said. Now it was time for him to move on. Heselden could not reveal where that would be, but it would be announced soon, he said. Succeeding Burdick would be his executive editor, Don Hatfield. Heselden was sure that having a local person move into this important job would be welcome news to everyone there.

Not everyone, I thought.

Burdick then spoke, thanking all for his good years in Huntington and for all the support they had given him. He walked over to the line of his department heads and shook hands and exchanged hugs and then did the same with many other employees. While he did that my fellow department heads gave me congratulatory handshakes. And then it was time to take the corporate folks back to the airport. We left amidst applause.

At the airport the Gannett execs walked toward the waiting jet and Burdick turned and handed me the keys to his company car and said "Good luck."

"Good luck to you," I said. "Thanks for everything."

He smiled and turned and walked to the waiting plane

When I returned to our building I went straight to his office—now mine. Louise Cazad, his secretary and now my secretary, was waiting with a hug. "I knew something was up and I figured maybe Mr. Burdick was leaving," she said. "I'm glad it's you—although I always thought you would end up in the news division at Corporate."

I sat at the publisher's desk—behind it, this time--and she brought me a soft drink and said every department head wanted to see me. She rounded them up and they came into the office, all smiles, all offering congratulations. I knew all were stunned to see me in this position; new publishers usually came from the outside. I realized some of their smiles were probably forced and that there had to be some hurt feelings. I had fought with the ad director, as editors and ad directors often fought. I had no doubt caused pain to the controller and the circulation director, not to mention the production director. Editors were viewed as arrogant souls who thought they were special, who didn't appreciate how hard those on the revenue side worked--all with good reason. I knew each one of them felt he knew more about his job than I did, which certainly was true. I would have to win them over, prove myself.

By then another announcement had been made, a couple thousand miles away. Hal Burdick had been named the new publisher of the El Paso Times--a much larger paper and a suitable reward for a man who, as Jack Heselden said, had done a good job.

We had no champagne but said "Here's to Hal" and gestured as if we did. And then one of the group said "And here's to our new publisher," and gestured again, which made me feel pretty good.

There were laughs and small talk and then they returned to their offices. Moments later Dwight McKenzie, the ad director with whom I had fought and argued, on whom I had thrust no small number of headaches, slipped back into my office.

"Just want you to know you'll have my full

support," he said. "I'll work hard for you."

"That means a lot to me, Dwight," I said. "Thanks very much."

And that he did as long as we worked together.

I left the office then and walked around the building, going into each department—press room, circulation, retail and classified advertising, business, composing room, newsroom—and spoke individually to every employee I could find. I told them I was honored to be given this opportunity and to be permitted to continue working with them as I had since walking into the building as an eighteen-year-old. I got applause in most departments, and more handshakes and hugs, except in the newsroom where I received a good-natured booing from my former colleagues along with the sneering comment, "Publisher? Gag!"

That evening at home I received a call from John McMillan, congratulating me on being promoted to publisher. "An obvious choice," he said. I was surprised and pleased.

The following day the newspaper carried a front page story about the change in publishers. And WSAZ-TV, the No. 1 television station in town, called to request a brief interview. They would be here shortly.

A cameraman and reporter soon arrived in the outer office and were shown into my office immediately. The reporter introduced himself and sat in the chair in front of my desk while the camera man set up his camera in the middle of the doorway facing me. When they were ready, the reporter asked me a question and I leaned back, trying to look confident and thoughtful, and stretched out my legs under the desk preparing a response.

What I did not know was that under the publisher's desk, hidden beneath the carpet, was a button that closed the door. My foot hit it and the door slammed into the rear-end of the camera man, knocking him and the camera into the floor.

So began my first full day as publisher. Not exactly a great way to start.

In the days to come congratulatory calls and messages came in—I had lived here all my life, after all, and knew many people in town. The common theme was that they were pleased this giant out-of-town company had entrusted a local boy with running the ship. I understood.

One call came from Mike Perry, president of the city's oldest and largest bank, which happened to be located immediately across the street. He asked me to meet him on the corner in fifteen minutes so we could "take a walk and talk."

He quickly came to the point. This is a reasonably small town, he said, and it needs to make use of all its resources and all its community leaders in order to move forward. "You've been the editor," he said, "and I understand the role of the editor when it comes to being objective and not getting too involved in the community. But now you're the publisher. And a town this size needs its local newspaper publisher to be involved. I'm hoping you'll do that. I'm not asking you to overlook stories or influence news coverage in any way. I just want you to realize that you're a businessman now and this town needs you."

It was a good thing to say and a good time to say it. I never forgot his words. I was grateful then and remain so today.

So my life and education as a publisher began. I accompanied Dwight McKenzie on calls to key advertisers. I prepared myself and was even able to take part in talks. I remember my very first was with the owner of a local furniture store who was upset that we had put into effect an annual rate increase. I told him we had made other adjustments in our rate card which could actually reduce his cost per inch, if he signed a new frequency and lineage contract. He did, which surprised both me and McKenzie.

I realized I needed to learn a lot more about advertising and the business side. I had not realized how little I knew about Circulation. I picked the brain of Circulation Director Tom Myers and learned about single copy sales and vending machines and district managers and subsidies and the difference between employees and contract dealers and "little merchants," as some called our youth carriers.

However, I knew more than I realized about Production. My years of overseeing pages in the composing room, of talking closely with printers, of following pages from my desk to the press room, had paid off. Not that I knew everything. I had to learn newsprint usage and the price of newsprint and where we were getting it and how often. I developed a new understanding of news-to-advertising ratios and what it really means to "go up four pages," which I used to call for as an editor who wanted more space, damn the cost.

Most of all, I learned to look at mid-monthly flash reports and monthly revenue and cost reports and what it meant to have a budget and have to follow it. This was forced on me immediately by time and circumstances, for this was the budget season and budget meetings were soon to be held in Cincinnati, the regional headquarters of Gannett Central, and at Corporate itself, which was in the process of moving its headquarters from Rochester, New York to Washington, D. C.

In the budget process each department head put together projected costs for his department for the coming year, and as editor I had been responsible for the newsroom budget. Like all editors, I always asked for more—more reporters, more travel money, etc. And like all, I never received as much as requested. Meanwhile revenue projections were being made by the advertising and circulation departments. And then everything was submitted to the publisher and the controller who would compile the revenues and the combined expenses. Never did they find the margin of return they desired or that they knew Corporate would approve. So round one would end with department heads being told to reduce spending requests and revenue makers being asked to increase their projections. Eventually the budget would be finalized and sent on to our regional headquarters for review and then, after more adjustments, on to Corporate.

I had submitted the news budget before the change in publishers was made. But I had not had a hand in the overall Huntington budget. I went over it with Ed Burns, made notes and tried to commit certain numbers and explanations to memory. But there wasn't enough time, especially for a news guy who had spent his career boasting about paying no attention to the business side. When we met with Bill Keating in Cincinnati, I depended heavily on Burns to get me through. As expected, some changes were made and now it was on to Corporate–without Burns—where I would be expected to explain and defend the Huntington budget by myself.

Again I studied the budget and met at length with Burns and McKenzie and made notes. But once at Corporate I was on my own. I waited nervously outside the "war room" until called. And when finally summoned I loaded my arms with heavy budget books and monthly reports and notes and entered. I was immediately intimidated by the number of serious faces around a very large table, staring at me. There were representatives from every corporate department—News, Production, Advertising, Circulation, Human Resources, Marketing, and above all, the emcees of this tragedy, Finance and Accounting.

Spread before them were copies of our budget books as well as our current year's results. Questions came first from Finance. Some of them I could answer, some I could not. I made the mistake of trying to bluff my way through a few and dance around others, but quickly learned that was not what one should do. Things went better when I simply said, "I'm sorry, I don't know."

I had learned years before that the two most difficult things to say are "That's my fault" and "I don't know, " especially if you are intimidated by a higher force (hello, Raymond Brewster; hello, John McMillan). It takes confidence to admit to either. And I had no confidence in that room full of corporate devils.

The purpose of this corporate exercise is, of course, to push local operations to increase revenues and reduce expenses, therefore adding to the bottom line. Corporate frequently imposed ad revenue goals that local ad directors considered unrealistic. And it always reduced expense requests, especially in the newsroom. What seemed especially unfair was Corporate's eagerness to compare the numbers from various sites which had little in common. The theme seemed to be "They don't spend that much in Richmond, Indiana; why do you have to in Huntington?"

When finally a publisher emerges from such a meeting, he or she feels defeated and deflated and wondering if he or she has been heard at all.

But when I came out of my first such engagement that day, I realized I now had a much better understanding of my own budget and my own operation than when I had entered.

In returning to my room, I found myself on the elevator with Mr. Corporate Business Bogeyman himself, Larry Miller. Hal Burdick had warned me about him. Miller had bored into me as if I were trying to put something over on him—and after all the meetings he had experienced with local publishers, he probably had good reason to feel that way.

"That was tough," I said.

"Nah," Miller said, suddenly smiling. That came as a shock. I didn't know he was capable.

"But I learned a lot in there," I went on, almost apologetically.

He nodded and smiled again. He seemed a totally different person than the man who had been staring holes in me minutes earlier.

Larry Miller and I had a lot of exchanges over my publisher's life, some confrontational, most cordial, always with respect, and some even in fun. He was a good man.

Back in Huntington, new budget in place, I concentrated on getting into the community. I agreed to serve on the Chamber of Commerce board and the United Way board and became a trustee in the Museum of Art and I joined the country club.

I traded in Burdick's four-year–old Olds 98 for a new publisher's car. I chose a sleek, two-door Olds Tornado. I did not know that Corporate preferred that local publishers drive four-door sedans, the better to pick up corporate visitors at airports. Nobody had mentioned it.

I had not wanted to be publisher. I had not wanted the pressure of making money. I liked being editor. As a Gannett editor I had never felt pressure from Corporate. The corporate news department was there when needed, there for advice, there to help. At least that was my perspective. But I had watched our publishers under pressure from Corporate. "Why are you behind budget? Why are you behind last year? You've got to cut costs." I wanted none of that.

But here I was. And strangely, I found that I enjoyed the position—not just because of the salary and perks, or the big office, although all were welcome changes. What I discovered about myself was that I enjoyed being in the position of doing whatever I thought should be done—helping employees, changing certain policies, even moving furniture or painting walls if I so chose. Mostly I enjoyed the fact that I had no one to report to on site; all my bosses were out of town. That was a first-time freedom.

30
THE NATION'S NEWSPAPER

I had been publisher only a matter of days when I received the invitation. A unique new newspaper was being launched and the announcement would be made during a special reception to be held outside the White House. All Gannett publishers were to attend. And so was the president of the United States, Ronald Reagan.

We had heard rumblings for some time. Gannett corporate execs were discussing creating a new kind of newspaper that would be circulated throughout the country. It was the brainchild of Al Neuharth, Gannett's flamboyant chairman and CEO. But he was having a tough time convincing his own finance execs. The company was doing fine without it, they said. Creating and publishing such a newspaper would be a huge financial risk, involving millions of dollars—nobody had any idea how many millions. The fight was waged behind mostly (but not always) closed doors. Would the board listen to the financial people or to Neuharth? And why did Neuharth want to take such a risk, anyway?

If I were to name the most unforgettable people I've ever known, Al Neuharth would be at the top of the list. The nouns and adjectives used to describe him over his amazing newspaper career run the gamut: egomaniac, ruthless, cruel, insensitive, defensive, irreverent, obsessed, s.o.b. (the latter the title he gave to his own autobiography). And, dynamic, creative, brilliant, energetic, charismatic, genius, and, yes, sensitive. He was also intensely loyal, and expected loyalty in return.

He was certainly controversial, in his work and in his persona. He wore only black and white in those days (in later years his hair turned grey and he shifted to grey suits and sports coats). When he visited your town, he expected the best hotel's largest suite to be ready and to have flowers and fine wine or champagne (Crystal, if you don't mind).

But it wasn't always that way.

Al Neuharth was raised "on the wrong of the tracks" in Eureka, South Dakota. His father died when he was less than two years old and his mother and he and his brother were left with a small house and no money. He worked on his grandparents' farm for pennies, literally, handling manure, and then was "promoted" to working with cattle from a horse. He passed newspapers and learned to build up his routes to make more money, such as it was. He served in the Army under Patton, whom he admired greatly, attended college, worked briefly as a reporter for the local newspaper and then for The

Associated Press. He launched his own sports weekly called SoDak Sports, only to see it fail financially—a blessing, he said many years later. If it had succeeded, he said, he probably would have stayed there as a member of the country club set. I doubt that. His nature and competiveness would not have allowed it. He moved on to the Miami Herald and then the Rochester, New York newspapers, and there he climbed the ladder until he ran the company that owned them.

When Neuharth became its leader, Gannett was a medium-size company made up of mostly medium-sized newspapers. In less than ten years it was the largest newspaper company, in combined circulation, in America. It was also a very profitable company. A lot of people contributed to that growth but the single most responsible person was Al Neuharth. And he was rewarded handsomely. He earned more than a million dollars a year as chairman and CEO. He had corporate jets and limousines at his beck and call. He owned homes from Florida to Lake Tahoe. He was known in newspaper circles everywhere. It would have been easy to sit back and enjoy his success. But that would have been boring, and that was not Al Neuharth. Besides, he had a thirty-year-old dream— of creating a different kind of newspaper.

He had failed with "SoDak Sports. He had succeeded in the mid-60s with Cocoa Today (later named Florida Today). And now he wanted to go even beyond that, with a national newspaper. Yes, it would be a risk to the company. But what company was better positioned to do it than Gannett, with great resources and, even better, a network of newspapers across the country? Present-day newspapers were predictable and boring, he said. This was a new age offering vast new opportunities, with communication satellites circling the globe, a growing number of young people more interested in visual imagery than printed matter, who wanted "quick reads" instead of long, dry articles. The world had changed, but its newspapers had not. It was the perfect time, Neuharth said. And Gannett was the perfect company to pull it off.

So here he was, working to convince others in the Gannett hierarchy, especially the "bean counters," to go along with his idea. In the end Al Neuharth won the argument. He usually did. John Quinn, always Neuharth's strongest ally, was all for the idea. Jack Heselden listened with interest. Even the usually conservative Doug McCorkindale, who headed the business side of Gannett, agreed to finance research toward the project, saying that "a million bucks or so isn't that much for a company like ours." Said Neuharth years later, McCorkindale was probably thinking that "if Neuharth comes up with some crazy idea we can always kill it."

Right.

Al Neuharth went public with his plan in 1981. He discussed it with Gannett editors and publishers at a breakfast meeting during a newspaper convention in New Orleans. We were gathered on the patio at Brennan's restaurant, and Sandy and I were in attendance. Neuharth and Quinn stood near a tree facing us all. Neuharth, in fact, climbed partially into the tree so he could be seen and heard.

And he told us about USA TODAY.

We had heard rumors as to what it would be-- basically a single copy newspaper delivery dependent upon heavy sales in hotels, on planes, and in offices. It would be published only Monday through Friday. Now its creator was telling us what the paper would be when finally launched sometime in 1982: upbeat, inventive, colorful, full of graphics, with short stories and pointed headlines. It would celebrate America rather than the world. It would be interesting and fun, and its enemy would be boredom. It would use satellite transmission of pages produced in Washington and printed on presses from one coast to the other, most of them owned by Gannett, others contracted to do so.

To bring all this about, he said, he would need our help. Every Gannett newspaper would be expected to lend a reporter or copy editor or two to help produce it until the paper got on its feet. We would hear more about that later. We should be supportive and confident about the new newspaper's success and not find ourselves among those who were shooting it down before it was born. We were to *believe.*

Earlier I had muttered to Sandy that such a venture was doomed to failure. No Sunday paper? Circulated across the country? Satellite transmission? What about all the local papers elsewhere, many of them owned by Gannett? Was Gannett creating something that would compete against itself? We're already competing for the reader's time. What makes him think readers even want a national newspaper? And how can small papers like my own lend them a reporter or two? What about the hardship on us? It'll never work, I said. I hope the company doesn't go broke.

But when the meeting broke up, perhaps influenced by the French white Burgandy but more likely by Neuharth's and Quinn's words, I was excited. Later, whenever someone asked me about Gannett's new venture, I responded that it was an exciting new idea. I sent a couple of our news staff to Washington as "USA TODAY loaners," as did every newspaper in Gannett.

All the doubters—inside and outside Gannett-- were wrong. USA TODAY worked. It took a few years before it was profitable, but the money invested was less than the purchase price of a few other large newspapers at that time. And USA TODAY, as we now know, went on to become the largest circulation newspaper in America.

I have never forgotten Neuharth's fight to put "product over profit," hardly a policy that everyone in the company agreed on. Here's a harsh assessment from his extraordinary book, "Confessions of an S.O.B.":

"Bean counters. Money crunchers. No matter what you call them they're all alike…They're intelligent. Well educated. Well intentioned…All of them know how to count money. A few of them know how to manage it. Very few know how to earn it. None of them is willing to risk it. Conservative, up-tight S.O.B.s. Narrow-gauged and no vision beyond the next quarterly earnings report...

"Smart financial people are very important to any business operation. But a CEO who permits the bean counters to set company policy or make long-range decisions is condemning that company to the status quo and ultimately to a slow death.

"Most of them think they can save their way to prosperity...They're likely to spend as much time policing pennies and peanuts as they are managing millions or billions of dollars. I've always tried to make it clear to the bean counters that they are a service department, not a police department. But they have trouble getting it."

I wouldn't go that far about all of them. As I've said, good controllers can save you from making big mistakes. But some of them? He's right on target. And it shows where Neuharth's priorities were—at least for his brainchild.

A fact worth noting: Gannett was run by newspapermen with news backgrounds during its greatest growth period, from Paul Miller to Al Neuharth to John Curley. Its stock prices, even with stock splits, were the greatest in its history. Before Curley stepped down, the stock was $90 per share. The bean counters and advertising sales types and television execs took over after that and Gannett was never the same—in product OR profit. At this writing the stock sits at less than $20 a share.

But on that night in September 1982, on a tented platform in the nation's capital, when no one knew for certain what the future held, here we were, all the publishers in Gannett, with the President of the United States, Ronald Reagan, the Majority Leader of the U.S. Senate, Howard Baker; the Speaker of the House, Tip O'Neill, and the founder of USA TODAY, "a country boy from South Dakota," as he later put it, Al Neuharth.

Said President Reagan: USA TODAY "…is a testimony to the kind of dream free men and women can dream and turn into reality here in America."

For a moment Al Neuharth could not speak. For just the briefest time, he was overwhelmed. And then quickly, he cleared his throat and became the confident, even cocky man with a swagger that we all knew.

That Neuharth would invite all Gannett's publishers, no matter how small their newspapers, to this occasion was typical. He always included every Gannett publisher at national conventions. It did not matter whether you were from Danville, Illinois or Huntington, West Virginia, or Cincinnati, Louisville, Nashville or Rochester, you were included. And, much to the envy of non-Gannett publishers, you would be there at Gannett dinners at which a Ray Charles would entertain. You took great pride in this, and you returned home feeling appreciated and motivated. You *mattered.* Unfortunately, it was a practice not understood or followed by Al Neuharth's successors. More's the pity.

Surely Al Neuharth was a man of ideas, most of them sound, some of them regarded as strange. For example…

After a short time as publisher I received a call from Bill Keating, who said he had a special assignment for me. I should fly to Los Angeles to perform an audit of USA TODAY vending machines there and file a report to Corporate. I would be teamed with another new Gannett publisher, Peter Horvitz of Chillicothe.

I was a bit confused. Check USAT vending machines in Los Angeles? Had I heard correctly? Why me? Why not a publisher in that area? Better yet, a circulation director there? What did I know about vending machines?

Keating said I should check as many machines as possible over a period of two days to determine whether their coin mechanisms worked, whether they had current day's papers or previous day's papers or were, in fact, empty, and the condition of each machine. Had they been tampered with? Bashed in? Corporate wanted to know. Instead of using circulation people, or publishers in the area, they wanted publishers from other areas because they would have a fresh and different eye. The exercise was nation-wide. Publishers from our western properties would be flying east to do the same thing. Every USA TODAY market would be checked out by Gannett publishers strange to the area.

I thought it was a crazy idea and a terrible waste of money. Nonetheless, I flew to Los Angeles and met Horvitz, whom I had known since we both attended a high-intensity publisher's seminar in Houston not long before. We rented a small car, and

289

for the next two days we rose at 4:30 a.m. and drove around the entire Los Angeles area to see what time vending machines were filled with USA TODAYs, which ones were current, which machines still worked, which were clean, and so forth. I had never driven in Los Angeles before, but Horvitz had, so he got the driver's role and I served as the runner. He would spot a USAT vending machine, stop, I would run out and check it. I would insert the proper coins, take out a paper, check what was left. And so it went for two days.

At the end of our exercise we compiled our statistics and Peter left to visit friends. I hunkered down in my hotel room near the airport to write my report. I was proud in that we had managed to check nearly three hundred machines. We found problems galore, from old papers to bad coin slots to dirty windows to bashed-in tops. When I finished, I sent my report on. And then I walked down the street to another hotel whose dining room I preferred, ordered a Heineken and then a bottle of Puligney Montrachet (since Corporate was paying) and enjoyed a fabulous meal.

The idea was Neuharth's, of course. And it turned out to be a good one, providing a nationwide look at how USA TODAY single copy sales in vending machines contracted out to distributors were being handled. And it was done by publishers rather than circulation directors, from other parts of the country, whose views were just about as objective as you can get. It produced good information, and despite the travel expenses, was no doubt cheaper than hiring some high profile company to do it.

Al Neuharth was not a saint. He brought pain to a number of people over the years. He was demanding and short-tempered and often unforgiving. But he transformed and advanced the newspaper world. And from a personal view, I do not forget that it was on his watch that I was promoted to publisher, and that unlike many Gannett publishers, I managed to survive in that position until my retirement. I also will not forget this inscription scribbled to me in my copy of his autobiography, *Confessions of an S.O.B.*:

"To Don Hatfield. A friend, a true professional, a great guy, and living proof that you need <u>not</u> be an S.O.B. to succeed! Admiringly, Al Neuharth."

31
SPECIAL TEAM, SPECIAL VISITORS

A publisher is doomed to failure without good department heads in key positions.In early 1983, some six months into my job as publisher, I felt we were in good shape in some of those, but not all. We were solid in news, with Managing Editor Fran Allred heading the newsroom and becoming a member of the Operating Group. I had kept the title of editor and we did not fill the executive editor's position.

We were also set at controller with Ed Burns, who had demonstrated to Burdick, to Corporate and certainly to me his value as the money man. I also felt comfortable with Dwight McKenzie as ad director and Tom Myers as circulation director, our two revenue-producing positions. Both had considerable experience and were "street fighters" as well as executives, having come up through the ranks. And like Allred and Burns, they had no problems disagreeing with the publisher when they thought I was wrong. I liked that.

In production, however, I had concerns. Our production director was a long-time employee with considerable experience. He was a quiet man, dependable and hard-working, but seemed to lack energy and I was not certain about his health.

In marketing and human resources, we simply were not up to standard with other Gannett newspapers. Marketing had become little more than a promotions job. Our human resources department consisted of one untrained personnel person at a time when human resources matters had become important and often delicate. Fixing that was a priority. I needed a human resources professional, someone trained and experienced who could step right in and handle every aspect of the job.

I had somebody in mind.

Nate Ruffin had been a member of the 1970 Marshall University football team. Because of an elbow injury he had missed the game against East Carolina in Greensboro, North Carolina and was not among the seventy-five players, coaches and townspeople who perished when the team plane crashed that terrible night of November 14, 1970.

He was sitting in the Keith-Albee theater when he heard of the crash, and went immediately to the airport to help however he could, only to learn that all aboard had died. He spent the rest of the night helping to notify his teammates' parents. It was a horrible, heart-wrenching experience.

In the weeks to come he suffered emotional and other problems. He felt enormous guilt that he was alive while his friends and teammates were gone. He had been so much a part of the team. If he had not been injured and had been with the team as he should have been, he would be dead, too. But he was alive. Why was that?

Often he found himself stumbling along lonely streets overwhelmed by grief and confusion. One night a strange thing happened. Walking through the underpass on Sixteenth Street, now known as Hal Greer Boulevard, heading from campus to the other side of the railroad tracks, it occurred to him he had forgotten where he was going. He thought of one of his teachers who lived in the area, who had believed in him and who had been close to him. He began to cry, and he heard himself say, "I can't go on like this." He fell to his knees and began to pray.

When he emerged minutes later from the darkness of the underpass, he felt alive again, almost exhilarated. Gone was the depression, the guilt, the anger, the confusion. In his mind and heart there was a new, clear understanding. He had been spared to help others.

"It was an epiphany," he said later. "I would give myself to God."

Nate Ruffin captained the Marshall team, known as the "Young Thundering Herd," the next season. He proved to be a great leader, an articulate spokesman for the team and across campus. He graduated with honors.

That had been more than ten years ago. Now he was in the human resources department—helping others—of a local steel company. He was active in the community, a man whose name was known by everyone. He was also outstanding at his job. There was one other thing about him that appealed greatly to me. He was African-American. We had no African-Americans on our management team.

First I called Corporate. This was a department head position and it was customary to report any vacancy at this level as well as any plan to fill one before any action was taken. I described Ruffin in glowing terms and was given the go-ahead to pursue him.

I called Nate and made an appointment for lunch. I told him I had recently been named publisher and that I needed a human resources director. I wanted to discuss the job with him.

He was surprised, reluctant, perhaps a little suspicious. He asked, as had Angela Dodson years before when as a new managing editor I had approached her for a job, "Why me?"

I was as direct and honest with him as I had been with her. Because you're good at what you do, because you've built a good reputation in human resources, because you're active and known in the community. And, because we need an African-American on our management team. Having none, we do not reflect the community we serve or practice what we preach. And no, you will not be a token hire. You'll have to work hard like everybody else in our Operating Group.

He said he had a good job and that he knew nothing about newspapers. I told him that did not matter. We would not be asking him to edit stories or sell advertising or run the business side. What he would be doing was oversee all human resources issues, take part in hiring and, when necessary, firing, keep up to date on federal regulations and corporate policies, know about benefits and pay scales, and in general protect his new publisher from making dumb mistakes. Salary was negotiable.

He said he would think about it. He did, and agreed to take the job.

Our Operating Group met in my office every Monday to talk about a number of matters—plans for the coming week, information that should be shared, problems our department heads might want to discuss, questions they might have of others. Nate was a big help because nobody besides human resources directors understands all the rules and regulations involved in personnel, and every member of the OG needed help in that area. He also was a good listener and took note of the information other members of the group passed on.

A good human resources director, like a good controller, can be of enormous help to a publisher. And Nate Ruffin proved to be the best—the best in Gannett, in fact. During his career he won five President's Rings for being among the top human resources directors in the company. He was later promoted to larger papers and eventually to Corporate. And then he moved to the Freedom Forum in Washington. Sadly, he developed cancer, defeated it once, but not twice. We talked by phone briefly before he died. He showed enormous courage. He was prepared to go, he said. He just hated to leave his family. It was an honor to have known him and to have worked with him.

Once Nate Ruffin joined us, I felt a growing confidence in our management team. During one Operating group meeting, Ad director Dwight McKenzie announced that he would be traveling to Pittsburgh to meet with representatives of Circuit City, which was opening a large new store near the mall east of the city. I told him to sign them to the largest contract we had to offer, and then jokingly added that if he did not, "Don't bother to come back."

Two days later he sauntered into my office and tossed a contract onto my desk and stood back, beaming. Sure enough, it was the largest contract on our rate card—and it was signed.

"Didn't think I'd pull it off, did you?" he said, laughing. Then he sat down and gave me a blow-by–blow account of how he did it. I was pleased, of course, but more so for him. He was quite proud. At the next Operating Group meeting I made certain to tell the other members of his accomplishment, which brought forth their applause and congratulations.

It was a good group. Unfortunately, our team did not stay intact for long. Ed Burns accepted an offer from the big bank across the street. I would have to find a new controller.

Again I called Corporate asking for recommendations, and I received a couple of names. I checked them out and did not have a totally good feeling about them. The "vibes" weren't there for me. Then Larry Miller, my corporate budgeting nemesis, called. He gave me a new name, a controller on another Gannett newspaper who for whatever reason did not seem to be hitting it off quite so well with his present publisher. "But I think you two might work well together," Miller said.The controller's name was Bruce Cannady.

We talked by phone and Cannady agreed to fly in for an interview. We met at length in my office and then went to an enjoyable dinner. The "vibes" were there. We returned to my office and I offered him the job. He said he would think about it.

"What's there to think about?" I said, only half-jokingly. I told him to tear up his plane ticket and stick around, we could have some fun. He resisted, I pressed. He said he needed more time. I said, 'For what?" Finally he gave up, laughing. "Okay, Don," he said. "I'll work for you."

And that, as Rick said in "Casablanca," was the beginning of a beautiful friendship, one that has lasted to this day. He was also the perfect controller for his newsroom-oriented publisher, and taught me a lot.

There would also be a change in Production, as I had anticipated. Harold Hopkins was retiring. There were those waiting in the wings, including a long-time composing room foreman. But I wanted to go another way. Since I had first gone into the composing room as an editor to check on my pages, there had been an energetic young printer who had impressed me. He often made up my pages, from the days of hot lead to those of "cold type," and while he did so we talked often about what we would do "if we ran this place." He was a hard worker, conscientious, well-liked, upbeat, honest, and I had always admired some of his ideas. His name was Jerry Epling.

But first, following procedure as always, I checked with Corporate. Did it have anyone in mind I should consider? Not really. Good production directors were hard to come by. I told them what I was thinking, and got permission to proceed "if you really think this person can do the job." Translation: it was my call, and if it didn't work out it would be my mistake, not theirs.

I sent word for Epling to come to my office when he wrapped things up. I told him I wanted to discuss the soon-to-be-open production director's job. He thought I was going to ask him about others who might be considered.

"Think you could handle the job?" I said instead.

He was stunned. He looked around the room as if he suspected he was being set up for some sort of joke. Then he looked back to me and a big grin came to his face.

"Do you?" he said.

"Yes."

"Then so do I."

Jerry Epling, like Nate Ruffin and Bruce Cannady, proved to be a good selection. Like Nate, he too won President's Rings for being among the best production directors in the company. Trust the vibes. Every time I did, it worked out. Every time I ignored them, it did not.

And now I could pay a little attention to the news department.

In addition to having Fran Allred as managing editor, I was fortunate to have Jim Casto as associate editor in charge of the editorial page. He was a knowledgeable, experienced newsman, a former reporter and city editor who possessed a high I. Q., and unlike some journalists, researched subjects well before writing about them.

Each week we met to discuss editorials for the next several days. And each day, he brought me the editorials—one of normal length, one very short--- for my approval before they made it into type. Years before The Herald-Dispatch had been "the Republican paper" in town and The Huntington Advertiser "the Democrat paper." Now that the two had merged a few years before, we did not concern ourselves with whether our editorials took a Republican or Democrat or conservative or liberal stance. Nor did we worry about taking the middle road. We made decisions for editorial stances based on what we believed was best for the community, the state or beyond. It was a great position to be in —to "call 'em as we see 'em,"

News coverage was not influenced by the editorial positions we took, as it should never be. News pages were for news, editorial pages for opinions, and never the twain shall meet. Nor were news stories or editorials influenced by opinion offered in a personal column, signed by the author and thus that author's own opinion and not necessarily that of the newspaper.

Most people have a difficult time believing that. Most believe that news coverage is planned with editorial biases and positions in mind. Especially if they dislike the news stories or disagree with the editorials. Most also believed that this giant newspaper company, Gannett, ordered us to take certain positions and make certain endorsements. Not true. Not once in my many years with Gannett was I told which causes or candidates to endorse or which positions to take editorially.

As one might expect, the new Herald-Dispatch, with its news coverage and editorials now free of political traditions and influences, was now viewed by Republicans in town as if we had deserted them and "gone over to the other side." And the Democrats in town, having lost what they considered to be "their" newspaper when The Advertiser folded, thought we were still in bed with Republicans. I figured if both sides thought we were slanting stuff, we must have been doing a pretty decent job.

We held frequent editorial board meetings at which we invited various office-holders, local officials, newsmakers of all kinds, giving them a chance to complain or discuss or educate us on a subject about which they felt we needed educating. A reporter—usually Tom Miller, our political and legislative reporter and my old sports department colleague--would sit in. Other reporters might attend as well, depending on the issue being discussed and whether there might be a news story in the session. When it was election time, we interviewed all candidates for the offices in which we would make endorsements. It was time consuming but the right thing to do.

We also invited members of Congress, United States senators and governors to visit for informal talks when their schedules permitted. The most memorable such visit was that of Sen. Robert C. Byrd, not only a legendary senator but practically a legend on the fiddle as well. He came to my office and Casto, Miller and Dave Peyton, reporter and columnist, joined us. With Byrd was one of his aides. Our talk began somewhat formally, with a few opening comments from Byrd, who seemed to me something of a cold fish, as if he might be a bit uncomfortable with those present. We asked various questions about what was going on in Washington, as one would expect, and after a short while he warmed up and things became less formal. And then Peyton, an expert on mountain music and who played the autoharp, asked if the senator had brought his fiddle.

"It's in the car," he said.

"Are you going to play us a few tunes?" said Peyton.

"Well, sure," said Byrd.

"If you will," I said, "I'll have all the employees gather in our community room to hear you. That would be a big thrill for them."

"Sounds good."

And so this powerhouse of the Democratic Party, this national figure, took his fiddle into The Herald-Dispatch community room, where by now several dozen employees from every department in the building had gathered, and began to entertain. He played until his aides told him he had to leave. He received great applause, and I walked up to him and said, 'Senator, that was special. Our employees loved it, as you could tell."

"Well, it was a lot more fun than our meeting," he said.

Unfortunately Sen. Byrd did not come that often. But one who did was John D. Rockefeller IV, better known as "Jay," who was at that time governor. He came when he happened to be in Huntington, and he was on a first-name basis with my secretary, Louise Cazad: 'Hello, Governor." "Hello, Louise."

One day he came in tennis shoes, khakis and polo shirt

"You didn't have to dress," I said.

"Hey, what is this?" he said. "Why are you giving me a hard time?"

Usually, Miller, Casto and I had plenty of questions for him. In the beginning, they addressed state issues. Then they moved on to more ordinary matters. Knowing him to be a student of Asian history and literature, I mentioned that my wife was reading "The Tale of Genghi" and kept a copy on our bed headboard.

"The whole thing?" he said.

I did not know it consisted of many volumes.

Another day I received a call in mid-morning from one of his state troopers saying the governor was in town for a meeting and wanted to see me afterward. I said I would welcome that but I had a luncheon meeting out of the office and would not be back until after 1 p.m.

When I returned to my office, I had just sat at my desk when his cars pulled up in front of the building and Rockefeller jumped out. He came through the front doors, quickly entered the outer office, said "Hello, "Louise," came straight into my office saying "Hello, Don," and then went into my private bathroom. He was there for a few minutes and then emerged smiling, explaining, "Now you know what I wanted to see you about."

It was during Rockefeller's terms as governor that Sandy was twice appointed to state commissions. Because of her volunteer efforts in the community, including that with Green Acres, a facility for the mentally challenged, she was appointed to the Governor's Commission on the Disabled as well as the West Virginia Disabilities Council. The appointments had nothing to do with my position as publisher, and everything to do with her good work and intelligence. I was once again proud of her.

32
A SUDDEN INTERRUPTION

As we approached the end of 1983, it was time for the Gannett year-end meeting in Washington, marking completion of my first full calendar year as publisher and my first annual performance evaluation. A highlight was being among the Gannett publishers invited to the White House for a special Gannett-only session with President Reagan. Afterward each of us met the President, shook hands, said a few words. He was as charming as everyone said.

The Gannett meeting went well and I looked forward to returning home for the holidays with my family. Having just been given the Gannett seal of approval, accompanied by a salary increase, I was on top of the world.

That Friday night Sandy and I hosted members of my Operating Group and their spouses for dinner at Guyan Country Club. There were jokes and drinks and good food and good times, and we talked about everything but business. I felt happy and fortunate and looked forward to the holidays as never before.

The following morning, a cool but sunny Saturday in December, I rose early and drove to the office to check on a few things and then dropped by a women's dress shop to pick up a few gifts I had bought for Sandy's birthday and Christmas. Returning home my heart stopped when I saw an emergency vehicle parked in front of our house, its rear doors open. I immediately thought something had happened to our youngest son, Joel. But suddenly he came running out of the house toward me, saying "It's Mother" and behind him came emergency medical workers wheeling a gurney carrying Sandy, lying motionless beneath a white blanket.

I ran shouting "What's happened?" as they placed her in the ambulance and hooked her to some sort of IV apparatus. I jumped inside and the ambulance sped off. I immediately asked again what had happened and one of the workers said they were not yet certain; she had collapsed and our son had called 911. We were on our way to St. Mary's Hospital, he said, which surprised me because it was about two miles away and Cabell Huntington Hospital was only two blocks away. They were monitoring her closely. She did not appear to be conscious but she was breathing. One of the workers, taking her pulse, suddenly told the driver, "Better hurry and give us the siren."

I was terrified. She had been sleeping peacefully when I left the house. When I returned they were putting her in this ambulance. What had happened? Our son did not know. The emergency crew members did not know. But they assured me she was breathing. And I prayed.

At St. Mary's she was taken into an emergency room where doctors and nurses bent over her and placed an oxygen mask over her face and attached more IVs. And I sat watching and wondering and then praying again.

Dr. Charles (Skip) Turner was carefully attending to her. I sat beside her having no idea what he was doing or what it meant or what her condition was. It seemed to be taking forever.

Finally Skip Turner turned to me and smiled and said softly, "I think she's doing better."

I sat there for some time watching and looking at what seemed to be an endless number of cables and tubes and monitors and people moving in and out. And finally she opened her eyes and looked at me and an ever-so-slight smile came to her face and it was the greatest smile in all the world.

Later, with nurses looking after her, Skip Turner walked me to another room and told me that Sandy, my invincible wife, had suffered some sort of cardiac problem. He was not certain at this point if it was a heart attack. Heart attack? How could that be? She did not smoke or drink, she weighed little more than an even hundred, she ate well, took care of herself, jogged and played tennis, had never had any health problems even while having three children. I told him all this and he said, "Well, we're not sure yet. We'll have to do a lot of tests. We'll see. The big thing is that she is doing better." She was sleeping peacefully, he said, and I should go home and come back later. I needed to take care of myself and she would be in good hands.

First I called Joel and told him what little I knew and that I would soon be home for a short while. I told him to hold off on notifying his brother Chris, now living in Boston but on his way home for the holidays, until we knew more. Then I called my wife's parents in Beckley, who often visited on weekends. Her father answered and I first asked if they were coming for the weekend. He said they were thinking about it but had not yet decided. I told him that it would be good if they did, and he must have heard something in my voice and said, "What's wrong?" And I told him Sandy was in the hospital and that doctors think she might have had a mild heart attack, and then quickly added that she was doing better and they thought she was going to be all right. No one had told me that but I felt I had to say it.

When I finished talking with him I looked up to see Fran Allred, our managing editor. I do not know to this day how she learned so quickly about Sandy's problem and where we were. But she had come to see if she could help in any way. I explained as well as I could what had happened. And then she told me, "You look terrible."

"I'm going home now and clean up," I said.

Joel was waiting on the front stoop and I gave him a hug and told him his mother was going to be all right, that we still were not sure what had happened. He told me his mother had called out to him, to his bedroom across the upstairs hall, and he had come immediately and found her in the floor by the bed. He had called 911 and sat with her until the emergency crews arrived. Thank God he had been home.

I poured myself a Scotch and sat down and stared into the garden and then closed my eyes and said another in a series of prayers. *Lord, please let her live.* And then I went to shave and shower and dress and then I had another Scotch, and then another, and then I went back to the hospital.

They had moved her to a room in Intensive Care. She was awake and smiling and I held her hand and told her that she was going to be all right, that she just had to be, I would not accept anything else. And despite my attempts not to, I started to cry. And being the ever-vigilant wife she asked me if I had been drinking, and when I confessed to the Scotches, she said, "Ahh, Don, why did you have to do that?" And I have never felt more guilty.

That night when I went to bed alone I realized perhaps for the first time in my life what was really important, what truly mattered in my life. It was not the world of newspapers or being publisher or being successful or making money. It was that extraordinary person who lay at that moment in the hospital. I convinced myself that she had not experienced a heart attack, but rather some lesser problem, and she would be just fine in a few days. But the following day Skip Turner told me the tests had confirmed that she had indeed suffered a heart attack. Again, I asked how that could be, given her excellent physical condition. He said there might be a blockage and they would schedule an angiogram and perhaps angioplasty.

After finding her resting comfortably and managing that wonderful smile, I drove to the airport to meet our son Chris. The plan was that his girl friend Connie would pick him up. She was there when I arrived and I told her about Sandy and she started to cry. Soon the plane arrived and Chris got off smiling, and when he reached us said to me, "What are you doing here?"

I had rehearsed how I would tell him: "Now, she's going to be all right," I began. "But your mother is in the hospital. Believe it or not, but they think she's had a heart attack."

His face went blank. We drove immediately to the hospital, and he rushed in to see her.

Word got around quickly. On Monday I received a phone call from Sen. Byrd. "Don, what happened to Sandy?" he said with surprising familiarity. And then he pledged whatever help I might need in the coming days. I realized this was the work of a good staffer in his office, but the call meant a lot to me anyway.

Not long after Gov. Jay Rockefeller called to also ask about her condition and to offer his help. Not that any help would have come, but again it was nice hearing it.

Even the basketball coach at Marshall, Rick Huckaby, called and followed up with a planter and card signed by the entire team. Sandy and I had long been Marshall basketball fans and knew Huckaby well. Marshall was going to host Cincinnati in a couple of days and the card read: "We will win this game for you."

But first Sandy had to have an angiogram. And there was another scare. The needle inserted into the groin caused her to hemorrhage, and doctors went running and cursing and clearly were in an emergency situation. What was going on? I literally grabbed one of the doctors. He blurted out that they had to stop the hemorrhaging or she could lose the use of her leg. Once more I was terrified. And once more I prayed. And once more my prayer was answered. The bleeding stopped. She would be kept in a special room, closely monitored. She would not be able to turn or roll over. She would have to remain very still. But they had found no blockage.

Still lying without the freedom of moving, Sandy asked that a radio be placed beside her so she could listen to the game, and insisted that I go so I could tell her about it. Reluctantly, I did so, and was thrilled to be able to return and tell her that, as Coach Huckaby had promised, Marshall had won it for her.

Her birthday was spent in the hospital, in a private room now, and there were gifts and champagne and even a few laughs. And after a week she was permitted to leave the hospital and return home in time for Christmas. It was one of the coldest and snowiest days in years, and I worried how that might affect her as we climbed into the car. But she was smiling and happy to be going home.

Her parents would be there to help care for her. But it was strange to have this energetic, type AAA personality depending on others and being so limited. She would come downstairs and read by the fireplace and then return to the bedroom, a trip she found to be exhausting.

But simply having her there was the greatest Christmas gift in the world.

As time went by, she recovered. No physical reason could be found for her attack. It was assumed that it was caused by exhaustion and stress, linked to her studying for a Master's Degree while caring for an invalid daughter and a son in high school. Whatever, her recovery was the blessing of my life. We had done wonderful things together. And now, with God's continued blessing, we would be able to do many more.

33
THE PUBLISHER'S WORLD

There was a time when newspaper publishers owned the newspaper they ran. They answered to no one but themselves and could do whatever they wanted about advertising rates, circulation pricing, and even bottom lines. If their profit margin was only three percent, well, for some that was enough; they didn't want to gouge their friends and fellow citizens to make more. But as the years went by and took with them those publishers, many of their sons and daughters decided they really did not want to be in the newspaper business. Some surviving families were so large and made up of people so diverse that they couldn't agree on important matters. And so family-owned newspapers were put up for sale, and more often than not were bought by large newspaper groups or chains. Hence the Gannetts of the world.

Publishers of these newspapers were no longer also the owners. They were professional managers, given short training on how to run the newspaper

313

according to the policies of the Corporation. These publishers were hardly in a position to do anything they wanted, especially when it came to rates, pricing and the bottom line. In spite of Al Neuharth's wonderful words about the bean counters of the world lacking vision, they ruled when it came to local budgets and profit returns.

Gannett in those days spoke of product and profit. Success was expected in both. The great thing about being a Gannett editor was that you did not have to worry about the profit part. You had only to concern yourself with the product--putting out a good local newspaper, one in tune with the community it served. And you had the vast resources of Gannett to call upon, from libel lawyers to talent tanks. Nor did you have to worry about Big Brother telling you what to put in or leave out of the news columns or which issues or candidates to support. Gannett trusted you and your staff to know about such things far better than they did in their Corporate offices.

Of course, you did have to deal with your local publisher, who in addition to making certain you followed your newsroom budget and news hole allocations, also had a hand in your editorial page stances. But all in all the news side was your show. And you knew that you had the support of Gannett's Vice President/News, John Quinn, who took pride in Gannett editors who stood up to their publishers.

It was a different world for a Gannett publisher. Yes, product was also part of his or her domain. But profit was the driving force. And margins that might have been satisfactory to the owner-publishers of yesteryear were far from satisfactory now. Try thirty percent. Or if you happened to be in a good town with little competition, how about forty?

A Gannett publisher was expected to follow the budget plan agreed upon in annual budget meetings ("forced upon" in the eyes of many publishers and ad directors). Once the budget was finalized, the call to arms every month was "make plan." Mid-month "flash" reports were submitted giving Corporate a heads up on how the month was going. At the end of every month, the brutal facts were submitted—revenues, costs and NIBT (net income before taxes). If revenues were not coming in as projected, one needed to make adjustments on the cost side to get as close as possible to "making plan."

What was unforgiveable was to fail to show an increase over the previous year. It was one thing to miss plan—most Gannett papers missed plan (I once heard John Curley refer to Gannett newspaper budgets as "fictions"). It was something else not to exceed the previous year. Do that many times and a publisher found himself in a new and lesser role somewhere. Similarly, those who did well were rewarded, with bonuses, stock options, stock incentive rights, and promotions.

Among the best were two friends and fellow editors-turned-publishers, John Curley and Gary Watson, and both had become my bosses. Curley, with whom I had played tennis during newspaper conventions and retreats and for whom I had once substituted in a week-long seminar at the American Press Institute, had become head of Gannett's Newspaper Division. Watson, whom I had known since his days in Boise, Idaho, was the new publisher in Cincinnati and president of Gannett's Central Division, replacing Bill Keating.

Both Curley and Watson knew something about Huntington. They knew that to make plan, even to show an increase over the previous year, was especially tough in Huntington, then part of the nation's Rust Belt. In fact, during a meeting in Washington Curley turned to me and said, "Don, you're going to have to face the fact that Huntington isn't what it used to be."

I was surprised. What's that? My town? The town I grew up in? What does he know?

He knew a lot more than I did, and those words proved it, even if they did come as a blow. Huntington wasn't what it once was, and our revenues proved it. We needed to make some serious changes on the expense side.

The two biggest expenses in publishing a newspaper are personnel and newsprint. You can reduce newsprint consumption, cutting the news hole and the number of pages, by only so much. So, you look at personnel--the work force.

Gannett, as usual comparing the budgets and operations of all its various newspapers, bluntly said we were overstaffed, especially in Production, and a number of people would have to be let go. That number, according to careful figuring by Corporate finance whizzes, turned out to be sixteen. Sixteen.

We had fewer than two hundred employees in the entire building. We probably were a bit heavy in the composing room now that newsroom computers were doing more such work, but elsewhere we were stretched pretty thin.

Layoffs would not be the answer. Those are generally thought to be temporary, although in reality they rarely turn out to be that. These cutbacks would not be temporary. They would be forever. Some of the positions could be eliminated through attrition, but not all. Not many people left our newspaper, especially in Production. This was West Virginia. Our employees were long-timers and loyal and rarely left for other jobs.

I convinced Corporate we should offer buyouts. If that did not produce enough takers, we would have to consider another course of action.

What would be the terms of those buyouts? And what would be the maximum amount of money I could use for them? Finally it was agreed that we would offer each employee in targeted departments (mostly Production) one week's pay for every year spent with our newspaper. There would also be a cap on how much I could spend

What I did not tell Corporate was that many in Production were long-timers. If they were the only ones who took the buyouts, we would run out of money before we got our sixteen vacancies. What then?

I also knew that there was a strong awareness in Production, especially in the composing room, that the newspaper computer age was only in its infancy and that one of these days there would be no composing room at all (a fear and an outcome that eventually came true, but not quite yet).

I asked each department head to announce the buyout program to all employees and I placed written announcements on every bulletin board. I also walked throughout the building, chatting with employees, answering their questions, managing to avoid the main question on everyone's mind: what if not enough people accepted the buyouts?

As fate would have it, there were some vacancies in the building we could freeze, and there were a couple of minor resignations. And finally, several composing room employees stepped up and, no doubt realizing that their jobs were eventually going to disappear and here was an opportunity to get many weeks' severance pay, agreed to the buyouts. And we reached our magic number: sixteen.

I found myself with somewhat mixed emotions —sad for those who were leaving, although many of them seemed happy to do so with a pocketful of money, and happy for those who were staying and out of danger. Mostly, I was relieved. We had put ourselves in a better situation when it came to making plan. I now could move on and get some other things done.

But I was met with an unwanted resignation— that of Charlie Bowen, our splendid city editor. He came into my office, sat down, and said he was leaving--not just The Herald-Dispatch, but the newspaper business. "I'm tired of holding hands and tying shoelaces," he said, referring to handling young reporters, which was his greatest strength. He had been writing magazine articles and a book on computers and computer software. Now he was going to do that fulltime.

I thought he was making a mistake, but wished him well. There were other matters to deal with besides the newsroom.

One of the things I liked most about being publisher was having the opportunity to do things for the community, especially with Gannett Foundation grants. The Foundation was the giving arm of the Gannett company, and its grants were made only to communities in which there was a Gannett property. All Gannett Foundation grant requests had to come through the local publisher. Gannett's thinking, commendably, was that local publishers knew best the needs of their community.

Each Gannett property was advised at the start of the year how much money it had been allotted to give away, with Gannett's approval, based on its previous year's earnings. In Huntington, I had been accustomed to receiving about $50,000 per year, over and above my budget. Obviously, a larger paper with more profits would have more money to give away.

But the Foundation came up with a new venture which would enable even small properties in small towns to award major grants. The program was called the Community Priorities grant, and it was quite competitive with only about twenty or so such grants being awarded to all Gannett properties.

One day representatives of Marshall University came to see me with a new idea and a different kind of request. They hoped to establish a special program called the Yeager Scholars program, named after Maj. Gen. Chuck Yeager, a local person who had achieved fame by being the first man to break the sound barrier in his famous X-15 plane.

I liked the idea but disliked the proposal they brought. There was no way it would qualify for a Gannett grant, much less a competitive Community Priorities grant. So I talked with them for some time in an effort to come up with a different kind of proposal. I told them the hot buttons for the Foundation were education, the underprivileged, minorities, and finally need and numbers—what the need was and how many people would be helped. If they could rewrite the proposal to touch on all these, I would be pleased to submit it.

Soon they brought in a completely rewritten proposal which was quite good. I entered it in the Community Priorities competition and hoped, although I must admit I thought it was probably futile.

I was surprised and thrilled when we won. Thus the Yeager Scholars program was launched at Marshall with thousands of Gannett seed dollars. Today that program has helped dozens of bright students get an education and it is on solid foundation. I was and am proud to have been a part of getting it going.

Among the things that had bothered me for

some time was how many times I heard the word "can't" and "don't" in our building. We can't make that change in your ad without additional cost. We can't deliver your paper to your doorstep because of where you live. We can't put that announcement in the paper. We don't use those kinds of stories or pictures. And on and on.

We needed to change. We needed to find a way to give our customers and clients more of what they wanted and less of what we wanted. We needed to say "Yes" more often, and when that was not possible, we needed to be able to make a compromise or offer a suggestion: "Instead of doing it that way, what if we try to do it this way?"

First I shared my thinking with our management team. I got my share of odd looks and heavy sighs along with all sorts of reasons we have to say "can't" and don't" in certain situations.

Let's find a way not to, I said.

Again, I went into every department and told employees my thinking. We can do better, I said. Our customers were tired of hearing what we can't do and don't do and won't do, I said. I asked for their help, and I promised them ours—meaning, their supervisors and myself. I was surprised and pleased to see so many nodding in agreement.

I chose as our slogan, "Yes, we can" (and this was more than twenty years before President Obama came up with the same slogan during his presidential campaign). I bought red tee shirts bearing the slogan "Yes, We Can" and distributed them to all employees. Would it work? Would it make a difference? I'm confident that it did, but to what extent I really can't be certain. At least we tried and we improved, and I felt good about that.

For some time I had held an annual weekend afternoon pool party at our house for the news staff, complete with beer, hot dogs, the works. Now that I was publisher, I heard from a couple of employees in other departments, asking why I had a party only for newsroom people. There would be far too many for one party, so I held three—one for the news staff, two others for the remaining employees. Sandy commented that the others were much better behaved than the news staff. Fortunately for her, she was not always there, spending a portion of her summers on Cape Cod.

Meanwhile, my editors and I were seeing more of the governor. Jay Rockefeller continued to drop by on his visits to Huntington, and now, in the last year of his second term, was considering running for the United States Senate. He usually came at the end of a busy day and occasionally after we met briefly in my office we would walk a couple of blocks to a restaurant called Permon's, atop the West Virginia Building. There were usually four of us--Rockefeller, editorial page editor Jim Casto, Tom Miller, and myself. Rockefeller and Miller, our long-time political and legislative correspondent, were especially tuned in to each other.

More than once it occurred to me that here we were with John D. Rockefeller IV, legendary name, legendary family. And he never seemed to carry any money. At least, he never offered to pay. In fact, after one such evening following his election as Senator, he sent me this letter:

"Our dinner last week was great, even if the weather was lousy. Thanks for your kindness, Don. I have always enjoyed the conversations we've had over the years and particularly appreciate the opportunity to share thoughts and ideas with you. I do hope we can continue this dialogue in the months and years to come.

"Thanks again for the dinner. It's ironic, I think, that I invited you to dinner and you ended up paying. "You see, being a United States Senator does have its advantages.

"Sincerely, Jay Rockefeller."

Some time after that he stopped in again to talk with us, and I happened to be out of town. Casto and Miller spent some time with him and they once again took him to Permon's. I was told later that when the check came Rockefeller said, "Don just thinks he's getting out of paying." And with that, he signed my name to the bill.

Of course, I was pleased to pay every time. If he had tried to pay we would not have permitted it any more than we would have for any other news source, official, politician or citizen. We had a strict policy of accepting no free meals, gifts, trips, tickets from anyone. "We pay our own way" summed it up quite nicely.

Jay Rockefeller was succeeded as governor by Arch Moore, who had already served two previous terms as governor and who ironically was both predecessor and successor to Rockefeller. We already knew Moore from those earlier years. He had sent to me the approved legislation for open meetings and open records laws in West Virginia in recognition of my newspaper and I having fought for that. I had also been invited to his Governor's Mansion at Christmas time, just as I had when Jay and Sharon Rockefeller and their small children occupied it. Now I was publisher and I immediately invited Moore to visit as Rockefeller had visited, and he was pleased to do so.

The meetings were quite similar, held in my office with Casto and Miller and occasionally another reporter. Moore knew Miller very well because of his many years in the Capitol and because Miller was regarded throughout the state as a tough but fair reporter. During one of his visits Moore sat in a chair opposite my desk and beside Miller, and Miller was posing questions, not all of them easy. Finally, Miller got to the subject Moore must have dreaded: rumors circulating involving mishandling of campaign funds.

Moore blew up, turned red, slammed the arm chair, stood and marched out of my office. I hurried after him, catching him at the front door of the building. He was still red with anger as he turned to face me with his right fist clenched and held at fighting level.

"One of these days, Don," he said. "One of these days…"

"Governor, you've got to know you're going to be asked about that," I said.

He wheeled and went directly to his waiting

car, state troopers standing at its side. I watched them drive away, surprised by his outburst, realizing Miller had struck a highly sensitive nerve, and wondering what it all meant. I was sorry our visit had ended this way—but not sorry Miller had raised the question.

Still, having had Moore's clenched fist thrust in front of my face I assumed I probably would never hear from him again, at least in friendly terms. I therefore was quite surprised when only a year later upon being transferred to another Gannett newspaper two thousand miles away, I received this letter from Moore:

"I have mixed feelings about the recent announcement of your move to Arizona. I am certain it will mean greater challenges for you, but no doubt it means leaving a lot behind in West Virginia. I know the people of Huntington and the region, and I in particular, will miss you.

"You have done a good job at the helm in Huntington. I know you will be successful in Tucson, but I hate to see our state lose good people.

"I also know that even though you will be living and working in another place, a part of you will always be with us. You have made a lasting contribution to the state and to our people. Few have the opportunity to leave much of anything behind them when they leave, but you have left the readers and subscribers of the Herald-Dispatch and the people of the Huntington area with a rich and rewarding legacy.

"Thanks for all your help in the past. My best

wishes go out to you for your continued success in whatever avenues your future may take you. Sincerely, Arch."

In 1990 Arch Moore pleaded guilty to five felony indictments including accepting illegal payments during his 1984 and '88 campaigns, extorting $573,000 from a coal company, and obstructing an investigation into his activities. He later attempted to withdraw his guilty pleas, but failed, and was sentenced to five years in prison. He served three.

Despite that, I liked Arch Moore. And I liked Jay Rockefeller. Both were good governors. When one considers that for nearly twenty years, from 1969 to 1989, West Virginia was served by the two of them, our state was pretty fortunate.

34
VICE PRESIDENT

I was a bit later than usual returning from a luncheon meeting at Marshall University and Louise was watching for me. "Mr. Watson called," she said. "He wants you to call him back as soon as you get here."

I immediately felt guilty about being late and missing his call. I feared he might think I was spending too much time out of the office. Louise got him on the phone and when he answered I rushed into my defense, still standing at my desk.

"Sorry I missed your call, Gary. I was attending a luncheon meeting at the university."

"Oh?"

"Yeah. I've really been busy."

"Too busy?" he said.

Something about the way he said that told me to be careful of my answer.

"Never too busy, Gary."

"Too busy to become a regional vice president?"

I was stunned. "Regional vice president?" I said, idiotically, as if I had not understood his words.

"Yeah. These crazy people at Corporate have asked me to become president of the Community Newspaper Division."

"That's great, Gary. Congratulations."

"Thanks. So, I thought maybe you might like to become one of my regional vice presidents."

For a second I was speechless. I eased into my chair and, repeating myself, said "Gary, that would be great. Just great."

Gannett had grown so large with so many newspapers of different sizes it had reorganized into two newspaper divisions—one for metro newspapers and one for community newspapers, of which there were far more. The community division was further broken down into geographic regions, each headed by a president and at least one vice president, in some cases two. Now there had been a restructuring. John Curley had moved up to Chief Operating Officer of all of Gannett and Watson was moving up to become president of Gannett's community newspapers.

Huntington had been part of Gannett Central. Now it would become part of Gannett East. I would be one of the region's vice presidents in addition to my duties as editor and publisher. The properties for which I would be responsible, each with its own publisher and management team, were four dailies in Ohio—Chillicothe, Marietta, Fremont and Port Clinton—a daily and two weeklies in

Tarentum/New Kensington, Pa., and my own operation in Huntington.

A retreat was scheduled near the Corporate offices to meet with our regional presidents. The newly appointed president of Gannett East was Bob Collins, now publisher in Camden, N. J. I knew Collins from his days as managing editor in Chambersburg, Pa., under then-publisher Hal Burdick before Burdick came to Huntington. My wife and I had sat with Collins during a dinner in Huntington some years before. Now he was my boss. I felt confident about that, remembering him as a fellow editor. I did not know of his reputation as a cut-and-burn executive.

That did not take long to discover at the retreat. After hearing from top corporate executives about the new structure and the responsibility we all shared in making the company ever more profitable, we broke into regional meetings. Mike Coleman, another fellow editor turned publisher and now also a new regional vice president, and I walked to the regional meeting together, wondering what we would hear from our new leader.

We were wearing sweaters and dress pants as we entered the room and I was struck by the way Collins was dressed: jeans, boots, a leather jacket, a gold i.d. bracelet on his wrist and a gold chain around his neck.

He started right in. We were going to be the best blankety-blank region in the whole blankin' company, he said. We would be reporting to him and we could forget all those other blanket-blanks in their corporate offices. We would all make our blankin' budget plans or else. When revenues didn't come in, we would quickly cut the blankin' costs to achieve the expected bottom line. He knew plenty about cutting costs and would be there to help. He would teach each of us "The Drill" and then we could take it into all our properties. It was all about finding unnecessary expenditures and cutting costs and he guaranteed results. After all, it was his drill, borrowed and improved upon from a veteran Gannett publisher.

I had never heard so many four-letter words. Nor had I expected to see a Gannett publisher— least of all my boss—in jeans, boots, leather jacket and gold chains. When Coleman and I left the meeting to walk back to our rooms, he said, "What do you think?"

"Not quite what I expected," I said. "He sounds pretty tough."

"Yeah, you're right," said Coleman. "Guess we'll see."

My first action as regional vice president would be to visit all my properties and talk with my publishers. I knew three of them and considered them to be friends. Dick Holtz, publisher in Marietta, had called the day my promotion to vice president was announced and said, "Hello, Boss." We both laughed because Holtz had been classified manager in Huntington when I was managing editor and we had fought as editors and advertising managers do. He had lived only a few houses from my house and when snow kept me from getting up my steep driveway, he would give me a ride to work. Jim Daubel, publisher in Fremont and Port Clinton, was an old friend from APME. And Peter Horvitz, publisher in Chillicothe, had worked with me on that infamous vending machine tour of Los Angeles and had been one of my "classmates" at a special high-intensity seminar in Houston when we both first became publishers. I liked them all personally and reminded myself that I should not let that get in the way of being their boss.

I could reach Chillicothe and Marietta easily by car. Tarentum and Fremont were farther, and Port Clinton sat on the shores of Lake Erie. So, I first went to see Peter Horvitz in Chillicothe.

The newspaper was located in a small old building which had once served as the Capitol of the state of Ohio. One really turned back the calendar when walking through the front doors. But there was a certain charm to the place.

Horvitz knew far more about financial matters than I (I discovered this when we were together at the seminar) and I admitted this to him during my visit. But, I said, it was my responsibility to help him however I could so that his property did, financially at least, what was expected by Corporate. A member of an old Ohio newspaper family, Horvitz understood perfectly without my saying much at all. He gave me a good tour of the building and I returned to Huntington feeling good about his being there. It appeared that Chillicothe was in good hands.

I paid a similar visit to Marietta and my old

colleague Holtz. The newspaper was located in a reasonably new building erected in what appeared to be a cow pasture outside town. I could have said it was built on nice, rolling, green land, but the fact is that there were cows mulling about. Not what I expected. But my visit was otherwise similar to that in Chillicothe: discussion about problems the operation might be facing, emphasizing the importance of getting the job done despite them, offering to help, and getting a tour of the building. We did not walk around the cow pasture,

Next I visited Tarentum, flying into Pittsburgh where I was met by Tom Bookstaver, the publisher. He was a former controller and this was our first meeting. He was noticeably nervous, which made for an awkward meeting, and I felt bad for him and tried to put him at ease while pretending not to notice. Tarentum, a few miles north of Pittsburgh, was a larger and more complex operation than my other regional properties. In addition to publishing the daily paper, it also produced two weeklies, boasted a sizeable commercial printing operation, and as if that were not enough was also an important print site (because of its excellent presses) for USA TODAY. We talked a long time and Bookstaver explained the various operations as well as his needs and concerns. Again, we toured the plant, drove around the region, and at the end of the day I flew back to Huntington.

Before I could make another trip there was another meeting at Corporate. Collins was quick to grill me on what I had done and had not yet done. I reported on my trips to Tarentum, Chillicothe and Marietta and said I had yet to get to Fremont and Port Clinton. He was obviously upset about something. It turned out that he had once been in Tarentum himself and knew all about that operation. He was bothered that I had spent only a day or less in my visits, especially Tarentum. "You didn't even stay overnight," he said.

He would make the Freemont trip with me, he said, and do "The Drill" and I would quickly learn what I should be doing during visits to my properties.

I returned home wondering just what "The Drill" was all about. As Collins said, I would find out.

We met in Fremont and went directly to the newspaper building where Daubel was waiting. We exchanged greetings and before we could get down to business, an editor burst into the room to inform us that the Challenger space vehicle had just exploded in the sky. We quickly turned on television, watching and listening, and then Daubel excused himself to check the newsroom on how the story was being handled. The Fremont paper was an afternoon paper and most of it had been wrapped up for that day's publication. We followed him into the newsroom and then the composing room where Collins looked over an editor's shoulder to see what was being done to page one. Apparently the editor thought it sufficient to add a bulletin on the Challenger disaster near the top of the nearly completed front page and leave the rest as is.

Collins shook his head. "My man," he said, "I'm about to tear up your front page." He took charge, ordering the editor to get a wire photo of the disaster and prepare a full AP story and place them at the top of the page with a huge headline, taking up the entire page above the fold. All were obvious and appropriate actions that any good editor would have taken. But I was surprised that Collins had barged in and taken over when the newspaper's publisher and editor were there. If he had not, Daubel may have himself. But we will never know.

Finally, the new page one reporting one of the year's biggest stories was done and we moved on to the conference room and "The drill."

Collins spread out monthly reports and financial statements as well as the Fremont budget. He asked that Daubel summon his controller and that he bring with him expense accounts, check requisitions, pay receipts, and bills. One by one he went through them.

"What are these monthly dues to a yacht club?" He asked Daubel. "You own a yacht?"

"No," Daubel said. "That's a private club on the water. Some people do keep their boats there, but it's sort of like a dining club, a place where you meet and entertain advertisers and customers."

"Here's another one to another yacht club. You belong to two of these things?"

"That's right."

"Get rid of one of them." He tossed the statements toward Daubel.

He continued through the expenses, frequently

commenting, "You need this? Get rid of it. How much does that save us?"

He asked   that other department heads be brought in one at a time. He grilled the advertising director on his numbers.   Why are we down in classified? Why are we missing in retail? What kind of fix are you putting in to get these revenues up where they're supposed to be? Why are the average rates so screwed up?   Way below your plan. Explain.

Average rate—the average dollar received for each advertising inch sold-- is the most fluctuating and consequently least predictable number one deals with in advertising in that it depends on so many factors--frequency, advertiser contracts, discounts. The good ad director watches the average rate and knows why it is where it is and can explain. Fortunately, this one could and did.

Then it was time to examine advertising expenses. What's the split of salary vs. commission for your sales people?   How many, if any, are on total commission?   Do you pay bonuses if they're over goal?   Where do you stand on payroll?   How many vacancies on your staff? And on and on.

An eye opener for me took place when the circulation director appeared. Before he entered the room, Collins told us his opinion about circulation directors: They all lie. They're the worst of the lot. They hide things. You can never trust their numbers.

Then he dug in. Tell me about your subsidies. Why does this guy get this subsidy and this other guy get a bigger subsidy? What, he's gotta drive up a mountain or something? How much per paper are you paying? How many returns are you averaging each day? That is a huge factor in your newsprint waste number. Cut back on returns.

Returns—left-over copies from vending machines and another difficult number to know. The perfect vending machine always has one copy left at the end of the day. But such perfection is not often achieved. If the machine is empty, you are concerned that you missed sales. If several copies are left, you worry over the amount of newsprint waste.

Newsprint waste—the key words for the production director when he entered. Where are you getting your newsprjnt? What are you paying per ton? What's the percentage of news to advertising, or do you know? How many pages are you producing each day? How many makeovers? How much waste is going on in your reel room (where the giant spools of newsprint are kept). Are you checking regularly to see if any damage is being inflicted there? Do you even know what your waste number is? That's too high. What are you doing to fix it? Reduce it by five percent.

And finally, there was the editor. Again, questions of newshole came up. Why are you averaging more news columns per day than your budget calls for? Cut that back by six columns a day. Why so many part-time hours here? Why so much overtime being paid to your reporters? We want no overtime in the newsroom. Corporate has preached that and now I am telling you. No overtime in the newsroom.

Now, there is a Catch 22 for you, forced upon every newsroom in the country by ridiculous federal government regulations and classifications. For whatever reason, reporters were classified as "non-professional" and were therefore "non-exempt" from federal wage and hour laws. They had to work strict forty-hour weeks and be paid overtime for any hour beyond that. Oddly, ad sales people were "professional" and exempt. Go figure, as they say.

So here was Collins, and Corporate, saying no overtime pay in the newsroom. Think about it. If a reporter happened to be working on a big story and his forty hours were up, he had either to quit and go home or be paid overtime. But if Corporate said no overtime, what do you do? Shut off his computer and order him out of the building? (I know of one editor who did just that). There was a small loophole. Columnists and "special reporters" working on their own without assignment were exempt. The temptation was to call everyone a special reporter, but how can an editor function without giving assignments to reporters?

Many editors allowed what they called "comp" or "compensatory" time. Whatever extra time a reporter worked over forty hours could be used as time off later. Many liked that because it could be used for long weekends or added vacation. But Corporate Human Resources ruled that "there is no such thing as compensatory time" and no matter what the pay period was, the rule applied to one forty-hour week with no carryover.

Having dealt with this problem as both an editor and a publisher, I still consider it absurd. No good reporter wants to quit and go home. Every one wants to finish a story, and most want to work without being encumbered by a forty-hour work week and a limit on how much time they can spend on the job. Which is not to say editors and publishers should be able to work reporters for long hours without pay. They should be paid for their work, period. But good sense should prevail. Putting these restrictions in the hands of a cost-cutting company or, worse, a tough regional officer can produce a real mess.

In any event, Bob Collins spent much of the session tossing statements this way and that, making notes, keeping track, and at the end of the day, with the help of the controller present, totaled everything and announced that he had "found" another x-thousands of dollars. And that was "The Drill."

Next Collins came to Huntington to perform The Drill on my newspaper. I must admit it was effective and I personally learned a great deal about my own operation, although it was pretty tough on at least one of my department heads. I too came to use The Drill during several of my regional visits-- but without the badgering and cussing.

It was interesting and sometimes exasperating to work for Collins. He would call and say "What the hell is that s.o.b up to now?"

I would reply, "Which s.o.b., Bobby?"

"Oh, you know, that #%&$# over there in... what's his name? His #$%$# numbers are way

338

down. Fix it."

He would frequently respond with "Yo!" when called. One day when he called me I answered "Yo!"

"'Yo'?" he said, and then started to laugh. "Where the hell did you get that?"

Another time he called just I was walking into the office and I took the call standing up.

"Are you sitting down?" he said.

"No. I'm standing up," I said.

"What do you mean, you're standing up?"

"I always stand up when you call, Bobby," I said.

"Ah, you #%&%," he said, laughing.

Before it sounds as if I am demonizing Bobby Collins, let me say that I learned a great deal from him, not only the methods used in The Drill, but other questions to ask and what to look for. I also learned that beneath that tough New Jersey exterior existed a quite decent man.

35
A TIME OF REFLECTION

A lot happened in 1985. In addition to becoming a Gannett regional vice president, I turned the magic age of fifty. Sandy said it was a special birthday and we should celebrate in some manner. After some thought, we decided to invite a few people who had been a special part of our lives to Guyan Golf and Country Club for dinner. It was one of the best ideas I ever had.

For starters there was Ernie Salvatore, the man who had hired me to be his part-time sports assistant when I was all of eighteen years of age, and who taught me more about newspapering than just about anyone. He was now the sports columnist for The Herald-Dispatch and we were closer friends than ever. There was Estelle "Bill" Belanger, who had been the Sunday city editor and columnist when Sandy and I were newly married. Over the years she had remained a very close friend with whom we had shared many things, above all our mutual interest in the arts. Now she was the arts and culture critic for the newspaper.

It occurs to me that while in the beginning I was "the kid" to Ernie and a budding young writer to Bill, as the years went by I became their boss. But that never got in the way of our relationship—so far as I know.

We also invited Jose and Amy Ricard, who had become recent close friends. Jose was an outstanding doctor in town who had escaped Cuba to come to this country many years before. While in Cuba, he had once treated Ernest Hemingway. And there was Keith Newman, family friend for twenty-five years and godfather to both our sons, Chris and Joel. He had believed more in my newspaper future than I myself. When I was no more than a copy editor on the rim of the afternoon newspaper, he told Sandy that "Don will run these newspapers some day." That was so absurd to me it actually irritated me. What he does not understand, I told her, is that publishers come from the business side, not the news side. Thankfully, I was wrong.

So I turned fifty with these past and present friends and Salvatore brought me a baseball bat in recognition of my having once set a high school batting record before he hired me. The bat was a fun and prized gift and I have it still. It was a special evening, as I had hoped it would be.

But as I had learned, one never knows what is out there.

Only a month later, we lost both our fathers, only two weeks apart—Sandy's father to a heart attack, my father to a blood clot following severe emphazema. First Sandy's father, and then mine—

two funerals, only days apart. In less than two weeks my sons had lost both their grandfathers.

And I had lost my father, the first person to put a newspaper in my hands, to explain the statistics on the sports pages, to point out the columnists. This man who had taught me how to bunt, who had warned me against trying to throw curve balls when I was young because "you'll throw your arm away," who had seen almost every football, basketball and baseball game I ever played, who was there when I committed three errors in one inning, when I scored my only touchdown in high school, when I won a basketball game by sinking two free throws with seconds on the clock, who had celebrated when I became a real sportswriter at eighteen and with every promotion I received after, who asked me each week, "What's new at the office?" and when I told him would respond, "What else is new at the office." A simple man who loved his family. A good man. Gone.

I suddenly felt much older. Maybe it was turning fifty. Maybe it was the deaths of our two fathers. Maybe it had something to do with my being publisher and being named a regional vice president and my assuming I had peaked in my career. And I wondered whether I would be able to last with Gannett another fifteen years until retirement.

For all sorts of reasons, it was a time of reflection. I had not become the writer of novels and short stories I had once wanted to be. I had published no books, and that was a disappointment.

But that was a small thing, I told myself. I had done very well.

It was not long after that I received a visit from the head of a small regional publishing house called Jalamap Publications. He said he wanted to publish a collection of my newspaper columns in book form. The name "Hatfield" should sell in West Virginia, he said. And given that I had a following of sorts of my columns, he felt it all made sense. He could not offer me an advance at this point, he said; but he would provide royalties once the book came out.

I felt like closing the door so he could not get away. Publish a book of mine? When do we start?

He planned to include about fifty columns that I would choose. That's just about the limit of pages he could afford, he said. Fine by me. I would go through all my past columns and pick out the best.

I had been writing personal columns for many years and had clips of some fifteen hundred or so. I went through every one. What surprised me was that the easiest ones to toss out were those that had seemed so important and significant at the time of writing. What stayed were columns that were more personal, the "Erma Bombeck"-like columns of which readers had said, "That's the way it is at our house" or "I wish I had written that." Most of those that were kept were fun and upbeat, though several were more serious, often written about individuals who had died ("your obit columns," C. T. Mitchell once called them).

Once I had selected the columns to be used, the

publisher and I argued over a title. I wanted to call the book "Cleaning Out the Attic." But the publisher wanted my name in the title. He won out and the title became "Don Hatfield Cleans Out His Attic." Next he set up a cover photograph which showed me at a typewriter rather than a computer. The book would come out in late December, 1985, just before the start of the new year. I would have a book after all--without leaving my newspaper career. I felt very fortunate.

36
WESTWARD HO

I entered 1986 determined to do a good job as publisher, editor and regional vice president in Huntington and hoped I would not screw it all up. I attended Corporate meetings, listened to Bob Collins's rantings about my properties not being on plan, kept in touch with them all, met daily with my managing editor and my editorial page editor, read editorials, checked news stories the editors thought I should know about before publication, met with members of my Operating Group, watched revenues and expenses and the ever-precious bottom line, met often w ith my advertising director, Dwight McKenzie, whose monumental task was to bring in the revenues that would keep the ship afloat, even in Rust Belt waters. And who, one day, had something to say to me personally.

He said point blank that I had changed since becoming a regional vice president, and not for the better. In fact, he said, he had never seen such a change in a person. He realized that in now reporting to Bob Collins and in being responsible for several other newspapers I was under more pressure than before. But I wasn't as easy to get along with, he said, and it created more pressure on himself and other members of the Operating group as well as on his sales staff.

I heard him loud and clear and thanked him for being so frank. He was right. I would do better. I was grateful I had an ad director who felt he could say such things to his publisher.

One afternoon in late summer Louise said that two employeees from our press room wanted to talk with me. It was contract time, she said.

The pressman's union was the only union we still had in the building. The composing room union had decertified itself during Buddy Hayden's days as publisher. I had not heard a word from the one remaining union since becoming publisher, although I had known our press room employees for years.

I recalled that some time ago union negotiations had been a big deal. They had been held off-site, handled by teams of lawyers and had lasted for months. But that was in the past. What should I do? Call Corporate? Of course. But, I decided, not just yet. First I would listen to what my press room friends had to say.

The two entered my office and sat in chairs in front of my desk. I knew them both, one better than the other. His name was Freddie. As an editor, I had been in his press room many times, watched the huge webs being pulled through the aging rollers, waited as the start button was pushed and the old press slowly chugged into operation, and checked early papers as they came off. I knew Freddie as a dependable, hard-working pressman. Now he was sitting in my office facing me. He was the first to speak.

He said "the boys" were happy that I, a "local boy," had become publisher. They would like it very much if I would take part personally in the negotiations, he said. In fact, they would like it especially if they could just negotiate with me and not have to bring representatives from the national union and have me bring in lawyers or Gannett Corporate types on our side.

Of course you would, I thought, warning myself not be taken in by this. More than likely they wanted to take advantage of my being a newsroom guy who had never been involved in labor negotiations.

On the other hand, Freddie seemed very sincere, and I found myself nodding.

"I'd like that too, Freddie. Let's see if we can make this work."

He said he would get back to "the boys" and see what they had in mind.

The contract now expiring had called for a three percent increase each year for three years. I figured they would be satisfied with the same this time.

On his next visit, he laid it out. "What the boys are looking for," he said, "is three, three and three. Three percent increase each year for three years. That's what we've had and they'll be satisfied with that."

Just as I had expected. But things were different this time around.

"In this economy?" I said. "That's more than the cost of living. It's less than two percent. And in this part of the world, the Rust Belt? You know that's not going to fly, Freddie. Look, we can go back and forth on this thing and make it last the rest of the year. Or I can tell you right now what I can do and we can settle the whole thing."

He looked at his partner, and then at me. "What did you have in mind?"

"Two, two and two."

He shook his head and stood. "I'll take it to the boys. And I'll have to tell the union."

"There's one other thing."

He sat back down.

"I want the right to give some of you more if I so choose."

We both knew what that meant. Merit pay. Unacceptable to unions everywhere.. He shook his head as if he had not heard me correctly.

"Freddie, I've known you for years. I've been in the press room at all hours, as an editor and now as publisher. I've watched you work your tail off. And I've seen others loafing over in the corner, doing nothing. Don't you deserve more than they do?"

He smiled and shook his head again. "Now, Don, you know we can't do that."

"Why not? You've got some very hard workers

in the press room. And you've got a couple who don't carry their weight. Right?"

He shifted uncomfortably in the chair but said nothing.

"You know I'm right. I'll make it two, two and two for everyone in the press room. But give me the right to make it greater than that for some of you."

I knew I was walking on new ground here. I hoped they would chalk it up to my ignorance about labor negotiations. I charged ahead.

"Don't think of it as merit pay. Everybody gets the same base increase. Think of it as a publisher's right to do more for those he thinks deserve it."

"I'll take it back to the boys," he said. "But I don't think they're going to go for it."

"I'm sure some of them won't," I said. "But some might. See what you can do."

A week later Freddie made another appointment. He came in smiling.

"Two, two and two," he said. "And you have the right to make it more."

"Freddie, I thank you more than I can say," I said.

"The boys wanted you to know they're doing this for you."

I knew better than that. But I said, "Tell the boys I appreciate that."

"I'll have to notify the regional leadership."

"And I'll have to get approval from Corporate. But I don't think that will be a problem."

I knew two percent would be acceptable, and I expected Corporate to jump at the chance to get a merit pay clause accepted, even though we would not call it that.

"I'll have it drawn up and give it to you," I said. "We've got some time. The present contract doesn't expire for a while."

But a surprising thing happened. After having the contract drawn up and giving copies to Freddie I received a call from Gary Watson. It came on a Monday.

"What are you doing tomorrow?" he said.

"Nothing special. Why?"

"Thought maybe you'd like to come over and see us," he said, meaning a visit to Corporate. "Thought maybe we could talk."

"Sure, I can do that. What did you want to talk about?"

"Well, you're probably tired of doing the same stuff over and over in Huntington. I thought maybe you might be ready for a new challenge."

Whenever representatives from Corporate had approached me over the years about moving elsewhere, I had always explained that for family reasons I preferred to remain in Huntington and, if possible, move up here. We had two sons, they had four grandparents nearby, and it was a good place to live, for our kids and for us. But by now, our oldest son Chris had been living in Boston for a few years and our youngest son, Joel, had just graduated from high school and was moving there to live with his brother and go to college. Both my father and Sandy's father had died just the year before. Although our mothers were still here as well as one

350

of Sandy's sisters and her husband, we no longer faced quite the same barriers in leaving--at least in my eyes. I had worked for the Huntington papers all my life and I had wondered whether I would ever leave and have a different kind of experience in another part of the country. I was publisher and regional VP and there was no higher job in Huntington. I had just turned fifty-one and wasn't sure what the future held.

"I just might," I said.

"Good. Maybe we can do some business while you're here. See you tomorrow."

I had Louise schedule a round trip to Washington the next day, and that evening told Sandy the news.

"What do you think they want?"

"I think they might want me to move to another paper."

"They didn't say where?"

"No. Not yet."

"Well, how do you feel about this?"

And I told her. Our sons are now in Boston. I have never worked anywhere else. I'm fifty-one. Before it's too late, I think I'd like to try it. "Depending on where it is, of course," I was quick to add.

As always, she understood. But she clearly was concerned. .

"I won't agree to anything before talking with you," I said.

"Of course," she said.

On the plane trip to Washington, I wondered

what Watson might have in mind. It occurred to me that Hal Burdick was expected to retire soon as publisher in El Paso. I had replaced him in Huntington. Would they want me to replace him again in El Paso? I hoped that was not the designated assignment. I doubted Sandy would go for that.

As soon as we landed I took a cab to the Twin Towers, one housing Gannett's Corporate offices, the other USA TODAY. Watson was waiting. He wasted no time as I sat in a chair in front of his desk.

"Gerald Garcia is stepping down in Tucson," he said. "He's leaving Gannett and going to another company. We thought you might be a good choice to take his place. You've done about all you can do in Huntington."

Tucson? I was so relieved I almost said "Yes!" on the spot.

Garcia was publisher of the Tucson Citizen and a regional vice president in Gannett West. The Tucson Citizen was known as one of the better newspapers in Gannett. It was much larger than my newspaper, and Tucson, Arizona was many times larger than Huntington, West Virginia. It would be quite a promotion. And Watson was offering me the job.

But I had promised Sandy I would not agree to anything without first discussing it with her, and so I listened.

Watson went on describing the situation. The Citizen was an afternoon newspaper in a Joint

Operating Agency, in partnership with the Pulitzer Publishing Company which published the morning Arizona Daily Star. Gannett and Pulitzer each owned fifty percent of the agency, known as Tucson Newspapers Inc. A general manager handled the agency, reporting to the two publishers. Regarding regional responsibilities, I would be in charge of the El Paso Times, the Santa Fe New Mexican, and a USA Today print and distribution center in Chandler, Arizona, just outside Phoenix.

Was I interested?

"Definitely,' I said. "It's a great opportunity and I'm grateful. But I will have to talk it over with Sandy."

"Of course. I wouldn't expect it any other way."

I had promised to phone her as soon as I knew something. I told Watson I needed to do that, and he understood, suggesting I use a phone in an outer office.

She answered almost immediately. "Did they offer you another job?"

"Yes."

"Where is it?"

"Tucson."

"Tucson, Arizona?"

"That's right."

"That is a long way."

"I know."

"What did you tell them?"

"That I would come home and discuss it with you and get back to them."

"Well, I thank you for that. How do you feel about it?"

I hesitated. How did I feel? Excited. Thrilled. Surprised. Fortunate. But I said, "We can talk about it when I get home. I'm flying out this afternoon."

When I returned to Watson's office, he was talking on the phone to Sue Clark-Jackson, the president of Gannett West. She would be my new boss. I had been in many Corporate group meetings with her but she wasn't quite sure who I was. She called me "Dan," and Watson interrupted to say, "It's Don."

She talked a little about Gannett West and the various properties it included. In addition to being the regional president, she was also president and publisher of the Reno newspaper. Her region included newspapers in Hawaii and Guam, California, Oregon, Nevada, Texas, New Mexico, and Arizona. She spoke of the properties for which I would be responsible—El Paso, Santa Fe, Tucson, and the USA Today site near Phoenix.

Watson interrupted again to say I would be talking with Sandy and getting back to them. Clark-Jackson said she would be pleased to have me and looked forward to my answer.

Watson resumed talking about Tucson, both the property and the city. The publisher of our partner newspaper was Michael Pulitzer, CEO of all of Pulitzer. But although as publisher of the Arizona Daily Star he once had maintained a residence in the Tucson area, he now lived in St. Louis where

Pulitzer published the Post-Dispatch and had its corporate offices. He was represented in Tucson on a daily basis by Emil Rould, controller of the Star, but came to Tucson for board meetings. The board was made up of only four members—Pulitzer, Rould, Clark-Jackson and, if I accepted the job, myself. Chairmanship of the board rotated between the two publishers. Michael Pulitzer was now chair but I would be in the coming year.

Tucson Newspapers Inc., the agency, handled only the business operations—advertising, circulation, marketing, production and systems, finance and accounting. It had nothing to do with the two newspapers themselves, or newsroom operations and expenses which existed outside the agency. The agency's general manager, Tom Jackson, reported to the two publishers, Michael Pulitzer (or, in his absence, Rould) and me.

As for the city, Watson said, "It's big and it's growing. I haven't been in this job long enough to know much about it. I'm not sure what they even wear out there, cowboy hats or ties."

I asked if he had any literature on the city that I might peruse on my return flight. He looked around and came up with a couple of copies of the Tucson Citizen and asked his secretary if she could find additional materials. Fortunately, she did.

When he had finished, I thanked him again for having confidence in me to do the job there and said I would call him first thing in the morning. He thanked me for coming "on such short notice."

I thought about that on my return flight. How

quickly things—entire lives—can change. On Monday morning I had no idea that twenty-four hours later I would be offered the publisher's job in Tucson, Arizona. I could not have imagined leaving Huntington and going west. Somewhere in Gannett East or in the Midwest would have been my guess. But Tucson? Neither Sandy nor I had ever been there. We had been to Phoenix for an APME convention some years before. But never Tucson. I would have to find out all I could about the town.

My quick reading told me that Tucson was the home of the University of Arizona, a major research university of more than thirty-thousand students and a member (which I already knew) of the Pac 10 athletic conference. It also revealed to me that Tucson was one of only twelve cities in the country that offered the "big five" professional organizations in the arts—symphony, theater, opera, ballet and museums. This would be welcome information for Sandy. She had told me more than once that she could never live in a town without a university. This city had one of the best. And it was rich in the arts. My selling job might be a little easier.

She would be leaving her mother and sister and her work with the French Department at Marshall University where she had just helped found a graduate exchange program with a university in France. She would be leaving her friends and moving to a city she had never seen and where she knew no one. She would be moving much farther away from our two sons in Boston and our disabled daughter now in an institution in West Virginia. And she would be leaving a turn-of-the-century home which she loved.

And, just three weeks before, we had realized a dream by buying a vacation cottage in Cape Cod. Arizona was a long, long way from Cape Cod.

Part of me knew it was unfair to ask her to make such a move. Another part of me believed— hoped—it would turn out to be good for her too. We would have more money, live better, meet new people, do new things, broaden ourselves.

I said all this to her, and trying not to sound too excited, told her that I really wanted to accept the job and would forever be grateful if she would agree. I would need her more than ever, I said. In the end she said, "Well, if this is what you want."

The next morning I called Watson. "You've got yourself a deal," I said.

"That's good to hear," he said.

"When do you want me there?"

"Garcia is leaving Thursday. We wanted you to be there then. But that's tomorrow. So you can make it Sunday."

"This Sunday?"

"Yes. And don't tell anyone."

He said he would get back to me with details. But I was thinking that I had worked in this building for thirty-three years and made a lot of friends in that time. I was thinking about my Operating Group and how loyal each director had been. How could I just leave and say nothing? "Don't tell anyone"-- the Gannett way. We're a big public company. We can't let anything out until it's time. That was the philosophy. But I had to say something.

"Gary, I can't just walk out on these people without telling them," I said. "At least, not my Operating Group."

He was silent for a moment, and then said, "Okay, you can tell them this weekend. But not before."

It was Wednesday. I had this day and two more to pack up thirty-three years, to close out my work here, to get ready to leave this special place which had been my only place of work since I was eighteen.Less than three days to wrap up everything in the publisher's office.

I thought then about the negotiations with the pressman's union, and summoned Freddie. He looked surprised when he came into the room.

"Freddie. Something has come up. I'm sorry but I absolutely must have that signed contract in my hands by the end of the day Friday."

"Friday? Why?"

"Trust me. Got to."

"I thought we had more time."

"I know. But we don't."

"Okay. I'll see what I can do."

I stood in the middle of my office and looked around. Three days to pack up and get out. I would need help. I asked Louise to come in, and I violated Watson's non-disclosure order.

"I'm leaving," I said. "I need your help."

In no time she had boxes, packing tape and marking pens and was emptying file cabinets and drawers. She would leave books on the shelves and paintings and photographs on the walls until late Friday so that no one would notice. She would say nothing. She had been through this before. She was great.

Watson called later to say that a room had been reserved for me in a hotel in Tucson near both the airport and the Tucson Newspapers complex. On Monday morning I would be met by Gerald Garcia and Sue Clark-Jackson and taken to the newspaper. My publishers in El Paso and Santa Fe and my general manager in the USA Today office would be there to meet with me. I would stay the week in Tucson and then could come back to Huntington to make arrangements for selling our house and other such matters.

I told Watson I would be taking Sandy on this trip. That seemed to surprise him, although knowing me it shouldn't have. "Okay," he said.

I shared all this with Sandy that evening.

"This weekend? You mean *this weekend?*"

"Yes. And we can't tell anyone until it's announced Monday morning when we're there. I mean, we'll tell our mothers and you can tell your sister, but wait until Friday, and tell them not to tell anyone else."

She looked around. "We've got three days."

"Yes."

Coincidentally, our oldest son, Chris, had just arrived from Boston for a brief visit. He came into the kitchen as we were talking and I told him the news.

"I think it's great," he said. He slapped me on the back and then disappeared down the cellar steps, returning with two bottles of champagne. "Let's celebrate."

On Friday I received the signed pressman's contract from Freddie. Louise began to pack up some of the books and paintings, and at the end of the day I summoned members of my Operating Group. Ironically, two of them were also leaving. Dwight McKenzie, my loyal ad director, was moving on for a bigger job in Missouri. Bruce Cannady, my controller and good friend, was on his way to the Northwest. And now I was going.

They did not seem surprised when I said I was being transferred to another Gannett property. I could not say where. The announcement would be made Monday morning, and a new publisher for Huntington would be introduced at that time. I could not tell them who that would be. But I knew, and I felt good about it. My successor would be Dan Martin, now publisher of Gannett's Port Huron, Mich. newspaper and, coincidentally, a native of West Virginia and a graduate of Marshall. I asked them not to tell anyone until Monday. I thanked them for their good work for me and told them I would miss them. I was congratulated and given best wishes, and a couple thanked me for what I had done for them. And then it was over and I left my Huntington office for the last time.

That night I told Sandy again how much I appreciated her sacrifice. I added: "I promise you we'll be there two to four years max. And then we'll come back east."

    We stayed for twenty-two years.

37
TUCSON

We flew to Tucson Sunday morning armed with information about the city. I read aloud to my wife with much enthusiasm as we flew over the country.

"The University of Arizona—more than thirty-thousand students and a member of the Pac-10, with such schools as UCLA, Southern Cal, Stanford and Cal. The Arizona Theater Company, Arizona Opera Company, Arizona Ballet Company, the Tucson Symphony--all professional companies. Two art museums---the Tucson Museum of Art and the University of Arizona Museum of Art. The theater company and the opera company are headquartered in Tucson but are shared by Tucson and Phoenix. The ballet company got its start in Tucson but is now headquartered in Phoenix. However, like the others it performs in both cities. Sounds great, doesn't it?"

"Sounds good," Sandy said. 'We'll see."

"And the University has an Artists Series that brings in all kinds of things," I continued. "And this magazine makes it seem as if there's an art gallery on practically every corner."

She went back to her book and I shut up for a while. The past few days had been trying without a doubt. It had been difficult and emotional telling our mothers and Sandy's sister that we were leaving. Even the night before had been awkward as we attended a Marshall home football game. The stadium was only a few blocks from our home and friends came by both before and after the game. I had taken Dr. Jose Ricard into the living room and privately told him we were moving away from Huntington in literally a matter of hours. We had become so close that he teared up and promised that he and Amy would be among the first to visit us in Arizona.

And now we were on the plane flying over mountain ranges surrounding the city of Tucson, Arizona and Sandy was looking out her window and saying, "It all looks so brown."

"Lots of mountains," I said. "I didn't realize there were so many and that they were so high."

"And so brown," she said.

We disembarked and walked through the airport terminal, so much bigger and busier than that in Huntington. We retrieved our luggage and walked outside to grab a cab to the hotel where reservations had been made for us. It was September and the sun was still hot and I looked for a string of cabs waiting at the curb as they did in large airports in the East but found none. Then I spotted several parked at some distance from the terminal entrance where we now stood. I suggested we take our luggage and go to them since it appeared they were not coming to us.

I asked the first cabbie if he would take us to the Holiday Inn Holidome. He refused, saying it was too close and he would wait on a larger fare. I had never been told that by a cab driver at an airport. I went to two more cabs before a driver agreed to take us there. "But it will cost you twenty-five bucks."

"But it's very close, isn't it?"

"That's what I'll be giving up if I leave my slot in line. Take it leave it."

We took it and in less than five minutes pulled up to the Holiday Inn Holidome. It sat by itself in what seemed to be a large overgrown lot. We looked around, at the mountains in the distance, at the road we had just left, at scrubby buildings some yards away. A garden spot it was not. I could feel Sandy's depression.

We registered and were taken to our room, a small Seventies-style Holiday Inn room. I was beginning to be as depressed as she was. I suggested we go to the bar before unpacking.

I ordered a beer and then another and then I looked at her and said simply, "Want to go back home?"

"Yes!" she said. "Can we?"

No, we could not. Everything had been set in motion. My replacement in Huntington would no doubt already be there just as I was already in Tucson.

"Not really," I said. "It will get better."

It was unfortunate that we were not met by someone, and that plans called for us to come to this airport hotel away from the city. We were given the worst possible first impression of Greater Tucson.

We had dinner in the hotel restaurant and returned to our room to unpack and then go to bed. Our bodies were, after all, in a different time zone, and we had risen early that morning to make our flight. But I did not sleep. I knew that the following day would be a big one, one of the biggest in my life. I knew that Sandy was very disappointed in what she had seen thus far and was already regretting that she had agreed to this move. Well, I told myself, things often look better in the morning.

And so they did. We dressed and went to the hotel coffee shop to meet Sue Clark-Jackson and Gerald Garcia. Sue arrived soon and welcomed us to Tucson and I introduced Sandy to her. We chatted briefly and she said Garcia would join us soon. He doesn't yet know who his replacement is, she said.

"Really?" I said. Of course, this was Gannett.

In a matter of minutes I could see him walking down the hall toward the coffee shop. He entered, spotted Clark-Jackson, and then saw me. He was obviously surprised. No doubt he had wondered who would succeed him and he was stunned to see this publisher from Huntington, West Virginia and Gannett East sitting there. I introduced Sandy and we talked briefly before climbing into his car, a Toyota Cressida, and heading for the newspaper where the announcement would be made.

He had chosen this hotel for us because it was close to the airport and only a few blocks from the newspaper building, he said. "It's a sizeable complex. The Citizen on one side and the Star on the other and TNI in between. All on a big piece of land. You've actually got two offices. One has been used for storage for a while because a former publisher moved to an office in the newsroom. It's a much better office and I had been planning to move into it before deciding to leave. So you'll have your choice."

Okay, I thought. We shall see.

The Tucson Newspapers property loomed before us, and was indeed impressive. A contemporary concrete structure that appeared to be one-level, with small angled windows and modern angled rooflines, and a courtyard with an iron gate in front. The Citizen wing sat to the left of the courtyard, the Star to the right, the agency operations in the center and beneath the Star newsroom, whose wing was actually multi-level. We pulled into the driveway at left, facing another large iron gate. Garcia punched in a code and we entered a private parking lot for Citizen employees, the gate clanging ominously behind us.

"We'll go in the back entrance," Garcia said. He then handed me the car keys, adding, "It's your car now."

We entered the building through simple double glass doors and then turned right into the Citizen newsroom. It was large and spacious, with parquet floors and high ceilings. Chest-high partitions separated departments, and I was interested to see rows of computer terminals placed on counter tops similar to the design I had come up with years before in Huntington. A large number of newsroom staffers turned from their desks and work stations to look at us as we walked through the newsroom, Sue Clark-Jackson in front, Sandy and I following, and Gerald Garcia trailing.

Clark-Jackson stopped at a counter top near the front of the room and stood facing the news staff and then began to speak.

"For those of you who may not know, I'm Sue Clark-Jackson, president of Gannett's West region, which includes Tucson. As you're all aware, Gerald Garcia has decided to take his talents elsewhere, and we wish him the best. So today I bring your new publisher and editor, Don Hatfield. And this is his wife, Sandy."

By now most of the staff were standing. There was polite applause. Sandy and I smiled and nodded as Sue continued.

"Don is a veteran publisher and editor and comes here from Huntington, West Virginia where he also served as a regional vice president for Gannett East."

And now it was my time to speak to my new staff. I made it brief.

"It's great to be here as your new editor and publisher. I look forward to getting to know all of you and working with you. I can tell you that the Tucson Citizen has a great reputation in Gannett and I am honored to be given this opportunity. I know I have big shoes to fill—Gerald Garcia is an outstanding publisher and editor. I'll do my best. Sandy and I are eager to get started and we look forward to making Tucson our home. Thank you."

There was more polite applause and then a tall man with grey hair and mustache approached and introduced himself as Dale Walton, the Citizen's managing editor. We had met before at APME conventions, and it was good to see a familiar face. He smiled broadly and welcomed us to Tucson. He asked if I minded taking time to talk with a reporter for a story for that day's final edition.

We were then introduced to a woman named Barbara Thompson, who would be my secretary and, as it turned out, one of the special people in my life. She smiled pleasantly and said she looked forward to working with me. Then came a young woman with a great smiling face. She introduced herself as Kathy Allen, the Citizen's promotions manager, which surprised me because I didn't know the Citizen had one. I had been told that all marketing resided in the agency. She suggested she take Sandy for a drive to see the city while I was being interviewed and meeting others. That was a great idea.

I sat down with the reporter, answered his questions about my background and how I felt about taking over the Citizen, and when the interview was over I moved on to the office that had been Garcia's. It was set off from the rest of the newsroom by portable walls and contained a desk, chair, small table and two straight-back chairs. Not what one would expect.

Clark-Jackson was making a phone call outside the office. Garcia was sitting at the small table inside.

"I'm glad you're the one," he said.

"Really. Why is that?" I sat at the desk which had been his.

"Oh, I just think you'll be right for the job."

"Thanks. I hope you're right. You've been a good editor and publisher here. Tell me what I'm getting myself into."

He sat back with his hands behind his head. "Well, you know we're the conservative paper in town. The *Republican* paper, in a lot of eyes."

That surprised me. "Why is that?"

"History, for one thing. It's always been the 'Republican' paper. The Star is the 'Democrat' paper--very, very liberal."

I knew little about Garcia, but he was Mexican-American, which to my then narrow thinking meant he was, like most minorities, liberal. So I said, "But you're not conservative."

"Well, I've tried to do what I think is best for the Citizen. And what is best is for it to be as different from the Star as it can be--the conservative alternative, since the Star is so predictably liberal."

I disliked the idea that the newspaper had to be either. A good newspaper, I thought, was objective, certainly on its news pages, but also that its editorial pages should not be labeled and predictable. But I knew I was being given good advice in a city about which I knew nothing.

About that time I heard a familiar, booming voice: "Hello, little lady."

"Hello, Mr. Burdick," my secretary said.

Hal Burdick, the man who had been my boss in Huntington, the man I had replaced there and who would now be answering to me, was on his way in. He stopped in his tracks when he saw me. He turned to Sue Clark-Jackson.

"You mean I have to put up with this?" he said.

"Afraid so, Hal," Sue said.

He stood there frowning and shaking his head, feigning disappointment.

"Hello, Hal," I said.

He looked up and that old twinkle came to his eye and that smile to his face and he walked over and shook my hand. "Congratulations," he said.

While we waited on the publisher of the Santa Fe paper to arrive Sue said she and I would move on to meet the directors of Tucson Newspapers Inc., the agency that controlled the non-news functions of the operation. They were waiting in the office of TNI's general manager, Tom Jackson. Sue introduced me as the Citizen's new editor and publisher, and I could feel every one of them sizing me up.

Sue said something about my background, and the director of human resources, Edith Auslander, said she was familiar with my work on behalf of minority journalists and that we had many mutual friends. That made me feel a little more at ease.

Someone then apologized for the weather--it

had been raining for a few days, apparently. And another said, "We actually have water in our rivers."

I thought: "Water in our rivers?"

I did not know that the rivers in Tucson run dry except when there were heavy rains such as those during the monsoon season. It was only the beginning of what I did not know and would have to learn about my new town.

After meeting with the TNI directors we went to the Pulitzer wing of the building where I met Emil Rould, the Star's controller and Michael Pulitzer's representative in Tucson. He was a low-key and pleasant individual and welcomed me to Tucson and TNI. We next met the Star's editor, Steve Auslander—husband, I soon learned, of TNI's human resources director. He would be my competition. And, as it turned out, my friend.

I was given a tour of the building, which had been constructed in the 1970's. We walked down clean broad hallways from Accounting to Circulation to Advertising to Marketing to Production, into the composing room and then to the press room with its huge full-color offset presses, very impressive to someone who had spent his thirty-three year career in the Huntington newspapers building with its aged rotary web press. We walked out onto the loading docks and then back, ending up in a large meeting room off a full cafeteria offering hot entrees, soups, sandwiches, and a salad bar. I was thinking that the "cafeteria" in Huntington had been a small room with a few tables and chairs and a soft drink machine. For food, you brought your own.

Sue and I returned to the Citizen newsroom where others were waiting, including Wayne Vann, publisher of the Santa Fe New Mexican, now part of my world, and Don Flores, the Citizen's assistant managing editor. I learned later that Flores was slated to become managing editor in Santa Fe, but that had not yet been made official.

For lunch we were taken by Garcia to the Plaza Club, a recently opened private dining club on the top floor of a mid-town office building. Window walls offered great views of the city and the mountains beyond. The interior was sophisticated and reeked with class. I thought, I'm going to like this place.

Over lunch in a private room I received reports on the properties for which I would be responsible. I said I would be visiting their operations soon.

Sandy's time with Kathy Allen proved to be eye-opening as well. They drove through nearby residential areas and through downtown, which offered theaters, music halls, restaurants, a large civic center, bank buildings, government complexes, but few stores and little shopping. Those were found in the city's four regional shopping malls, I was told. Four?

That evening Garcia took us to the Gold Room at Westward Look, an older resort that had been something of a dude ranch, situated high in the foothills of the Santa Catalina mountains. The views were spectacular, the food outstanding if pricey, and the wine plentiful. Coming from

Gannett East, where Bobby Collins held tightly to everyone's budget, I was astonished Garcia was spending so much, and even more so when he tipped the maître d' twenty-five dollars in addition to what he had given our waiter. This was truly a new world.

When we returned to our Holiday Inn room, I asked Sandy how her day had gone. She mentioned a residential area called El Encanto which, she said, was lovely but very expensive, with homes priced in the high hundreds of thousands. She had thought about a condo downtown, but after looking at what downtown had to offer and the outside of several condo complexes, she had changed her mind.. Then she mentioned that day's edition of the Tucson Citizen, which happened to be on our hotel room table.

"Look at this," she said, pointing to a front page photo of several women sitting in a restaurant. Beneath was a story headlined: "Women now permitted to dine on main floor of Old Pueblo Club."

I looked at the story. It seemed the Old Pueblo, long a private dining club downtown, had for years forbidden women unaccompanied by their husbands to dine in the top floor dining room. Nor could they be members.

"What kind of city is this?" she said.

Still, I felt much better about my new assignment when we went to bed that night. I was not sure that Sandy did, although she had said little. I decided not to push it.

We spent the next few days with Sandy being shown houses and condos by a real estate agent and I meeting individually with the Citizen's news staff. Some were suspicious, my being this stranger sent in by the giant Gannett. Most were cordial. One, Peter Madrid, the Citizen's sports editor, winced and said "Oh no" when I told him I had written sports for seven years before moving to the news side. I liked him immediately.

One of those rare life-changing events occurred Saturday, as if I had not already experienced such by moving here. I received a call from the controller at the University of Arizona who identified himself as Ben Tuchi. He said he had previously worked at West Virginia University and would like to invite Sandy and me to be his guests for that Saturday's Arizona-USC football game. We were delighted to accept.

During a pre-game reception he introduced us to several others with university connections: Dr. Helen Schaefer, who was married to the previous UA president, Dr. John Schaefer, and Dr. Allan Beigel, senior vice president of university relations. He was an impressive man, with white permed hair and a white mustache but a young face with a great smile and laugh. He was wonderfully welcoming, talkative, cool.

Helen Schaefer mentioned that we would have to meet her husband John, who was unfortunately not here at the time but rather in New York attending a meeting.

"And you didn't go with him?" Sandy asked.

"No," she said, "I don't fly."

Sandy reacted in mock horror. "Mon Dieu, better to risk death than not to visit Manhattan."

Allan Beigel roared. "You've got to meet my wife," he said, and went to find her.

Moments later a jovial dark-haired woman wearing a red Mickey Mouse shirt showed up with him. And it was then that Joan Kaye Beigel entered our lives.

She was laughing and upbeat and full of questions for Sandy and they hit if off immediately. They talked about New York and theater and plays each had seen. And then it was game time, and I was thrilled to be in attendance at a Pac-10 game, and one featuring USC at that. After the game, we all went to a Mexican restaurant where I learned that "cerveza" was not a brand name, but the word for "beer" in Spanish, and that before eating a tamale one had to remove the husk.

The following day Sandy returned to Huntington to put our house on the market and to prepare for the move. A few days later she received a phone call. It was Joan Beigel.

"Remember me?" she said. "I'm the one in the Mickey Mouse shirt."

"Of course I remember you, Joan."

"I know you're busy getting ready to move out here to this place where you know no one. I just wanted you to know you have a friend in Tucson."

Nothing could have meant more.

In the years to come, Allan and Joan Beigel would become our best friends, and Allan would become one of my prime news sources and closest confidantes. John and Helen Schaefer would prove to be lifelong friends as well. But on this day, Sandy was enormously grateful to know she had "a friend in Tucson," this fun and crazy native of New York City named Joan Kaye Beigel.

I spent that week getting acquainted with my new news staff, driving around my new city, looking for a house, and giving up my small Holiday Inn hotel room for an apartment on the east side, where I would stay until we found a house. It was brand-new, part of an addition to a complex of units in which, I was told, some members of the Cleveland Indians major league baseball team stayed during spring training. It was only autumn, so I would have to wait until spring to check that out. I hoped that we would be in our own home by then.

At the end of the week I headed back east to attend the APME convention, fortunately being held that year in Cincinnati, not far from Huntington.

I welcomed the return. It would give me the chance to help Sandy with the move, to get rid of a few things—clothes, books. Mostly, it would give me the opportunity to revisit the newspaper for the farewell I had not been able to have before heading to Tucson.

When I entered the newspaper building, I was met with cool stares, which surprised me. I had worked with these people for years. But I had also left them, and without saying goodbye. This was West Virginia. If you left you were somehow being disrespectful. Especially if you had not explained yourself.

After a few hellos and handshakes, it got better. Then I went into the pressroom and sought out Freddie. He looked at me somewhat suspiciously.

"You knew you were leaving the day you told me we had to hurry up and sign the new contract, didn't you?" he said.

"Yes, I did. I was afraid a new publisher would want to start all over in the negotiations and I thought we had a pretty good thing for all concerned."

He thought for a moment before answering, and then nodded. "I see."

"I just wanted to make sure you guys would be all right." I wasn't sure he believed me but it was true.

"Okay," he said. "Makes sense, I guess. How's Tucson?"

"Big operation."

"So I've been told."

I thanked him for his faith in me and wished him good luck. I haven't seen him since.

The next night I took members of my former Operating Group to the country club for dinner. We told stories and laughed but it wasn't the same. When the evening ended they presented me with a basketball signed by all the players on the Marshall University basketball team. I have it still.

38
BRAVE NEW WORLD

I was excited to return to my new world in the desert. From my apartment balcony I looked directly into the face of the Santa Catalina mountains. Walking outside the apartment, I could look south over a generous portion of the eastern part of the city and at other mountain ranges in all directions. This was Tucson, Arizona. A different world. West Virginia seemed far away, in both geography and time.

Tucson sat in the middle of the Sonoran Desert, surrounded by four mountain ranges—the Santa Catalinas to the north, Rincons to the east, Santa Ritas to the south, and Tucson Mountains to the west. There were also the Tortilitas to the northwest and the Chiracahuas at some distance to the southeast.

The city was large in every way. More than five hundred thousand people lived within the city limits and more than seven hundred thousand in the county (that since has grown to more than one million). It occupied some 227 square miles, and driving across town, from the Rincons to the Tucson Mountains, covered more than forty miles.

The city of Phoenix, with all its satellite cities (Scottsdale, Tempe, Glendale, Mesa, Chandler and others) lay only a hundred fifteen miles to the north on Interstate 10. And Mexico was only sixty miles south on Interstate 19.

South and west of Tucson were two Indian reservations--the Tohono O'odham (which had been known as the Papagos) and the Pascua Yaquis. Just south of Tucson sat a lovely old mission, San Xavier del Bac (the "White Dove of the Desert"), established in 1692. Further south on I-19 was the retirement community of Green Valley, and beyond that the tiny arts colony of Tubac, and then finally Nogales, Arizona, separated from Nogales, Sonora only by a fence and gate of entry into this country.

Atop the Catalina mountains, more than nine thousand feet high, sat the village of Mount Lemmon, with its ski slopes and lifts, which seemed remarkable to me, here in the desert below. Yet one could get there in less than an hour, driving up the narrow, twisting Catalina Highway. More than twenty vehicles had gone over the edge of the highway, tumbling to rest below (they were finally pulled out in a few days' operation shortly after my arrival).

There were two large military bases, one-- Davis-Monthan Air Force Base--located smack on the southern edge of the city. Here were attack fighters ready for action as well as the nation's

379

military plane graveyard. There was also Fort Huachuca, an Army base, in Sierra Vista, a town to the southeast.

Within the city of Tucson was another city all its own called South Tucson, where signs and billboards were written in Spanish and where one could find outstanding Mexican restaurants. South Tucson had its own city manager, council, and police force.

The University of Arizona, founded in 1885 as Arizona's first university and older than the state itself, was located in the heart of town, and had an enrollment of more than thirty thousand (at this writing that has climbed to forty thousand). Its football stadium (seating 57,000), basketball arena (14,500) and its University Medical Center, sat along Campbell Avenue, the city's major north-south corridor. The university was clearly the big player in town.

There also was Pima Community College, a two-year institution with five separate campuses and a total enrollment of some eighty-five thousand.

Tucson boasted quite a movie-making history, going back to the 1935 filming of "Arizona," when a set was constructed just west of the city. That set had grown over the years to be used for countless movies and television shows featuring such stars as John Wayne, Montgomery Clift, Dean Martin, Elizabeth Taylor, Ava Gardner, Kirk Douglas, Lee Marvin and Sidney Poitier (whose Oscar-winning "Lilies of the Field" was filmed here), to mention only a few. The large set resembled a town all its own and served also as a major tourist attraction called "Old Tucson," where visitors often were warned "live set" when films were being made.

The tourism industry was huge. Two large resorts had been opened only the year before my arrival, both in the foothills of the Catalinas. There was La Paloma, with its twenty-seven- hole golf course designed by Jack Nicklaus, and Ventana Canyon, with two eighteen-hole courses, set deep and almost indistinguishable in the Catalinas. And there was the historic Arizona Inn, opened in the Twenties just a few blocks from the university, which over the years had attracted many of the stars mentioned above as well as such others as Spencer Tracy, Clark Gable and Gary Cooper. Some made Tucson their home or kept vacation places here. Paul McCartney and his wife Linda Eastman owned a ranch to the east of town, near the Rincons. Elizabeth Taylor had once owned a house here. Lee Marvin was still a permanent resident whose home sat on a dirt road just off North Campbell Avenue in the foothills. And Katherine Hepburn and Spencer Tracy frequently stayed in a special cottage on a dude ranch in the Foothills called Hacienda del Sol, which to this day refers to the structure as "the Hepburn cottage."

More than forty golf courses dotted the Greater Tucson landscape (that now has surpassed fifty). And of course for decades the city's dry climate had attracted both tourists and those hoping to improve their health because of it.

There were major events throughout the year—

the Tucson Open, a major stop on the men's professional golf tour; the LPGA, one of the women's professional golf tournaments; a rodeo with its accompanying parade through downtown; the country's largest gem show; major league spring training with the Cleveland Indians; and major concerts.

Tucson also was the center for astronomy in the nation if not the world. There were huge telescopes atop Mount Lemmon to the north, Mount Graham to the east and the Kitt Peak National Observatory to the west. And most of the mirrors for telescopes throughout the world were made right here—at a lab on the university campus located, amazingly, beneath the university's football stadium.

What incredible diversity--ethnically, culturally, artistically, economically. Great science (Tucson would later become known as "Optics Valley,"), a great university, tourism, major league baseball, major college sports, military bases, movies and movie stars, the arts, a touch of the old west and yet as modern as tomorrow, with a smaller city inside itself, Indian reservations nearby, and an entire country only sixty miles away.

What a challenge to cover all this. What a large news staff would be necessary to really do the job right. And here I was, a newcomer from the East, a new editor/publisher unknown to a news staff new to me but not to each other and not to the town.

How to begin?

Taking over the Tucson Citizen was certainly

no save-and-rescue operation. This was a good newspaper with a solid reputation and, as the oldest continuously published newspaper in the state of Arizona, great tradition. It had been around since the late 1800's and much of the time had dominated the local newspaper scene—although, like afternoon newspapers everywhere, its circulation now trailed that of the morning newspaper by a considerable margin.

The news staff numbered about eighty individuals, most of whom were well educated, talented, savvy and sophisticated. They were a diverse group in every possible way—by age, experience, gender, ethnicity, personal tastes and, so far as I could tell at this early point, political persuasion if they had one. They had come from many points across the nation, but one thing they appeared to have in common was that they were all very much a part of the unique Tucson landscape. They seemed to believe in and care for this place— a great quality and a great advantage in many ways.

And here comes this new publisher about whom they knew nothing, dropped suddenly into their midst by this giant corporation from the East known as Gannett. Clearly, what we had here was a matter of their sitting back and waiting for him to prove himself.

How does one do that?

I called for a full staff meeting in the community room adjacent to the cafeteria, to be held just after final edition close. I asked my secretary, Barbara Thompson, to order pizzas and soft drinks, and to put out the word that everyone was expected to attend.

But first I put together a short questionnaire, consisting of just four questions:

--What in your opinion are the strengths of the Tucson Citizen?

--What are its weaknesses?

--How would you describe working conditions here?

--What would you do if you were editor and publisher?

I did not leave space for a signature. I wanted everyone to respond openly without fear of retribution or being labeled or categorized. Barbara made a sufficient number of copies to be distributed at the staff meeting. I also asked her to come up with a small box to serve as a suggestion box, and for it to be so labeled.

The room was filled with Citizen news staffers, all curious as to what this was all about. They lined up by the opened pizza boxes in the back of the room, filled their paper plates, and then settled into their folding chairs. They sat eating, having private conversations, and waiting.

After several minutes, I stood to speak.

I thanked them for coming, said I hoped they enjoyed the pizza, and explained that we would have such a meeting every month. I would use the meetings to pass on various kinds of information from Corporate or the Tucson newspaper agency or whatever I thought they should know. I would welcome questions, I said, and I would try to answer them all. I pointed to the suggestion box Barbara had put together and said it would be placed in the newsroom hall for all of them to use, dropping off questions or suggestions. They need not sign their names, I said. I would then address them at the following staff meeting. (As I learned later, that could create some awkward moments, but how better to know what was on their minds?)

I then told them about the questionnaires. They did not have to fill them out, I said, but if they did it would be a big help to me to better learn about the Citizen and the staff. I urged them not to sign the questionnaires so that they might respond more freely. Meantime, Barbara was distributing them.

I then opened it to questions that might already have occurred to them. They were understandably hesitant, until Dale Walton asked me to talk a little about my background in newspapers. I spoke briefly about walking in off the street as an eighteen-year-old looking for a job as copy boy and ending up as a sportswriter, and went on from there. I tried to be light and humorous whenever possible—difficult, when you don't know your audience.

I finished by saying no one should feel he or she had to wait for a staff meeting or a response to a suggestion box comment in order to talk with me or ask questions. My door, I said, would always be open and each one of them would be welcome. I said that while the Citizen was a very good newspaper, to keep it that way and perhaps make it even better I would need their help. We were all in this together, I said. And my goals were to make the

Citizen the number one news source in Greater Tucson and to kick hell out of that newspaper "across the moat," meaning the Arizona Daily Star.

The pizza was gone and the questions had dried up and I realized it was time to end the meeting, which I did, again with thanks to all for attending. As Barbara and I walked back to my office, she whispered, "A nice start." Later, a couple of staffers stopped by to thank me for the pizza and the meeting, but most went on to their desks or home. Walton dropped in to say, "I think that went pretty well," and I thanked him for his words and for his questions during the meeting.

Not all the questionnaires were returned, but most were. I spent the rest of the day reading them and making notes. A couple of things quickly became obvious. Many members of the staff— female, I presumed—believed Citizen management did not treat male and female members of the staff equally, not just in opportunities, but especially in salary. I would have to look at payroll and experience and see if there was any truth to that. Others believed certain male editors were sexist. A few thought that work loads were uneven. Most thought the Citizen was understaffed, especially compared to the morning Star. A couple said Gannett was cheap.

But also clear was that nearly every staffer who responded believed that the Citizen was a good newspaper, that it served the community well, that it was the newspaper closest to the community. There was considerable pride.

I was grateful that so many had returned the questionnaires and that they had been so frank.

The following afternoon I looked up to see a tall young woman standing in my office doorway. I waved her in. She introduced herself as Julie Szekely, a staff writer, and apologized for missing the staff meeting, having been off the previous day. We chatted briefly about her background and mine and as she left, she paused for a moment and then said:

"When I walked into the newsroom this morning there was a buzz I haven't heard around here for a long time. Everybody was talking about the staff meeting."

"I hope that's a good thing," I said.

"That's a good thing," she said.

That meant a lot to me.

Each day after that I took a different editor to lunch in the caféteria, starting with Dale Walton who as managing editor ran the newsroom. He was an old world kind of managing editor, hands-on in the very best way, and the oldest and most experienced member of the staff. You could tell he knew what a news story was and was not and how to treat each accordingly. I also got the feeling he would prove to be both loyal and trustworthy, and indeed he was.

After that I met individually with all the department editors: editorial page editor Ted Craig, a grizzled and obviously opinionated long-time conservative; news editor Keith Carew, a somewhat cantankerous sort on the surface but a dedicated newsman inside; city editor Mark Kimble, who I could see would be one to pin me to the wall, keep me honest, and take no b.s. (in other words, a very good city editor); features editor Bruce Johnston, quiet and intelligent; business editor Judy Lefton, friendly, outgoing, willing; sports editor Peter Madrid, a good person who, as I said earlier, moaned when he heard I had spent seven years as a sportswriter; photo editor P.K. Weis, gruff and temperamental, but a good man and a great photographer); copy desk chief Keith Busch, a superb protector of the language who liked things best when left alone; art director Joel Rochon, creative and bright; makeup editor Paul Schwalbach, who was clearly restless and uncomfortable during our brief lunch; and librarian Charlotte Keenan, who knew the Citizen's morgue like the back of her hand.. A very good group.

We talked about their staffs, their needs, their thoughts about the Citizen. Again, I urged them to come to me with any problems or questions, and said I would be depending heavily on them, which was certainly the truth.

Each day I walked around the newsroom, talking with members of the staff when they had a break in action. There were assistant editors and managers, copy editors, reporters and writers in each department, columnists, critics and reviewers, feature writers, news clerks and library assistants. I talked with a couple of the Citizen's critics, letting them know of my and Sandy's interest in the arts. And I spent time in Sports, talking with the

Citizen's sports columnist, Corky Simpson, and its basketball writer, Jack Rickard, letting them know of my background and interest in sports. Some were a bit suspicious of me, as they probably would be of any new boss, especially one sent in by Corporate. I understood that.

The Citizen also had two freelance columnists, Richard Salvatierra and Ernesto Portillo. Each wrote one column per week and was paid for that column. Portillo had come to Tucson from Mexico some years before and owned a Spanish language radio station. He wrote his column in Spanish and provided a brief translation to accompany it. His wife, Julieta, worked as secretary to Steve Auslander, the Star's editor. Over the next several weeks the Portillos invited us to their home for dinner, and we had good discussions about Tucson, its history and its Hispanic tradition.

Salvatierra was a retired career foreign service officer who had spent time in Cuba and parts of Europe. He was a native of Tucson, had played baseball for the University of Arizona, and had returned here in retirement with his wife Clara. His column dealt with foreign affairs. He was also a dedicated conservative—make that *Republican*—and in the years to come we would have many discussions about some of the ways we did things at the Citizen. He felt that the newspaper should run no conflicting opinions on its editorial and op ed pages, including personal columns that differed from its editorials. That was confusing to the reader as to where the Citizen stood, he said. I responded that we stood for offering different and contradicting opinions to readers, believing they would benefit from reading differing opinions and that they were intelligent enough not to be confused by them. He would only shake his head.

Often he spoke of the *liberalmedia* as if it were one word.

But he proved to be enormously helpful to me both personally and professionally. He invited me to dinners of the Tucson chapter of the Council on Foreign Relations. He took me as his guest to the Tucson Literary Club, at the time a club of men only which met monthly to have drinks and dinner and hear the reading of an essay by one of its members. He soon put me up for membership (Sandy also became a member a few years later when the club finally decided to break its male-only rule—a change my friend Salvatierra never quite got over).

He was an avid tennis player and asked me to join him in a weekly men's doubles league at Westward Look resort. Participants included professors, doctors, lawyers, business men. I met many people through that program, all because of Salvatierra.

We also played singles every Saturday and Sunday when Sandy was out of town. He was about sixteen years older than I, but moved like a cat, and seemed to get back every ball. I once approached the net, shaking my racquet at him and saying, "Why don't you act your age?"

We became close friends, his family and mine,

and over the years spent many good times together at both his house and ours. He was always the first guest to arrive at our Christmas Eve parties. A good man, and my good fortune to have him there when I arrived.

So that made up the news staff of my new newspaper. It was more than twice the size of the news staff of my paper in Huntington. And that did not include the employees on the business side, handled by the agency, who numbered more than six hundred. When one added those to the news staffs of the Star and Citizen, the Tucson operation totaled more than eight hundred employees. Although Gannett had placed Tucson in its Community Division because of the Citizen's circulation, this was clearly a metro operation.

Barbara checked the suggestion box each day. One afternoon she found two separate notes urging me to bring bottled water into the newsroom. The newspaper building was located near an area once found to have some sort of contamination in its soil that had caused several illnesses, they said. I told Barbara to check into it and from that day on we had bottled water brought in.

As promised, I looked into the salary structure and the pay as well as the years of experience and the job responsibilities of each employee. I have always believed in rewarding those who do the job, and merit increases would naturally result in some reporters making more than others, regardless of gender. Obviously, those with more experience would make more than those with less simply because they've had more time to prove themselves and receive increases. On the other hand, if two have the same responsibilities and the same experience, one should not find a big difference in salary. But this was the situation I found regarding a female and a male who were regarded as the stars of the staff. He was being paid quite a bit more than she.

I called her in and told her that I had examined salaries and thought she was being underpaid and therefore I was raising her salary immediately. I asked that she not share that in detail with others.

But one thing I have learned is that employees somehow always know what others are making. A few days later the male reporter came into my office. He said he had heard I had given the female writer a good raise. I said I had, that she was underpaid, quite behind him even though they had the same experience, job title and responsibilities. He said that he should be given a raise as well. I told him she had only been brought up to his current salary level, and that there would be no out-of-season raise for him; we would approach that at evaluation time.

He responded by telling me the Star had long been seeking his services, and that if I did not give him a raise immediately he would leave the Citizen and go over to that newspaper. I told him this was not the way I operated, that I did not respond very well to threats, and if he felt that way he indeed should take his talents to the other side. I wished him luck.

He sat stunned.

"Was there anything else?" I said.

He stood, looking at me in what appeared to be disbelief. "Well then, all right," he said.

I called Dale Walton in, told him what had happened and to get with the finance people and have the writer's final check drawn up.

That reporter did go to the other side. In a matter of days he called Walton and said he had made a mistake and asked Walton to talk to me about his coming back to the Citizen. I told Walton that he could not come back. He had made his decision and it was his to live with.

I could tell Walton did not quite agree with me.

"Is this the way people have gotten raises around here—by threatening to leave?" I said.

"Sometimes," he said.

"Not anymore," I said.

The reporter never approached us again after that. But over the years he and I often ran into each other in hallways or the cafeteria or in the community, and he was always friendly and respectful. Neither of us ever mentioned his leaving the Citizen.

The incident made me realize that I had much to learn about the news staff and past Citizen policies and practices. I would have to learn much more about a lot of things.

Meanwhile I continued to look for a house. I quickly learned that Tucson was not Huntington when it came to the price of houses as well as everything else. Having given a Tucson real estate agent a ballpark figure as to how much I wanted to spend, I was being shown houses that were considerably less than those we had owned in Huntington. I would have to spend more. Finally I was shown a house in the Catalina Foothills that, while smaller and yet more expensive than I would have liked, was of high quality and overlooked part of the city. Sandy was still in Huntington, packing and selling our house.

As luck would have it, my replacement in Huntington, Dan Martin, made an offer, and after some negotiations, we reached agreement. When I called to tell her about the house I had seen, as I had about several other houses, she remarked that it was the first time I had shown any enthusiasm for any property. She would soon be coming to Tucson and we would look at it together. I warned that it was considerably smaller than our turn-of-the-century house in Huntington. But our sons were gone now, both living in Boston, and, we told ourselves, we would not need more space. Time proved us wrong about that. In any case, we bought it. The moving vans would be here Thanksgiving week.

39
THE GREAT SOUTHWEST

Now that I had made a start with the Citizen news staff, I moved on to the Tucson Newspaper agency's directors and employees. This was not quite the same, in that they did not report directly to me but rather to the agency's general manager, Tom Jackson. I had already met with Jackson a few times to discuss circulation numbers, advertising lineage, financial reporting and other matters. I had plenty of questions in each area. I told him I would like to meet individually with his department directors to get to know them better, if he did not mind.

I met first with Edie Auslander, TNI's human resources director who had mentioned in our introductory meeting that we had several friends in common. She was an intelligent, charming woman who had been both college journalism professor and Star reporter. She was of Hispanic descent and definitely TNI's pipeline into the Hispanic community. Tucson, after all, had once been part of Mexico, and the percentage of Hispanics (the term used before Latinos and Latinas came into favor) in Tucson was at the time about thirty-three percent and growing.

Edie had learned of my wife's Hispanic roots. Sandy's maiden name was Soto and her paternal grandparents had come from La Caruna, Spain. I had thought "Soto" was a strange name, but.in Tucson "Soto" was like "Smith" back East. Sotos were everywhere.

Edie said she would help introduce Sandy to the community, both Hispanic and non-Hispanic. I quickly discovered that Edie Auslander knew just about everyone in town. We were extremely fortunate to have her.

I next met with Wayne Bean, our production director, who was quite impressive. Already I had been impressed by his operation. His production numbers were good. Color reproduction in both papers was outstanding. Every part of the building was clean—even the composing room and the pressroom, a rarity in my experience.

I began by telling him I just wanted to learn more about him. He told me he had been born and raised in South Africa where he had participated in international swimming competition. He might have been an Olympian if not for the country's racial policies, which kept it out of the Olympics. But he had competed in many countries.

Then he said, "There has been a lot of tragedy in my life, Don."

He told me that his son had been killed at the age of seventeen when a car under which he was working suddenly collapsed. Then he spoke of an explosion in the newspaper building some years before which had taken the life of the TNI controller and critically injured the Star's managing editor as well as Bean himself. He showed me his left arm and hand—quite scarred and with fingers missing. (I would soon learn that his past injuries had little effect on his golf game. As many times as we played over the years, I never once came close to beating him.)

Mostly I was impressed with the way Wayne Bean carried himself. Tall, erect, proud, handsome with a small mustache. He commanded respect from employees throughout the building. (Gary Watson, at the time president of Gannett Newspapers, once told me "Wayne Bean is the best production director in all of Gannett.")

My next session would be with TNI's circulation director, Steve Pope. Already he had dropped by my office to invite me to be his guest at the Arizona Theater Company's production of "House of Blue Leaves." (It was an excellent production with an outstanding cast and I only wished that Sandy could have been there. As soon as she returned, I took her to the play and we became long-time supporters of ATC. She even became its president—but more on that later).

I spoke frankly with Pope, stressing that I thought the Citizen was not getting enough of his department's attention. The Star was growing rapidly in circulation, with more than 80,000 sales daily and one hundred thousand on Sunday. The Citizen was not, languishing in the low fifty-thousands. I understood that the Star, as a morning paper, would naturally gain and the Citizen, like afternoon papers all over the country, was challenged, especially in a two-newspaper town. But this was a big growth area, I said, with a population increase of more than two percent every year. The Citizen should be getting some of those newcomers, I said, and I expected to see that in the future.

He got the message. In two months the Citizen's circulation topped the sixty-thousand mark. However, those numbers were later challenged and reduced by the Audit Bureau of Circulation. Pope had turned in numbers that included many heavily discounted for marketing purposes, which were not recognized by the ABC. Nor were they permanent. The Citizen soon dropped back to the low fifties in circulation.

I met briefly with the current advertising director, discussing among other things an absence of small advertisers in our pages. I could not help but think about the Huntington operation, where we had to scratch and claw for all our advertising, coming up with shopping center pages and neighborhood pages and whatever else we could do to attract the small advertiser who could not afford a full or half-page ad. I told him about that and he said, "Well, maybe we could look into that."

And I met with the TNI controller for whom I

had many questions about financial reporting. It seemed we occasionally were pushing some expenses into the next month, hoping to make the current month look better. Not a good practice.

Both the ad director and the controller appeared to be uncomfortable with my questions, or with me, or both. As it turned out that must have been so. Both left, the ad director not long after I arrived, the controller some months later. I was not disappointed. We would replace them with better people.

It was now time to find out more about the regional properties for which I was responsible— Santa Fe, El Paso, and a USA TODAY print and distribution center in Chandler, Arizona, just this side of Phoenix..

I had never been to any of the three cities. To get to Santa Fe, one had to fly from Tucson to Albuquerque, then rent a car and drive the rest of the way. I had heard great things about Santa Fe for years. But when I reached the town, I was surprised to see how small it was. The population was a bit less than sixty thousand. There were no tall buildings and no "city feel" whatsoever, especially for someone who had spent his life in the East. But I soon learned that here was a special place with special charm. Art galleries everywhere. Unique shops. Interesting restaurants. A town square and plaza wonderful for sitting, walking, reading, or buying small treasures. There was Canyon Road, a narrow street lined on each side with small galleries. And the Georgia O'Keefe museum. And a gallery in the center of town which sold nothing but works by the great southwest sculptor, Alan Hauser, many priced in six figures.

The newspaper, the Santa Fe New Mexican, had been owned by a man named Robert McKinney who once had been, among other things, President John F. Kennedy's ambassador to Ireland. He had sold the newspaper to Gannett several years before and still kept an office in the small New Mexican building and still claimed the titles of publisher and editor-in-chief, although he rarely came there.

It was a small building and a small newspaper, with a circulation of perhaps 20,000. Its general manager, Wayne Vann, gave me the usual tour. It did not take long. Vann was an outgoing man who obviously liked to impress, especially with someone who had suddenly become his new boss. He told me how well he had worked with my predecessor, Gerald Garcia, that they had played golf together and had good meals together and it was always a pleasure to have Garcia visit. He explained that Santa Fe was a somewhat unique property. There was the matter of Robert McKinney still wanting to know what was going on even though he had sold the paper. And there was the reality that the New Mexican had less circulation in its own town than did the Albuquerque newspaper which kept a bureau there. In fact, he said, that bureau alone had a larger news staff than the New Mexican. I agreed that was a problem, especially if the Albuquerque papers came after the New Mexican's advertisers.

"They are," he said

I met with his directors, including his new managing editor, Don Flores, the Citizen's assistant managing editor the day I arrived in Tucson. It was good to see him again. He seemed excited about his new job.

The New Mexican's controller was a young man from Rochester, New York named Charlie Lang. He was polite and responded to my questions but otherwise had little to say. Still, I was impressed with his sincerity and grasp of his position.

Vann and I talked privately about his numbers. He was below plan in virtually every category. He said the economy was down in Santa Fe, that it was a small town with few advertisers and not much growth. I didn't buy all that, given Santa Fe's tourism industry, but I listened. We discussed the process—his monthly report, monthly financials, and what I expected. I said I looked forward to working with him, that I hoped for open and honest communication with him, and that I really did not like surprises. I did not mention golf.

El Paso proved to be another quite different and interesting place. Perched on the banks of the Rio Grande across from Ciudad Juarez, Mexico, it was a mix of the Old West and a modern city. One could imagine some of the paved city streets having been dusty roads not so long before. It boasted a population of, surprisingly, more than five hundred thousand people, many of whom were of Mexican descent. And yet it was dwarfed by its neighboring city across the border. There was a great old hotel with a rich history. There were boot-making and boot repair shops and leather shops downtown and a modern shopping mall nearby. It was the home of the University of Texas at El Paso, a good and growing institution with major college sports, as well as the Sun Bowl, which brought money to the city every year.

Juarez, meanwhile, had a population of more than a million, and fine restaurants, tall buildings, and the feel of a true city. (I was always surprised that when I visited El Paso, which proved to be often for various reasons, we frequently dined not in El Paso restaurants, but in posh restaurants in Juarez where customers wore diamonds, furs and dark suits.)

My old boss, Hal Burdick, welcomed me to his town and we talked for some time about the uniqueness of El Paso, the position of the El Paso Times, its strengths and some of the problems it faced. As the city's morning paper it enjoyed a circulation of about 85,000 daily and 100,000 Sunday—much larger than that of the afternoon paper, which was owned by Scripps-Howard. Another joint operation, but unlike that in Tucson this one was not fifty-fifty. Gannett was by far the majority owner and called the shots, so there was no need for the kind of agency and general manager serving both sides as in Tucson. The Times' future looked solid. Besides that, it had been in good hands, as Burdick had long proved himself to be a good publisher who produced good results, even in El Paso where the average household income was one of the lowest in the nation.

He provided the customary tour of the building and paused as we approached the mail room, or distribution center, where papers come over from the presses to be stuffed with advertising inserts and other supplements before being bundled for distribution. In most newspaper operations, especially one of El Paso's size, this was done by inserting machines, some more refined than others. The supplements were placed in the machines which then inserted them into the newspapers and the papers were then bundled and bound.

"I'm going to show you our inserters," he said, and then opened the door.

There were no machines inside. What there were, were dozens of women, nearly all of Mexican descent, lining steel-topped tables from both sides, inserting all the supplements by hand. Make that both hands. They opened the papers with one hand and slid the supplements into them with the other, shuffling faster than any black jack dealer I have ever seen. Their hands moved so fast they were a blur. And they seemed never to make a mistake.

"That's amazing," I said.

"Now you know why we're asking for an inserting machine in our capital requests."

"I'm not sure you need one. These women seem to do the job better than any machine."

"We need one," he said.

He called a meeting of his directors and introduced me as the new regional vice president responsible for the El Paso Times. I spoke only briefly and then took questions, although there weren't many.

I heard later that one of the directors said to Burdick, "This guy was your editor in Huntington and now he's your boss? How do you feel about that?"

"I'm proud of him," Hal responded. Good man, as I have said before.

When he and I talked later I asked him how he thought my meeting had gone.

"Fine," he said, adding: "You've changed."

"I have? In what way?"

"Just changed."

Well, yes. I was a publisher now. And a regional vice president. And now his boss. Of course I would seem different to him from the editor who had reported to him a few years before. But I thought of similar words spoken to me by Dwight Mc Kenzie, my ad director in Huntington. I hoped I had not lost something along the way.

Burdick then shared with me the news that he would be retiring at the end of the year, which I already knew. I told him he deserved a good retirement and thanked him again for all he had done for me. It did not seem that long ago when I had done that before, standing on the tarmac in Huntington as he turned over his publishing duties to me.

"I don't know if they have decided yet who will replace me," he said.

"If they have, they haven't told me," I said.

That changed soon. Not long after I returned to Tucson I was informed by Gannett that a new editor had been chosen for El Paso. His name was Tom Fenton. He was a veteran Associated Press newsman who had run AP bureaus in South America and West Germany. Al Neuharth had met him in Europe, had been impressed by him, and had convinced him to join Gannett. A native of Kentucky, he had connections in El Paso, with UTEP and otherwise, as did his wife, Ellie. Now he would become editor of the El Paso Times. And—surprise—he then would move up to publisher when Burdick retired.

I returned to El Paso to meet with Fenton and introduce him to members of the El Paso Operating Committee as the Times' new editor. No mention was made of a plan to make him publisher when Burdick retired. But I learned later that at the time of Fenton's introduction as editor, one of the directors whispered to another: "You've just seen our new publisher."

Smart man.

My one remaining visit did not require a plane ticket. The new USA TODAY print and distribution center, located just off Interstate 10 in Chandler, Arizona, was only about a hundred miles north. Sandy and I drove up together. The general manager was waiting for me just as those who ran the Santa Fe and El Paso operations had been. But this was totally different. There was no operating group of directors to meet with, and no editor. There was a great color press and a huge loading area. The center not only served as the printer for the satellite-transmitted pages of USA TODAY, but distributed them throughout a wide area, including Tucson and El Paso.

My assignment here was quite temporary. We both knew that Gannett was putting into place a new division to be made up of all the print sites for USA TODAY. And once that happened this one would no longer be reporting to me.

My prime function as a regional vice president was to help see that my properties were profitable. I had read the latest financials from this print site and they showed very low profit with expenses way beyond revenues. I mentioned this to him and he smiled and explained that USA TODAY print sites basically had only expenses with only a few revenues from commercial printing. Advertising and circulation revenues were recorded at Corporate. No one had explained that to me. I felt pretty foolish.

As expected, not long after my visit the Chandler USA TODAY operation became part of a new Gannett division and therefore was no longer my responsibility. I was not sorry about that.

Before the year was out I met the Corporate jet at Tucson International Airport and joined Gannett execs John Curley, Gary Watson and Sue Clark-Jackson for a flight to El Paso to install Tom Fenton as publisher. It was something of a celebration, with Burdick retiring and Fenton taking over. There was good food, good wine, toasts to both.

Fenton was a tall man with a boyish face and a great smile. He wore western boots with his suits, but with sophistication, no doubt honed by his foreign assignments. He had covered the war in the

Falkland Islands. He had taken crash courses in Spanish and then German for his bureau assignments in South America and Europe. He was intelligent and had class.

His wife Ellie was bright, upbeat, and clearly a full partner in Tom's life work as Sandy was for me. She had attended a university in Mexico City (which, oddly enough, Sandy and I later happened to visit). She would be, with Tom, perfect for El Paso. Of course the four of us would become friends.

40
GETTING TO KNOW YOU

From the very beginning, I wanted the Citizen to be *the* Number One source for local news in Tucson, the recognized authority on everything local in town. We would be more local than the Star in every way. We would not attempt to have a full-blown world and national news report but we would "own the local news scene." I shared these goals with the Citizen staff and they were received with enthusiasm.

We had a solid city reporting staff, an educated, experienced, committed group. We enjoyed an edge in business reporting, having launched a weekly local business tab section (the Star had none), and because the Star was viewed as "anti-business." We published a weekly entertainment tab. The Star did not. We were strong in sports, with more coverage of high schools than the Star, with good coverage of university athletics, and with a talented sports columnist in Corky Simpson.

But we were not quite where I wanted us to be in our coverage of the arts.

We had one writer who covered and reviewed dance and theater. He was a good writer and worked quite independently as critics should. His dance reviews were excellent. His theater reviews lacked the same level of perspective. We talked about it and although he thought at first I was telling him to write only positive reviews, he came to realize that was not my intent. I simply wanted reviews of substance, good or bad.

We alternated writers in covering music, which made some sense in that there are so many forms of music, from country to pop to jazz to classical, with all kinds of shades in between. Tucson had its own symphony orchestra and an outstanding chamber music organization which offered a fine season as well as an annual festival which attracted some of the finest chamber groups in the world. I wanted a music critic who had the background and ability to cover the classical scene. After a short search we made an offer to a former Tucson critic working in New York, but he turned us down. Finally we came across a local man named Dan Buckley, who wrote about music in the Tucson Weekly, the city's good alternative newspaper. He was himself a composer and performance artist, and worked in a music store. There was something about Dan Buckley that made me smile and I found myself thinking "This is not your normal music critic." As I had done so many times in Huntington, I followed my "vibes" and hired him. It proved to be a good choice. He would win national awards with a series we called "The Music of America," in which he traveled to areas around the country noted for their music— Austin, New Orleans, Memphis, Nashville, the Appalachians, New York.

We had no one covering visual arts even though Tucson was huge in this with three museums and galleries everywhere. So the hunt was on again. We turned to another writer whose work appeared in the Tucson Weekly, a woman named Charlotte Lowe. She was a feature writer, lacked the experience in visual arts that Buckley had in music. But she convinced me that her knowledge of and long-time appreciation for art and her hard work combined with her obvious writing talent would offset that. Once again, I followed my vibes. And once again it worked. Now we had writers in every major art. No one else could make that claim.

Now the Citizen was even more different from the Star. That fit well with advice given me by an attorney named Jack Donahue.

Donahue was one of my first visitors in Tucson. He felt we needed to talk as soon as possible so he could brief me on the Tucson Newspapers' joint operation and its history. The agreement went back to the 1940's and was challenged in the 1960's as a violation of anti-trust regulations. Donahue and his law firm defended the Tucson newspapers in that action. The suit went all the way to the United States Supreme Court, where the JOA's right to exist—that is, for it to be exempted from anti-trust laws--was overturned. However, before the court's decision could take effect, Congress passed the "Surviving Newspapers Act" which exempted newspaper joint operations from anti-trust laws if they could show that without the exemption one or both of the newspapers would fail and thus a "separate and competing voice" would be silenced. That was not difficult. Newspapers were very expensive operations. If both newspapers had to own their own buildings and presses, establish their own advertising, circulation, production and financial staffs, making a profit would indeed be difficult for at least one of them. By sharing those expenses, both could survive (and in this case, thrive). So Tucson had been the test case and the decision affected every JOA in the country for years to come.

Donahue, an intelligent and conservative man, advised me that whatever I planned to do with the Citizen I should keep in mind that to protect the Tucson JOA the Citizen "should be as different as possible from the morning Arizona Daily Star," its partner. Since the Star was predictably liberal, it followed that the Citizen should always be conservative. It did not take me long to realize Donahue was pushing his own conservative agenda with this advice. Still, I knew he was right about keeping the two newspapers different from each other. He wanted to do that for political reasons; I wanted to do it to sell newspapers.

I told him I agreed the Citizen should be different from the Star and that we were. I pointed to our weekly local business tab, our weekly entertainment tab, our emphasis on local coverage. That wasn't enough. He reminded me that the Citizen "has always been the conservative paper in town, a clear-cut choice to the liberal Star." I should not permit that to change, he said.

He was a kind man and invited me to join him for a round of tennis. As it happened, that was on the same Sunday morning that Sandy and I had been invited to the house of our new Tucson friends, Allan and Joan Beigel. What I did not realize was that Joan was holding this brunch in our honor, so that we could meet people. I joined Donohue for tennis and Sandy and I arrived late for our own party. I was embarrassed.

But the affair turned out to be one of the best things that could have happened to us, not only socially, but to me in my new job as publisher of the Tucson Citizen. Most of those present were close friends of the Beigels, and not surprisingly many were also among the movers and shakers of Tucson. Among them were Justice Stanley Feldman of the Arizona Supreme Court and his wife Norma, Dr. John Schaefer, the former president of the UA and his wife Helen, and Stan and Judy Abrams, he a developer and she owner of a public relations firm. All became our friends. The Beigels, Schaefers, and Feldmans, became our most special friends, with whom we traveled, dined, spent Christmas Eves and New Year's Eves together. When Feldman was elevated to Chief Justice of the Arizona Supreme Court, we were invited to the ceremony.

Word got around quickly to various Hispanic groups (thanks to our human resources director, Edie Auslander) that the wife of the new Citizen publisher was Hispanic. Sandy soon received several invitations to their meetings and was asked to join their organizations. One such organization was the Hispanic Professional Action Committee, known as HPAC. I was asked to speak at one of their meetings and looked forward to doing so.

It went well early on, but when I invited questions I found myself being nailed to the wall by one HPAC member in the back of the room. My predecessor, Gerald Garcia, was Hispanic; I was not. That seemed to pose a problem for the man in the back of the room. He wanted to know how many Hispanic employees there were at Tucson Newspapers. I had no idea. He asked if the Citizen's lawyers were Hispanic. Again, I had no clue. I turned to Edie, sitting nearby, and asked her. She wasn't sure what lawyers the Citizen used. And on it went.

After the meeting the man remained in the room and Sandy and I passed him as we walked out. He introduced himself as Jose Canchola. He said he and I should have lunch, just the two of us. I said I would welcome that. I worried that for whatever reason, I had made an enemy. But I was wrong. I had made a friend—not only in Jose Canchola, but with his family. Years later we were present for his daughter Carmen's wedding and for the Canchollas' fiftieth anniversary.

I said earlier that in coming to Tucson we were

moving to a city in which we knew no one. But I learned that two former Gannett publishers were living here in retirement. One was Jim Geehan, a former Tucson Citizen publisher who, ironically, had been the first Gannett person I had met when the company purchased the Huntington newspapers fifteen years before. It was Geehan, then publisher in Binghamton, New York, who had told me that while I might be concerned, I would later be pleased Gannett had come into my life. He was so right about that. Geehan had moved on to become publisher of the Tucson Citizen, then had been named head of Gannett News Service in Washington, D. C. In that role he had asked me to speak at a GNS meeting. Now in retirement, he and his wife Betty had moved back to the Tucson home they had kept from their earlier years. They invited me to dinner and it was good to see them again and to know they were here.

I was also getting to know more people from the community simply because they came to my office asking for Gannett Foundation grants. There was Lorraine Lee of Chicanos Por La Causa, a kind and intelligent woman who was committed to improving the lot of Hispanics—make that Latinos and Latinas. She became a friend of ours, and we saw each other many times at various events. There were women from Angel Charities, a non-profit organization that raised thousands of dollars each year for children's programs and assistance. Several of these women also became our friends for as long as we were in Tucson.

And there was Jane Goodall. I knew the name and was aware of her studies with chimpanzees, but not much beyond that. She was seeking a Gannett Foundation grant for her institute. I was impressed by her presence and honored when she presented me with an autographed copy of her book. But I was thinking that her request was more national in scope and would not qualify for a local Gannett Foundation grant which had to address the needs of a specific community. I suggested she apply to the Foundation itself at its offices in Washington. I would notify the Foundation of her visit to my office and her intent to apply directly to it. She was understanding and left saying, "Well, see what you can do." I do not know if she received a Gannett grant but as the years have shown, she managed to raise millions elsewhere and her work has proved to be enormously important around the world.

There were other visitors as the months went by. I was astonished when the Honorable Mo Udall, long-time congressman from Arizona, came by with two of his aides to welcome me to his state. At this point he was suffering from Parkinson's, but he could walk with assistance and despite great difficulty in speaking, managed to carry on a good and intelligent conversation. I was honored he would come to see me. He was a great, generous man with a wonderful sense of humor. He once ran for President, and when he withdrew from the race did so with his usual honesty and modesty. That led to a book, *Too Funny to be President.* Although a Democrat, Udall counted as one of his closest friends Republican John McCain, U.S. Senator from Arizona. Sometime later, as Udall lay all but immobilized, it was McCain who came most often to see him, sitting by his bed and talking with him. McCain later told me, "I wasn't sure he even knew I was there. But I had to go see him."

And there was McCain himself, who appeared before our editorial board shortly after my arrival. I mentioned to him that a former fraternity brother of mine, Gen. Al Wheeler, sent his regards. I had seen Wheeler on a return trip to Huntington. Hearing of my move to Arizona, Wheeler had said, "If you run into Sen. John McCain, give him my best. We're friends."

McCain was surprised. "I know Al Wheeler," he said.

More on McCain later.

We made special efforts to heighten the Citizen's presence in the community and to meet as many people as we could. We marketed ourselves as Tucson's local newspaper, and we coined the phrase, "The Citizen *is* Tucson." One would feel it in our pages and know it from our involvement in the community. We set up a speakers bureau of editors and reporters willing to speak to local groups. We held neighborhood sessions in which we sought to learn what was on the minds of those we served. I took positions on local non-profit boards such as the United Way. So did Sandy.

In fact, Sandy proved to be well ahead of me in getting plugged in throughout the city, joining organizations such as HPAC and accepting positions

416

on the boards of the Tucson Symphony, Arizona Theater Company, Tucson Museum of Art, the Food Bank, even the local Job Corps. She served on the university's Office of Cultural Affairs and was selected by UA President Dr. Henry Koffler to help organize "Festival in the Sun," a year-long festival of the arts that attracted nationwide attention. Koffler also asked her to participate on a special committee on minorities. In time she would be appointed to more boards and organizations, including the university's Children's Research Center, and the Arizona-Mexico Commission—the latter by the governor..

Tucson was very much an early morning town and many of the board meetings were held at 7:30 a.m. A few took place in the southern part of Tucson, several miles from our house. But Sandy made them all. Through her I met many Tucsonans, some of whom--notably Fred Acosta of the Job Corps—became both friends and news contacts. Acosta called me often on my direct line to pass on news tips and information

Sandy was of enormous help to me, especially given the amount of time I spent traveling to national meetings and to my regional properties. Gannett truly got two for the price of one with us, for she promoted the Citizen not only in Tucson, but in Phoenix and even parts of Mexico as well. Although many at Corporate liked and respected her, no one there ever fully understood all that she did.

She also met with my newly formed arts staff.

In retrospect, this was a mistake, because the staff misunderstood. In Huntington, she had been friends with most of the news staff from the time I was just starting to the days when I was editor and publisher. Here, she was "the publisher's wife." My arts writers were suspicious. Why would the publisher's wife invite them to lunch to talk about the arts? They assumed she would put pressure on them to write positive, flowery articles on all her pet projects. They did not know her. Instead, she talked about the importance of the arts and the importance of their work. She hoped to make them feel special. I do not know if that worked; I was not present. I do know now that we were naïve not to realize that we were strangers here, and that to this staff I was the publisher, the boss, "el jefe," and she was and always would be the publisher's wife, even if kinder and friendlier than most.

Knowing of my interest in sports in general and basketball in particular, the Citizen's basketball writer, Jack Rickard, invited me to lunch with Lute Olson, the University of Arizona basketball coach. Olson was a national figure. He had been at the UA for three years after a successful run at Iowa. He was a handsome man, tall, silver-haired, with a commanding presence. I mentioned to him that my wife was quite a basketball fan and that she had asked me, during an exhibition game the night before, if Arizona was using a "box and one" defense instead of a man-to-man. Olson replied, "That's probably when we had Turner in there. He tends to play zone no matter what defense we're in." We both laughed.

I was impressed with Olson and liked him immediately. But I would be cautious in expressing that. I would not want my sportswriters to think I favored him in anyway, so that they could feel free in writing and commenting.

The same caution held true on the news side as well, and for this reason whenever Allan Beigel and I were in the presence of my editors or reporters, I referred to him as "Dr. Beigel" and he referred to me as "Mr. Hatfield." Some reporters are always looking for signs that their publisher has certain "sacred cows" in the community—especially a publisher who is new to them and thus unknown.

Over the years Lute Olson's popularity and reputation in Tucson became such that people jokingly referred to him as "Saint Lute." He took Arizona to four Final Fours, won the national championship in 1997, and was elected to the Basketball Hall of Fame. His wife, Bobbi, was also much loved. She and Sandy became friends, and we saw them socially on occasion, although we never became close, or even had dinner together. Sandy, who regularly went to the university campus for meetings or to sit in on classes, occasionally dropped by the basketball arena to watch the Wildcats practice. Once, at a party, I returned from the bar to discover that Sandy was not where I had left her. I found her sitting with Olson at a nearby table, and asked him, "Is she trying to tell you how to run your basketball team?" He smiled. "Come on over," he said. "You might learn something."

Sadly, in 2001, Bobbi Olson died of cancer. There was a huge public observance at McKale Center, the UA basketball arena, and a private invitation-only church service for family and friends. I was surprised and honored when one of the Olsons' daughters called to ask that we attend. "Daddy would like you to be there," she said. As we were leaving the service, he gave Sandy and me each a hug and thanked us for attending. So perhaps we were closer than I thought. In any case, by the time of Bobbi's death I had already retired from the Citizen, so I was no longer concerned about letting it be seen that I liked the man

I do not think, in these my later years, that most newspaper people worry about such things these days. But there was a time when credibility meant everything, and that meant objectivity, no matter who one's friends were. It did not always work. But one did not want to be vulnerable to such accusations. My sportswriters at the Citizen were quite aware of our interest in and support for the Arizona Wildcats. We went to every game and sat on the front row. These were not dumb people; of course they would not want to court my disfavor. But I worked hard to dissuade of them of such thoughts and to convince them to write whatever they thought should be written.

Some got it, some did not. Sometimes, writers will go the other way in an attempt to show their independence from their bosses. Good for them--- so long as they are being fair and, more than anything, honest in their reporting.

Our efforts in the community were given a big boost with the visit to town of Gannett chairman Al Neuharth and his "USA Today Caravan." Neuharth and some of his associates traveled around the country by bus (although he sometimes flew in to join those on the bus once it had arrived) to hold town meetings designed to find out what was on the minds of Americans everywhere. I scheduled the meeting for the ballroom of the Doubletree Hotel and placed ads and news stories in our pages and sent out press releases to other media. I would do the welcome and introductions, a USA Today editor would serve as moderator, and Neuharth himself would stand at the podium and respond to questions and comments and even pose questions to make sure the audience was involved. I prayed we would have a decent turnout.

Not to worry. The place was packed, standing room only, and many stopped to look at the brightly painted USA Today bus parked outside. The evening went extremely well. There was news coverage on television and in my own newspaper, focusing on the many comments and discussions from the floor. It was a great idea by Neuharth— one of his many great ideas. And for me it went a long way to getting the attention of Tucsonans and sending the message that there was a new kind of Tucson Citizen in town.

For years after, I held similar town halls, including several designed just for teens, but they did not have Al Neuharth or the USA Today bus and although quite worthwhile, they understandably never generated the interest this one did.

There were other visitors of a different nature early in 1987---a few of my former reporters from Huntington. First came Kevinne Moran, reporter and friend. She not only came to town, but stayed, accepting a reporting job on the Citizen. There also was Angela Dodson, whom I had hired years before with the help of my friend Bill Congleton to break the racial barrier on the Huntington newspapers. She was now on the New York Times news staff and was visiting Tucson as a board member of the Institute for Journalism Education's Minorities Editing program at the University of Arizona.

And there was Jennifer Dokes, who had left Huntington before I did to take a job on the Phoenix Gazette. I had tried to talk her out of it at the time. "You don't want to go to the desert," I said. "There are rattlesnakes and scorpions and mountain lions out there." And it was she who phoned on my first day in Tucson to say, "You don't want to go to Arizona; there are snakes and scorpions out there…"

We gathered at our house and it was like a reunion. I was delighted and proud.

Not long after came another. Margaret Bernstein, who also had been a reporter for me in Huntington, had just completed a loaner stint at USA Today. A native of Los Angeles, where her parents still lived, she had heard of my move to Tucson and thought, "That's only eight hours from my family." Her mother had the same thought and sent her a box full of information on Tucson. Bernstein updated her resume and mailed it to me, hoping for a job. I had no openings at the time, but did eight months later. And to the desert she came—another good reporter, and another good friend..

41
SEASONS OF CHANGE

It was time for a meeting of the TNI Board in Tucson. Michael Pulitzer flew in from St. Louis, and I looked forward to meeting him. I anticipated that he would be an imposing figure, perhaps even difficult. I couldn't have been more wrong. He was low-key, friendly, smiled at each person who spoke. The meeting was brief and cordial. General Manager Tom Jackson gave his report on the agency financials. There were few questions and no disagreements between the two companies. The gavel was passed from Michael Pulitzer to me as chairman of the four-person board. Then he announced that this would be his last meeting as Pulitzer's top representative on the board. He was replacing himself with the publisher of Pulitzer's St. Louis Post-Dispatch, Nick Penniman. Dinner that evening was a pleasant affair, with Pulitzer's wife present. I was sorry that he would no longer be on the board; I would like to have known him better. But he was still head of Pulitzer, and I knew I would see him again, which I did.

That was not the only change regarding TNI. Jackson resigned, taking a position with the Pulitzer company as head of its suburban operation in Chicago. He would be leaving in June. I was not surprised. Gannett was a pressure-packed company and I was a publisher who asked questions and complained when I thought our side was getting short shrift from the agency. Now Gannett and Pulitzer would have to find a replacement. .

And much of my time was spent traveling, with trips to Santa Fe and El Paso for my regional responsibilities, to Reno for Sue Clark-Jackson's regional meetings, to Washington for Corporate meetings, and New York, Washington and Seattle for national publishers and editors conventions. And there were regional subsidiary meetings. These were high-stress sessions in which the publisher and department heads of an individual newspaper appeared before Gannett's top executives. It was examination time and was not unlike a court appearance. The newspaper's representatives sat facing the Gannett execs, who were seated at a large table. Each department head—circulation, advertising, news and, of course, finance---reported on his or her area, trying to be as positive as possible. Then each had to field questions from the corporate brass. I do not know if these sessions were designed to be confrontational, but they often turned out that way. At the very least, they were intimidating. I had been there and I had seen department heads so nervous they could hardly speak. I myself had experienced anxiety during these meetings and would again when my own newspaper went through such a session.

Now it was time for the Santa Fe New Mexican, one of my responsibilities, to be so examined. Its numbers were not good. Circulation was down, advertising was down, expenses were not down enough, so the bottom line was below budget. I had told the newspaper's publisher—in Santa Fe that title was general manager—to be prepared to answer tough questions. I also told him it would be important that he and his directors appear to be together on their answers, to show that they were a team. Alas, things fell apart soon, with some of the department heads going one way, some another, a couple actually disputing each other. The fallout was that the publisher/general manager would be replaced.

There soon would be another trip to Santa Fe to install his successor. Diane Borden, a former editor and teacher recruited by Gannett, had been in Reno learning Gannett publisher ropes under Clark-Jackson. She would take over in Santa Fe and report to me as her regional vice president. I had heard good things about her and looked forward to working with her.

One of Gannett's corporate jets happened to be available in the West region. It picked up Clark-Jackson and Borden in Reno, then Sandy and me in Tucson, and we headed directly to Santa Fe. An Albuquerque stop would not be necessary. The plane was brand-new and all class, inside and out, with beige suede seats and interior walls. One almost hesitated to touch them.

Clark-Jackson said she had been given a somewhat unusual assignment by Gannett chairman and CEO Al Neuharth, who had a vacation home in Lake Tahoe, not far from Reno. He liked burning pinion wood in his fireplace and it could be found in Santa Fe. Since she would be there, could she possibly pick up a good supply and bring it back to him?

As odd as that might seem, it was not all that surprising given that we were dealing with Al Neuharth.

Clark-Jackson agreed to, of course. One did not say no to Al Neuharth. Nevertheless she was worried how and when she would find the pinion wood, especially considering that she would not have much time.

"Don't worry about it," Sandy said. "I'll take care of it."

And she did. While Sue and I were introducing Borden to her new associates in the Santa Fe newspaper building, Sandy was in our hotel room on the phone. That night at dinner she reported that all was in order. The wood would be delivered to the plane when we left.

"Fantastic," said Sue.

The next day, as we prepared to board the corporate jet, a faded red pickup truck pulled up to the gate and drove onto the tarmac. It was piled high with coffee-sack bags filled with cut-and-trimmed pinion logs and tied neatly at the top. The driver and his passenger, Mr. and Mrs. Rios, stepped from the truck and asked where they should put the wood. Sandy had found them while looking under "firewood," had talked with Mrs. Rios and explained that as strange as it might sound, she needed a   truck load of pinion delivered to an airplane at the Santa Fe airport. Sandy introduced herself and thanked them for fulfilling her request so efficiently and neatly. The plane's crew stared at the load, and then motioned to the baggage area beneath the plane. The process of unloading the truck and loading the plane began.

When the baggage area was filled there were still bags left on the tarmac. I wondered what we would do with them, but the crew began loading them into the new suede-lined cabin, piling them in the aisles.

The Rioses stood proudly in having completed their mission.   They were paid, they smiled and thanked us and said they would be ready if we wanted to do it again sometime.

"I don't think so," Sue said.

We flew back to Tucson with our feet atop bags of pinion wood.

"This is probably a story we do not want to tell," Sue said.

When we landed in Tucson and Sandy and I stepped out of the plane and onto the tarmac, Sue said, "Wait a minute. Here, take one." And a crew member tossed one of the bags of pinion wood to our feet. We picked it up with our luggage and drove home.

Some time later when Clark-Jackson and I were talking about our pinion wood adventure, she smiled and said, "You haven't heard the punch line. One day I was looking out my office window and I noticed these trees covering the mountains in the distance. I asked one of my employees what they were. He said, 'Pinion. Why?'"

So Al Neuharth had pinion wood all around him, without having to get it picked up in Santa Fe, but didn't know it. Ah well. It was fun and it makes a good story.

While in Santa Fe, Watson, Clark-Jackson and I discussed the TNI situation. Who would make a good successor for Tom Jackson in Tucson?

I mentioned something about the position being a desirable one, and Watson said suddenly, "Do you want the job?"

"No thanks," I said, believing I already had a better job. After all, Jackson had been reporting to me. Besides, I didn't want to give up being involved in editing and publishing a newspaper. Running the agency even if it was supporting two newspapers and owned by two large companies had no appeal to me.

A couple of names came up. One was that of Harry Whipple, a Gannett national advertising executive who previously had been a publisher. I knew Whipple and liked him. So did Gary and Sue. After some discussion, they decided to pursue Whipple as a possible replacement for Jackson. They would have to convince the Pulitzer side, but Gannett seemed to have its way with Pulitzer at that time. Although Pulitzer was the legendary name, Gannett was far larger and had all that corporate expertise.

In three days, Whipple was in Tucson. Not surprisingly, he was offered the job and accepted. I was delighted. I knew we would work well together. I hoped the Pulitzers would feel the same. He would start in July. And he would not disappoint.

So now I had a new general manager in Tucson, who reported to both Pulitzer and Gannett, a new publisher in El Paso, and a new general manager in Santa Fe. I did not worry about Whipple; besides, his office was only a few steps away. The El Paso and Santa Fe changes would require a few trips there. One, to Santa Fe, came quite unexpectedly when Clark-Jackson called from Reno to tell me she'd just talked with Diane Borden in Santa Fe, and I should hop over there to see how things were going and offer my support. Less than an hour later I was on a plane. The suddenness of that trip convinced me to keep a small shaving kit and a change of underwear in my office. The visit went okay. Borden and I had dinner together and I told her again to call me whenever she had a problem or a question.

But there were far more important matters going on involving Santa Fe, and they were playing out in the courts. I was only vaguely aware that there was some sort of lawsuit going back to the previous owner and Gannett. But I knew nothing of the history behind it.

It seemed that when Robert McKinney sold the

newspaper to Gannett in 1976, he retained a separate agreement, he claimed, to remain as publisher and CEO for five years and as editor-in-chief for ten years. He kept an office in the building, but was rarely on the premises. But Gannett did not bestow the publisher or editor titles on those who actually ran the operation, instead calling them general manager and managing editor. In 1978, reportedly upset that the newspaper had not endorsed his choice for governor of New Mexico, McKinney sued Gannett, claiming breach of contract and demanding that the newspaper be returned to him. That suit stayed in the courts for nine years.

In September of 1987, the courts rejected Gannett's motion for a rehearing of a decision in which McKinney's claim had been upheld and ordered that the newspaper be returned to McKinney. He would have to pay back Gannett for the paper.

The court's decision had a number of ramifications. Obviously, Gannett no longer owned the newspaper; consequently no longer was it one of my responsibilities. And no longer was Diane Borden to be in charge. But the remainder of the newspaper's employees, including Don Flores, the managing editor who was running the news and editorial operations and who had been the assistant managing editor in Tucson when I arrived a year earlier, were now McKinney's employees.

Borden was extremely upset when told, and felt not only blind-sided but betrayed by everyone in

Gannett including her friend and mentor, Clark-Jackson, and me, her regional vice president. When I tried to convince her I was not aware that all this was coming down, she was not convinced. She was told that Gannett would find another situation for her, but she left the company.

The time was set for McKinney's return to Santa Fe to take over the newspaper, and Gary Watson asked me to be there during the changing of the guard, and to make myself available if needed. I was not to go to the newspaper building unless invited by McKinney. And I was not to contact any of the newspaper's employees. To do so would be "tampering" as long as they were still employed by the newspaper. However, I could talk with them if they contacted me first. They had been notified that I was in town, staying at the El Dorado where I was to remain for as long as it seemed necessary. Fortunately I took Sandy with me. If I had known we were going to be there for nearly a week, I would have gotten a suite instead of the small room we had.

I stayed in the room and waited for any call that might come. None did. And then it was D-Day. McKinney arrived with a flourish, I was told later. Dressed in a double-breasted suit and broad-brimmed hat, he swept through the front door like McArthur returning to the Philippines. I also heard that some of the employees had no idea who he was or why he was there, and that he was clearly disappointed when there was not a rush of open arms extended to him.

I had been advised by Watson to notify McKinney that I was in town and available should he wish to talk with me as the representative from Gannett. I will not forget how he responded when I identified myself on the phone.

"Well, so it's the great Don Hatfield," he said.

I was astonished. I had assumed he had never heard my name and would have no idea who I was. I explained that I was in Santa Fe and if he wanted to see me I would be pleased to come to the newspaper or he could come to my hotel.

"I don't think that will be necessary," he said, and hung up.

I continued to sit in my hotel room and wait.

There were a few department heads at the newspaper whom Gannett would be interested in keeping. We were especially concerned about Flores. He was a solid editor and we even had a place for him. But I could not tell him that. I felt sure I would hear from him, and so I did.

He was hurt and confused and said he wasn't sure what to do. He and his new wife had just purchased a home in Santa Fe. He did not know McKinney or what it would mean for him to stay there. McKinney had not yet summoned him or come by his office, he said. He wanted to know what to do.

"Do what you have to do," I said.

I knew that wasn't much help. But I could not go beyond that.

"See what he has to say," I added.

He called back an hour later. "I've met with

Mr. McKinney," he said. "He's ordered me to publish a story on the sale of the paper, written by a friend of his, and I don't think it's really accurate and I know it isn't very complete. He refused to allow me to assign one of our reporters to do the story. What should I do?"

"Do what you have to do," I said again.

I called Gary Watson to inform him. "You're handling it just right," he said. "Get back to me if you hear from him again."

"I will."

"And Don?"

"Yes?"

"I'm glad you're there."

That meant a lot.

Don Flores called back within the hour. He was choked up. "I've just resigned," he said. "I refused to run the story. But I don't know what to do."

"Congratulations," I said. "You're the new editor in Visalia."

I explained that I had not been permitted to approach him as long as he was an employee of McKinney's newspaper, but that Gannett needed him, wanted him and had a place for him. I praised him for his courage and apologized for the situation that we all found ourselves in.

I did not hear from any other employees. That was disappointing, especially regarding the paper's controller, Charlie Lang. Lang, ever the loyal, play-by-the-rules employee, stayed with the New Mexican and did what he was told—for a while.

After several days and no additional calls

except my contacts with Gary Watson, Sandy and I headed back to Tucson. It had been one of the most unusual weeks in my newspaper career. I never did meet McKinney face to face. I no longer made trips to Santa Fe to check on the newspaper there, which was unfortunate. I had grown to like the place. It had not only been one of my responsibilities, but it had also been interesting. I was grateful for the experience.

By the end of the year, Charlie Lang called to say he'd had enough of the new regime in Santa Fe and wanted out. It so happened the Tucson Citizen needed a controller, a veteran part-timer having left shortly after my arrrival. Welcome to Tucson, Charlie. This will be the beginning of a great relationship.

We also had been searching for a new advertising director at TNI. After several interviews, the position went to a woman named Cathy Davis, an experienced Gannett ad person who had worked with Clark-Jackson in Binghamton. It was a welcome change.

Lang would start the first week in January. He would need an office. I had never liked the tiny partitioned office I occupied in the newsroom. The two best offices in the building were sitting empty to the east of the newsroom and were being used as stock rooms. In earlier years, they had been the top executive offices, spacious, well designed. It had been Jim Geehan who moved from the publisher's office to the newsroom in order to be closer to the news staff when he perceived that things weren't going so well without his physical oversight.

I could understand that. The Citizen's executive offices were separated from the newsroom by walls, several doors and various outer offices. Strange, given that the owner/publisher who had been involved in the building's design was a kind, generous, friendly man. Visitors found it necessary to go through various check points if they hoped to see the publisher. The building itself had iron gates in front with a security booth and guards. Making it through there, visitors found themselves in an outdoor plaza with steps to the right leading to the Star's newsroom and steps to the left leading to the Citizen's side. Here they passed through glass doors into a large entry room facing a ticket-like booth with solid black double doors on each side. In the booth sat the first clerk. Given approval to enter the newsroom, they went through the doors to the right. If they hoped to see the publisher or controller or editor, they went through the doors to the left. And there was a smaller room with a desk and secretary, a narrow door leading to the newsroom, another door to a conference room, and a short hallway to the left leading to the executive offices. If they made it past the secretary, they were led through the hallway where they found another secretary and two large offices. In one resided the publisher, in another either the editor or the controller (it varied over the years).

Members of the news staff had to walk through the narrow door from the newsroom into the small room and through the same short hallway to reach the publisher or editor. Another longer hallway led from the publisher's corner office to another work area and two other offices. These were actually closer to the newsroom so news staffers more often came through another narrow door at that end. No wonder Geehan had moved his office to the newsroom.

Enough of that. And enough of that small closet-like offfice I occupied. I would move to the corner publisher's office, which was far nicer and roomier. But understanding Geehan's thinking some years before, I did not want to be separated from the staff so much. So, I tore down the walls—literally. I had the ticket-taker booth removed along with the double doors right and left and the walls that held them. Now members of the news staff could walk directly to the executive offices without facing any walls or going through any doors. Also, they could use the executive conference room for their own meetings or interviews.

I had the parquet floors cleaned (the former owner had been a man of taste, not only for installing the handsome parquet floors throughout the newsroom but also for the Oriental rugs he placed atop them in his office—rugs that were no longer there, I should add.)

The stock in the executive offices went back to where it belonged--two stock rooms in the same part of the building, one of which contained a walk-in safe. I bought new furniture for my office—a desk, two small couches, two chairs to be placed in front of the desk, a round table with four other chairs, and five tall book cases which I lined along one wall. I added a few works of southwestern art and moved in.

Lang would occupy the office to my left, which was good. I never wanted to be far from my controller.

Down the hall from my new premises was an executive rest room. There were also larger rest rooms for the staff at the other end of the newsroom. I was told a story about earlier years when the editor, who was not well liked by the staff, visited the executive rest room one day only to be shocked by the presence of one of the news staff. He immediately left, exclaiming, "Don't they know they have one of their own?"

It was not like that now. The executive rest room was open to all. So was my conference room. And so were all the doors to all the executive offices.

Sandy, meanwhile, was suffering from painful back problems, no doubt a result of all those years of caring for our invalid daughter, Lisa. In March she underwent surgery, which proved to be successful, at least at the time—she eventually had three more as well as a hip replacement. She recovered quickly from that first operation, in time to travel to Kansas City for the Arizona Wildcats' first Final Four appearance. Unfortunately, the 'Cats were upset by Oklahoma.

But there was a major victory involving Gannett and the Citizen yet to come. It was time to renegotiate the joint operating agreement.

The present agreement with Pulitzer was fifty-fifty in terms of revenues and agency expenses. This was unusual; in most JOA's the larger circulation paper—almost always the morning cycle paper--holds the majority interest. And certainly the Arizona Daily Star had far greater circulation than the Citizen. Thus there was concern in Gannett that Pulitzer would push for a greater share in a new contract. When I had been transferred to Tucson I was told by Watson and others that it was highly important that we maintain the fifty-fifty ratio in Tucson if at all possible.

Because the Star was a seven-day publication and the Citizen six, its news staff larger and its newsroom expenses consequently greater, Gannett paid a minimal subsidy to Pulitzer. It did not take an Einstein to figure out that with revenues in the agency split evenly between the two owners, and with the Pulitzer-Star side having greater newsroom expenses than the Citizen, Gannett would enjoy more net profit than Pulitzer if the subsidy did not cover the difference.

Negotiations for a new agreement were handled by corporate officers and lawyers from both sides. In the meantime I was to produce a quality product, different enough from the Star that readers would feel they must have it, keep watch on the local scene and communicate regularly with Corporate. That did not work quite as well in reverse; I had no idea what was going on there. But I understood that legal matters could not be made public, or even shared broadly, at this point.

I passed on to Corporate every bit of information about the Citizen from the community, hoping to prove that we were indeed Tucson's local newspaper, the "voice of Tucson." If we didn't have the numbers to back it up, I stressed the reader loyalty factor. I also kept an eye on Citizen expenses as well as the agency's revenues. Here, Harry Whipple, the agency's new general manager, was extremely cooperative.

When the corporate dust had cleared, it was time to take the endeavor into a joint meeting involving Pulitzer and Gannett executives to hash out the new agreement. The meeting took place in Phoenix, and I was there with the Gannett brass, which included Watson, Sue Clark-Jackson, and chief financial officer Larry Miller. I waited outside the meeting room. It was almost like waiting for the smoke to emerge signaling a new pope. The day stretched on.

Finally the word came. Pulitzer and Gannett had reached an agreement to continue the joint operating agreement in Tucson for the next twenty-five years. What's more, it would remain fifty-fifty. Unbelievable. There would be one change. Instead of a subsidy paid by Gannett, newsroom expenses for both papers would also go inside the JOA and be split evenly. Small matter. We were thrilled.

That evening Watson, Clark-Jackson, Miller and I went to a fine Italian restaurant called Avanti to celebrate. It was the only time I ever saw Miller taste a sip of wine; he never drank. It was a joyous evening.

With newsroom expenses going into the JOA, it also meant that all financial and marketing staff would go there. But neither Citizen controller Charlie Lang nor Citizen public relations staffer Kathy Allen wanted to work for TNI. We turned Kathy into a reporter and kept her in the Citizen newsroom. But Lang chose to leave the Tucson newspaper operation rather than work for TNI. He soon found an accounting position elsewhere in the area. We stayed in touch and remain close friends to this day.

There were other major changes in the new agreement. The board, having been made up of only four members, would be increased to six, with Watson joining as a Gannett representative and Steve Auslander, the Star's editor, coming in on the Pulitzer side. Harry Whipple's job as general manager of the agency would be upgraded to president, and he would be reporting to the full six-member Tucson Newspapers board instead of just to me on the Citizen side and Emil Rould on the Star side. Both Rould and I remained on the board, along with Nick Penniman and Auslander on the Pulitzer side and Watson and Clark-Jackson on the Gannett side. Board meetings would be held every quarter or if necessary more often, rather than twice a year as before. And Whipple would get direction from the full board at these meetings instead of running up and down steps to the right and left to see Rould and me on practically a daily basis. It worked much better in this way, even if it lessened my power and control.

I felt a sense of achievement even though I had not been involved in the negotiations. The fact was that I had come to Tucson when it was feared Gannett might lose its fifty-fifty split, which would have established Pulitzer as the majority owner. And that had not happened.

42
IT'S ABOUT THE NEWS

But what about *my* newspaper, the Tucson Citizen? What about the editor part of my titles? What about the fun part of the business—producing a daily newspaper that people want to read and need to read? What about informing and educating readers? What about the newsroom, that zoo of creativity?

I did not want to get too far from that, with my responsibilities as publisher and regional officer. I had seen too many newspapers go down in quality with neglect from the top. I could not allow that to happen. The key would be staying in touch—communication, planning, my personal involvement when possible. And letting the news staff know that the news, the work that they did each day, was still the priority.

I continued to conduct monthly staff meetings with pizza and Pepsis. I attended our weekly news story planning sessions whenever possible. I attended all editorial board meetings. I walked around the newsroom, seeing and being seen.

One assumes that a newspaper, regardless of size, will publish the day's local news. A good newspaper goes beyond that. A good newspaper plans and publishes enterprise stories and investigative stories, projects that take time and planning, that go behind the scene, that perform a public service.

We had done that in Huntington. I think of the time we enrolled a nineteen-year-old college intern, who looked to be about fourteen, in a junior high school so she could report on what junior high kids of the day were doing and talking about. And the time we placed a reporter, Doug Imbrogno, incognito in the state hospital to see whether there were abuses there as rumored. And when Kevinne Moran exposed questionable if not illegal practices involving Huntington's housing inspector and local slumlords. And Dick Stanley's investigative stories revealing that the jailer was trucking prisoners to work his own farm and while using his "jail cart" for what amounted to black market sales.

Of course we would do enterprise and investigative reporting in Tucson. The Citizen always had, and I always had. It was a perfect match.

In a story planning session one day, I asked, "Who really runs this town?"

The editors looked at each other. Well, it depends...

And thus was born a special enterprise report

called "Who Runs Tucson?"

We discussed how we would determine who the real powers were in our city. We would do that in several ways. First, we would announce the project to the public and ask our readers' help: Whom did they consider the most powerful people in Tucson? Next we would interview dozens of people--city and county officials, lawyers and judges, car dealers and real estate brokers, restaurant owners, university administrators. We would examine the makeup of the boards of every non-profit organization in town.

Most of our staffers would be involved to some degree, but the overall master assignment went to my Huntington/Tucson/China reporter, Kevinne Moran.

We were quite surprised at the response we got from readers. They sent lists that included not only familiar names, but the names of people we'd never heard of. One school administrator nominated herself.

After several weeks of compiling responses and interviews, we gathered in my office to discuss what we had. We counted the times each name came up. We debated the strengths of those whose names appeared most often.

At first we were going to name a "top ten" and a "second ten." But the results didn't fall that cleanly. When the dust had cleared, we had five names who were quite obviously the most powerful people in town. Then we had a drop-off before the next group of fifteen. And that's the way we went with it.

If we had named a single "most powerful" person, which we did not, it would have been Tucson's city manager, Joel Valdez. We had expected it to be some wealthy developer.

Not that we didn't have one in our top five. We did. His name was Don Diamond, and he owned so much land, had developed so many properties and had so much money and influence he was clearly, as expected, one of the most powerful people in town.

As one also would expect, included as well was the president of the University of Arizona, Henry Koffler—not because he openly exercised power over the town, but because he ran the largest single entity in our fair city.

Also named was a long-time local citizen named Roy Drachman, who had been instrumental in bringing to Tucson Hughes Aircraft (now Raytheon) and major league spring training (with the Cleveland Indians). He also had been involved in just about every major decision made in our town for decades.

And there was Jim Click, auto dealer, banker, humanitarian, big-time political contributor and benefactor to just about every charity in town. The most powerful man in Tucson, many said. Still, he did not use that power to run anything but his own businesses.

The "second fifteen" was made up of people who were powerful in some segments of the community. And they ran the gamut, from business owners to developers to volunteers. They were male and female, Anglo and Hispanic, African-American and Asian, wealthy and middleclass.

Who runs Tucson? In the end, we reported that nobody runs the city totally. Clearly, Valdez ran the "City of Tucson" as city manager, but not beyond that. Koffler ran the university, but again, no more. Diamond and Click were forces. And even though he was retired, nothing really could happen in town without Drachman's involvement. We were a wonderfully diverse city. But we tended to do our own thing, often go our own way. Maybe that was one of our problems—and one of our blessings.

We put together a tabloid section listing not only the top five and second fifteen, but the top vote-getters in various segments: women, Hispanics, sports, media, etc. We published every name that had been submitted to us by our readers. We ran a page one story in the Citizen, keyed to the special section. We increased the newspaper's press run, expecting higher than normal single copy sales. And we printed thousands of extra copies of the section itself for those who might want to order it or get back copies.

Readers immediately turned to the list of everyone who was mentioned, many clearly hoping to see their names included. The section itself was the subject of several talk shows in town. We made copies available to schools, the university, virtually anyone who asked.

The project took time and planning and patience, not to mention money. But it was a marketing gem and, more importantly, a good service to the community.

There were other such efforts. We learned of a doctor at University Medical Center who was having personal problems to the degree that it affected his ability to practice. Yet he continued to do so, in spite of mistakes that proved damaging to patients, possibly fatal in one case. We had an excellent medical reporter named Carla McClain who jumped right into the story, and it was top of page one. The doctor was put on leave. Another public service.

The Citizen was also blessed with a veteran reporter named Tom Shields, who possessed good research skills and great patience. He was a quiet man who worked well without direction, and the perfect reporter to whom one could pass on a tip and say "Check this out" and know it would be done.

We heard that there were several major cracks in the Hoover Dam in northern Arizona, and that the federal government had ignored them because of the cost of repairs. Downstream from the dam were communities which would be endangered should the dam break. I thought of the Buffalo Creek disaster several years before in West Virginia, when an earthen dam collapsed, wiping out several villages and settlements and inflicting more than one hundred fifty casualties.

Shields checked with federal authorities and, when he could not get the answers he sought, filed FOI (Freedom of Information) requests. In time, boxes arrived containing previously undisclosed information, and our calls were returned. Shields visited the area surrounding the dam and talked with countless citizens. And finally our story was published, leading the front page.

Not long after, federal authorities sent in workers to repair the dam. Costly, yes. But there were no breaks, no floods, no communities destroyed, and no deaths. A public service, to be sure. Our story, and Tom Shields, were nominated for a Pulitzer Prize.

Some time later Shields was assigned another story of considerable importance. For decades there had been serious airplane and helicopter crashes in and over the Grand Canyon, resulting in many deaths. Now there had been another. We told ourselves, "We ought to look into this."

The Grand Canyon is one of the great tourist attractions in the world. This is true not only for those who drive there and peer over the rim, or walk down its steep slopes in blazing heat, but for those who view the Canyon from the air as well. The area around the Canyon is covered with small aircraft operations advertising flights and views over the Canyon for very low prices. Nobody seemed to govern or schedule these flights, and they filled the skies. At the same time, Air Force pilots were reportedly flying unofficial dare-devil missions through the Canyon "just for the hell of it." There were even small plane crashes that went unreported because there had been no deaths in them. What's more, the control tower at the tiny airport there was located on the wrong side of the airport so that there was a permanent blind side.

Once again, Shields exercised his FOI requests. And this time, even more large boxes arrived, all to be stacked up in one of the empty offices in back. Here Shields sat day after day, poring over all the information inside the boxes. Finally, he produced a special report on the "Deadly Skies of the Grand Canyon," again at the top of page one. And again submitted for a Pulitzer Prize.

After our story appeared new regulations and restrictions were put into place and for a while the number of incidents involving planes and helicopters was reduced. Sadly, that did not last long. Since then there have been several more crashes and deaths. Still, it was another example of good public service reporting, of good enterprise reporting.

We also did an investigative story that took us across the border. Federal authorities, joined by the Pima County Sheriff's Department, were moving in on a Mexican drug smuggler named Jaime Figueroa Soto, known as "Arizona's most notorious drug lord." He had brought countless truckloads of drugs into this country, and had fine homes in Tucson and Scottsdale and lesser houses from which he ran his operation.

What do we know about the Jaimes of the world, the smugglers who manage to bring in multi-millions of dollars worth of drugs? We knew very little. We decided to find out more about this one. Where was he from? How did he operate? How long has he been doing this? How has he managed to get this far? What ties did he have?

We assigned the story to a reporter we had recently acquired from the New Times, the alternative weekly in Phoenix. He was not only a skilled reporter, but wrote with style and grace, on subjects from corruption to the arts. His name was Ruben Hernandez.

The editors and I met with him to discuss the assignment and his traveling into Mexico, wherever the story took him. I advised him to call us regularly, and to use caution, and I went on like this until he interrupted.

"I know, always sit with my back to the wall facing the door," he said, smiling. "I know the routine."

What was a man born and raised in the Watts area of Los Angeles going to learn from a white guy from West Virginia? I shut up.

The assignment turned into a series of articles. We may not have learned about all the Jaimes of the world, but we learned about this one. And so did our readers.

Jaime, meanwhile, went to prison.

The enterprise projects we carried out at the Tucson Citizen went beyond local hard news into sports.

In February 1989, Arizona All-American Sean Elliott lacked only 46 points to become the all-time scoring leader of the Pacific 10 Conference. The record was held by former UCLA great Lew Alcindor, later known as Kareem Abdul-Jabbar. Coming up were two home games, on Thursday against USC and Saturday afternoon against UCLA. If Elliott could average 23 points in each of those two games, he would break the record. That was no easy task against such strong teams, but Elliott was averaging more than that for the season. And he would be playing on his home court.

We had an idea. What if we printed in advance a special edition saying he had broken the record, and had it ready for distribution at the arena as soon as he did so? We would not have the score of the game or his point total. But it would be quite a souvenir edition for the 14,500 fans who would be there. And it would a great marketing piece for the Citizen.

We gathered in my office to discuss it. Included was Mike Welsh, then TNI's marketing director. Of course, printing up thousands of copies would be costly—and, a gamble. If Elliott failed to score 46 points over those two games, we would be stuck with all those special editions and have to eat the cost of printing them and of the newsprint.

But, nothing ventured, nothing gained. Besides, we were confident in Elliott. We decided to go for it, assigning stories, researching, gathering statistics.

By Thursday the edition was completed. A banner headline on its front page announced that Elliott had broken the all-time Pac 10 record. The main story was written as if the game had been played, but without the score or Elliott's point total. Also included were several feature stories on Elliott, photos, and his statistics over the years. We would put it on the press after Friday's regular press run, and we would print several thousand copies to be taken to the arena. We felt good about our plan. Forty-six points wasn't so many for a player of Elliot's caliber.

On Thursday night we were stunned when he scored only 12 against USC. That meant he would have to score 34 against UCLA Saturday. Not very likely.

We convened another meeting Friday morning to cancel the project. At least we would save all that newsprint. But, strangely, no one wanted to. Not even Mike Welsh. "God hates a coward," someone said.

Nobody wants to be a coward. We made the decision to go on with the plan And I silently prepared myself to be hit with considerable criticism from Corporate over scrapping all those copies and wasting all that money. But I said nothing to the others; they were up for it and I didn't want to take that away.

On Saturday afternoon, I sat in the arena watching Elliott play the game of his life. He drove, he floated, he rebounded, he drilled three-pointers, he slammed home dunks. Everyone in the arena was counting his points. Could he pull it off?

When he finally reached his 34th point, the crowd erupted, and at each end of the court a TNI employee held aloft a copy of the Tucson Citizen announcing that Elliott had broken the record. It was spotted immediately. Fans started pointing toward the paper and cheering. We were not permitted to sell our papers inside the arena, but we had employees and bundles of our special edition positioned immediately outside every entrance and exit. Word quickly spread, and as fans left the arena thousands snatched up copies.

I was, as one might expect, quite relieved. I had gone from potential goat to hero, and all because Sean Elliott had scored 34 points. Gannett even asked me to write a report on how we pulled it off.

Not all enterprise stories are as much fun as "Who runs Tucson?" and Sean Elliott's new Pac 10 scoring record, or as impersonal as those about the Hoover Dam and the Grand Canyon. The personal stories sometimes can cause pain, and require even more careful handling.

We were working on a story about one of the biggest developers in Tucson. How did he get to be so successful? So wealthy? So powerful and yet keep such a low profile, out of the spotlight? How much was he worth, really? How much land did he and his various companies own, and how did he amass it? Were there questionable acquisitions involved? What about blind trusts and covered-up connections?

Such a story requires considerable research— digging through purchases, accounts, corporate and partnership filings, and beyond. This is not always easy; one often comes across limited partnerships in which not all the partners' names are recorded. One follows up with interviews with various sources. Lastly, the reporter goes to the subject of the story:

Here's what we have, what do you have to say about it?

In this case, our reporters came across no illegal acts. At the most, there may have been a question of powerful people putting the squeeze on those less powerful in terms of rents, leases, land. Some might even question the ethics involved. I thought of what my old publisher, Buddy Hayden, had said: Private business is private until private business wants to make it public. Well, I hadn't agreed totally then, either.

The subject of the story happened to be a very good friend, one who had been to our home many times, with whom we had often wined and dined. In fact, Sandy and I were going to his house for dinner and on to a performance of the Arizona Theater Co. on the very day that my editors had scheduled the story to appear.

"This is going to be a bit awkward," I told her as we drove into his driveway.

His wife answered the door, full of smiles as usual. Sandy stepped in, and as I started to follow my friend suddenly appeared in the doorway, a copy of the Citizen rolled up in one hand, his arms folded. He said nothing, stood tapping the rolled-up paper against his folded arms.

"I've been reading the Tucson Citizen," he said, stepping aside so I could enter.

"Good. We need all the readers we can get."

"Would you care for a drink?" Still tapping his arm with the paper.

"A beer would be good."

He got beers for us and we sat on a couch in the living room and he proceeded to tell me where he felt the story was incomplete and where it was unfair. I told him the reporter had interviewed him and he had the opportunity to get things straight before publication. I said if there were errors of fact we would correct them the following day, and I invited him to write a guest column if he so desired.. He acknowledged all that, but still couldn't understand why we had done the story in the first place.

"I'm just a private citizen," he said.

"Not true. You may not be an elected official, but you're as public as anyone in this town, in spite of yourself."

In the end we agreed to disagree, enjoyed dinner and went on to the theater.

He was a good man and did a lot for the city. And he remains a good friend to this day. To his credit, not once during the preparation of the story had he called me to try to get the story stopped, even though he knew it was in the works.

It is not unusual for a publisher or editor who is active in the community to have several such awkward circumstances in which he must publish a story about a friend who would rather it not be published. But it goes with the job. To hold a story or underplay a story even once in order to please a friend would be the first crack in one's credibility. And like one's reputation, once that is damaged there is no recovering.

But not all stories that reporters turn up are

worthy of publication, even though they may think so. Sometimes the editor has to make the call. In one matter, I was the one who stopped a story, and that bit of action earned me charges of "protecting his country club friends" from a couple members of the staff.

An editor brought me a story written by one of our reporters but not yet put in print, saying, "I think you ought to see this."

It told of a private cigar and Scotch party to be held at a local resort in which a "female dancer," a stripper, would perform. It was a stag affair, and was being put on by a couple of well-known Tucson citizens and their friends. Names were used, but without attribution or response from those named.

"Where's the story?" I said after reading it, meaning, I don't see anything here that's worth being in the newspaper. "These things happen all the time. Even women are holding them with male strippers. They're hardly against the law. These are not public officials; they're private citizens. If they want to have a party like this, they certainly have that right."

"I thought you'd feel that way," the editor said. "I guess they think it's a story because of the names involved. They're pretty well known."

"We haven't called them, apparently."

"We tried; they hung up on us."

So I called one of them, got through, and told him I had a story in my hands about this stag party and that some of my staff thought it ought to be run. Was he really going to be involved in this? I asked.

If so, did he want to speak to the reporter?

"To tell you the truth, I don't know a hell of a lot about it. Let me get back to you."

He called in minutes. There is no party, he said. It's been called off.

No party, no story. And if there had been, there still would have been no story. We weren't publishing a gossip column. If a few of "Tucson's Best " wanted to make fools of themselves in private, were breaking no laws and were not affecting others, what was the big deal?

The big deal to some of my staff was that I was protecting my pals and had killed a story that would have been embarrassing to them. There isn't much reporters like better than revealing something embarrassing about politicians, government officials—and "leading private citizens," especially if they happen to be wealthy. "Afflict the comfortable and comfort the afflicted," as the saying goes. But one must make sure the story merits publication, and in my opinion, then and now, this one did not.

But those staffers might have been pleased to know that the handling of another story, involving a wealthy developer, also a friend, did cause me a problem. In doing a story about the developer's latest project, the reporter got quotes from both sides, including environmentalists. In displaying the story on the front page, a designer had chosen to "lift out" a quote, with a thumbnail photo. The quote came from one of the environmentalists, who called the developer "the devil." So there was his photo with "the devil" beneath it.

I normally do not see the made-up page before the presses roll, and when the papers came off the press I neglected to look that closely. And then the phone rang. It was my friend, the developer, who was more upset than I had ever seen him. The "devil" label had hurt him deeply, and he could not understand how I could have permitted it to run. I tried to explain that it was a pullout quote for display purposes and that I had not known about it, and I apologized. Understandably that was not good enough. He could not forgive me.

"I of course will not be able to come to your house on Christmas Eve," he said.

It was a long time before he even spoke to me without a wall of awkwardness between us. It was very unfortunate, and in no way did he deserve it. He has contributed multi-millions to the university and to various charities in town.

In any case, such enterprise projects and investigative stories as those mentioned are examples of what a good newspaper does, routinely and consistently. Fortunately, a few major newspapers continue that tradition. But one does not find much risk-taking or enterprise or investigative reporting in most of the small and medium-size papers remaining in this country. Or on their web sites, where most seem to be placing their emphasis. What a loss.

But it was there during my days as editor and publisher of the Tucson Citizen. And that was the fun part. Not the corporate meetings, not the monthly reports, not the budget sessions, not the fighting for our fair share of attention from the Tucson newspaper agency, not the quick trips to El Paso and Santa Fe--but dealing with the day's news.

I recall a comment by John Quinn, Gannett's great news executive: "Being a city editor is the most fun you can have with your clothes on."

I would vote for managing editor. That way you work with all the newsroom departments.

43
IT'S ALSO ABOUT THE PEOPLE

The top editor on any newspaper must make many decisions in his work, and they are not always in agreement with members of his staff. It is not a matter of the editor or the staff being more ethical than the other, although I realize some staff members would challenge that. News staffers do not always consider the consequences of publication. Editors must. By "consequences," I do not mean offending big advertisers or observing sacred cows. But someone has to consider the broad view and make the final decision, whether he or she is the top editor, the publisher or, in my case, carries both titles. For example, an editor might decide that a photograph is too gory to publish in a family newspaper; the photographer who shot the photo might believe that its news value outweighs all other considerations.

Ironically, that can also work in reverse, the staffer not wanting to run a story or photo when the editor believes it should run.

Margaret Bernstein was by now an experienced news staffer, a reporter who had demonstrated intelligence and maturity in news jobs in Huntington, during an internship on USA TODAY, and now on the Tucson Citizen. For that reason we promoted her to assistant city editor. Among the responsibilities in the position was serving as city editor for the Saturday newspaper, which came out early with only one daily edition.

So I was surprised when I picked up that day's newspaper to find what I considered to be an outstanding news photograph used on the local page rather than page one. It showed police, guns drawn, moving in on a suspect hiding beneath a bridge. The suspect was clearly African-American.

I called Margaret in and asked who had made the decision on where to play the photo. She said she had. In fact, she said, she did not even show it to the page one editor because she did not want it used there. She did not want to advance the stereotype of "cops chasing down another black man."

Margaret was, and is, an intelligent and highly sensitive person, and a close friend quite dear to Sandy and me. She is also African-American.

"What if the suspect in the photo had been white?" I asked.

"Then I would have offered it for page one."

That troubled me greatly. If the photo has such news value that it deserves to be on the front page, whether the suspect is black or white should have nothing to do with it. She was basing her news

462

judgment not on the news, but on something else—her own life-long concern with how blacks have been treated in this country and in its media.

Black children, she said, have seen enough of this kind of thing. They do not need to look in their newspaper and see another picture of another black man being hunted down by police.

We had quite a discussion to the point where her eyes welled up in frustration that I could not understand. And then she said, "We make decisions all the time about something besides the news value of a story or photo."

She was right. As with photos too gory for readers to see. We spare them that. Is that any different?

That was a long time ago, and I still am not sure whether Margaret was wrong, or I was wrong. In retrospect, I wish I had not even brought it up. She had a right to her judgment and her opinion. And she did make a valid point. Recently, I related all this to Sandy and to my oldest son, Chris, over lunch. They both sided with Margaret. So, what do I know?

Margaret knew far more about such matters than I. One day in Tucson she was shopping at an inexpensive women's clothing shop. That night police officers came to her apartment. It seemed that after she left the shop, one of its clerks had called police and reported that she had stolen a purse. The clerk got Margaret's license plate number and passed it on to police who tracked it to her apartment. They asked that she confess to the theft.

Margaret was stunned.

She recalled the incident this way in a recent email:

"I was an assistant city editor at the time, undoubtedly making more than the clerk who reported me. My God, people, my father is a probation officer. I don't steal."

She reminded me that the following day when she told me of the encounter, I called Tucson Police Chief Peter Ronstadt, told him that the idea she would steal a cheap purse was preposterous and strongly suggested, according to Margaret, "that he better tell his overzealous detectives to cease and desist from harassing me. They did."

Unfortunately for me, and for the Tucson Citizen and its readers, both Margaret Bernstein and Kevinne Moran left us that year, Kevinne moving with her husband and new daughter for his new job in Portland, Oregon, and Margaret for the Cleveland Plain Dealer, where she became a metro columnist. It was my good fortune to have had both as reporters, and to still have both as friends.

As I have mentioned, occasionally reporters become too close to the people on their beats. It had been brought to the attention of our sports editor, Peter Madrid, that our long-time basketball writer had grown too close to Arizona coach Lute Olson, which creates the possibility of his not being objective in his writing. Madrid felt we needed to make a change. So we moved the writer to another beat, where he flourished, and replaced him with a talented young woman who had experience covering a variety of sports from boxing to baseball. However, in a time all too short, she too proved to be too close to those she covered—in this case, not Olson, but at least two of his players. Her writing reflected that. It was time to make another change.

We had on our staff a young man from Santa Fe named Steve Rivera who covered various sports for us and who showed great promise. He seemed the right choice for this most public of all our beats. He soon gained the respect from everyone involved—players, coaches, fans, and even Olson's wife Bobbi—for his honesty, accuracy and toughness. He was the perfect kind of writer to have on such a key beat in a place like Tucson, where the university truly is the lifeblood of the community. In fact, in a few years he would be included on a list of the top college basketball writers in America by ESPN'S Dick Vital.

As for Rivera's getting too close to Olson, he shared with me an incident some time after it occurred. He had written a story Olson did not like and Olson had complained angrily, even poking Rivera in his chest with his forefinger. When Olson quieted down, Rivera said simply, "Don't do that again, Coach." Olson never did.

I enjoyed running the Citizen. I enjoyed the people who made up its news staff., just as I had enjoyed those on the Huntington newspapers.

And I was enjoying living in Tucson—especially for the people.

If I were to list the most remarkable people I've ever met, right at the top would be a woman named

Bazy Tankersley. Also known as Ruth McCormick of the Chicago Tribune McCormicks. Favorite niece of the legendary Col. Robert McCormick. Former head of the Washington, D. C. Times-Herald, a member of the Chicago Tribune's board of directors, and now owner of one of the largest Arabian horse farms in America. Known as Al-Marah, it took up some one hundred acres on Tucson's east side, at the base of the Santa Catalina Mountains.

Bazy Tankersley lived to be ninety-two, and at the end was still mentally sharp, still very much aware of what was going on in the world of politics, which she always loved. Sandy met her before I did, and was invited to her home while I was out of town. Once I returned, we were invited again. I may have known nothing of Arabian horses and horse farms. But we had the world of newspapers in common.

Bazy's story has been written in books, magazines and newspapers several times over the years. It's surprising a movie hasn't been made. The choice of Col. McCormick to someday succeed him as head of the McCormick empire, Bazy was sent at age twenty-eight to the nation's capital to take over the Times-Herald, which McCormick had just purchased. She was married at the time. But she fell in love with her managing editor, Garvin "Tank" Tankersley, and decided to divorce her husband and marry him. Her uncle was furious. He gave her an ultimatum: reject Tankersley, stay married, and someday you'll run the Tribune Company. Divorce your husband, marry your managing editor, and you're finished. At the time, Bazy thought her uncle was being quite hypocritical. He had already had two wives himself and was remarrying. In any case, she followed her heart, married Tank, left the Times-Herald and the McCormick world—somewhat. She retained her position on the Chicago Tribune board and kept her press card, which she carried as long as I knew her.

And in Tucson, she created one of the world's great Arabian horse farms, with world-class breeding equipment including sonar. Today the farm itself covers eighty–eight acres, has an indoor air-conditioned arena, several buildings for managers and farm hands, barns, breeding stables. Adjacent to it is another ten acre parcel that includes her large and aging farmhouse of some seven bedrooms and a huge, comfortable library—and another building across the swimming pool that is strictly for entertaining. It has two kitchens, large enough to serve more than one hundred twenty-five people, a dining room that comfortably seats sixteen, a room I once called a "great room," which irritated her—call it a living room or front room, whatever—a glassed-in Arizona room, patios, bathrooms.

Bazy long enjoyed having "salons," interesting dinners with interesting people expected to converse intelligently on whatever is going on in the world—especially the world of politics and education and, for some of us, newspapers..

Sandy and I were blessed to be invited many times over the years to these wonderful evenings.

They would begin with drinks on the terrace or in that first room—usually no more than one, sometimes two at the most, and then we would be ushered into the dining room. There Bazy would be standing with a note in her hand on which she had scribbled seating assignments, and she would direct us where to sit. She always placed the person she wanted most to talk with to her immediate left. Another person of interest would be placed to her right. And so on. For my first several visits, I was placed beside her on the left. Then I found myself on the right. The first time I was assigned to sit in the middle of the table, I felt wounded. What had I done? I told myself there were interesting new people she wanted to get to know better and she had placed them beside her. Which was, of course, true.

We reciprocated by inviting Bazy to dinner, to lunch, to university and community events, and to our house for our annual Christmas Eve party. She loved Sandy.

When I arrived at her house, always waiting for me in his chair would be her husband Tank, who by now was having difficulty getting around. He wanted to hear about the latest newspaper convention I had attended, what was being discussed, what other newspapers were doing, and on and on. He was a quiet man, a great listener, a good man.

Bazy founded a private prep school in Tucson called St. Gregory's that to this day enjoys the highest academic achievements in the area. I was invited to speak to the students once and found them to be challenging, energetic, intelligent to the point of brilliance. I was invited, with my friend Dr. John Schaefer, to deliver an annual address there (our subject was the future of print, he discussing books, I newspapers).

She had come by her interest in politics honestly. Her maternal grandfather was the legendary Ohio senator, Mark Hanna. She was also descended from Joseph Medill, whose name adorns the outstanding Medill School of Journalism at Northwestern University. And, of course, in the newspaper world there was her uncle, the Colonel.

An evening, or a lunch or dinner with Bazy was never boring. In fact, I could not keep up. In all honesty, I have never enjoyed politics, despite my many years in newspapers. And I certainly was not as well informed as she, either in politics or world events.

She conducted a summer session at her ranch in northern Arizona to which she invited authors, professors, United Nations officials, friends, and others for four days of discussions on world matters. She called the annual event "the Straw Bale Forum." One day she took Sandy and me to lunch to "discuss a proposition." She wanted me to take over the forum. She was getting too old to run it, she said. I was surprised because I had never even attended, In summer, we vacationed in Cape Cod. I also realized I was not qualified to take over for her. I had to say no, the only time I ever said that to her.

Bazy Tankersley. Quite a lady. It is our good fortune to have known her. And knowing her was one more valuable experience in my new world of Tucson, newspaper-wise and otherwise. She expanded my world.

It was about to be expanded further with a special trip deep into Mexico. Early on we had driven the sixty miles from Tucson to the twin border towns of Nogales, Sonora, and Nogales, Arizona. It was a Sunday afternoon. We parked on the Arizona side of the border and walked across into another country. Driving home later that day I remarked that in the past our Sunday drives might take us a few miles from Huntington, perhaps into two other states—Kentucky and Ohio. Now our Sunday drives took us into another country. It was fascinating, walking along the crowded streets of Nogales, Mexico, stopping at all the shops and booths selling just about everything one could visualize, at prices far lower than one had seen in years. I quickly purchased a leather bag for just a few dollars. And we bought four leather and wood chairs, which we had vendors literally toss over the fence to us once I retrieved my car on the American side. In those days, it was not dangerous to spend an afternoon sightseeing in Nogales. Unfortunately, in recent years that has changed.

Now we were going beyond the border towns. We were invited to join a group representing the University of Arizona on a trip to Mexico City, with a stop in Guadalajara. It was a friend-building and educational trip for the university, and the schedule included dinners, visits to museums, and an afternoon at the University of the Americas in

Mexico City. There was also free time to see more of Mexico City, which was far more European-like than I had expected. We found ourselves in a sidewalk café on the Via de la Rosa that reminded us of those in Paris. We thoroughly enjoyed going to the great museum and seeing the expansive murals of Diego Rivera. And we enjoyed meeting representatives of another country and another university over dinners. I knew that our friend Allan Beigel had been responsible for our being invited. But there were other non-university locals along as well, including our friend Norma Feldman. It was a good trip that taught me much. This was a different and welcome kind of travel for me, not a business trip to one of my regional sites or to regional or corporate headquarters, or to conventions.

That was only a small bit of our activity that year. There were our quarterly TNI board meetings, at least three of them held in Tucson, which brought Gary Watson and Sue Clark-Jackson of Gannett and Nick Penniman of Pulitzer to town. Somehow we always managed to work in a round of golf and dinner at one of Tucson's finest restaurants.

I recall one such visit involving several execs from both companies as well as a few of our own TNI department heads. Watson told me the board meeting would last into the evening so I should not make any dinner reservations for them as I normally did. But shortly before seven o'clock he came over to me and whispered that the meeting was going to be over sooner than he had expected. Everyone was ready for a drink and dinner, he said, and he wondered if I might call "that favorite little restaurant of yours and see if we can get in."

He referred to Le Bistro, a small French restaurant whose owner and chef I knew very well and which my wife and I frequented more than any restaurant in town.

I called George Badoux, at that time the owner, and asked if I could bring a few Pulitzer and Gannett folks to dinner.

"How many?"

"Seventeen."

"Mon dieu. When?"

"Oh, probably the next twenty, twenty-five minutes."

I could not quite make out his reply, but it didn't sound good. It was Monday, normally a slow day, so his chef and maitre d' were both off, leaving him to double as chef and front man, and only a single server to help out.

Then he said, "Okay."

When we arrived, we were greeted by both George and his chef, Laurent Reux, who directed us to a private room just off the entrance. There was a large table, set for seventeen, with large silver buckets at each end. In one bucket were bottles of white Burgandy being chilled, and in the other were several bottles of cold French beer. At the front of the room was a chalk board showing that evening's menu, including one item reading: "Halibut a la Hatfield."

"You come here a lot, Don?" Watson joked.

It was a great evening, the perfect end to a busy

day. I never appreciated George and Laurent more. They were just two more people who made Tucson special for us.

Though six of us made up the TNI board, three from each company, it clearly belonged to Watson as president of Gannett's community newspaper division and Penniman who headed Pulitzer's newspaper operations. The two obviously liked and respected each other and at times would simply get up during a board meeting and disappear into the hall together. When they returned, decisions had been made, subject to a vote by the rest of us.

I liked Penniman. He was a gentleman and easy to talk with, on the golf course, over dinner, or during breaks in the board meetings. We talked about subjects besides newspapering—travel, books, wine, good food. His wife Linda and Sandy liked each other and even did some shopping together during a convention trip to Chicago.

Sandy was looking specifically for items for our new home. We had sold our first Tucson home, which had been too small from the beginning. We learned something about ourselves with that house, which was that even though our sons were gone the two of us needed more space, including a den or library. We looked for a larger house for months and found a jewel sitting atop a small hill in an area called Catalina Foothills Estates Number 10, or "Cat 10." We had made an offer on the house in October of the previous year which had been so far below the asking price that the owner had been insulted and did not want to see us again. By spring he was less insulted and we were able to negotiate the purchase. It was an open, Santa Fe style with windows floor to ceiling—and those ceilings were beamed and more than twelve feet high. Standing in the great room, one looked south over all of Tucson and north into the face of the Santa Catalina Mountains. There was a feeling of space, with views from our back terrace of all four mountain ranges surrounding Tucson. It remains one of Sandy's two favorite houses, the other being our turn-of-the-century home in Huntington.

On the corporate scene, meanwhile, Al Neuharth turned sixty-five and, in line with the policy he himself had established of mandatory retirement at that age, had to step down as Gannett's chairman and CEO. He was replaced by his hand-picked successor, John Curley. Neuharth retained his position as CEO of the Gannett Foundation, which had no such retirement policy. He had left a lasting mark on the company, and with his creation of USA TODAY, the entire newspaper industry.

44
MAKING A DIFFERENCE

Sen. John McCain was back for a meeting with our editorial board, this time under somewhat different circumstances. He came into my office and then we walked to the conference room. The familiar spring in his step seemed to be missing as well as his upbeat smile. He looked tired and somewhat down, which was surprising. But much had happened since our last conversation.

In 1989 McCain and four other U.S. senators—Dennis DeConcini of Arizona, John Glenn of Ohio, Alan Cranston of California, and Donald Riegle of Michigan—found themselves involved in a scandal and referred to as "the Keating Five," linking them to Charles Keating, a wealthy Arizona developer and head of a large savings and loan company. The five were accused of improperly intervening in the federal government's investigation into Keating and his savings and loan operation, which reportedly had bilked its shareholders out of millions of dollars. The five senators, all with solid reputations to this point, had met with regulators on Keating's behalf. Now they were being charged with interceding because Keating had contributed heavily to their campaigns, and had done them favors such as—in McCain's case—a free ride on his jet for a vacation. All five responded that they were only doing what was expected of members of Congress in regard to their constituents and their communities.

McCain said he had done the same thing "dozens of times" for others. That was what members of Congress did, he said.

So here we were in my conference room, sitting at the low round conference table. McCain was asked about the Keating Five incident as I knew he would be. He began to respond in an almost rehearsed manner, and then stopped abruptly and covered his face with his hands.

The room grew silent. Then McCain looked up.

"I'm sorry," he said. "It's just that I've always taken great pride in my reputation, my credibility, in doing the ethical thing, and now this comes along, and…I'm sorry."

I was touched. Here was this former prisoner of war, shot down in Vietnam and thrown into a Vietnamese prison where he spent the greater part of the next six years. Here was this man who had been offered his freedom by his captors because he was an admiral's son, and who had rejected that offer because his fellow American prisoners would not also be freed. This man of great courage and unbelievable service to his country was choked up in my conference room.

In a few minutes he explained his involvement in the matter, said he had broken no rules, that he had simply arranged a meeting with Keating and the regulators, had not attempted to have any charges dismissed.

The Keating five investigation lasted for twenty-two months, from 1989 to 1991. In the end, Glenn and McCain were cleared, found guilty only of "using bad judgment." The others were censured for unethical interference with regulators. DeConcini continued to insist he had done nothing wrong. And Keating went to prison.

I saw both DeConcini and McCain several times after that, not only in editorial board visits but at social events. DeConcini retired—fed up, he said, of having to raise money for re-election campaigning. He wrote to me, commenting on someone's claim that my newspaper had been "soft" on him.

"Your paper has been more fair than other Arizona papers in printing our op-ed pieces and with others who disagree with news reports regarding the Keating matter. But it certainly has not been 'soft' on me, in my opinion. I have no complaints regarding the Tucson Citizen but I know you well enough to know that you call it like it is and when I am criticized I attempt to accept it the best way I can. Certainly you have been a leader in the area of objectiveness in running an Arizona newspaper. To be objective is not to be hard or not to be soft, it is to be fair. I accept that you have done so with this senator."

And McCain. during a reception in Phoenix, told me, "I like your paper."

"Thank you," I said.

"I mean it," he went on. "I think your paper is very fair. I don't always agree with everything you write, but I think you do your job."

I thanked him again.

Some years later he wrote a good book called *Faith of My Fathers*. I asked his aides if he would autograph a copy for me and another for a friend who had fought in World War II. He was happy to do so.

Even after my retirement from the newspaper, Sandy and I occasionally ran into him. While attending a reception and dinner at Ventana Canyon, a resort in Tucson, we were talking with friends when he walked up. He looked at me and said, "Where the hell have you been?"

"I retired," I said. "Don't your people tell you these things?"

"Ahh," he said, grabbing my neck with those short arms made stiff by his wounds in Vietnam, arms that were surprisingly powerful. And he grinned that grin of his.

At the time the United States was about to go into Iraq, and Sandy said, "John, do we really have to do this?"

"Yes, Sandy, we do," he said. But before she could ask why, he was confronted by several well-wishers and we never got an answer. It proved to be the last time we saw him personally.

McCain ran for president in 2000, and in his typical independent, maverick style, did not enjoy the full support of some of those in his Republican party. And following surprisingly unscrupulous acts by his opponents prior to the South Carolina primary, he lost the nomination to George W. Bush. Eight years later he ran for president again, and this time it was a different John McCain from the one I knew. No longer was he the maverick. He wanted the nomination so much that he changed his style, and this time he won it. But he did not win the presidency, losing to Barack Obama.

Since that time he has been the old McCain again, saying what he believes should be said, whether it pleases his party or not. I have always liked and admired John McCain. I cannot forget his courage in that POW camp, nor that day he choked up in my conference room. It is a memory I will carry forever. In some ways I am sorry he did not become president because I know it would have meant so much to him.

But once again I am getting ahead of my story.

By mid-1990, I had become quite tired of the corporate scene and the travel and stress that went with being a regional vice president. There were frequent calls about El Paso, why numbers were down there, what our publisher there was doing to improve them. I dreaded those calls, getting the same old questions and providing the same old answers. A friend of mine at corporate had given up her regional responsibilities because she too had grown tired of it all. I thought about that a great deal. I had been a regional vice president for five years. That was plenty. I was as close to Corporate as I wanted to be. But could I afford to risk stepping down? Would I want to be a quitter? What would that do to my reputation? And would that not reduce my salary?

I didn't have to make the decision. On Oct 1, 1990, Gary Watson called from Corporate. On the line with him was Brian Donnelly. Watson had been president of Gannett's community newspaper division and Donnelly president of its metro division, which had no regional vice presidents. Watson informed me that there had been a change. The community and metro divisions were being combined, and he would become president of Gannett's entire newspaper division. Connelly would become his vice president and continue to concentrate on metro papers. And there was one other major change: Tucson was being placed among the metro papers.

"You've always said Tucson belonged in the metro group," Watson said. He was right.

He was silent for a moment, and then he said, "Of course, this means you'll no longer be a regional vice president."

. I said nothing. I was so relieved I would no longer have regional responsibilities that I did not know what to say.

"So, you'll have more time to play tennis now," he said. .

When I did not respond, he took that to mean I was upset.

"Well, we won't be cutting your salary or anything like that," he said. "I think this is best for Tucson."

"I agree," I said.

"This also means you'll now report to Brian," he said.

Donnelly spoke then. "I look forward to it, Don."

"Thanks, Brian. So do I "

I was thinking how much I would miss Watson. We had been together for a long time. I needn't have worried. He remained on the TNI board, continued to come to Tucson, and we saw each other just as much as before.

And that is the way my life as a Gannett regional vice president came to an end. It had been great, for a while. I was glad for the experience and glad that it was over. I would have more time to spend on my own newspaper, more time in the community I had come to like very much, and more time to spend with Sandy.

By now she had become president of the Arizona Theater Co. For years it had performed in the small Leo Rich Theater, part of a city-owned downtown complex that included a large music hall. Now the company was moving into the restored Temple of Music and Art, a relic from the 1920's that had survived the wrecking ball when dozens of young Tucsonans chained themselves to its front fence to save the old theater. Now it had been returned to a gleaming white stucco building featuring a main theater as well as a small hall for rehearsals or readings. And Sandy was to cut the ribbon.

I sat out front in the sun as the mayor said a few words, joined by a few other dignitaries, and then handed her the scissors. She cut the ribbon deftly, to considerable applause. I was proud of her and grateful to be there instead of on the road somewhere.

As we moved into a new year, Gary Watson had an idea. He had been to enough TNI board meetings by now to know something about Tucson and its newspaper history. He was aware that for years the legendary name "Pulitzer" was the power name in the Tucson newspapers operation. Far more people had heard that name than that of Gannett. He was also aware that Michael Pulitzer himself had once lived in Tucson and served as publisher of the Arizona Daily Star. And as everyone knew, the Star was much larger than the Citizen and enjoyed the strength that any morning newspaper holds over an afternoon paper in a two-newspaper town. In short, he was afraid that Gannett and the Tucson Citizen weren't getting the respect they deserved.

He decided we should throw a party. Make it first class. Invite all the power brokers in town, everyone who was "someone." Big advertisers, developers, politicians, university officials, etc. He would see to it that the top brass of Gannett, the nation's largest newspaper company, was present.

The event was set for March. The venue we chose was the Tucson Country Club, among the most prestigious clubs in southern Arizona. There was a splendid buffet—lamb chops, tenderloin, shrimp, smoked salmon, fine cheeses, and outstanding wines. The invitations invited guests to "come and meet the CEO of Gannett, John Curley," as well as other Gannett and Tucson Citizen executives. And the invitation came from Sandy and me.

I do not remember how many invitations were sent, but there were very few who did not come. The country club was packed. We set up a receiving line with Curley, Watson, Donnelly, and myself, and personally greeted everyone who came through the entrance. Later, we broke line so that we could mingle and talk with our guests. Among them was Lute Olson, the Arizona basketball coach who had become a national figure. Missing was Henry Koffler, president of the university, but only because he was in the hospital at the time.

Curley found it amusing. "Well, you got the basketball coach, but you didn't get the president," he said.

"Only because he's in the hospital. He sent his regrets."

As it turned out, Curley, himself quite a sports fan, talked with Olson more than anyone.

I do not know if that event changed anyone's thinking in Tucson. The Citizen was still the smaller afternoon paper. But at least now people knew that this company called Gannett, considerably larger than the Pulitzer company, was quite a presence in town. And that it obviously was making quite a commitment to the community.

Great idea by Watson.

It's unfortunate that Henry Koffler was unable to make our event, because he would soon be retiring as president of the university. An intelligent man of classical taste, he had been good for the university, had seen it continue to move forward after its being set on that path by his predecessor, John P. Schaefer. Schaefer had taken it from a good university to a major research university of considerable reputation. Now Dr. Koffler too was retiring.

The big question was not only who would replace him, but how that appointment would be made—especially in my mind. This was because Arizona State University, our sister university in Tempe, had only recently named a new president and that process had been conducted in almost total secrecy. Not one candidate was known until the final choice was made. The state's Board of Regents, which governed both universities, determined the process, conducted the search, and made the selection, in private.

I believed strongly that the public had the right to know about a public university, supported with its tax dollars, choosing a president, that it certainly ought to know some of the names being considered before the final choice was made. I understood that every name in a preliminary field of prospects could not be shared with the public; many of those were not even candidates, merely prospects. But I believed the public should know the names of those who did apply for the job, and certainly those who became finalists and were to be interviewed. That had not happened in the Arizona State search. I was determined to see that it did in the University of Arizona selection process.

Our education reporters had a lot to cover in Tucson—higher education, with the university, the Regents, and the multi-branch Pima Community College, as well as many secondary schools. We did all that with two reporters—Joe Garcia and Gaby Rico. Both were good and, as good reporters need to be, relentless.

I told them to keep after the university and the Regents and to report regularly on how the search for a new president was going. They reported back to me that the Regents were not about to share any information on that, believing that candidates' names should not be revealed because it would compromise them and limit the search. Many won't apply if they know their names will be made public, they said, because they fear losing their present jobs.

I could understand that. So I told Garcia and Rico to press the Regents for the names of the finalists, or all candidates to be brought in for interviews.

But the Regents would have none of it. Okay, I said, then we'll sue.

Two members of the Regents, Donald Pitt and Esther Capin, were friends of mine. In fact, that very evening Sandy and I were to have dinner with Esther, who just happened to be president of the Regents, at Le Bistro.

On our way I told Sandy that I might be suing Esther the next day. Sandy asked that I not mention it, at least until the end of our dinner. We had, as usual, an enjoyable meal, with good conversation and good wine. And when deserts came, I mentioned the university's search for a new president. I told her, though she already was aware of our position on the matter, that I felt strongly the public needed to know the names of the finalists before the final decision was made.

She gave me the reasoning we all had heard, and I told her I understood. But, I said, the people's right to know is more important. Therefore, I said, "Tomorrow my newspaper may be filling suit against the Regents."

"Oh, I hope you won't be doing that," she said.

"We're not asking for every name on the list," I said. "Or even all those who apply. But we do believe the public has a right to know the names of those called in for interviews. If you will agree to provide that, we'll forget the rest including the lawsuit."

She said she would take it to the Board.

The next day she called to say the Board had agreed. It would provide the names of finalists being brought in for interviews before the final section was made.

"That's great, Esther. That's the right thing to do."

I felt we had performed a service for the people of Tucson. But somewhere along the way, as word of those who were being considered for interviews somehow trickled out, Garcia and Rico had a question: "Are any Hispanics among those to be interviewed?"

Their tips had been sound. There were no Hispanics. Strange, for a city like Tucson, where there were so many Hispanics, many of them integral parts of the community. Surely across the country in this national search, there were Hispanic academics qualified to be considered as finalists for president of this university so close to Mexico.

They wrote the story and local Hispanic leaders jumped all over it. The Regents suddenly announced that the presidential search had been extended.

Soon the list of candidates to be interviewed included Dr. Manuel Pacheco, president of the Houston branch of the University of Texas. There was a visit, an interview, a study of his qualifications, and before one knew it he was among the finalists. And when the final selection was made, Pacheco was the choice.

The public had seen a list of finalists before the choice was made, as we had sought. The candidates included a qualified Hispanic academic leader as many had wanted, and as we had urged in editorials. The University of Arizona had a new president, one of considerable promise. And readers of the Tucson Citizen knew what was going on, all the way.

I told Garcia and Rico they had done a good job for the newspaper, and a great service for the community. That's what good reporters do.

Manuel Pacheco and his wife Karen served the

university from 1991 to 1997. They shared their home with countless members of the community, guests from across the nation as well as from other countries, the well-known and the not-so-well-known. Sandy and I were there several times and enjoyed sitting at table with many interesting people, once including Prince Edward, the Duke of Kent, who was visiting the university. (I had watched on television countless times as he and his wife had handed out trophies at Wimbledon). Sharing was what the Pachecos were all about. They brought the university to the community in a very real way. The Regents, in my mind, had made a good choice.

Some time after Pacheco took office, I was visited in my office by Donald Pitt. Here was this good friend who had taken Sandy and me to join him and his wife Susan to watch Phoenix Suns games—he was a part owner. We had shared good times, many dinners, and he and Susan had been to our house every Christmas Eve. It was unusual for him to be coming to my office; we usually saw each other elsewhere. When he entered, he closed the door behind him. I wondered what this was all about.

"I want to tell you something," he said. "I don't think you newspaper people always realize what's involved elsewhere. In our search for a new UA president, you insisted that we identify finalists and those being interviewed. Do you know how many people we lost because of that? There one very special candidate in particular. He had to drop out when he learned that his name would be made public. If he did not get the job, he would be washed up where he was. That's the world of Academia. You people don't realize that. He would have been a great president. Okay, Pacheco seems to be a good man, so it turned out all right. But it might not have. You could have cost the university someone truly special. It's easy for you to say the public needs to know this, the public needs to know that. And most of the time I agree. But frequently there is another side, and a reason for doing things in another way. And I just don't think those of you in the media always consider that."

Neither of us ever mentioned the matter to each other again. But he did leave me thinking. And maybe I wasn't quite as proud and cocky as before.

Meanwhile, life went on in the wonderful world of Pulitzer, Gannett, and TNI. Harry Whipple had proved to be the solid leader of the agency that I thought he would be. He was a man of enormous patience, especially with me. He was my friend, but I must admit I was not always as nice to him as I should have been. Always, this came about when I thought the Citizen was not getting its fair share of attention—meaning, marketing and circulation. Sometimes I became quite angry and found myself almost yelling at him. He would listen and when I calmed down, would say, almost softly, "Don, what's wrong?"

We played golf together, dined together, talked privately. And he never reminded me of what a jerk I had been. I knew what an almost impossible job he had. Serving two masters equally is not easy. But I had a difficult job too, in running the smaller paper and making sure we got what we should be getting from the agency. And I had concerns. I feared Whipple was going to take my paper down the same path that my former afternoon newspaper in Huntington had been taken, only to die a slow death. Whipple succeeded in convincing both companies to cut back on my newspaper's circulation in southern Arizona, where we were stronger than the Star, and transfer that circulation to the Star. The thinking was that the agency would have one cycle of delivery trucks instead of two, thus cutting in half the agency's travel expenses there, saving on gas, tires, drivers, and so on. The agency would simply tell Citizen subscribers that from now on they would have to take the Star instead. He promised, he would build up Citizen circulation elsewhere.

I had heard this before, in Huntington, where the publisher had moved the evening paper out of eastern Kentucky, telling subscribers there from now on they had to take the morning paper. That idea flopped when they did not, instead subscribing to the Lexington and Louisville papers. Now here we were doing the same thing in Tucson.

Gannett and Pulitzer agreed to Whipple's plan because it would save on expenses, thus increasing profits for both owners. But I was not a very good member of the TNI board, because I didn't care whether profits were increased if it meant my newspaper was making the sacrifice. Anyway, I lost the argument. No surprise there.

I feared the next two steps would be to eliminate the Saturday afternoon Citizen as well as the second, or final, edition of the Monday-through-Friday Citizen. I told him not to even think about it, and not to bring it up with others on the board. He did not, and that did not happen, at least during his watch and mine. Eventually, however, my fears proved well-founded. The Saturday Citizen was killed and the 1 p.m. final edition of the Monday-through Friday paper was dropped. All three moves, as I had seen years before, were steps toward the newspaper graveyard. At least I wasn't there to see it.

45
CHANGE ONCE AGAIN

January 1992 brought us a Gannett "on-site" meeting, a corporate visit considerably more civilized than the regional subsidiary meetings we once had shared with other Gannett newspapers. The meeting was still an evaluation of sorts, with the top Gannett brass coming to town to look over the property, meet with the publisher and agency president, talk with department heads, check on revenues, costs and the ever important bottom line. And enjoy a fine dinner, hosted and "emceed" by the local publisher.

Harry Whipple and I worked together to prepare for the meeting and dinner. As president of the agency and the man most responsible for its financial performance, he would head up the main sessions. He would prepare his vice presidents— advertising, production, circulation, finance, marketing, human resources. I would concentrate on the Citizen side, its expenditures and especially the news operation. And as publisher I would emcee the big dinner. However, the agency would be billed for it—meaning Pulitzer would pay fifty percent of this Gannett meeting.

Harry, some of his vice presidents, and I met the corporate jet and brought our Gannett visitors to the Tucson newspaper complex. Some of the corporate visitors met with members of Whipple's executive staff. Gary Watson, meanwhile, came into my office. He closed the door behind him and sat facing me.

"I'm taking Harry back with me."

"You are?"

"We're moving him to another property."

This seemed very sudden. I was surprised I had not been involved in the discussion. Obviously, Nick Penniman of Pulitzer and probably Mike Pulitzer as well had to have been involved because Whipple also reported to them.

"Do you have a replacement in mind?"

"Larry Aldrich. We brought him with us. He'll stay."

"Larry Aldrich?" This was even more of a stunner. Aldrich had never been a publisher or general manager, had never, in fact, worked for a newspaper. He did know the Tucson operation pretty well, having been involved in the rewriting of the joint operating agreement and serving briefly as secretary to the TNI board during the negotiations. A member of the corporate legal staff, he had come to Gannett from the federal government where he worked in anti-trust matters, particularly involving newspaper JOA's. I knew him and liked him. Still, I was surprised.

"He's never worked for a newspaper," I said.

"He knows the Tucson operation," Watson said. "He'll do the job." Then, smiling, he added, "Besides, he has you here."

I did not know whether he was being light, or serious, or throwing me a bone. But it was true. He would be responsible for the business side, not the newspaper itself. That was still my responsibility as editor and publisher. Also, he would be reporting to the six-member board and I was one of those six. That's the way it had been with Harry Whipple, and that had worked fine. Still, I had concerns. Would he understand where I was coming from when I pushed for more support for the Citizen?

I said none of this to Watson. Instead, I said, "Where are you taking Harry?"

He hesitated. "That won't be announced until tomorrow, when we get there." He paused again. "Well, I know you won't tell anybody. It's Cincinnati."

"That's great. That's a great move for him."

"Yeah, it's a JOA, only not 50-50 like this one. There, we're the majority owner."

"He'll do a good job. I'll miss him."

Our on-site visit went well. Whipple's department heads handled themselves as the professionals they were. And our financial numbers looked solid. Even Larry Miller, Gannett's chief financial officer, seemed pleased—although he and

I did have our usual editor-finance chief argument during his brief visit to my office. He asked why we sponsored so many things and gave away so much money in the community. We should be using our Gannett Foundation grants for that, he said, not take it out of our own expenses.

"Treat the money as if it were your own," he said.

"If it were, I'd give away more," I said, adding, "the way you do." I knew he personally contributed considerably to his church and to several charities.

He ignored me and went on to the next question about newsroom expenses, targeting as always the amount we had budgeted for travel. "Your travel budget is bigger than Poughkeepsie's and you're about the same circulation."

"As I've mentioned before, circulation is not the factor. Population, geography--those are the factors. Do you realize my education reporter has to drive forty miles just to get from an east side school to a west side school? This is not Poughkeepsie."

"Ah," he said, "you editors are all alike."

As the day drew to a close our Gannett visitors met with TNI department heads to announce that Whipple was being promoted to another Gannett property and that he would be replaced by Larry Aldrich. Shortly after, all TNI employees were asked to gather in the cafeteria conference room and there Aldrich was introduced as their new boss. He spoke briefly, saying he looked forward to working with them and occasionally inserting a few humorous comments. Good job, I thought.

Dinner was held at the Westin La Paloma resort, where the Pulitzer and Gannett visitors were staying. It was a fine affair, with good food, good wine, and good conversation. Then it was time for a few remarks from the host publisher, that being me.

I began by welcoming everyone, and then introducing our corporate visitors. When I came to Larry Miller, whose reputation for cutting costs and holding on to every Gannett dime possible was known by all, I said, "And now, a great humanitarian, Larry Miller."

The room erupted in laughter.

"That will cost you ten thousand dollars," Miller called out.

In truth, Larry Miller rarely gave me many problems about Tucson expenses once we got our budget approved. Fortunately, the Tucson operation made good money. "Big bucks in Tucson," Gary Watson once told Gannett publisher and regional officer Frank Vega when the three of us were dining in Washington, D.C. And big bucks there were.-- total annual revenues of more than $100 million and a profit margin of more than thirty percent.

And now that newsroom expenses for both papers were being split by the two owners, I could do some things that wouldn't fly elsewhere. For example, every year I gave Christmas gifts to every member of the Citizen staff--hooded sweatshirts, sweaters, turtle necks, all adorned with "Tucson Citizen" on the chest. I also held a staff Christmas party every year, at first serving Mexican food and beer at a quaint old house in the Botanical Gardens, later expanding that to an expensive buffet and drinks at La Paloma. I wanted to reward the staff and make everyone feel special. Not once did anyone at Corporate mention either expenditure to me.

So now we had a new man in town, Larry Aldrich. Over the next several weeks Sandy and I took him to dinner several times and to the theater, and I took him to lunch to meet various people in the community. I felt it important that he get to know them and they him as soon as possible. But he hardly needed my help. He was an articulate, intelligent man of charm and humor and made friends easily and quickly, and soon became a familiar face in Tucson.

Unlike Whipple, Aldrich made it clear that he was running "Tucson Newspapers." That caused some confusion because he ran neither newspaper, not the Arizona Daily Star, not the Tucson Citizen. What he ran was the agency, previously known as "Tucson Newspapers Inc." or "TNI" and now as "Tucson Newspaper Partners." More than once I had to explain that Aldrich did not run the Citizen— I did. In fact, at one of his first meetings of the Greater Tucson Economic Council, I was approached by Jim Click, one of our biggest advertisers and a man I had known for several years, who said: "I've just met your new boss. Seems like a nice fellow."

"He's not my boss," I said. "He reports to the board and I'm on the board. He runs TNI, not the

Citizen."

Click looked puzzled and said, "Well, whatever."

It was a situation that, unfortunately, would be repeated many times during the next several years.

In May, Harry Whipple called to ask about my editorial page editor, Peter Bronson. He was thinking about Bronson for the same position on the Cincinnati Enquirer, at the time Gannett's largest newspaper other than USA TODAY. Bronson was a columnist as well as editor of the editorial pages for the Citizen and had quite a following in Tucson. His columns were so well researched that sometimes they resembled investigative reporting, but with a touch of opinion. Our conservative readers loved him, our liberal readers hated him, but just about everyone read him—the best thing you can say about any columnist. So I did not want to see him leave. But this was a big step up, a much larger newspaper, many more readers, and considerably more money. Of course I couldn't stand in his way. I recommended him highly to Whipple, saying he would be perfect for Cincinnati, which had the reputation of being a very conservative city. Harry said he would arrange an interview.

I then told Bronson about the call, that he would be hearing from Whipple, and that I didn't want to see him go, but it would be a great move for him. In less than a month he was gone. He would become a very popular columnist in Cincinnati. No surprise to me.

I knew it would be difficult to replace Bronson

on the Citizen, and not just because of his column's popularity. The editorial page editor position on our paper was a demanding one. We published two pages of opinion each day—the editorial page and the op ed page. These contained two locally written editorials every day, syndicated columns, letters to the editor, guest opinion columns, staff columns, and editorial cartoons. All had to be selected, edited, displayed on the pages, and headlines had to be written on each one. The editorial page editor also organized and conducted our editorial board meetings, extending invitations to newsmakers and others, and our monthly citizens editorial advisory councils. As if this were not enough, he also wrote a weekly personal column. And he had to meet regularly with the publisher to discuss editorial positions and other matters. To do all this, he had only himself and his assistant editorial page editor. If you had an editor who could do all this and still write a lively and popular column, you were fortunate indeed. We had been fortunate to have Bronson. Now we had to find his replacement.

After making several contacts and inquiries I settled on a former Citizen newsman named John Lankford. He was lively, energetic, and wrote extremely well. I was warned about one problem: in his career he had demonstrated a restlessness that had led him to move from one job to the next. In fact, he had left the Citizen years before to join the news staff of the city's top local television station, only to leave that job, too, after a short while.

But given his abilities, especially his writing

talent, I brought him in for an interview. And those old vibes returned. He would be a good fit for us—if I could trust him to stay. So I brought up that concern early in our talk. He admitted he had moved around far too much, and blamed it on the restlessness of youth. He had outgrown that, he said. He wanted to return to the Citizen, where he had been happy before, and this time he would stay. Sandy and I took him and his wife to dinner and celebrated his joining the Citizen staff.

We worked well together with few disagreements. His columns were good, as I expected them to be. He got along with everyone. I felt good about the staff that summer. Sandy and I decided to invite every member, with spouse or friend, to our house for a party of Mexican food, wine and beer. It lasted well into the night, with Lankford holding forth from a lawn chair. .

It was also the summer of '92 that I was asked to become a member of the University of Arizona Foundation Board of Directors. Although I had been asked to serve on most boards, this was one I had actively sought. It wasn't a matter of ego, although most of its members were among the most powerful people in town. Rather, the attraction for me was that it served the university and education, which had long been priorities for Sandy and me. I told my friend Dr. Alan Beigel of my interest and he passed it on to the Foundation's president, Dick Imwalle. And when the next round of membership vacancies came up, I was invited to join the board. I was thrilled. This would prove to be a relationship that would grow and last for years..

I also became involved, to a lesser degree, with the Muscular Dystrophy Association, which had moved its headquarters from New York to Tucson and whose striking new building was located in the Catalina Foothills not far from our house. I was asked to become a "national vice president," which involved very little work. Because of this and my position as publisher, Sandy and I were invited to an MDA reception featuring Jerry Lewis, the actor, comedian and long-time face of the MDA and its annual Telethon. Sandy talked with him for several minutes about disabled children, and somehow the conversation got to our having a severely disabled daughter. Lewis put his hand on Sandy's shoulder and said, with sincerity, "You know what it's like, don't you, Dear." Sandy was touched. A few days later I received a letter from Lewis:

"Dear Don: It was a pleasure to meet you and Sandy last night at the kick-off for our February gala. Sam (Lewis's wife) and I are happy to count you among our many new friends in Tucson.

"I deeply appreciate all your support for MDA in Tucson. Thanks for all your help in ensuring the concert will be a tremendous event for MDA and for the city. God bless you. Love, Jerry."

Below his signature was this handwritten addition: "It was good talking with you and your lovely wife. J."

Sandy continued to be active, and not only in Tucson. Serving as president of the Arizona Theater Company took her to Phoenix as well. And being appointed to the Arizona-Mexico Commission by then-Gov. Fife Symington took her not only to Phoenix but also Mexico. I was privileged to go along as spouse. It was good for me in several ways, especially in meeting people I otherwise would not have met.

The Commission held panel discussions during its sessions and that year one touched on journalism as practiced in Mexico. I thought that was a topic that merited more attention. By coincidence Tucson Citizen reporter Ruben Hernandez had been asked to participate on a Commission committee to explore the matter. Together he and I planned and conducted a day-long seminar in Tucson involving journalists from Mexico and Arizona. Discussions were ripe throughout the day, including lunch. I knew the meeting was worthwhile when one of the Mexican journalists chastised those of Arizona for "abusing the freedom of the press you have in your country." "You Americans take it for granted," he said. His words created a whole new direction for the discussions. We followed up with a story and editorial on the joint meeting.

As the year neared its end, an interesting sports story developed that would create an ethical problem for the Citizen and for me in early 1993. Our sports columnist, Corky Simpson, served as one of the voters in the weekly Associated Press football poll. Each week he voted for Alabama as No. 1, while other voters listed several different teams in that slot. In those days, the team that finished the final week of the AP poll in first place was declared the national champion. When Alabama finished its regular season undefeated, several other voters moved over to also choose the Crimson Tide as No. 1, just as Corky Simpson had been doing all year long. Alabama completed the matter with a victory in the Jan. 1 1993 Sugar Bowl and was declared the national champ. Someone in Tuscaloosa discovered that Simpson had voted for the Tide as No. 1 all season long, the only writer in America to do so. Suddenly he became a hero there, and was invited to attend a championship celebration featuring a parade in Tuscaloosa.

When Simpson told me about it, he said he didn't know whether he should go. Alabama was willing to pay his way, he said, so it wouldn't cost the Citizen anything. I reminded him that our policy was that we accepted no freebies, that we "pay our own way." However, I added, we didn't have it in our budget. Therefore he should thank them but reject the offer.

He came back to my office the next day. A private plane would be taking others from our part of the country to Tuscaloosa and there was room for him. It would cost no one anything.

I thought of the marketing publicity the Citizen would get with its sports columnist in the parade. I told him to accept the ride but that the Citizen would pay his hotel expenses.

Corky Simpson rode in a convertible at the head of the parade and the Citizen enjoyed the national publicity—for a very brief time. The Associated Press reported that it was not involved in the celebration, that it continued to be impartial, and that Simpson did not represent the AP. Also, it pointed out that he was no longer a voter in the AP poll, his term having expired at the end of the season.

I called Lou Boccardi, the CEO of the AP and a friend, to explain how all this had come about and to apologize if I had unthinkingly involved the AP. I did not consider my allowing Corky to ride in the parade to be unethical, I said.

"Well, we could debate that," Boccardi said.

Some time later the sports columnist of the Arizona Daily Star wrote about the incident but incorrectly reported that Simpson had been kicked off the AP football voting committee. He repeated this on a sports talk radio show. Not so. Corky's term had expired. But the Star didn't bother to report that. Angered, I made the mistake of calling the talk show and trying to set things straight. I must have sounded like an idiot.

In the spring of 1993, less than a year after promising that he was at the Citizen to stay, my new editorial page editor, John Lankford, came into my office, looking nervous and uptight, saying he needed to talk. And then he said he was leaving. His doing so had nothing to do with me or the Citizen staff, he said. Everyone had treated him well. I was the "best publisher I've ever worked for," he said. It was just himself. He couldn't explain it. He just had to move on.

Well, I had been warned.

This time I would not look outside for a

replacement. Some time before I had reorganized the newsroom to split the operation into two divisions—content (reporting, writing) and production (editing, page design). I had appointed an assistant managing editor over each, promoting former city editor Mark Kimble and business editor Judy Lefton into the slots. I now decided to turn once again to Kimble, who had done well in every newsroom assignment given him. I upgraded the editorial page editor position to associate editor of the newspaper, and convinced him to take the job. It was one of the best decisions I ever made. Kimble expanded and excelled in every aspect of the position, proving to be an outstanding columnist, a solid editor, a great representative for the Citizen in the community, a popular member of a weekly public television news show, and the most dependable member of the Citizen staff.

I could always count on Kimble for a straight answer, even if I hadn't asked a question. He was not shy when it came to telling me I was wrong, or questioning something I had done or said. But this was not a man without humor. Nor was he boring or ordinary in any way. He was a Mickey Mouse freak. He went to Disneyland every year. He wore a Mickey Mouse watch. Every tie he owned was a different kind of Mickey Mouse tie. And on the wall in his office was displayed an expensive Mickey Mouse cartoon cel, properly framed, not far from his Indianapolis 500 racing poster. Yes, he went to the big race every year as well. I used to wonder what visitors to his office thought when the first thing they saw was a Mickey Mouse cartoon cel and the second thing a racing poster. But then, he was a newspaperman, and I thought of what my old coaching friend back in Huntington had said about newsrooms being zoos.

That would not be the only major change for our newsroom. Dale Walton, our long-time managing editor and my right arm, decided to retire. I was partly the cause. I had been notified by Corporate that as of the end of the calendar year it would no longer provide health care coverage for retirees. If Walton were to retire before that, he would get health care coverage throughout his retirement. If he continued to work beyond the end of the year, he--like all of us including myself-- would not. I called him in and told him about it. I made clear I did not want to see him retire, but I felt I owed it to him to tell him about the coming change. The next day he told me he would retire in order to keep the coverage. I could not blame him.

Managing Editor is a top-level job on any newspaper and choosing one requires checking with Corporate. I notified Sue Clark-Jackson, regional president in Reno and my immediate boss, and Phil Currie at Corporate, long one of the company's top news executives who would become Gannett's VP/News. Both Clark-Jackson and Currie had lists of key people ready for promotion, and up came the name of Ricardo Pimentel, then managing editor of Gannett's newspaper in Stockton, California. Both Sue and Phil thought he would be a good fit in Tucson.

A Gannett meeting was coming up in Washington and Pimentel would be there. We met at a dinner and talked briefly. He seemed a likeable sort. Later he visited Tucson for an interview and I offered him the job, which he accepted. He, his wife Laura and Sandy and I went to dinner at Le Bistro to celebrate. We became good friends immediately.

Which is not to say we always agreed. Early on he wrote a personal column for our op ed page and brought it to me. It spoke of Tucson's "white flight" from downtown to the Foothills, and compared it to what had happened in Detroit. It struck me he was going too far with that comparison, and that there had been little "white flight" to the Foothills in Tucson. I chalked it up to the fact that he had been in Tucson only a short time and did not understand its past as well as its present. No one "fled" downtown Tucson to get away from Hispanics, I said, using the word then more in fashion than the "Latinos" usage we now hear. In fact, many of my neighbors were Hispanic, I said. They didn't flee downtown; they had never lived there. They had come to the Foothills because they preferred living there over downtown. He was surprised and frustrated and visibly upset. I suggested he rewrite the column. Eventually he did, and it was published, but I'm sure neither of us was satisfied with the new version.

Looking back, I can see I was wrong, as I said in a recent e-mail to Ricardo. Chalk it up to my ignorance, I said.

In October of 1993, Sandy and I were chosen by Pima Community College to be the recipients of its annual awards recognition dinner for service to the community. The dinner was the college's major fund-raiser of the year. This would be the first time in the nine years of the awards that a couple, rather than an individual, would be honored. I was very pleased for Sandy, who would finally receive the recognition she deserved for all she had done in the community.

We asked our good friend Stanley Feldman, chief justice of the Arizona Supreme Court, to serve as guest speaker, Bishop Manuel Moreno to give the invocation and Rabbi Arthur Oleisky to handle the Benediction. We were honored that all three agreed. We were also pleased that so many of our friends bought tickets and that so many companies sponsored tables, including Larry Aldrich and TNI, the Citizen, and even the Arizona Daily Star, my competitor.

Both Sandy and I spoke following Justice Feldman's remarks, and this gave me the opportunity to thank Sandy in public for all she had done for Tucson, for the Citizen, and for me. It was a splendid evening and we were grateful.

46
FREEDOM OF SPEECH
FOR ALL OF US

It struck me that for more than a year there had been certain incidents in Tucson that posed a threat to freedom of speech, more specifically freedom of expression in the arts.

The first involved a local high school in which the drama teacher had planned to produce the award-winning play, "The Shadow box." She would edit out some offensive language for the production, she said. But apparently some heard excerpts of the play with the original language and found it "offensive." The school canceled the play and at the end of the school year the teacher was let go.

Next came the seizure by police of photographs at a small art gallery. The photographs, which had appeared in museums and galleries, were reported to include shots of nude adults and one of a nude child. They had been seen by children from a nearby school peeking into the gallery windows. After a complaint by someone, police seized the photos—twelve of them to be exact—on the grounds that they were pornographic. The deputy prosecuting attorney told us the police had done "the right thing," and that the photographer—a veteran professional who had included in the gallery display a photo of her four-year-old son—faced up to twelve years in prison. The prosecutor and the police refused to allow reporters to see the seized photos.

All this was reported, of course, and there was considerable reaction in the community. Surprisingly, after several days the police and the prosecutor suddenly said the photos were not pornographic after all, the photographer would not be charged, and our reporters could look at all the photos if we so desired--except for one, which still might be considered offensive. It showed the four-year-old holding a chicken in front of his genitals.

The third incident involved this same police department and the Arizona Theater Company. This time police, again acting on a single complaint, told the theater company that it would have to ban anyone under the age of eighteen from seeing the prize-winning play, "M. Butterfly," because it involved a scene on stage of a nude male. The company would also have to post a sign saying so, and if it refused both orders it would be shut down.

All this got considerable attention—in our newspaper, certainly, and nationwide. It aroused the attention of a national organization called "People for the American Way," a group of free speech activists from the East Coast that included such notables as actors Christopher Reeves and Mercedes Ruehl. They were particularly concerned about the high school cancelling the planned production of "The Shadow Box" and the teacher being let go. They decided to come to Tucson to give a public reading of the play and to discuss it.

My newspaper and I were only too happy to be involved. Working with others in Tucson as well as the organization, we scheduled the reading for the Temple of Music and Art, with a panel discussion to follow. We found panelists who we hoped would represent both sides in the matter and convinced Stanley Feldman, chief justice of the Arizona Supreme Court, to moderate.

At the time I wrote the longest column of my career. Some excerpts:

"If the photographs were 'not even in the realm of pornography,' as the police now say, why were they taken in the first place?"

"Who is to determine what is art and what is pornography? Police officers? Deputy prosecutors?"

"Why are police officers bothering with an art gallery at all at a time when kids are being gunned down in school yards and shoppers are being attacked at malls?"

Regarding the play, "M Butterfly," I wrote: "And all because one theater-goer considered one scene showing a nude male to be obscene. And this a play that had achieved worldwide praise for its depth and sensitivity.

"That a single person...filing one complaint can create such strong and immediate action by law enforcement agencies is not only unsettling but downright dangerous.

"Who and what is next?"

Moving on to the scheduled reading and panel discussion of "The Shadow Box," I wrote:

"Perhaps we ought to urge that some members of the Tucson Police Department and the prosecutor's office attend the panel discussion. They might learn something.

"Whatever the benefits or outcome of Monday evening's discussion, let's just hope we're not seeing a trend here—a high school play cancelled, a professional theater company told by police what it can and cannot do, an art gallery raided.

"If such actions continue, any of us could become potential targets. And we all will be the losers."

Following the reading and discussion, our newspaper co-hosted a reception in the library of the Arizona Inn. There, before a roaring fire in the fireplace, we talked to the panel participants and several of those who had attended. Reeves and Ruehl were especially complimentary that so many in Tucson had stepped up in support of freedom of speech and freedom of expression in the arts. And we were especially complimentary to them and their colleagues for taking time to come to Tucson for the reading and discussion.

I was proud of my newspaper's role in all that, and frankly, proud of my column, which received a number of good comments. But I knew at the time I would receive plenty of criticism as well. Many complained that my views were far too liberal for a newspaper that had been thought of as conservative. They did not share my opinions and they were disappointed I had published such a column. I was not surprised. I told each of them what I told most people who called to complain about a story, editorial or column: If you will write a letter or guest column taking issue with what we've printed, we'll be happy to run it.

When I arrived at the Tucson Citizen in 1986, I was well aware of its history as the oldest newspaper in Arizona, having been born in 1870, and as the traditional "Republican" and "conservative" newspaper. I understood, as I had been told, that the Arizona Daily Star was traditionally and predictably liberal, and that the Tucson Citizen, partly because of JOA anti-trust legislation and partly because of its own interest in survival, should be different from the Star. I also had told myself, and others, that it was more important for the people of Tucson to have two separate newspaper voices than for me to "get my way." Still, I was not quite prepared for some of the issues that would confront me early on.

Ted Craig, the editorial page editor when I arrived, was very conservative. His editorials showed that, and so did his arguments during editorial board meetings when we discussed editorial stands. Peter Bronson, at that time Craig's assistant, was of the same persuasion even though he once had been a college protester of the Vietnam War and other matters. So right away, I found myself down two votes to one. Fortunately, the editorial board also included another editor and a reporter.

I once was asked how many votes I got as publisher in my own editorial board meetings. My joking reply was "as many as it takes." In truth, I tried to follow the votes of the board without exercising my power as the man in charge.

Sometimes I winced, as when Craig and Bronson wanted to editorialize in support of the mining of harbors during the Reagan presidency. And, when they wanted to editorially endorse the Republican in a race for mayor when it was clear that he was by far the weaker candidate (he lost by a wide margin despite our endorsement).

But there were at least two times I did play the publisher's card.

The Arizona Legislature was taking up a bill to establish a holiday commemorating the birthday of Dr. Martin Luther King Jr. Bronson, who had replaced Craig after his untimely death from melanoma, turned in an editorial before we had even discussed it, saying the bill should be killed. Bronson offered several reasons, from the "cost of another state holiday" to certain aspects of King's life which he claimed should prevent him from being so honored. Disregarded was the fact that many states had already established a holiday honoring King.

I tossed back the editorial and stood facing him.

"All my life I have fought for the rights of minorities," I began. "I am not going to stop now, whatever the hell this newspaper's history may dictate. We will not editorialize against a holiday in honor of Martin Luther King. In fact, we will endorse it. Every black American deserves it, and Dr. King deserves it. So you can tear this up and start over."

Bronson looked at me with both surprise and disdain. "I refuse to write that."

"Fair enough," I said. "Then I will."

People often ask why editorials aren't signed. It's because they reflect the editorial opinion of more than one person. They represent the editorial stand of the newspaper itself and the collective thinking of an editorial board made up of several people.

I did not blame Bronson for refusing to write the editorial supporting a King holiday. He was a man of principle and stood up for his own opinions. But in this case, his opinion did not match mine, nor those of most of the Citizen news staff, nor the direction in which I wanted to take the Citizen.

A similar stand-off came some time after that when Bronson wanted to editorialize in support for capital punishment. I gave him pretty much the same words: "I have always been opposed to capital punishment. I have a problem with taking someone's life in a civilized society. I am not going to change now."

He gave me the usual argument, a collection of facts and a report on many vicious crimes, and then he brought out that old favorite of those who believe in capital punishment:

"What if a criminal took the life of someone you loved, say your wife? Wouldn't you want to see him dead?"

"Absolutely," I said. "In fact, I would want to kill him myself. But that does not make it right."

For the most part, however, Bronson and I got along very well. And when he left to take the Cincinnati job, he told me I was the best publisher he'd ever worked for. That meant more to me than when John Lankford had said it, because I knew Bronson meant it.

Many people do not understand how editorial endorsements are made on most newspapers. I can only speak about how it was done on newspapers for which I have been responsible.

First, we invited all the candidates in to make their case to our editorial board, usually made up of about five people. Obviously, we also had considerable information on each candidate, based on our own news stories and interviews. Then, once the candidates had appeared before our editorial board we sat around the conference room table and discussed the merits of each. Sometimes there was near-unanimous agreement. Sometimes there were disagreements to the point of arguments. But when we emerged from the meeting, there was the understanding that, okay, this is the person we're endorsing for this race.

It should be said that our choice would be reflected only in editorials and only on our editorial page. Endorsements would never affect the news. Most people don't believe that, but on the papers

I've headed, that has certainly been the case.

The local public television station filmed such an endorsement meeting in my conference room, and the program received good comments when it was shown.

A woman once asked me at an art museum reception if I had made up my mind yet which candidate I was going to support in some race. I responded that "our editorial board hasn't interviewed any of the candidates yet, so I have no idea how it will go."

She smiled accusingly and said, "Oh, come on now. Don't hand me that."

I paused, then said, "Well, that's the way we do it, whether you want to believe it or not."

Nothing brings out letters and calls more than an endorsement or an editorial criticizing something close to someone's heart. We editorialized many times against Arizona's mandatory sentencing laws. Finally one day I received a call from the prosecuting attorney who had long championed the practice and who had, indeed, abused it. Incredibly, he said, "I get the idea your newspaper is against mandatory sentencing."

"Well," I said, "I'm glad we finally got through to you. Yes, we most certainly are."

It does not always take an editorial to get people riled up. One day our switchboard was suddenly alive with calls from local citizens who proclaimed in nearly identical opening statements: "Why are you running these lies about our schools?" Then they hung up before anyone could answer.

I fielded some of the calls myself and went to both the managing editor and editorial page editor to ask if I had missed something. What stories or series we were running about schools? As I thought, at the time we were not running any. I was puzzled. The next time one such caller got through to me, I quickly said, "Hold on, please. Could you be more specific? We're getting all these calls but we don't know what you're talking about. What stories on schools?"

"I don't know," the caller responded. "I was just listening to Rush Limbaugh and he said the media all over America is telling lies about our schools and we should, all go to the phone and call our local editors and tell them to stop."

Amazing. I wrote a personal column about that, saying I was glad Limbaugh hadn't told his listeners to shoot their local editor or I obviously would be a dead duck by now. Of course, my column stirred up even more protests. Ah well.

Over my years in this business I have fielded many such protests. One caller in Tucson was angered over a photo on our front page which showed a returning service man being embraced at the airport by his wife. The service man was black, the wife blonde. The caller wanted to know how I "dared" put such things in our newspaper, much less on page one. When I tried to discuss it, he responded: "Well, you better never bring those ideas up here in the Foothills where I live."

I did not tell him I too lived in the Foothills.

Another day an elderly woman called to complain about a photograph, also on the front page, which showed workers lifting an injured driver out of a truck cab. The woman said she could see the man's "pubic hair" and charged that we had purposely done that "to sell newspapers."

My wife and I looked closely at that picture. The woman must have been using a very large magnifying glass. We could see nothing.

Sometimes callers want to do more than get your attention and argue. Sometimes they want to hurt you. Our sports columnist, Corky Simpson, once wrote a quite positive column about the return to glory of a local high school football team. He mentioned that it had climbed from the bottom, a season some years before in which the team had lost a record number of games. I—not Corky--received a call from an irate member of that losing football team who said we had embarrassed him and he was on his way to show how tough he was and I should be expecting him. I alerted the guards at our main gate, but he never showed.

It brought to mind the time in Huntington a man came to my office after we had published a brief reporting that he had been beaten up by an older man. He was going to show me that no older man could get the best of him.

Sometimes I think people just want to argue. We were running a widespread promotion campaign on billboards, television, radio, and in-house in which I told readers: "If you care about Tucson, you *have* to read the Tucson Citizen."

A caller took issue with that. "I care about Tucson, and I'll be damned if I have to read your paper," he said. "Who are you to tell me what I have to do?"

My explanation that this was a slogan born out of a marketing campaign fell on deaf ears.

The feeling that we were "telling people what they have to do" sometimes came up with our endorsements. Some charged that endorsements were our attempt to tell readers what to do. I always answered that endorsements were made strictly as guidelines. In most cases our readers had not had the opportunity to meet or listen to the candidates, and we had. We were trying to serve readers by saying, "We've met with them and here's what we think, for whatever it's worth."

Of course, most people are going to believe what they want to believe.

I have never been convinced that editorial endorsements make much of a difference in elections. News stories certainly may. But I'm not sure a newspaper giving its blessing to one candidate over another ever changed many minds. Most people not only know which candidate they're going to vote for, but also why, and often feel pretty strongly about it. Good enough. The most important thing to me was always that people vote, not for whom they vote. I've never understood why so many stay at home and fail to vote. It's one of the most precious rights we have in this country.

But most of the time I have welcomed whatever criticism readers wanted to send our way.

Freedom of speech belongs to everybody, after all—
not just newspapers.

47
FIGHTING THE GOOD FIGHT

Life without regional responsibilities proved to be very good for Sandy and me. We tried to learn more about the state in which we now lived. We traveled to the Grand Canyon, which left us in awe. "One feels so insignificant here," Sandy said. We visited a small town in Arizona's White Mountains called Greer, which reminded me of the community of Wayne back in West Virginia. We stayed in an old lodge there and walked through Aspen trees, those marvelous creations whose tiny yellow leaves trembled in the autumn sun, an experience Sandy called "a true blessing."

We spent more than one Thanksgiving in Sedona, north of Phoenix, marveling at its incredible red rock formations and staying in a special place called L'Auberge. We teamed with our friends Allan and Joan Beigel for a weekend in Bisbee, where we spent the night in the historic (and according to legend, haunted) Copper Queen Hotel. We stopped at Tombstone and Sierra Vista along the way. We drove with the Biegels to the top of Mount Lemmon, more than nine thousand feet high. We drove south of Tucson to Patagonia and the horse country of Senoita. We hiked in Sabino Canyon, just minutes from our house, and in the Chiricahua Mountains, more than an hour to the east. There was much to see, and now we had the time.

Unfortunately, our friends the Beigels split up, going their separate ways after all those years of married life together. Too bad. They were a great couple to be with. The four of us made a good team. Sandy and I would continue to see them both, and Allan would continue to be a great news source. But it wouldn't be the same.

We also met with various groups and individuals. We enjoyed a Sunday breakfast at La Paloma with Sen. Dennis DeConcini and his wife and came to know the DeConcini family very well. Sandy attended the wedding of the senator's widowed mother to a most extraordinary man, Dr,. Morris Martin, a former professor at Princeton and product of Oxford. He would become one of our closest friends.

I joined the Board of the Greater Tucson Economic Council (GTEC) a public-private organization involving the city and county and private developers. I become more active in the Arizona Newspaper Association as a director and officer. By coincidence its new executive director was a former Huntington reporter and promotion director, John Fearing. He had come a long way since doing occasional features for the Huntington

Sunday paper when I was its managing editor. We worked well together then, and now, and were able to bring some good changes to ANA .

There was still a fair amount of business travel, to publisher and editor conventions, and now, under Larry Aldrich, TNI retreats. They provided the opportunity for his management team as well as the editors of both papers to get away for a few days for discussions, planning, "bonding" (a word I've always disliked), a bit of golf and several good meals.

Aldrich and Whipple before him had put together a good team. Ted Bergh had been an excellent VP/Finance, and when he left to join Whipple in Cincinnati, his assistant, Jane Engel, took over without the operation missing a step. Terry Egger had come in from San Diego as our new VP/Advertising and was outstanding from the start. He would later become publisher of Pulitzer's St. Louis Post-Dispatch and then publisher of the Cleveland Plain-Dealer. Tom Henry was a solid marketing director with lots of good ideas. Larry Martin had moved from Virginia to become our VP/Circulation. And still on board were Wayne Bean, VP/Production whom Gary Watson had once called "the best production director in Gannett," Edie Auslander, as VP/Human Resources, and Mark Williams as our systems director. Egger, Martin, Bean and Auslander would go on to win Gannett President's rings for being among the company's best in their positions.

I put on my good-guy face and listened and

cooperated during the retreat sessions, although I put forth my usual arguments for the Citizen to get more support from the agency. It had become obvious to all that the Star was getting more and the Citizen less from Aldrich and TNI. I could understand that, even if I didn't like it. The Citizen, as an afternoon paper, was losing circulation and would continue to do so, while the Star, a morning paper in a growth area, continued to gain. All the more reason, I argued, to provide more resources for the Citizen.

Aldrich's job was to show overall growth in advertising and circulation and certainly in the bottom line. His concern was not whether the Citizen's circulation grew so long as overall circulation grew. And it was easier to grow the morning paper's numbers.

In this fifty-fifty agency operation, Gannett stood to profit just as much when the Star did well as when the Citizen did well. And in one of our board meetings, even Gary Watson commented that TNI's efforts should "play to our strengths." Aldrich took that and ran with it. .The morning paper was, after all, "our" strength. I knew that, but it was frustrating.

The Star had been considerably out front in developing an on-line operation, calling its venture "StarNet." Good name. The Citizen, though considerably behind in this area, would also have to create an online presence. I gave the assignment to Joel Rochon, the Citizen's staff artist and leader in all new ventures, and pretty much left him alone.

He knew far more than I did about the world of wonders known as online publishing. Although I had been among the first editors to be involved in computer newsroom technology twenty years before, I had not kept up. I had several elementary questions.

Rochon said we needed a special name for our operation, as the Star had come up with StarNet. I asked why we couldn't just call it Tucson Citizen Online. He said that wouldn't do.

I said if we went online, would we not be competing with ourselves? Why should people buy our paper if they could get the entire thing online for free? He said because everybody's doing it. (Later that very question was raised by newspapers, most of which are now charging readers to view their online sites.)

I told Aldrich we would need lots of help from TNI. Aldrich understood that, but his priority at this time had to be the Star's venture, which was a good one and advanced considerably beyond us.

My relationship with Aldrich was an interesting one. He and his wife Wendy were friends of Sandy's and mine. We dined out, he and I golfed together, we talked regularly, at least early on. He often shared his concerns about what it was like serving two masters in Pulitzer and Gannett. No easy job. I understood that. But I had my own problems, and TNI was one of them.

Tom Henry, TNI's previous marketing director, had come up with an idea that would benefit the Citizen only. We would publish a monthly golf magazine, taking advantage of the region's huge interest in golf as well as that of the many tourists who came to Tucson. The Star would not have such a publication. I loved the idea.

I called in our golf writer, Jack Rickard, and asked him how he would like to be editor of a new Citizen publication called "Tucson Golf." He looked skyward and said, "I've gone to Heaven."

We launched the magazine with a party at the Westin La Paloma resort, whose twenty-seven-hole layout had been designed by Jack Nicklaus. We sent out invitations and had a good crowd. Rickard, who had golfing contacts all over the Southwest, produced stories for the publication like a three-man team. Each one was readable and interesting. The lay-out was crisp. It was a product to be proud of. And other papers copied it.

The problem was that advertisers were not that interested in buying ads in a Citizen-only publication. They were accustomed to their ads appearing in both papers. But the Star had no similar product. As time passed there were fewer ads and fewer pages in Tucson Golf. Finally I met with Terry Eggar, who had not been our VP/Advertising when the decision was made to create the publication. I told him we weren't getting the advertising support we needed. I complained that his sales people were not making Tucson Golf a priority.

"Frankly, Don, it is *not* a priority," he said. "We need to sell advertising in both papers, not one, especially that one being the afternoon paper with its smaller circulation. I'm sorry, but I wish we didn't have Tucson Golf."

"Well then, why am I using up my newsroom resources to publish it when you aren't willing to use yours to sell it?"

"If I were you, I wouldn't," he said.

Tucson Golf died not long after that. Everyone, including the TNI board, agreed it made sense to discontinue it. Again, I understood; but, again, I was not happy about its demise. Too bad. It was a good publication.

Oddly enough, there was some thought in TNI that the Citizen was the better newspaper. The Star's strength was its morning cycle, several said. The Citizen's strength was its better local news and sports coverage. In fact, Larry Martin, our VP/Circulation, told me privately that he wished the Citizen were the morning paper and the Star the evening paper. If that were the case, he said, combined circulation would be growing even more.

And that gave me an idea. What if the Citizen also came out in the morning? What if we went head-to-head with the Star?

I asked Martin what he thought that would do, if we could pull it off.

"Your circulation would go up and the Star's would go down," he said.

The problem was that the two newspapers shared the same press. Would it be possible to start printing the Citizen immediately after the end of the Star's press run? If so, could we get it delivered before readers had left home for work? Granted, the

Star would get there first, but if the Citizen came not long after, would the fact that it offered better local coverage be enough to switch papers?

I talked with Wayne Bean, our VP/Production. He said he would look into it. I talked with Aldrich. He thought it was an intriguing idea. The thought of head-to-head competition between the two papers was enticing.

Aldrich and I agreed to take it up with the board—at least with Gary Watson, Sue Clark-Jackson, and Nick Penniman. Before we could meet, however, our plan fell apart. Martin and Bean said in looking carefully at press on-and-off times and changing work schedules, they just did not think we could get the Citizen delivered to readers in time.

Besides, said Aldrich, the Star, Pulitzer, the board, and perhaps even the JOA agreement itself may not have permitted it.

Well, it was an exciting idea for a while. And wouldn't it have been fun.

Spring of 1994 brought something that was exciting and fun—another Final Four for the Arizona Wildcats. As I have said, UA basketball was huge in Tucson. McHale arena, which seated 14,500, was sold out for every home game every year. It was difficult to get a season ticket unless one inherited it, married it or came up with a huge contribution to the athletic department and even then one might have to be placed on a waiting list. In some cases, UA season tickets were battleground objects during divorces. And the Citizen's sports pages reflected this interest. Every year the Wildcats qualified for the NCAA tournament, which always merited a meeting with editors and writers in my office to discuss coverage.

One thing I have learned in years of watching major college sports is that the best team does not always win, especially when it's tournament time. The team that wins is the hottest team, and even then it takes a little luck. The 1994 UA team had two talented, future NBA guards, but it was not one of the best teams in the school's history. Still, it won its first and second round games to advance to the Sweet Sixteen in Anaheim, California.

Sandy and I made the trip, of course, joining several friends on a special charter. Two close friends in our neighborhood, Louis and Marjory Slavin, picked us up for the drive to the airport, all of us wearing UA cardinal red. I told Sandy we would enjoy our time in Los Angeles but I did not expect the UA would advance beyond this stop. I was wrong. The Wildcats defeated Louisville and Missouri to advance to their second Final Four in six years. It would be held that year in Charlotte. And we would make that trip as well.

Again there was a meeting of editors in my office to discuss assignments and personnel. We would send four members of the staff to the tournament—our basketball beat writer, our sports columnist, a photographer and a city-side reporter for feature stories. We would have a page one presence each day of the tournament week as well as several stories and photos on the sports front.

The 'Cats had lost in their previous Final Four appearance in 1988 to Oklahoma even though they had been expected to win. This year they were not expected to advance past their semifinal game against Arkansas, and they did not. But the Final Four is a great sports event, the best, and we were excited to be there.

That summer Sandy had a bit of travel on her own. She and her best friend, Joan Beigel, went to Paris for two weeks. I was happy for her. While she was away my friend and former controller in Huntington, Bruce Cannady, made his annual summer trip to Tucson for a weekend of golf and good food and drink. He continued to do my taxes every year and refused payment. So I "paid" him by flying him in from San Bernardino and treating him to golf and dinners at good restaurants. Yes, it was far more expensive than if I had paid him. But we had great weekends together.

Ricardo Pimentel, meanwhile, was proving to be the good, energetic managing editor I knew he would be. When I had to be out of town I felt good knowing he, Mark Kimble, and my administrative assistant, Barbara Thompson, were in charge.

It occurs to me that I have not written much about Barbara, who was as important to me as anyone at the Tucson Citizen. As mentioned earlier, she was there as secretary to the publisher when I arrived in 1986. That was my good fortune. She was well educated, with degrees in sociology and psychology, including a master's. She had worked as secretary to an attorney who later served in

Congress, and she had been with the Citizen for several years. She was close to the Citizen news staff and she had experience with TNI.

Early on, I am sure that I took some "getting used to." I joked a lot, shared my thoughts when perhaps I shouldn't have, allowed anyone who wanted to see me to do so. She did not try to keep people out, "protecting" me as had Louise Cazad, my good secretary in Huntington. I liked that. She was not hesitant in letting me know something that she felt I should know. And when I kidded her, she learned to give it right back.

One day she corrected me on some matter and I remarked, "Now, Barbara, you know I'm perfect."

"Yes," she said, "but you're so modest sometimes I forget."

Whenever I screwed something up, I would say, "Barbara, that's the first mistake I've ever made in my life."

"Wrong again," she would say.

She became close to Sandy as well, and often went beyond her duties to help us in various ways— scheduling appointments, making arrangements, reservations, whatever.

She was so respected in the newsroom that I expanded her duties to include oversight of our newsroom clerks and assistants and changed her title from secretary to assistant to the publisher. She scheduled our monthly staff meetings and ordered the pizza and soft drinks. When we held community meetings or town halls, she was there early to make sure everything was set up properly.

She helped with job reviews and staff pay raises.

She was especially good in handling our Gannett Foundation and Community Grants processes, scheduling meetings for those who sought money and keeping track of the many written requests that came in. We set up a small committee to evaluate all the requests and determine which ones we wanted to provide with our limited Gannett Foundation dollars so that our decisions did not simply reflect the tastes and biases of the publisher. Our work paid off for the community when we were successful in winning a $350,000 Gannett Communities Priority grant for the Prima Vera Foundation and an offshoot, Primavera Buildings. It was a non-profit facility for homeless men which provided them a place to eat and sleep but only if they went out each morning and worked in jobs found for them through the Prima Vera Builders.

That was one of the pluses of being a Gannett publisher—the opportunity to help others, to help the community. And Barbara seemed to value that more than any part of her job.

When I served as treasurer of The Associated Press Managing Editors, it was Barbara who did all the work—keeping the books, paying the bills, handling convention details. She accompanied Sandy and me to the convention in Boston, where she manned the treasurer's desk, which was a long day's job.

I once gave her an almost impossible assignment. One of our female staff members regularly wore very suggestive attire, and some of the other female staffers complained. I should put an end to that, they said. I wasn't sure how to do that. It promised to be very awkward. So I called Barbara in and asked if she would take care of it. She looked at me for a moment, then said, "I'll try." I do not know what she said to the young woman, but it worked—for a while.

She was a wonderful observer, especially of the Citizen staff—from clerks to top editors. Again, if she felt I should know about something, she told me. Regarding one editor, she once warned: "Don, I don't think you realize it, but this person does not have your integrity."

In retrospect, I should have listened more.

She also shared with me her thoughts about those she considered trusting and trustworthy. "Ricardo is a good man," she said early in Pimentel's time at the Citizen. "He cares about the staff and he is loyal to you."

One day she shared with me the terrible news that she had lung cancer. She told me in a steady voice, but with a tear. She did not want my sympathy. She just felt I should know. She would be undergoing treatment and would need some time off here and there, and she might be more tired than usual, but she still planned to work.

She beat the cancer for some time, staying with me until she retired just a few months before I did. "Why are you leaving now?" I said.

"I want to be out of here before you are," she said.

She is gone now—the cancer returned after she retired. But when we worked together, sometimes it was as though she knew my thoughts and what I wanted to do before I did. My only regret is that I did not tell her what she meant to the staff and to Sandy and me.

But, Sandy says, "I think she knew."

48

AN EMPTY CHAIR, A DIET COKE

Mark Kimble and I decided to put together a Readers Advisory Council made up of   local citizens to get their views on how we were doing things at the Tucson Citizen. We would meet monthly to discuss stories and editorials we had published and seek their thoughts on those we ought to publish. We would involve intelligent, well-read Citizen subscribers familiar with our newspaper.

Ray Clarke was the executive director of the Tucson Urban League, whose headquarters was just a few blocks from the Tucson Newspapers complex. He had visited the Citizen newsroom for editorial board meetings in which he discussed various issues and needs at the Urban League. A native of Cincinnati, he had come to the University of Arizona to play football. He proved to be an outstanding cornerback and later played briefly in the National Football League for the Atlanta Falcons. As head of the Urban League, he was often in the news and was well known throughout the community. He was well educated, articulate, and straight forward. I was impressed with him from the first time we met. He was perfect for our newly formed Readers Council. I asked him to serve and he agreed.

I turned also to our weekly free-lance foreign affairs columnist and my good friend, Richard Salvatierra. A retired foreign service officer, he was intelligent, thoughtful, a true gentleman, and as I mentioned earlier, ultra conservative. A perfect match for the liberal Ray Clarke. I knew the differing--and at times clashing--views of the two of them would provide exactly what we were looking for in this group.

I also asked Donald Shropshire, the retired CEO of Tucson Medical Center, to join us. He was a moderate, level-headed, soft spoken, well-educated southerner. And there were others who came occasionally.

Salvatierra long had charged that by publishing different points of view, we were confusing our readers. All our columnists should be in agreement with our editorial stands, he felt. I of course disagreed. So did Ray Clarke. Differing opinions were important to our country, he said.

Clarke gave us good marks for "always showing both sides" in our news stories. Our paper was full of "he said, she said, he said," he remarked. But, he added, "you never tell readers who's right, whom to believe."

I explained that one did not do that in news stories, but could and should do that on editorial pages. Perhaps we should do it more, I said.

That wasn't enough for Clarke. Our news stories should show the way, he said. They should be so well done that the reader would know who was right, whom to believe, simply by reading them.

Shropshire was meticulous in clipping stories and editorials from our pages and bringing them in a manila folder to our meetings. He would pull out each one, sometimes asking why we had done a story or editorial a certain way, other times flatly saying he thought our story or headline had been incomplete or unfair or confusing. I always listened carefully, not only because I knew he had put considerable time in doing this, but also because I knew odds were that he was right.

We met monthly in my conference room, after regular office hours. The sessions were always interesting. It was good to watch Salvatierra and Clarke take issue with each other. Both did so in such a civilized manner. And I always learned something from Shropshire's clippings.

Ray Clarke became a good friend. He and his wife Deborah joined Sandy and me for dinner occasionally, and it was always an enjoyable evening. The Urban League was fortunate to have him as its leader. The city of Tucson was fortunate to have him. I was fortunate to call him my friend.

With the Readers Council firmly in place, with Ricardo Pimental handling the newsroom, I felt good about the Citizen.

On the TNI scene, meanwhile, Larry Aldrich

was pushing for a building expansion. Some of his vice presidents' offices were inadequate. We needed a community room big enough to handle larger groups than our present cafeteria conference room allowed. Aldrich himself occupied an office that was less than satisfactory. He talked with me about his plan prior to taking it to the board. Surprisingly, the board approved.

The expansion would be built at the front of the complex, with a large community room adjacent to the Citizen wing, an improved courtyard, better entrances to TNI, and a second level extending partially over a large entry hall that would provide a conference room for his management team.

At the time my office occupied the northeast corner of the Citizen wing, with a small portal-like window facing north to the Catalina Mountains and an identical window facing east over the TNI parking lot. Unfortunately as it turned out my north window had to go. Well, what the hell, I told myself. Don't sweat the small stuff.

And it was small stuff compared to the dark news waiting around t he corner.

Dr. Allan Beigel, my best friend, was on sabbatical for study and research at Harvard. He had remarried and was living temporarily in Boston, with frequent trips back to Tucson. His role at the university had diminished since the change in presidents. No longer was he "the most powerful man at the university," as some had referred to him when he was President Koffler's key vice president. He had continued for a while as a vice president to

President Pacheco, then had rejoined the faculty.

I had returned to Tucson from the Cape a few days before my 60th birthday. Sandy and I had celebrated there as she would not be in Tucson for the birthday itself. Allan and his new wife, Nancy, were in town that weekend, and invited me to dinner to celebrate my reaching "the big 6-0" mark. It was Saturday evening, June 15, 1995.

Nancy had learned that she was pregnant, and I toasted to their good fortune. But I noticed that Allan was not his usual talkative, animated self. Dinner was enjoyable but brief. We said goodbye and the following day he and Nancy returned to Boston.

On Monday, in an office at Harvard, Allan collapsed. He was taken to a Boston hospital where a number of tests were run. A few days later he called me with terrible news. He was suffering from a malignant brain tumor. "Inoperable," he said.

I was stunned. How could this have happened so suddenly? Only days before we'd had dinner together. He revealed that he had a bad headache that evening, but hadn't mentioned it because it was my birthday.

Inoperable? I immediately rejected that. He should get a second or third opinion, I said. Inoperable? Who said so? How can they be sure? Inoperable? That did not seem possible.

But I was talking to a man who was a medical doctor himself. The tumor was located in such a place in his brain that an operation to remove it was not possible, he said.

Then chemo or radiation will take care of it, I argued. They found it early. You're young. You've got years ahead of you. You'll get through this.

He was silent for a moment. Then he said, "I hope you're right." But there was resignation in his voice.

In November Sandy and I flew to Boston to see our son Chris as well as Allan. We drove across the Charles River to Cambridge to join Allan and Nancy for brunch in a hotel restaurant. He was clearly not well. His treatments had left him weakened and unsteady. His memory, however, was good, and he talked about issues facing the University of Arizona, including threats to the UA telescopes atop Mount Graham. I was encouraged that he could think that clearly. I left with major concern, but some hope.

The following day Chris, Sandy and I drove to the Cape for Thanksgiving. It was cold in our cottage, which had no heat other than a large fireplace. We had Thanksgiving dinner at the lovely old Chatham Bars Inn. We raised our glasses in a toast to Allan and his recovery. We walked the cold, windswept beach near the cottage. We returned to Boston and after a couple more days, flew back to Tucson.

Allan and Nancy returned to Tucson in the spring of 1996. In March a luncheon was held in his honor at the Arizona Inn. The room was filled with friends and family. Sandy and I sat at Allan's table, and I was among those asked to speak. I tried to be light, which was impossible. I thanked Allan for a being my best friend since my arrival in Tucson ten years before.

He sat stone-faced at the table, looking down, saying little. The schedule called for him to say a few words. I was not convinced that he could. But when it was time, he stood and, holding onto the back of his chair, thanked everyone for being there and for their support.

Nancy gave birth to twin daughters. I could not help thinking that he would not be there to see them grow up. Thankfully, he had seen his two daughters with Joan grow into intelligent young women.

In April Sandy and I took two large pizzas to Allan and Nancy's house for dinner. We would try to cheer him up, if possible. Nancy helped him to the table in his wheelchair, and positioned the newborn twins nearby. Allan looked at them as Nancy put a couple of slices of pizza on his plate. He had great difficulty eating, but we all acted as if everything were as normal as if we were going to Caruso's garden for spaghetti, the way we used to.

He became bedridden soon after that, and then fell into a coma. Sandy went to the house every day and read to him. There was no sign that he was aware of her presence. But she continued to do it.

When June arrived, Sandy went to the Cape as usual. We talked every night, as we always had. But now our conversations began with word on Allan and his condition.

On June 22, he left us. Only fifty-six years of age. One year, almost to the day, after learning of his tumor.

That evening Stanley and Norma Feldman and I went to Le Bistro and sat in the booth where we had sat so many times with Allan. Stanley ordered his customary single malt scotch, Norma a glass of white wine, and I a beer, and then Stanley added that we would also have a Diet Coke, Allan's favorite drink. We placed it where he would have sat had he been there. And then we toasted him.

The death of Dr. Allan Beigel was front page news in Tucson and even merited news-obit stories in the New York Times and the Boston Globe. He had served as vice president of the American Psychiatric Association, was active in the World Psychiatric Association, and had served on President Carter's Commission on Mental Health. He was known nationally and internationally as an authority on community mental health care. He had contacts everywhere. The Tucson papers ran editorials about his passing.

Several of us were asked to jot down a few thoughts about Allan for Rabbi Arthur Oleisky who would be performing his service. Later, I wrote a personal column in the Citizen which began this way:

"He could make your day. And he could drive you nuts. He could be almost numb to those around him, yet he was among the most sensitive of people. He had countless friends—and he had enemies.

"Allan Beigel. Gone now, at the age of 56.

"He was my friend. My first friend when I came to Tucson 10 years ago, and my best friend until the very end one week ago.

"Life, as they say, is not fair. If it were, he would be with us still, not struck down by an inoperable brain tumor. What a terrible irony—this quick, wonderful brain under attack, as though targeted by fate."

As I said in that column, Allan Beigel understood the news media better than anyone I have ever known who was not in the media—and better than some who were. He has been gone a long time now. I still miss the hell out of him.

But life goes on. At TNI, we had a new VP/Marketing named Mike Soliman who was a native of Egypt, had been educated in Geneva and at Georgetown University, and most recently worked in marketing at the Toronto Star. We became good friends almost immediately, having much in common—strange, given our backgrounds. He was a scratch golfer, loved good food and drink, and good jazz. He spoke French with Sandy and called her "M'Belle." He became a regular at Le Bistro and joked with owner-chef Laurent Reux in French and English. He was a man of some sophistication.

But while we were gaining a promising new director at TNI, we were losing at the Citizen. In November I was advised that Ricardo Pimentel was being considered for the top editor's job at Gannett's newspaper in San Bernardino, his home town. That would be a good promotion--a higher job at a larger circulation newspaper. If I ever wanted to stand in somebody's way of advancement, this was it. Of course, I wouldn't do that. Which is not to say I didn't try to talk him out of it, telling him how valuable he was to the Citizen —and to me. I was not exaggerating.

He said he would have to think about it. I was thrilled when he came in the following day to say he had decided to turn the job down if it was offered, and would stay at the Citizen. To celebrate, I asked that he and Laura join Sandy and me at Le Bistro. It was a long and wet evening; we toasted his decision to stay and left cheering each other.

The day after that he came into my office and said he had changed his mind. He would be going to San Bernardino as its editor. "I want my own paper," he explained. I certainly could understand that.

So now I had to find a new managing editor again. Just as Sue Clark-Johnson (whose marriage had changed her name from Jackson to Johnson), had recommended Ricardo, now did she strongly suggest I consider her assistant managing editor, Michael Limon, for the opening. The final decision would be up to me, she insisted. I should bring him to Tucson for an interview. If he didn't seem to be a fit, that was fine and I could look elsewhere. She had said the same concerning Ricardo not quite three years before. Fortunately, that had worked out.

Normally I am not shy about letting my true feelings be known--ask Harry Whipple or Larry Aldrich or, well, just about anybody. But would I *really* want to go against my boss's recommendation? I hoped Michael Limon would be another Ricardo, and looked forward to meeting him.

Pimentel left the Citizen in December. Limon came to Tucson three days later. He looked us over, we looked him over. He went back to Reno.

I was concerned that those old "vibes" I followed so often did not go off during our interview. He was obviously bright, experienced, and according to many a very good newsman. But something didn't quite click for me. What was it? His confident, almost cocky manner? Or was I just looking too much for another Ricardo?

Michael Limon accepted the position of managing editor of the Tucson Citizen in January of 1997. He would be there when I retired three years later. It was not always smooth sailing.

Meanwhile, I had been approached by the University of Arizona Foundation leadership about moving up to vice chair of the board, which meant chair-elect. That was exciting and appealing. But I had concerns. Our reporters covered the University and occasionally that included the Foundation as its development arm. Would it be a conflict for me to be chairman of the Foundation when our reporters had to write about it? The chairmanship was not a paying job. I would not be "feeding at the public trough." The board was made up of volunteers.

I went to see the one person on our staff who I knew would give me a straight answer—Mark Kimble.

"Oh, it's a conflict, all right," he said. "At least, it could be." I could sense he was against the idea.

"But it will come down to you. Will you be able to handle the job there without letting it affect what you do here?"

Kimble was an alumnus of the University and a big fan of its sports program, especially its basketball teams. But I knew he didn't think I should accept the UA Foundation position.

I thought about it, then went back to his office. "Yeah, I can handle it," I said. "Don't worry. Do your job the way you've always done it. I will never try to get you to do anything else, no matter how involved I am at the Foundation. Same goes for our news operation, and I will tell our editors and reporters that."

"Okay," he said. "Good luck." But I wasn't sure he meant it.

Allan Beigel would be proud of me, I thought. He had been the one who recommended me as a Foundation board member back when the Foundation reported to him before it became independent from the university. Now I was going to become vice chair and if all went well, chairman a year after that. I regretted he would not be here to see it.

49
WINS AND LOSSES

It was a time of new faces. At the Citizen, Michael Limon. At TNI, Jon Heimerman in Finance, Randy Cross in Circulation, Paul Ingenari in Advertising, and before the year would be out, Jim Rowley in Marketing. Gone were Terry Eggar, who had become general manager of the St. Louis Post-Dispatch, Larry Martin and Jane Engel. And soon to be on his way, Mike Soliman. For various reasons, Larry Aldrich's award-winning management team was in the midst of major change.

There was also a change at the University of Arizona, with the arrival of a new president, Peter Likins, replacing Manuel Pacheco, who had become chancellor of the University of Missouri system.

But my priority was the operation of the Tucson Citizen. For years I had depended on my managing editors to run the newsroom and had given them considerable freedom. They ran the daily news meetings, they planned the day's news report. I trusted them to do the right thing, to support me, and to always keep me informed. I would do the same for them. Fran Allred in Huntington and Dale Walton and Ricardo Pimentel at the Citizen had filled their roles very well. They were dependable, honest, and trustworthy. I expected no less from Michael Limon.

I introduced him to as many people and to as many facets of Tucson life as possible. Sandy and I took him and his wife, Robin, to dinner at Le Bistro and introduced him to owner-chef Laurent Reux. I invited him for rounds of golf at La Paloma and Tucson Country Club. At my various meetings in the community, I announced that he was the new managing editor of the Citizen, and when practical took him along to be personally introduced.

Limon was a bright, engaging young man of many interests. He was outgoing, energetic, gregarious. He would have no trouble meeting people and becoming a part of the community. He would represent the Citizen very well. He was also, as advertised, a good newsman. I felt confident that in my absence he could and would keep things going smoothly.

But the Citizen was about more than publishing the day's news. We sponsored the "Citizen of the Year" award in conjunction with the Volunteer Council of Tucson at its annual awards breakfast. We selected Tucson's top ten restaurants each year and presented them with Tucson Citizen "Silver Spoon" award plaques. We honored members of our own staff with awards for those whose work was judged to be the year's best. We named a reporter of the year, an editor of the year, an employee of the year. Originally we presented the awards at our staff Christmas party. But Limon pointed out that for those who did not win, there was a downside to the party. So we changed the process to announce the winners during a staff meeting in our conference room.

We also held an off-site retreat each year for the Citizen's senior editors to discuss needs, issues, plans, and to listen to whatever each editor had to say. We always included lunch and at the end of the day, drinks. Limon fit right in.

When it came time for "March Madness," the NCAA basketball tournament, he was a big help with his knowledge of sports and feel for good sports pages.

Not that we were expecting much from the University of Arizona basketball team that year. The Wildcats had finished fifth in the Pac 10 Conference and had lost their last two games of the season, at California and Stanford. We weren't even sure they would get a bid.

When they did, we held our usual NCAA tournament planning meeting. Arizona would be traveling a good distance and we did not expect many fans would follow them. We assigned our basketball writer, sports columnist and a photographer to make the trip. We did not bother to include a city reporter for color stories on fans.

Arizona opened the tournament with a close win over South Alabama. Two days later the 'Cats struggled again before getting by College of Charleston. Still, they had advanced to the Sweet Sixteen once again. There they were heavy underdogs as they faced the No. 1 team in the country, Kansas. Surprisingly, they upset the Jayhawks to advance to the Elite Eight, against Providence. Again, it was close, but the Wildcats pulled it out. They were going to the Final Four— their third time overall and second time in three years.

Again we gathered in my office to discuss coverage. We added a city reporter to our coverage team. We scheduled a number of stories to run on the front page, the local page, and in the sports section throughout Final Four week. We planned a special section.

The Final Four would be held in Indianapolis. There would be a chartered plane for fans and another for the university's official party, which included the president, other administrators and officials, the athletic director, the players and coaches, and a few special guests of the university.

Just as Sandy and I were making reservations to join friends on the fans' charter, I received a call from Dick Imwalle, the University of Arizona Foundation CEO. He and the Foundation's chairman and their wives were to be included in the official party, he said. The problem was that the chairman couldn't make the trip. Imwalle was asking me, as vice chair, to go in his place.

Join the official party for the Final Four? Where do I sign?

I did have concerns, however. I thought of Mark Kimble warning me about possible conflict of interest. Citizen reporters, after all, would be covering the event and writing about a number of things including those who would be attending. Also, I knew I could not accept a free trip from the university.

I told Imwalle that Sandy and I would be thrilled to join him and the rest of the official party. But, I said, we would have to pay our own way. The Citizen's policy was that we accepted no gifts, and that included travel. I couldn't let the university pay our way.

The university doesn't pay, he said. The NCAA pays. It provides all expenses for the official party of every university in the Final Four. He told me to work it out with somebody at the university.

I contacted Rocky LaRose, the associate athletic director. She said she had no idea how I could pay or what the cost would be. They would not know the expense totals until after the Final Four. She suggested we wait until then. They should be able to put together some kind of number I could pay, if I insisted on it. I agreed.

It was a great trip in every way. It was interesting and enjoyable being on the official charter, traveling with the team, being greeted by a motorcade in Indianapolis and taken to a hotel where our rooms awaited. The Final Four is one of the great sports events in America, no matter which city happens to be hosting. It's fun to walk down the streets, to mingle with those from other universities, to meet new people and attend pep rallies.

In its Saturday night semi-final game Arizona played perennial power North Carolina, like Kansas one of four No. 1 seeds in the tournament. Once again, Arizona was the underdog. If by some miracle the Wildcats managed to win, waiting for them probably would be another No. 1 seed, powerful Kentucky.

Again, Arizona pulled off a huge upset, defeating North Carolina to advance to Monday night's championship game. Kentucky also won its semifinal game, as expected. The title game would involve two teams of Wildcats. Arizona had never won a national championship in basketball. Kentucky had won several.

On Monday night, Dick and Susan Imwalle and Sandy and I attended a big Wildcat rally, then had a little beer and wine and snacks before moving on to the arena—the huge RCA Dome that the Indianapolis Colts called home. Unfortunately, our seats were not chair-backs, but temporary steel bleachers erected for the tournament. Sandy had been having considerable back pain in recent months, and this was not good news for her. But she did not complain.

Amazingly, as the game moved on, Arizona was more than holding its own and, in fact, was leading. Could this be happening? This team that had finished fifth in its conference? With less than a minute to go, it appeared certain the Cats would win. Then Kentucky hit a three-pointer to send the game into overtime. I was crushed. To be so close to winning the national championship, and now to lose it in overtime.

But they did not. Led by Miles Simon, they never let Kentucky in it in the extra period. When the buzzer sounded the scoreboard read, Arizona 84, Kentucky 79. Simon, cradling the ball in both arms, fell slowly to the floor on his knees. Arizona had won its first national championship.

I gave Sandy a bear hug and a kiss and we high-fived the Imwalles. And I whispered to Sandy, "If only Allan could be here to see this." No one would have enjoyed it more than my friend Beigel.

Arizona coach Lute Olson was beaming. He had made four trips to the Final Four in his career, and now for the first time he would be bringing home the championship trophy. His wife, Bobbi, came onto the floor to join him, and they embraced.

Following the ceremonies on the court, there was another presentation—that of the crystal Sears trophy emblematic of the national championship--in a somewhat dark room in another part of the arena. Members of the official party crowded in, joined by a few other fans. I looked beside me to see Steve Kerr and Jud Buechler, then of the Chicago Bulls and both Arizona alums.

We did not get to bed until the wee hours—and there was a 6 a.m. call to join the official party for the return flight to Tucson. When we landed, the group moved on to Arizona Stadium where thousands of fans were waiting. The players rode in convertibles, waving. Copies of that day's Tucson newspapers, both the Star and Citizen, were being sold on every corner and in the football stadium. Citizen writers and photographers and our editors back in the office had done an outstanding job of capturing the historic event, on the front page and throughout the paper. I was very proud. For days, we received calls from fans wanting copies. Fortunately, we had saved the plates and put them back on the press for reprints.

But the trip had taken its toll on Sandy. She had been suffering acute back pain for some time. Now, the trip to Indianapolis, the steel bleachers of the RCA Dome, the lack of sleep the night of the championship had increased her pain and our concerns.

The Arizona Daily Star, meanwhile, had published a sizeable story on the university's official party, naming many of those who had been included in this "free ride." Prominent in the story as being among those who cashed in was my name as editor and publisher of the Citizen.

I was quite upset. I walked across the TNI courtyard to the Star newsroom and into the office of Steve Auslander, the Star's editor and my friend. I held a copy of the story the Star had printed and told him it was incorrect—or, at the very least incomplete. Either way, it was unfair. I was paying my own expenses and Sandy's, I told him, reimbursing the university for all our expenses—travel, hotel, whatever else there might be. I asked that the Star run a story saying so. Auslander said he would take care of it.

The following day there was a two-inch short

buried inside the Star and reporting that I had "said" I was paying. Not much of a correction.

Our expenses came to something over $2,700. I wrote out a check to the university immediately, even though the NCAA had picked up the official party bill. Let the university figure out how to handle it, I thought. At least I paid our way and we had accepted no freebies.

In May Sandy was able to attend the theater, in this case the play "Love Letters," with Hollywood stars Robert Wagner and Jill St. John. We were invited to an after-theater party by Bob Shelton, the founder of Old Tucson Studios who had made it a tourist attraction as well as a working movie set. Shelton had many Hollywood contacts (he'd been a close personal friend of John Wayne) and he and his wife Linda were talking with Wagner and St. John. They spotted us and waved us over.

Shelton introduced us by name and added, in reference to me, "This is Tucson's William Randolph Hearst."

"Hey, Don, great blue," Wagner said, pointing to the French blue dress shirt I was wearing beneath my jacket.

That stopped me, not only because it was unexpected, but because it triggered a memory from my teen-age days. I had seen a magazine photo of Wagner wearing a new kind of sport jacket. I liked it so much that I searched several men's stores in Huntington before finding one similar to it. I bought it and wore it frequently. Now, years later, here was this still-popular Hollywood star telling me he liked something I was wearing. A small thing, a coincidence, but for a moment it stopped me cold and took me back some forty years.

As the summer wore on, Sandy's back pain become far worse, and surgery would again be necessary. She was eager to have it in hopes of eliminating the pain. Our surgeon friend came out of the operating room with a big smile. "I nailed it," he said. "On a scale of one to ten, this was an eleven."

When she awoke, he told her the surgery had been a success and that after three or four days the pain would go away. But it never did.

50
MYSTERY OF THE MISSING PILOT

It was a national story with a Tucson dateline. It began in 1997, extended into 1998, and has been written about many times since. It broke in the Tucson Citizen, and from that point on the Citizen stayed in front of all media in its reporting despite catch-up attempts by the country's major newspapers and networks.

It necessitated one of the most difficult decisions I faced in my forty-seven-year newspaper career. It was also a story for which my newspaper and I were heavily criticized—and commended. In some ways, it has haunted me ever since.

In April, 1997, three A-10 military jets took off from Davis-Monthan Air Force Base in Tucson, heading for a routine practice bombing run over a testing range near Gila Bend, Arizona. Before the bombs were dropped the plane at the rear of the tight formation—piloted by Capt. Craig Button—suddenly veered off. In a minute, he was five miles away from the two other pilots before they noticed his absence. No radio contact could be made. His homing device had been switched off. Capt. Button and his plane had vanished.

Searches began immediately. Air Force planes roamed the skies for any sign of a crashed A-10, concentrating on the mountains of northern Arizona and Colorado.For days there was no information—only speculation and many questions. Had the pilot become ill? Suffered some kind of attack? Become confused? Blacked out? Could something have happened in the plane's cabin to cause that? Or had he intentionally flown elsewhere? Was he possibly meeting terrorists with his load of bombs and weapons?

Citizen reporter C. T. Revere was assigned to the story from the start. We sent him to Colorado in an attempt to learn more. He produced daily updates which we published on the front page each day. The Associated Press picked up our stories and our newsroom received daily calls from other newspapers and networks, CNN most frequently of all, wanting to know what we had. The story had captured the interest of the country and no newspaper or television station was on top of it the way we were.

One week after the plane's disappearance searchers using radar tracked the missing A-10 to the central Rockies, some 800 miles off course. Interviews with people in the area turned up sightings of smoke and a "glow" the night the plane had disappeared.

It was three weeks before searchers, slowed by

spring snowstorms, found the wreckage and its human remains above the tree line of 13,365-foot Gold Dust Peak, near Vail, Colorado. DNA tests later positively identified the remains as those of Capt. Button. He had not ejected. The plane had not been on auto pilot. It appeared he had purposely crashed his plane into the mountain.

But why? What would cause a career Air Force officer to do such a thing?

Returning to Tucson, C. T. Revere worked literally night and day on the story. He talked with Air Force officials, visited bars near the base where he spoke with both civilians and servicemen, made countless calls. Some of the things he heard seemed bizarre. Like all good reporters, he kept digging, asking more questions, hoping to find a theme, something in common from his many sources. He kept his editors informed, but he was not ready to write just yet. He needed more--confirmation of some kind, if possible. And if not, at least stories that matched. Once he had that he would once again go to the Air Force for its comments.

Michael Limon came into my office each day to update me on where we stood with the story. Then one day he and Revere and other editors came into my office and presented me with what Rivere had written.

I read it and then I read it again. And then I began asking questions. "We are quoting anonymous sources here. How many do we have? One won't do it."

Revere had more than one sources on all the

items but one, and it was major. I insisted we find another source. "Go back and try to get one more on this one," I said.

I heard heavy sighs. I knew my staff was eager to run the story before anyone else got to it. But we were dealing with a strange and extraordinary account here, a strong, sensitive and unquestionably controversial matter. I said we would wait until the next day and see whether Revere had been successful in getting a second source.

The following day he and the editors returned to my office. He had found his second source.

I read the story again, suggesting changes here and there. It was rewritten several times and each time I personally read it. Finally, it seemed ready. Here is the final version:

"The investigation into the crash of a wayward A-10 attack jet is focusing on the personal life of the pilot, who investigators suspect committed suicide because a homosexual affair was about to be made public, military sources have told the Tucson Citizen.

"A source close to the investigation, who spoke on the condition of not being named, said Capt. Craig Button apparently intentionally smashed the $8.8 million plane into a Colorado peak because his private life was about to be revealed by an estranged lover. The alleged ex-lover was a pilot stationed with Button at Davis-Monthan Air Force Base.

"Numerous rumors and theories have circulated about why Button flew his Thunderbolt II from

Arizona to Colorado. But a military source said Air Force investigators believe fear of embarrassment over the alleged affair is the most plausible explanation. 'The Air Force really believes that could be the answer,' said the source.

"Investigators suspect the suicidal Button targeted a peak bearing his first name in a mountain range named after his home state, a source said. Button was raised in Wantagh, N.Y., and his parents live in Massapequa, N.Y.

"'Investigators do believe it was premeditated. If he had cleared Gold Dust Peak, the next peak was Craig Peak, which is part of the New York mountain range,' the source said."

There was more. Revere had done a hell of a job. I ran out of questions for him. But I still had many concerns; I still had this bad feeling in my stomach.

I thought of Capt. Button's parents reading this story. I thought of his friends and fellow officers. I asked myself what we would gain by publishing it.

And then I knew the answer to that. It wasn't what we would gain. It was that we were fulfilling our reason to exist—to inform the public, to try to answer questions our readers had. We were a newspaper; we reported the news, good or bad. That's what we did.

I cleared the story. And I braced for the storm. I knew we would be blasted with criticism.

The story, which we copyrighted, ran Friday, May 2, at the top of page one with this headline:

Military's theory: A-10 pilot feared gay ex-lover would reveal affair

The headline was larger and bolder than I would have liked, although I had approved basically what it said. I immediately regretted not looking at the page design and the headline type before we went to press; I knew the boldness and size of the type would suggest "sensationalism" to many. But that had been done in the early morning hours, before I arrived at the office. Perhaps I should have gone in earlier.

Our paper came off the press at 9:15 a.m. Soon the story went all over the nation, transmitted by the Associated Press and Gannett News Service and broadcast by countless radio and television stations and networks. CNN, "Inside Edition" and several radio stations wanted to put C.T. Revere on the air. Told he and we would not consent to this, the CNN reporter asked, "Well, what do you want us to do?" As if we wanted them to do anything. The "Inside Edition" representative, told the same thing, responded to Revere: "We can make it worth your while."

"Forget it," Revere wisely answered.

Several newspapers called for faxes of the Citizen story, including The Washington Post, Los Angeles Times, New York Post, New York Daily News--nearly two dozen in all. The Daily News asked for our future stories as well, suggesting it would pay us to "string" for them.

The criticism I expected came quickly and

loudly--phone calls, letters attacking us for our insensibility, our "sensationalizing."

Said one caller: "I can't believe the Citizen published this story. It is a disgrace. You didn't have to do this. Those big banner headlines and this terrible story, and all of it unsubstantiated. You and your anonymous sources. You outdid even the worst of the tabloids. What about this boy's parents? How do you think they feel?"

Said another: "I want to take issue with the handling by your newspaper of the Capt. Craig Button story. I think this is a huge disservice to his family. It bothers me that after such things as plane crashes, the media continue to bother the family, which has already suffered enough. Now you bring out this homosexuality issue, and it isn't even substantiated."

And another: "I just wanted to say what a disgusting article you published about the A-10 pilot, without verification, without knowledge. What do you think his family is going to think of that, especially if it turns out not to be correct? Now you wonder why we call the press 'vultures.'"

But one reader called only a few hours after our paper came out to say he had talked with Capt. Button a week before his flight and "I think you're right on target."

Another called to say, "Congratulations on your reporting. I know this was not an easy decision, but without you this probably would not have been reported, ever. The military always likes to cover things up, as you know. This took a lot of guts.

Thank you."

On Saturday, May 10, I addressed the issue in my weekly personal column. Here is what I wrote:

"Last Friday the Citizen reported, in a copyright story, that military sources said the focus of their investigation into the crash of an attack jet from Davis-Monthan Air Force Base had shifted to the personal life of the pilot who died in the crash and their suspicion that he had committed suicide because he feared that a homosexual affair was about to be revealed.

"We were very careful about what the story said—and did not say. Literally every word was weighed, and the story rewritten several times. I personally read every version and every proposed headline.

"We wanted to make certain it was clear to the reader that we, the Citizen, were not claiming this was what had happened. We do not know. Rather, military sources were saying it, and we were quoting them. What's more, the sources were not saying at this point that it had been established factually; only that this was now the focus of the investigation. We did not name them because they spoke only on that condition, fearing retribution."

I reported that we had received considerable criticism since publishing the story, and then I posed the question: "So, why did we do it?" And I tried to offer an answer.

"Because there was such tremendous interest in the story and the mystery of what happened, and most of all, why. Why would an accomplished pilot suddenly veer off from his formation, fly hours and miles in another direction, avoid radio contact with his group, and crash into the side of a mountain in Colorado?

"It was a question being asked around the country, and certainly here in Tucson.

"Already there had been absurd speculation and theorizing: that he was attempting to 'steal' the plane, that he had been somehow captured or lured by 'space aliens.'

"For days we had followed the story, sending Revere to Colorado, talking with countless sources and possible sources, official and otherwise.

"And then we were told—by military sources, mind you—that the focus of the investigation had shifted to the pilot's personal life and the suspicion he had committed suicide for fear of being 'outed' by a gay ex-lover, also a pilot.

"How could we not report that? How could we not report the newest focus of the military's investigation, even if it was painful?

"The investigation was, is, news. Its focus and direction was, is, news. Informing the people of the day's news is what we do, why we're here.

"It is not always easy, and it certainly is not always pleasant."

After my column ran, I received a few more calls and letters, these a bit different.

Said one: "What is the purpose of a newspaper? Is it to report only what the reader wants to hear or to report all news good or bad? I personally think the people who present and edit the stories need encouragement for a job well done….sometimes the truth hurts…I commend the Citizen for doing a difficult job."

And another: "I commend Don Hatfield for his May 10 column on the missing A-10. I feel that he explained with care the decision process in publishing the story, and I feel he fulfilled your public trust by doing so…thanks for doing your job."

And this: "I'm not a friend of the press but I feel that credit must be given to Donald Hatfield's handling of the Craig Button story."

Still, the decision I had made to run the story continued to gnaw at me. What if our sources were wrong? The Air Force had ruled that Button had committed suicide by crashing his plane into the mountain. But what if he were not gay, not trying to avoid being "outed" by a gay ex-lover as our military sources said. And even if our story and our sources were correct, what about the pain caused to Capt. Button's parents?

The Air Force Office of Special Investigations launched its own investigation, including a "psychological autopsy." It interviewed more than two hundred people. It used psychologists to help with the findings. Naturally, the Air Force did not make the report public When we heard of its existence, we immediately filed a Freedom of Information request. Was no one else in the country willing to do that but us? Whatever, after some time, the report was turned over to us.

The report said that Capt. Button appeared to

be in "mental turmoil," perhaps over "unrequited love" for a former girlfriend (the woman said they were friends and had not been in a relationship). It also cited his relationship with his mother, one of anguish and frustration. A Jehovah's witness, she opposed his being in the military .A friend who was interviewed said Button had received a phone call the night before his fatal flight which seemed to upset him a great deal.

The report made reference to the homosexual allegations and a newspaper story that reported a call from a man who claimed to be Button's gay lover, made just days before his death. But, the report said, "No credible evidence to support theories of homosexuality, financial difficulty, family conflicts, militia ties or any other possible motivation has been discovered."

It never offered a definitive answer as to why Button took his life.

It did reveal that its investigators had found in Button's bed-stand the Bible and a religious pamphlet which described "God asking a father to sacrifice his only son on a burning pyre at the side of a mountain."

Over the years the mystery of why Button had committed suicide was never solved, and another mystery developed over the four 500-pound bombs his plane carried. They were never found. Had he dropped them somewhere over Arizona or Colorado before crashing into the mountain top? Had they been buried deep into the soil by the impact of the crash? No one knows.

And now, years later, how do I feel about all this and the Tucson Citizen's—and my—role in the story?

I believe we did what we had to do.

51
INTERESTING TIMES

In 1998 I found myself facing an anniversary—
my forty-fifth year in newspapers. I had not even
thought about that until receiving in the mail from
Corporate a gold watch, suitably engraved with my
initials. That was a surprise. I had thought gold
watches were for retirements. I had just turned
sixty-three. I wouldn't be thinking about retirement
for another two years—unless Corporate had other
ideas.   Fortunately, it did not. The watch was
Corporate's way of recognizing my many years in
this business, and it was good to know that someone
there was aware of it.

I thought about those forty-five years. Thirty-
three of them with the Huntington newspapers,
twelve in Tucson. An eighteen-year-old kid when I
began, a fifty-one-year-old man when I found new
life in Tucson. And now sixty-three.

I thought of all I had learned in that time. I
thought about all the young reporters who had
trusted me enough to come and work for my papers

in Huntington, and all those staffers who had welcomed me in Tucson. I thought of.my first days as a regional vice president of Gannett's southwestern newspapers. I remembered arriving from the East with what I thought was a great idea. The cities of El Paso, Santa Fe, and Tucson were heavily Hispanic. Consequently one marketing plan should work for all three, right?

Then I learned that the three markets were in no way the same or even similar, and that the Hispanics in the three cities differed greatly, to say the least. Most of those in El Paso had Mexican roots, many of those in Santa Fe were more tied to Spain, while Tucson had quite as mix, with Hispanics not only from Mexico, but also from Central America, South America, and Cuba. I learned too that in the world of politics there was no such thing as an Hispanic voting block. I dropped my marketing idea quickly.

But it is always good to learn, especially if one learns before making a big mistake.

All in all, it had been forty-five years well spent. And I looked forward to the next two years, my final two, with enthusiasm. .

In the Citizen newsroom we faced something of a new challenge, and it came in the world of sports.

Arizona had been involved with major league baseball for decades, hosting a number of teams for spring training. Tucson had been the training home of the Cleveland Indians since 1946. Greater Phoenix had been the spring training home for several different teams over the years. Now, in 1998, the state of Arizona was about to enter the major leagues fulltime as the home of the National League's new Arizona Diamondbacks.

Phoenix already had fulltime professional sports, with the Phoenix Suns in the National Basketball Association, the Arizona Cardinals in the National Football League, and the Phoenix Coyotes of the National Hockey League. Jerry Colangelo had been instrumental in building and guiding the Suns franchise and in the construction of the new America West Arena. Now he was the key individual in building a new state-of-the art domed baseball stadium called Bank One Ballpark, or simply, "the BOB," and in founding the Diamondbacks.

He made certain to call his new major league baseball entry the Arizona Diamondbacks instead of Phoenix Diamondbacks so that the entire state would feel involved. He also selected Tucson as the site for the Diamondbacks' spring training as well as its center for rehabilitation. And he obtained Tucson's Triple-A minor league franchise and made it the Diamondbacks' top farm team. All of which resulted in the construction of a complex featuring a main stadium, Tucson Electric Park, several practice fields, and the rehab center.

All this was great news. However, for newspapers it meant more sports to cover. With the Suns, Cardinals, Coyotes, and Diamondbacks as well as Arizona State University in Phoenix, we would have four major professional sports teams as well as major college sports just a little more than a hundred miles up the Interstate. And we would have three major league teams—the Diamondbacks, Colorado Rockies, and Chicago White Sox--doing their spring training in Tucson. Toss in the hometown University of Arizona, a national power in college sports, and we had a pretty full plate when it came to our sports coverage.

It was clear to me we needed to increase our sports staff by at least one more person and perhaps move that person permanently to Phoenix. But my request to Corporate for an additional staffer fell on the proverbial deaf ears.

My decision then was whether to assign one of my present sports writers to Phoenix. But we simply did not have a large enough staff to do that without cutting back on local sports coverage. I decided that we would rely on The Associated Press to cover Phoenix professional sports and ASU and send one of our Tucson writers there only occasionally.

The Star, of course, did just what I had considered doing. It moved a sportswriter to Phoenix fulltime, and it didn't have to add staff to do so. There were plenty of bodies in the Star newsroom.

Larry Aldrich committed TNI dollars to the purchase of Diamondbacks season tickets, not only to show support for the new team, but so he could use them for advertising and marketing purposes. And he would take members of his management team and the editors of the Star and Citizen to the Diamondbacks' opening night.

Bank One Ballpark was an impressive place that night, with a roof that opened and closed and two huge shutters high in the outfield walls that swung in and out to let breezes in when needed. There were restaurants and game rooms on its plazas and a swimming pool just beyond the right centerfield fence. I thought of my father and the days he took me to Crosley Field in Cincinnati to see the Reds play. If only he could see this place.

We sent a sportswriter to Phoenix when we felt it was merited, but we continued to concentrate on what was happening in Tucson. The Citizen, after all, *was* Tucson.

The year proved to be a busy one for me with considerable travel. There were budget meetings in Reno, corporate meetings in Washington, a TNI retreat in Sedona, the newspaper publishers convention in Dallas, UA Foundation meetings in Phoenix and La Jolla—that jewel of a village just north of San Diego--and in San Diego a second time, for the Holiday Bowl football game between Arizona and Nebraska (the Wildcats won).

The La Jolla meeting was interesting and even coincidental in that it included a reception at the home of University of Arizona alumni Karl Eller and his wife, Stevie. Interesting, because it was a beautiful home on the ocean and it was filled with interesting people. Coincidental, because years before, for a brief time, Karl Eller had been part of Gannett. That had come about when Combined Communications, of which Eller was a major owner, reached an agreement with Gannett to join forces. Gannett thought of it as a purchase in which it was acquiring the Oakland Tribune and Cincinnati Enquirer, among other assets. Combined considered it more of a merger. As part of the deal an Office of the Chief Executive was established with Eller in a key role. He quickly set his sights on Al Neuharth's job as Gannett's CEO. While visiting Neuharth at his Florida home, he used the phone to call his wife and confided that he felt he could take over Gannett. What he did not know was that Neuharth was listening in on an extension. Neuharth wrote about it in his book, *S.O.B.* Years later, Eller wrote about it as well in his book, *Integrity Is All You've Got*. As one might suspect, the two accounts are quite different. In any case, Eller never managed to pull off the coup, and soon left Gannett, although with lots of Gannett stock in his pocket. For years after, whenever I saw him he would tell me to "get on those guys at Gannett to get our stock up."

The Ellers were good hosts and great donors to the UA, contributing many millions of dollars, including some $24 million to the UA College of Business which understandably is named after Eller. And the striking new UA dance building is named in honor of Stevie, also following a sizeable contribution. Both honors were well deserved.

The Dallas publishers convention was interesting for an entirely different reason. Guest speaker for the main dinner was George W. Bush, then governor of Texas. While he addressed the room full of publishers from the lectern, his mother and father—former President George H. W. Bush and First Lady Barbara—sat directly behind him on the stage. Gov. Bush's speech was quite good, focusing on education. When Sandy and I left the dinner, I said, "We've just seen the next President of the United States."

"Do you really think so?" she said.

"Did you see all the power on that stage? Do you think President Bush and the former First Lady were up there for fun? I'd say we've just seen the beginning of a new campaign."

It was not long until George Bush the Junior announced that he was running for President. No surprise here.

Another interesting and more enjoyable dinner meeting came at a Gannett gathering in Washington. For whatever reason, I was asked to sit at the table of Gannett CEO John Curley and that evening's guest speaker, Pulitzer Prize-winning historian Doris Kearns Goodwin. She had won the Pulitzer for her superb book, *No Ordinary Time: Franklin and Eleanor Roosevelt,* and had received great acclaim for two other works, *The Fitzgeralds and the Kennedys* and *Lyndon Johnson and the American Dream.*

By extremely good fortune, I was seated beside her at the small table of eight, and we talked all through the meal. I knew she was a great baseball fan, having seen her interviewed several times on Ken Burns' wonderful PBS documentary, "Baseball." And I knew that at this point in her life she was a big Boston Red Sox fan, as was I. We talked about the upcoming key series for the Sox and she commented, "Pedro (Martinez) is pitching tomorrow, and I've got tickets. Got to get out of here and get home."

But first she had to address the group. She spoke eloquently about her LBJ and FDR books, but came alive when she discussed her most recent book, *Wait Till Next Year.* It was her personal story of growing up in Brooklyn and listening to Dodgers games on the radio, keeping score for her father so she could recount the game in full when he returned home from work. She was a kind, totally unassuming woman of great intellect and great warmth.

Back in Tucson, it seemed we had new neighbors. A new couple had moved into the house immediately to the west of us. I asked about their names and was told, "I don't know, but I hear he used to work for CBS."

Then I heard the name. *Richard Threlkeld, CBS News, Moscow.*

How many times I had heard that. Now he was my next door neighbor--with his wife, Betsy Aaron, also a journalist who had worked for ABC, CBS and CNN. Both had retired, more or less, and had chosen to make Tucson their retirement home.

Sandy and I took over a bottle of red Bordeaux to welcome them to the neighborhood. In a couple of weeks Betsy called to thank us again and to say that the wine was excellent. The call came from Moscow. Yes, they traveled a lot. Of course we became friends. Journalists living next door to each other? How could we not?

We dined together many times, usually at Le Bistro, Threlkeld in his familiar off-white khaki sports jacket of many pockets large enough for notebooks. We talked about news and politics, television and newspapers, good bosses and bad, mutual friends in the business, good books and bad. They had contacts everywhere. It occurred to me that while my entire career had been focused on covering the local scene wherever I was, theirs had involved the world. Sometimes I had no idea whom they were talking about, but they treated me as if I were the insider they were. I listened and learned. It was a treat.

They came to our Christmas Eve party every year, often bringing a close friend and fellow network veteran, John Harris. It was interesting to see our Tucson newspaper friends congregate around them, usually in the kitchen, and our doctor and lawyer and business friends gather in another part of the house. Except for Stanley Feldman. The Chief Justice, a man of many interests, might be found listening and talking with any group.

Threlkeld was working on a book about his time in Moscow, called *Dispatches From the Former Evil Empire.* When it came out some time later, he walked up the driveway to our house and handed me a copy which he had signed: "To Don and Sandy. From one ink-stained wretch to another. Best, Dick and Betsy."

(The Threlkelds later bought a house in the Hamptons in New York and divided their time there and in Tucson. In a few years they left Tucson permanently. We kept in touch and I sent them a signed copy of my new book of short stories. Tragically, a few days after receiving it, Dick was killed in a car crash during a mid-morning run to pick up a few things. He died much too early. He was a good man whom we were most fortunate to know.)

My work with the UA Foundation increased dramatically as I moved into the chairmanship. There were board meetings and committee meetings in both Tucson and Phoenix. And again, there was the opportunity to get to know people.

Bob Elliott was one of those. A successful CPA in Tucson, he served as treasurer of the Foundation board. He was also in the "media biz." A former UA basketball All-American and NBA player who had held Arizona's all-time scoring record until Sean Elliott came along, he had served as a radio color commentator for the Phoenix Suns and was now, in addition to his fulltime CPA work, an on-air analyst for college basketball games for Fox Sports Arizona.

We became friends and began playing golf together. Elliott, who stood about 6-8 or 6-9, had just taken up the game. He could hit the ball forever, but its direction was the great unknown. I took advantage of this and in the beginning often won. That would not last very long. Elliott, like all great athletes, worked hard on his game and before I knew it was burying me on the links. No more were those long drives disappearing left and right. Now they were vanishing in the distance.

One day I noticed the golfers in a foursome eyeing us. Finally they approached and one asked Elliott, "Excuse me; we were just wondering if you were a professional basketball player?"

"Well, I was once," he said, smiling.

He explained that he had played for two different teams, including the Philadelphia 76ers. They were quite impressed.

When they walked away, I couldn't help kidding him. "You sonofagun, you ate that up, didn't you?"

He flashed a wide grin and shrugged, as if to say, "Well, what can you do?" I was happy for him. Great guy.

There were lots of pluses about living in Tucson. People were right at the top.

52
TAKING STOCK

When does it stop being fun? Does it happen simply with the passage of time? Is it when one has been doing the same thing too long? When the excitement of the job seems to have waned? When the "juices" no longer flow as they once did and the "vibes" are no longer there? Does it come in the realization that printing stories which bring pain to others bothers you more than it once did?

Or is it when other forces seem to have taken control of one's daily efforts?

Gradually the fun of running the Tucson Citizen and working in partnership with Tucson Newspapers, the joint agency that controlled everything about Tucson's two daily newspapers except the newspapers themselves, had been fading. I could see it everywhere. At the agency, where Larry Aldrich had dramatically changed directions and priorities. In my own news staff, where several were leaving to accept other jobs, some of those with my morning competition across the moat. I could see it in the Gannett Corporate news division. And worst of all, I could see it in myself.

Aldrich, my friend, seemed like a different person. He told me repeatedly that the Citizen soon would be going out of business like many afternoon newspapers in the country. He predicted that we would be gone in another two years, four at the most. People just don't want afternoon newspapers, he said.

He brought in a special motivational speaker, a psychologist to meet with his management team, in a group setting and individually. He expected Steve Auslander of the Star and me to join in. I went to one of the group meetings. I never went back. And I never met with the man individually, although Auslander did.   My action gave credence to Aldrich's frequent complaints to others about me— that I was not always willing to go along with everything he wanted. I plead guilty.

More than once he explained our jobs to others by saying that "we work for the same people." He obviously did not consider me to be over him in any way, even though I was a director on the board to which he reported. He told me there were only two people on the board who mattered—Nick Penniman of Pulitzer and Gary Watson of Gannett. As time went by he seemed to consider himself the only real contact with the two. He did not think of me as being Gannett's eyes and ears in Tucson. A mistake.

Aldrich wanted a long-range plan for the entire enterprise. And where would the Citizen fit in with that, given that he had already said to me and others that we wouldn't be around in a few years?

He held an off-site meeting to discuss such matters, to plan for the future, and he asked that editors of both the Star and Citizen join many employees of the agency. Dutifully (though it was hardly my duty), I attended with several of my editors. We were quite outnumbered. The room was filled with TNI managers and directors and top-level members of the Star staff.

After listening for some time to discussions about plans to advance TNI and the Star, I finally asked why I was hearing of no such efforts for the Citizen. Aldrich stood and responded, before the entire audience: "Don, you've got to realize that the Citizen is irrelevant."

What? Surely he did not say that, especially in front of all these Star and TNI employees, not to mention my own Citizen staff.

"Excuse me?" I said.

"The Citizen is irrelevant. That's just the way it is."

I was steaming. I told myself to cool it, not to make a scene. I sat down and said nothing more. I have regretted that action—or inaction—to this day. What I should have done was to respond, "Well, if the Citizen is irrelevant, then what are we doing here?" And I should have summoned all the Citizen editors to follow me out the door. That I did not is one of my great regrets—and I have very few.

I said nothing about Aldrich's remark to anyone at Gannett Corporate until my final review a few months before my retirement. And then I told Sue

Clark-Johnson of my frustrations in Tucson and of Aldrich's comment that the Citizen was irrelevant. She was very surprised and asked if I would share that with Watson, which I did.

As for the Gannett news division, things just weren't the same. A lot of time had passed since John Quinn was VP/News. I missed his consistent defense of the news side, of his editors in the field, and his strong belief that local news was best handled by local editors who knew their communities far better than anyone miles away at Corporate. For all my years as editor and then as editor and publisher, I was never told once what to put in the paper or what to leave out.

But in the 1990s Gannett embarked on a new program called "News 2000." And things changed. Gannett always had competition among its papers, making monthly and yearly "Best of Gannett" awards. There were programs in which some editors critiqued the papers of other editors (not a good program, in my mind, because again these people did not know the communities served by the papers they were judging). All this involved time—in selecting entries and preparing and shipping them. I relied on my managing editors to handle this, and most did a good job. And the awards meant something to members of news staffs, especially if they were annual awards, which were accompanied by a check.

Now came News 2000. And this involved more work than ever. Editors throughout the company complained, but the program rolled on. In essence, Gannett newspapers were told to plan the content of their newspapers according to the "pyramid blocks" of the News 2000 program. These blocks addressed "core values" such as community interest, immediacy, "watchdog" journalism and First amendment issues, diversity, presentation, consistency and "anticipating change."

Most editors thought of all this as Big Brother interference, as Corporate telling them how to edit their own newspapers for their own communities. Also, it involved a lot of extra work for news staffs already stretched in order to cover the day's news and produce a good newspaper.

My old friend Phil Currie, heading the corporate news operation, was instrumental in the creation of News 2000—although I doubt it was all his. He brought in an editor named Mark Silverman to oversee the program, including the participation of all Gannett's newspapers. I had known Currie since his days as part of the news division's recruiting and training team. He had been a good friend of Sandy's and mine for years, and I had great respect for him as a newsman. He had always provided support when I needed it. If he were heading this, I told myself, it must be worthwhile. So I was not among the many who complained—at least, openly. I will admit that like all newsrooms, ours was one in which there was grumbling about planning news coverage designed to match "pyramid blocks," more grumbling when it was time to submit our reports, and even more if we received a bad grade.

We were told that for too long we had been practicing "spinach journalism—eat it, it's good for you." Meaning, I suppose, we had been force-feeding our readers with the wrong news and information. Don't give them what you think they need; give them what they want. I had always considered the proper mix of a good newspaper was to provide readers both what they want and what they need.

News 2000 was one of my disappointments in Gannett. But looking back, it probably was a valuable program in making some editors and news staffs address subjects that they may have been neglecting. Not one of the News 2000 pyramid blocks was unimportant. I think the weakness in the program was in its implementation, not its goals and ideals. What was most disappointing is that it took Big Brother to remind editors of the "core values" of good newspapers, and the idea that Corporate was now looking over our news and editorial shoulders more than they had and more than any of us liked.

Currie suffered criticism from many Gannett news staffers for some time. In fact, it followed him even to his much-deserved retirement, and that was unfair. He was a hell of a news person who was committed not only to the news, but to people.

There were also programs and many buzz words elsewhere at Corporate. "Bundling," "branding," far too many for me to recall at this point but all a bit of a turnoff. It was as if Corporate was another world with its own language. Strangely enough, I felt better about such things when I was with Gary Watson, whether it was at corporate headquarters or TNI board meetings in Tucson. He was not just my boss, but a friend of long standing. Whenever we talked, I forgot some of my disappointments and concerns about Gannett. I suppose that is the mark of a good boss.

In the spring of 1999, during a Citizen staff pizza-and-Pepsi meeting, I was asked an odd question.

"Isn't there a retirement coming up you'd like to tell us about?"

"A retirement?" I wondered to whom she was referring. No one was retiring on the Citizen and I wasn't aware of any key retirements at TNI. "Not that I know of. Did you have somebody in mind?"

There were smiles and shifting of feet and coughs and she said, "Well, yeah. You."

"Me? Not unless you know something I don't know," I said, laughing. But no one else was laughing.

"You're not retiring this year?"

"No, I'm not. Where did you hear that?"

"Well, when then?"

It almost sounded as if she wanted to get rid of me. What I did not realize was that several members of the staff were concerned, perhaps not so much with my leaving as with who would replace me. I could see that they were serious, and that the entire staff was waiting on my answer. So I got serious as well.

"Gannett has had a policy that every CEO in

the company must retire when he or she reaches the age of sixty-five. I assume, although I am not certain at the moment, that policy still is in effect. I won't be sixty-five until next year—in June of 2000, as a matter of fact. Unless they want to get rid of me sooner than that, I plan to stick around at least until then."

She smiled and thanked me and a few others smiled, and then I ended the meeting, still quite surprised, and returned to my office. One of the staff followed me and offered an explanation. There was a fear in the newsroom, she said, that Michael Limon, our managing editor, would be my successor. They did not want to work for him.

That did not come as a shock. Not long before, a Citizen staffer had written anonymously to Gannett CEO John Curley to complain about Limon. I had defended him at the time.

Also, she continued, some believed that once I retired the Citizen would be closed.

I told her I had no idea who would replace me and that since that was more than a year away, Limon might not even be here; he might be transferred elsewhere by then. As for Gannett shuttering the Citizen, I said it made the company a lot of money and there were no indications that had even been considered no matter what they may have heard from TNI and Larry Aldrich.

Nonetheless, we started losing members of the news staff. A few accepted jobs on other newspapers. Sports Editor Peter Madrid was one, moving to the Arizona Republic in Phoenix. A couple of others were moving to the Star, including Kathy Allen, Sandy's friend and mine, and Elena Chabolla, our online editor.. Both told me they were leaving because I would be leaving and they feared the Citizen would fold when I left. I thanked them for the compliment but said that was not the case. Gannett made a very good profit from this operation and wasn't about to give that up.

What I did not tell them was that it might be possible for the two owners to shut down the Citizen and still continue the 50-50 JOA, that Gannett and Pulitzer would actually make more money that way because there would not be the expenses of the Citizen news staff or of producing the paper and delivering it. I did not think that would happen, at least in the near future, but I did have that fear. It had happened elsewhere, including St. Louis, Pulitzer's headquarters.

It was about this time that I had a visit from two key members of the agency, Randy Cross, VP/Circulation, and Jim Rowley, VP/Marketing. It seemed the Star was planning a huge makeover. In essence, it would be going more local, involve itself in the community more, and "be more like the Citizen."

Really.

Cross and Rowley thought that was a great plan. I have no doubt they had been part of it all along, nor did I have any doubt that Aldrich was involved as well. He had mentioned to me that the Star was planning a redesign, but he had said nothing about it going the way of the Citizen.

Cross and Rowley said they would be marketing the Star along these lines. Therefore, since none of us wanted two newspapers that were alike, they felt the Citizen should change. That way they could promote and market the two papers differently.

"Let me see if I have this straight," I said. "Everybody likes the Citizen but the Star is the morning paper and the bigger and stronger paper so it should become what the Citizen has been and the Citizen should go off and be something else. Right?"

They looked at each other and then nodded. "Well, basically, yes."

"And what should the Citizen become?"

"Well, that's why we're talking with you. We thought you'd have some ideas."

"This is really bullshit," I said. "I can't believe you guys are asking me this. I'm sure Larry Aldrich feels this is the way to go as well."

"Yes, he's on board."

"I'll bet he is."

I was silent for a long moment. Then I said, "Well, you and the Star can do whatever you want. But the Citizen is not going to change. We're still going to be the best local news source in this town, and we're not going to be programmed by somebody in Marketing or Circulation or anybody else, unless I am told differently by Gannett."

They looked at each other again and then stood up. "Okay," one of them said.

They left and I sat wondering why Aldrich

hadn't accompanied them. Guess he didn't want to hear me howl.

I never mentioned this to Gannett, nor did Gannett ever mention it to me. And the Citizen continued to do and be what it had done and been during my time here.

As it turned out, there was a key retirement in TNI that year. Edie Auslander, our long-time head of Human Resources, left to join the University of Arizona Foundation. That would be, in my mind, a huge loss for Tucson Newspapers, especially in the community.

Meanwhile, there was also a major change in Pulitzer and at the Star. Nick Penniman stepped aside, to be replaced by Bob Woodworth, who brought in a new publisher and editor for the Star. Her name was Jane Amari, and she had considerable experience on several of the country's major newspapers. Michael Pulitzer finally had given up the title of publisher of the Star. Steve Auslander was moved to editor of the editorial page, where he had been years before. Amari was now my new competitor.

I must say I was not all that friendly to her. At this point, I was frustrated and somewhat bitter about TNI's efforts going almost entirely to the Star. She and I frequently attended Aldrich's management team meetings, and I offered little more than my defense of the Citizen and pretty much ignored her. The same held true at meetings of the TNI board, of which she was now a member.

I'm sure that I felt some resentment toward her,

not for any personal reason, but because in my mind her paper was getting everything from the agency and the two owners and my paper was getting little to nothing. I reminded Aldrich that "this is a fifty-fifty JOA." And he reminded me that involved revenues and expenses. There was nothing in the agreement that said the amount of support each paper received in terms of marketing and promotion had to be fifty-fifty. Unfortunately, he was correct.

There is no question that Aldrich's job—his position—was a difficult one. Serving two masters always is. Now and then he shared that with me. In my office one day, he confessed to being increasingly tired of it all. "Some days," he said, "I feel like getting out of all this and just moving on." I understood. Despite our disagreements I still considered him my friend, after all.

When Gary Watson came to Tucson for that November's board meeting, I had a number of things to discuss. I waited until we were sharing a cart and had just completed a round of golf. Then I told him the staff knew I would be retiring the following year and that several were leaving because they feared that when I did either the Citizen would be shut down or Michael Limon would be my replacement.

As always, he understood. It was rare for Gannett to announce retirements or replacements before they actually occurred, he said. "But in this case, maybe it's needed."

I told him I thought that would be a great idea, and the sooner the better.

And I remembered something he had told me over dinner a few years before. *Whenever you leave, we won't bring in the same kind of publisher you've been. It's different now.*

I knew what he meant. When I arrived, TNI was run by a general manager who reported to me and to Emil Rould of the Star. Now the head of TNI had the title of president and reported to the six-person TNI board. The role had changed.

I wondered if he had anyone in mind, but I didn't ask. When he was ready he would tell me. Instead, taking advantage of the fact that we were sitting in a golf cart at La Paloma, I asked if Gannett would allow me to keep one of my two country club memberships. He said he would see what he could do.

53
TIME TO GO

New Year's Eve, 1999. Remember? The world was supposed to go crazy. Computers were going to crash around the globe, not properly designed to handle the arrival of a new century—or something like that. Christian Fundamentalists were convinced the world was going to end. Didn't it say so in the Bible? And with computers dead around the world, everything would stop. Planes, trains would be at a standstill. There would be a shortage of food, of power, of supplies. Armed battles would rage as those who were without attacked those who had prepared. Normally rational men and women hoarded food and water and got out rifles and shotguns. And everyone waited.

Sandy and I joined friends at Le Bistro for dinner. I avoided the wine, ate sparingly, and excused myself, heading for the office. If the world were going to end, we would have to report it, right? Well, in truth, there was concern about computers at the magic hour of midnight. So I went to the office, where most of the Citizen staff had gathered, and we watched television to see if any part of the planet had yet exploded. And we waited until midnight to see if our computers were affected. And when they were not we toasted the new year with soft drinks. It was 2000.

As we now know, nothing happened. Not the computer crashes, not Planet Earth being brought to a halt. There were no armed conflicts. And thousands were left with a stash of food and water.

But my world was changing. The arrival of January 1, 2000 meant the beginning of the end of my long newspaper career, for this would be the year of my retirement.

Gary Watson had made his decision on my replacement and it was a good one. "Of course," I said when I heard the name, "great choice."

Mike Chihak was the publisher of Gannett's newspaper in Visalia, California. He was a hometown boy, born and raised in Tucson, a graduate of the University of Arizona, a former Citizen photographer, reporter, and city editor. He would be coming home.

Chihak would move to the Citizen with the title of executive editor, Watson said. And when I retired in June, he would move up to publisher. He would start Monday, January 17. I should introduce him to the staff as the executive editor, Watson said, not as the publisher, "although they can probably figure that out."

I knew Chihak, not only from corporate meetings, but because he often visited his family in Tucson and usually dropped by our newsroom. I was pleased not only for him to get the job, but for the staff. I knew he would be a popular choice. And

I knew they would be relieved to know the Citizen wasn't going to be shuttered and Michael Limon was not going to be their new publisher.

Chihak arrived in Tucson the weekend of January 15 and on January 16 joined Sandy and me at Le Bistro. We celebrated his arrival and his promotion, although that would not happen for another six months. He was excited to begin. He welcomed the opportunity to work with me for six months, he said, to learn from me and how we now did things at the Citizen.

The following day, immediately after deadline, I summed all members of the staff to the large entry hall adjacent to the newsroom. Chihak stood off to the side. It was no surprise to the staff to see him there; they were accustomed to seeing him in our newsroom.

"As most of you know," I said, "I will be retiring in June. This morning I want to introduce the next publisher of the Tucson Citizen, Mike Chihak."

Chihak stepped out to cheers and applause.

"Mike begins today with the title of executive editor. When I step aside in June he will assume the title of editor and publisher."

As I expected, it was a popular choice. Chihak told the staff he was honored to return to the Citizen as publisher and editor and looked forward to working with everyone. I followed by saying Gannett had made a great choice. Nearly every member of the staff shook his hand, and some gave him hugs, and then all returned to their jobs to put out the next edition and Chihak and I went into my office.

"Well, what do you think?" he said.

"I think they're very pleased to have you."

"I hope so. I'm certainly very pleased to be here."

Then I talked to him about Michael Limon, who I knew would be disappointed not to be chosen my successor. He's a good newsman, I said, and can be a big help to you. Chihak said he would talk with Limon and assure him that he was needed and that he looked forward to working with him.

We would run a news story announcing his appointment as executive editor, I said, but not as publisher. That would come later.

We had a temporary office for him and he went there to arrange things, and I sat in my office and thought about what had just happened. I looked around the office, at the books, the photographs, the old IBM Selectric typewriter that still sat nearby, close to my desktop computer. It was a great office. "One of the best in Gannett," someone had said. I had come a long way from that steel-topped table in the corner of the Huntington newsroom.

I took Chihak to Larry Aldrich's office to share the news of his appointment, and then to the offices of all the TNI directors and vice presidents for introductions and a tour of the building, which had changed and expanded considerably since he had worked here.

During the next several days I introduced Chihak to key people in the community, but it wasn't as if he was a newcomer to town. He had grown up here, after all, and no doubt knew more people than I did. I made sure to invite him to dinner with our friend Joan Beigel, who could be a help to him in the community.

In a matter of weeks, Aldrich dropped by my office, closed the door and sat in one of the chairs in front of my desk.

"I'm leaving," he said.

That was a surprise, but not a shock. I knew that he had grown tired of the pressure of pleasing two companies, especially now that one of them had a new CEO.

"It's just too much," he said. "I've had it."

I asked what he would do, where he would go. He said he would remain in Tucson, but wasn't yet sure what he would do. He had passed the Arizona bar exam and could practice law if he chose to do so. Whatever he decided, I knew he would be fine. I told him I would miss him, although I myself would be there only a few more months. He seemed like the old Larry Aldrich.

"You look relieved," I said.

"I am."

If there were other factors involved in his leaving, I was never aware of them. I let it go at that, and we remained friends and saw each other often in the community.

His replacement was Cathy Davis, who had been our first new advertising director not long after my arrival in Tucson. She had left us to join Phoenix Newspapers, and now here she was back at

TNI to run the place. She had been a good ad director and I had always liked her.

The next couple of months seemed to zoom by. I met with various people to complete plans for my retirement and with a few others who might offer something for me to consider doing. I had thought about teaching, and met with the chair of the UA journalism department. I knew most journalism programs offered endowed chairs (Gannett had sponsored one at Marshall University) or an endowed professorship. I was surprised to learn that the UA journalism department had no endowed chair and only one endowed professorship which the department head himself held (as he quickly informed me). I might be interested in becoming an adjunct professor, he said, teaching beginning reporting. It paid $1,500 per semester per class. I told him I didn't think so.

Before I realized it, June had come and I was flying to Washington for Gannett's annual meeting —my last. It would be highlighted, as always, by the President's Ring dinner. I had never won a President's Ring, although I had been a finalist for one early in my Tucson career. There was the usual reception and then we gathered in the large banquet hall for food and wine and more wine and then the customary speeches by Gannett's top executives, followed by the awards.

The room was filled with Gannett publishers and corporate executives. I sat with friends drinking wine and listening to a few brief remarks, and then Gary Watson took over the microphone.

"Forty-seven years," he began. I sat up with a start. Was he talking about me?

"I want to recognize a special executive who has forty-seven years with Gannett. Later this month, Don Hatfield will conclude a brilliant career with our company as he and his wife and lifelong partner Sandy make the transition into retirement."

I was stunned. I had not seen this before at Gannett. Watson went on .

"Let me share a few highlights of Don's career. A descendant of one side of the legendary feuding Hatfields and McCoys, Don was educated at his hometown Marshall University and went to work for his hometown newspaper on June 18, 1953.

"In his 33 years at the Huntington Advertiser and later the Herald-Dispatch, Don served as a reporter, columnist, editor and publisher.

"In 1986 a younger division president convinced Don and Sandy to leave their West Virginia roots and head for the desert Southwest and Tucson.

"Over the past 14 years Don has served as the publisher and editor of the Tucson Citizen with style, grace and commitment...

"With Sandy at his side, Don has made both his newspaper and his community a better place to work and live.

"I would think that Don's most enduring legacy will be the generation—or maybe even two generations—of journalists who benefitted from his wealth of experience and, as happens as time moves by, from his wisdom.

"Those who know Don well recognize and understand that beneath that easy-going manner of his heritage burns a keen sense of competition and a passion for our business.

"He is the consummate newspaperman."

Watson then asked me to come to the stage where John Curley, Gannett's chairman and CEO, and Doug McCorkindale, deputy chairman, also stood.

When I reached the stage, Watson presented me with a Gannett President's Ring. I stood looking at it and then at him, and he asked me to say a few words. I was all but speechless.

I thanked Gannett, and Curley and McCorkindale and Phil Currie and Bobby Collins and Sue Clark-Johnson, my two regional presidents, and then I stepped down and walked through the crowd, now standing and applauding, to my table. I had never expected anything like this. I was honored and touched. If only Sandy had been here to share this, one of the great moments of my life. As soon as the dinner was over I sped to my room to call her.

The following day I returned to Tucson to wrap things up. Only a few more days to go.

By coincidence, my two-year term as chairman of the University of Arizona Foundation was also ending. As chairman I had the responsibility of heading a committee to work out a new contract for Dick Imwalle, the Foundation president and CEO. We knew he had been courted by other universities and foundations and that he wanted a multi-year contract if he were to stay. We wanted that, too; we didn't want to lose him. When the committee agreed on terms of the contract, it was up to me to meet with him. I set up lunch.

Straight to the point, I told him the Foundation's executive committee had agreed to offer him a five-year contract with built-in merit increases, if he continued to do the job. I then presented him with the salary schedule and the contract.

He studied it for a few minutes, then said, "I think that's very fair." And he signed.

We finished our lunch and he asked what I planned to do in my retirement. I said I had thought about teaching but that in a meeting with the UA journalism department chair learned that the pay for an adjunct professor was surprisingly small. I would soon be leaving for the Cape, I said, and planned to stay there until the end of August.

He mentioned that the Foundation was embarking on a huge campaign and would have to expand its staff. "If you're interested, there might be something there."

I told him I would like to hear about it, and he said he'd put something together and send it to me on the Cape. I left our lunch with a new possibility to consider.

My official retirement party (as if that wonderful evening in Washington hadn't been enough) was scheduled for June 15--my birthday, oddly enough. Mike Chihak made all the arrangements for a big dinner at Tucson Country

Club, inviting most of Gannett's top executives as well as those from TNI and the entire Citizen staff. Coming from Gannett would be Watson, Phil Currie, and Dick Clapp, Senior VP/Human Resources and a friend and fellow Cape Cod summer resident.

Unfortunately, when the Gannett group arrived at the Washington airport for the flight to Tucson, the weather failed to cooperate, and they were unable to get off the ground. But Sue Clark-Johnson and her husband, Brooks—who had served with me as a regional vice president for Gannett West—did come.

My son Chris flew in from Boston. But sadly, my son Joel could not make the dinner because of illness.

Otherwise, it was a splendid, once-in-a-lifetime (obviously) affair. Although Watson and Currie weren't present, their prepared comments were read. In addition to Watson's, which reflected his earlier words in Washington, there were these from Currie:

"I have known Don Hatfield for a longer time than either of us will admit. I admire him for all of the things Gary has mentioned and more. And I would underscore one point.

"You cannot be a really strong journalist without a passion for the business, without caring about the quality of the work that is done by you and by those under your guidance, and without caring deeply about the impact that work can have in and on our community .

"Don Hatfield has that passion and that caring, and that makes him a very special person. And he has a caring way that always has left him contributing a big piece of that passionate heart for his staff, his company and his community.

"It has been an honor to work with Don over the years--and it is an even greater honor to know him as an outstanding human being."

Well, pretty heady stuff. But just so my head would not get too big, there were words from Mark Kimble, the Citizen's associate editor and my good friend. He roasted me over my West Virginia roots, my manner in the newsroom, especially during editorial board meetings, and several other things. There was laughter all around, the most from me. And then he ended this way:

"I think it's pretty clear that to all of us at the Citizen, Don is a lot more than just our boss. He's also someone who brought a lot of innovation and new ideas to the Citizen. He is a journalist with very high standards, and he expected all of us to live up to them. And even more important, he has become a friend."

Finally there was a short speech from my son Chris, who offered many dear and touching comments, some focused on the work I had done with and for minorities. That was truly special.

There were gifts: a trip to Europe for Sandy and me from Gannett, a computer package from the Citizen, a shipment of several bottles of expensive white Burgandy from Sue Clark-Johnson, and a surprising and wonderful gift from TNI—a small sculpture created in my honor by Southwest sculptor Kurt Brill, to be placed in the Tucson Museum of Art. Even my friend Laurent Reux of Le Bistro presented me with a gift—a case of red Bordeaux.

And then it was over. The party and, but for a few days the following week, the career.

I left with one final personal column. It opened this way:

"It all began 47 years ago in Huntington, West Virginia.

"And entered a new and wonderful phase 14 years ago in Tucson, Arizona.

"And now, in a matter of days, it comes to an end."

It finished this way:

"To all newspaper people, especially those on the Citizen news staff, I would leave with a couple of thoughts.

"As Sandy has said, what you do, what I have done over the years, is important. It matters.

"But never forget that you are dealing every day with extraordinarily powerful tools:

"Words.

"They can be used to inform and educate and enlighten and help and even, now and then, to save.

"And they can be used to hurt and do untold damage.

"Use them with care.

"Journalists—reporters and editors—have far more power than they realize.

"Use that power with care.

"I leave this profession with thanks and with pride and with respect for what it is and what it means. And with some humility. I will miss it greatly.

"But the time is right..."

On Friday, June 23, 2000, I walked out of my office, out of the Citizen newsroom, out of the newspaper world. Forty-seven years. It had been a blast.

54

IN RETROSPECT

I began my career on a small afternoon newspaper in Huntington, West Virginia. I ended it on a larger afternoon newspaper in Tucson, Arizona. Neither newspaper exists today. Many other afternoon newspapers have also disappeared in that time. Unfortunately, so have several morning newspapers. Clearly, the golden days of newspapers are behind us.

But there was a time when newspapers were special. Editors and reporters were important. Columnists were treated like celebrities. Everyone read them and everyone felt they knew them. No home was complete without at least one daily newspaper. If your town had two, morning and evening, your home probably had both. If you were fortunate enough to write for a daily newspaper, you carried a certain pride. People knew who you were. You mattered.

Or was that all in my mind?

I have been extremely fortunate to have lived and worked in a time when newspapers were not only relevant, but considered a necessity in every home.

And I have enjoyed many more highs than lows:

--Getting that first job as an eighteen-year-old kid wandering into the newsroom at just the right time.

--Attending the American Press Institute at Columbia University in New York, which opened a new world.

--Working for Gannett, a company which gave me every opportunity to learn and grow.

--Being elected to the Associated Press Managing Editors Association Board of Directors.

--Being promoted to publisher, a position I had not sought and for which I was not prepared. Someone must have seen something in me and gave me the job anyway.

--Moving to Tucson, truly another new world in every way.

I have been fortunate in working with and learning from bright, committed people of all ages, colors and persuasions.

And I have been most fortunate in having Sandy at my side through it all...sitting in cold high school football bleachers awaiting the birth of our first child while I took notes and interviewed coaches...spending enormous time with Corporate execs...entertaining guest after guest to help her husband and his newspaper...participating on several boards to show my newspapers' commitment to the communities we served...

traveling with me to my regional properties, including those dull days spent in a Santa Fe hotel room waiting on the final blows of the previous owner's takeover of our paper there.

I remember her sitting with John Quinn over a late night drink and telling him Gannett should have bought Ted Turner's new television news venture, to which he agreed. And in a restaurant having no hesitation in telling my boss, Gary Watson, that his recommended Super Tuscan was a bit too fruity, not at all like her favorite Bordeaux.

She always made me look good. She always made me feel that what I—what we—were doing *mattered.*

I once told a fellow editor that I had two dreams: winning the Pulitzer Prize and scoring a hole-in-one. "Well, I've been fortunate enough to do both," he said, and then spent a half-hour telling me about his hole-in-one.

I never won the Pulitzer and I never made that hole-in-one. But I have no regrets. I realized far more important dreams and achieved more than I ever could have imagined.

I have occasionally been asked about my philosophy in running newsrooms and newspapers. I never thought of it in a formal way. There were no rules handed out. One learns through trial and error, and one matures. But looking back, I realize that over the years I did develop certain values and practices:

--Never lie to get at the truth.

--Never break the law to get a story.

--Try to know what your next move will be before you have to make it.

--Keep it fun, especially in the newsroom.

--Use every vacancy as an opportunity to re-evaluate the position and to replace the outgoing person with someone better.

--Be yourself. Don't try to be someone you're not. Staffers will forgive your whims and flaws if you're honest about yourself. Otherwise they will think you're a phony.

--Don't lie to any employee. It always comes back to haunt you.

--The most difficult things to say are: "That's my fault" and "I don't know." Work on it.

--Don't promise what you may not be able to deliver.

--Respect your employees and they will respect you.

--Communicate. Let people know what's going on; it's the best way to avoid rumors.

--Understand that people would rather believe what they hear in the hallways than what management says. Try to improve on that.

--Praise in public and criticize in private. A cliché, but it works.

--Do not insult (I remember once telling a reporter, "If this isn't the worst piece of writing I've seen this year, it's a hell of a close second." A mistake on my part.)

--Don't hold a story without explaining why to both the editor involved and the reporter.

--Try to make others think your idea was theirs.

--Listen.

Not exactly profound, of course. But they worked for me.

I have also been asked what I think about today's newspapers. Well...

Too many have given up on publishing the day's news, on planning and executing real journalism, going behind the scenes, asking tough questions. Too many have grown soft and predictable. They rely on stories about every holiday, every anniversary, every notable date in history to carry the day for them. They seek and print responses from readers on every conceivable aspect of life on this planet without regard to qualifications or verification or even names. At one time we would not publish even letters to the editor without verification and full names. Now we give anyone the opportunity to libel and slander anyone else without even identifying themselves.

My good friend Dr. John Schaefer and I once were asked to speak on the future of the printed word, he on books, I on newspapers. I said among the many problems facing today's newspapers were often the newspapers themselves, and I cited some of the sins above.

Fortunately the great newspapers have not fallen into this pit.

I am convinced there will always be a few fine papers like the New York Times and Wall Street Journal and others. But more cities will be without seven-day printed newspapers.

However, being distributed on-line rather than

in print does not mean they no longer will exist. Virtually every newspaper still alive has an on-line site. I would like to see today's newspapers market their online sites as being the newspapers they have always been. Today I read two daily newspapers— the Boston Globe and the Arizona Daily Star—on line. I think of them still as the newspapers they were and are--same good reporting, same columnists, just distributed differently. In this way perhaps we can ignore comments about the "Death of Newspapers," and continue to celebrate them.

But enough of this preaching. Let's just say my life in newspapers was a wonderfully worthwhile way to spend my days on this planet, and I am grateful that time came when it did.

In the months that followed my retirement I was notified that I had been voted into the Arizona Newspapers Hall of Fame. The person who nominated me was, surprisingly, Jane Amari, the editor and publisher of the Arizona Daily Star, to whom I had not even been friendly. When the award was presented I looked down from the podium and said, "Jane, I wasn't even nice to you." To which she responded, "Ah, Don, that was just business."

But what a business. And what a way to go out.

55
POSTSCRIPT

When I left the world of newspapers in June 2000, I was not ready to retire from life. Fortunately, when one door closes, as they say, another often opens.

In September, just three months after leaving the Tucson Citizen and Gannett, I joined the University of Arizona Foundation as Vice President for Corporation and Foundation Development. I had gone from unpaid chairman to paid vice president. Paid is better.

The following summer Sandy and I used our Gannett retirement gift for a trip to Paris and London. We repeated the trip with our sons Chris and Joel in 2005 on the occasion of our 50th anniversary. Among my gifts to Sandy was an endowed scholarship in her name for French studies at Marshall University.

I stayed at the UA Foundation until June 2006 when I retired once again. This time it took. For the first time in my adult life I had no office to go to each day. I had feared that. But I did not miss it one bit. Sandy and I would be able to spend more time together.

Unfortunately, her health would interfere. In May 2007, she was diagnosed with breast cancer. As if that weren't enough, she was badly in need of a hip replacement. And there was, as always, the chronic back pain. Following breast surgery she completed six weeks of daily radiation. A week later, she received a new hip.

During that time our sons were unable to visit Tucson to offer any help. They had their own work and their own lives. This prompted both to urge us to move back to Huntington.

Joel was especially convincing. Tucson was a long way from family, he said, and he and his brother could not be there to offer the help we needed now that we were getting older. We had not planned to move, but there was truth to Joel's appeal. Sandy was as reluctant to leave Tucson as she had been to leave Huntington twenty-two years before. But, in November, 2007, we sold our house, said goodbye to our friends, and left the desert we had come to love. In Huntington my priority would be to take care of Sandy as she had always taken care of me. And I would return to the writing I had left forty years before.

In spite of her health problems, Sandy

immediately became active in the community once again, chairing the Dean's Council at Marshall University's College of Fine Arts, serving on a capital campaign for its new Visual Arts Center in downtown Huntington, hosting Marshall social events including almost the entire National Symphony Orchestra, in town for an Artists Series concert.

In 2009 Sandy had another back surgery—her fourth—this time for spinal stenosis. Although the surgery was successful, the chronic pain did not go away. But she continued to go to meetings, we attended Marshall football and basketball games, and we still had a decent social life. In 2010 we again went to Paris and London. Meanwhile, I resurrected some old short stories and wrote new ones.

In 2011, with the help of my friend and colleague Charlie Bowen of Bowen Books I published *A Pocketful of Cinders,* a collection of nine short stories. My son Chris did the cover illustration. We held a book signing at a downtown hotel, sold several books, enjoyed friends. Life was good.

And then...

Chris, who had done well in Boston, serving on staff at the Museum of Fine Art for fifteen years and then at M.I.T. for nine, became ill. He returned to Huntington and moved into his brother's house. He later suffered a broken hip in a fall. Because Joel's house had no downstairs bedroom and bath, he came to our house to recuperate. Joel, reasoning that we could not take care of Chris, came with him.

On February 2, 2014, Chris died in his sleep from liver and kidney disease. He was only fifty-four. We all were crushed. We had been a very close family. Joel was shattered; he had loved his brother very much. Tragically, in his pain Joel turned again to drugs, a problem he had faced more than once over the years. Only two months later, in April 2014, Joel too died, from an accidental overdose. He had not yet turned forty-seven.

How does a mother deal with the loss of two sons in two months? Our daughter Lisa, profoundly handicapped all her life, had passed away some years before. Now Chris and Joel. Three children, all gone. I feared the worst for Sandy. But she was strong as always. "We're back where we started," she said. "Just the two of us."

We spent that Christmas and New Year's in Tucson with friends. We could not face the holidays in our Huntington home, which seemed so empty now. We would take one day at a time and try to look forward, which is really all one can do. And we hoped that the next year would be better.

In July 2015 Sandy once again had a battle with cancer. This time it was appendiceal, which forms in the appendix and then spreads. She had major surgery in Huntington, followed by an examination and diagnosis in Pittsburgh, and was put on months of chemo, stretching into the next year. She was determined to defeat cancer a second time. She did.

During her recuperation I convinced her to gather all the poems she had written over the years and we would have them published in book form. And in November, 2016, with the help again of Charlie Bowen, her book of poems, *Songs From the Night Blooming Garden,* was published. We held a book signing at Guyan Country Club, dozens of books were sold, and we both were extremely proud.

Our relief was short lived. Only three weeks after her book signing, she went through yet another surgery because of a basil cell carcinoma of the nose. A cancer surgeon removed the tip of her nose followed immediately by a plastic surgeon who restored it. The surgery was pronounced a success, but she went into shock caused by the loss of electrolytes and was hospitalized even longer.

We felt we were home free after that, but all the visits to the hospital resulted in her acquiring a serious intestinal infection. She was bombarded with antibiotics, and appeared to recover.

However, the years of surgeries, radiation, chemo, antibiotics, took their toll. Sandy's body, despite her courage and determination, was beginning to fail. An examination in June showed that her heart was functioning at only twenty-five percent efficiency. On July 8, Joel's birthday, she fell twice during the night and, unable to walk, was hospitalized again. After a week she was moved to a rehabilitation facility where she stayed for ten days. Then home again—but not for long.

She grew quite weak and after only four days was taken by ambulance to the hospital—the fourth time in seven months. I feared it might be the last time. I was right.

Now her heart was functioning at only eight percent—not enough to support the kidneys, liver, and lungs. She would need dialysis. She spent several days in ICU hooked to a machine—long her worst fear. But as always, she did not complain.

Teams of doctors--specialists in kidneys and cardiologists—worked with her daily. But her heart was not going to improve. Because of her age, a transplant was out of the question. She was taken off the machine and moved out of ICU to a regular room, which pleased her, and she greeted each day with hope. But after a month doctors told me nothing else could be done for her, that she would soon be discharged. Her options would be a nursing home, assisted living, hospice house, or hospice at home. We had spent most of the year, months of long days and nights, in hospitals. Sandy wanted to go home.

Not once had she or I acknowledged to each other that this might be the end. I told her that she was very ill, then lied by adding, "But you're not dying." "I know," she said. If she would not give up, how could I? We would make her as comfortable as possible and wait to see if somehow, even if her heart could not improve, perhaps the kidneys would. She would require twenty-four hour care, but I could arrange that.

I started to tell her how wonderful she had been, how much she had given me and our children. But she interrupted me. "Don't," she said simply.

We brought her home by ambulance on Sept.1.

Hired professional caregivers awaited, and would be there around the clock. Hospice staff would come three times a week for an hour. She looked around the room and smiled. "It looks so nice," she said.

For two days she was reasonably alert, although frequently drifting into sleep. I sat by her, whispering that she had been an incredible wife and mother, thanking her for all she had meant to our children and to me, hoping that she could hear me. Often she would smile, although not really opening her eyes. But after a few days, she became unresponsive.

On Sept. 13, 2017, less than two weeks after coming home, my Sandy, my love, my life, my incredible best friend, my partner in every conceivable way, left us. It did not seem real. It did not seem right. She deserved so much more. At least now, I tried telling myself, she would be out of pain and at peace. But the words seemed hollow.

The following days were all but overwhelming as preparations were made for services that would be as deserving as possible. Her funeral was conducted at the church where we had met sixty-four years before, where we were married and where the funerals of our three children had taken place. Afterward, friends and family came to our house where there were toasts and remembered good times.

Three months later, on Dec. 19, her birthday, a celebration of her life was held in Tucson at the Arizona Inn, her long-time favorite place. Again there were kind words spoken and again her poems were read, copies of her book were placed on sale in the Inn's gift shop, and the University of Arizona Poetry Center announced that it was adding her book to its permanent collection. How honored and humbled she would have been.

I stayed in Tucson for a month in the midst of friends and former colleagues, and then returned to my life in Huntington. Nothing felt the same. Nothing was the same. Nor would it ever be. No children, no grandchildren. And now no Sandy.

The sense of loss is at times overwhelming, and there are sudden unavoidable moments of loneliness. Yet thanks to a few special people I do not feel truly alone or forgotten or at all bitter. And I am comforted in the realization that I have had a wonderful life--more than sixty years with Sandy by my side, two sons who were bright and sensitive, a long, fascinating and rewarding career as a newspaperman, and many, many friends.

On my desk is a small card sent to me after Sandy's passing. It reads: "A circle of caring surrounds you."

I feel that. I am fortunate, as I have been all my life. And I am grateful.

SPECIAL NOTE

I am indeed fortunate in having many friends in Huntington and Tucson who have been of great help to me, especially since the passing of my beloved Sandy. Three have become my unofficial new family: Tammy Stewart, my late son Joel's girlfriend who has been like a daughter to Sandy and me. And Paula and Brandon Horton, who with their two small children have become the grandchildren and great grandchildren I never had. I love you all, and I thank you for being here for me.

Don Hatfield
April 2018

ABOUT THE AUTHOR

Don Hatfield is a former writer, editor and publisher for newspapers in Huntington, WV, and Tucson, AZ. He has published several short stories and many magazine articles. He is the author of *Don Hatfield Cleans Out His Attic*, a collection of his newspaper columns, and *A Pocketful of Cinders*, a collection of short stories.

Made in the USA
Middletown, DE
28 May 2018